Scott Hagan, with sensitivity and a skill for igniting truth in your heart, creatively invites you to experience an eternal touch of the Holy Spirit in poignant and practical ways.

–JACK W. HAYFORD
FOUNDING PASTOR, THE CHURCH ON THE WAY
CHANCELLOR, THE KING'S COLLEGE AND SEMINARY

THEY FELT THE
SPIRIT'S
TOUCH

SCOTT HAGAN

Charisma
HOUSE

THEY FELT THE SPIRIT'S TOUCH by Scott Hagan
Published by Charisma House
A part of Strang Communications Company
600 Rinehart Road
Lake Mary, Florida 32746
www.charismahouse.com

Unless otherwise noted, all Scripture quotations are from the New
American Standard Bible. Copyright © 1960, 1962, 1963, 1968, 1971,
1972, 1973, 1975, 1977 by the Lockman Foundation. Used by permission. (www.Lockman.org)

Scripture quotations marked KJV are from the King James Version of
the Bible.

Scripture quotations marked NIV are from the Holy Bible, New
International Version. Copyright © 1973, 1978, 1984, International
Bible Society. Used by permission.

Scripture quotations marked NKJV are from the New King James
Version of the Bible. Copyright © 1979, 1980, 1982 by Thomas
Nelson, Inc., publishers. Used by permission.

Scripture quotations marked THE MESSAGE are from *The Message:
The Bible in Contemporary English*, copyright © 1993, 1994, 1995,
1996, 2000, 2001, 2002. Used by permission of NavPress Publishing
Group.

Cover design by Karen Gonsalves

Library of Congress Cataloging-in-Publication Data
Hagan, Scott.
They felt the Spirit's touch / Scott Hagan.
    p. cm.
ISBN 0-88419-928-2
1. Bible. N.T. Acts--Biography. 2. Bible. N.T. Epistles of
Paul--Biography. 3. Christian life--Biblical teaching. I. Title.
BS2430.H24 2003
226.6'0922--dc21

2003010610

03 04 05 06 07 — 87654321
Printed in the United States of America

This book is dedicated to my four children:

Joslyn,

Tyler,

Kramer

and Spencer.

When it came to having kids, Mom and I went four for four, with four home runs.

Acknowledgments

Let me say a word of thanks to:

- My E-group: I can't reveal your names...at least not yet. Karen and I love and appreciate each of you for bringing laughter, spirituality and accountability to our lives.

- Greg Heeres, an unexpected friend during an unexpected season of life: Thanks, Barnabas.

- My fabulous staff and ministry team at Grand Rapids First: It's still new, fresh and at times confusing, but we are getting there. And most importantly, we are getting there together.

- Joan TeRoller, Sue Sanders and Sue Sauer—my superstar team: Karen and I deeply appreciate all you do for our ministry and family.

- Bob and Beverley Hagan: Mom and Dad, thanks for moving to Michigan. Enjoy the winter! From my first year of Little League in 1972 until now you have supported me without wavering. Dad, you taught me how to tell a good story. Mom, you taught me how to love without limit. I'm not as good as either of you at those things quite yet, but maybe I will get there one day.

- My GR First church family: People think "GR" stands for "Grand Rapids"; it really stands for *great relationships.* You have been daring, flexible and mega-loving. There are three words from my heart to you—I love you.

❧ Wayne and Kathy Benson, and Perry and Barb Kallevig: Being a part of kingdom dominos has been a challenge for all of us. But look at the friendships it has brought. To God be the glory!

❧ Stephen Strang and Lee Grady: Your personal investment in a rookie writer has meant so much. Thanks for being humble and staying close enough to shore to help those who are just learning to swim.

❧ Barbara Dycus and Deborah Moss: Your graciousness ministered to my sluggishness on several occasions. Thank you for treating me with such esteem *every time* I called.

❧ Dan Duka, Kevin Compton, Rich Wilkerson and Bob Johnson: Thanks for being some of the men who have shaped my ship over the years.

❧ Neva Swinson: You don't simply lighten the load; you flat out remove it entirely. You have served your way into our hearts. Thank you for such sacrificial ministry to our children.

❧ Bob and Maryann Coppinger: Thanks for letting me hijack your office to get this manuscript finished. You are treasures from the Lord.

❧ Max Lucado and John Grisham: I've never met either one of you (yet), but your writing gifts have affected me deeply. Thank you.

❧ Brenda Haggard: Thanks for a masterful study guide. You did a great job!

- Phil Aud, David Beiser and Darnisha Taylor: Your anointed worship, songwriting and voices have been central to my experience with God during this past year. I love each of you dearly.

- And to my wife Karen: Your role as general during "operation deadline" was outstanding. After twenty years, you're still my beauty to rescue.

Contents

They Felt the Spirit's Touch

Chapter 1

The Story of Apollos

Now a certain Jew named Apollos, an Alexandrian by birth, an eloquent man, came to Ephesus; and he was mighty in the Scriptures...and he began to speak out boldly in the synagogue. But when Priscilla and Aquila heard him, they took him aside and explained to him the way of God more accurately.
—Acts 18:24, 26

Our house had one bathroom. The cushions on the downstairs couch, a tear. My blue jeans, an iron-on patch over the knee. But the real clincher was the family car, a 1966 Rambler. The problem? The year was 1974. In other words, by my tenth birthday, I had pretty much figured out that when it came to riches and fame, our family stood out like a tree in the middle of a dense forest.

Please don't get me wrong; love abounded, just not in the form of fancy material things. But the important stuff was all there. Like full cereal boxes at breakfast. A Christmas sock

1

hanging by the fireplace. A new Eveready for my transistor. But *elaborate*, for us, meant things like a new soap-on-a-rope for the bathtub. Or being able to lick store-bought Popsicles with two sticks instead of homemade ice pops with none.

Maybe it was getting to stay up late one night a year in our flannel "jammies" to watch *The Wizard of Oz*. Mom would let us spread out the big red plaid blanket on the floor while she filled the biggest green Tupperware bowl you have ever seen with popcorn. If you saw the big green bowl on the table… if you could smell a cold cube of butter being slowly melted on the stove…if the navy blue Morton's Salt container had been moved from the pantry to the counter…then you knew tonight was big.

But we kids understood our part, too. Without a pause or rewind button, we had to learn to budget our bladder. An unplanned trip to the bathroom could cost you an entire year of waiting to see the scene you just missed, all because you couldn't manage the two Pepsi floats you downed before Dorothy met her first Munchkin.

With that being said, growing up a Hagan in the 1970s wasn't all bad. It did offer me one important fringe benefit the rest of the world didn't have: It gave me a lifetime membership to my Grandma Addie's kitchen. I never needed permission to enter. Actually, no one did. Grandma had an "open cookie jar" policy. If you could spot it, you could bite it. But on one occasion, that policy got me in big trouble. Grandma was out to have my hide. It also made me mad enough to punch the guy in the nose if I ever met him. This was his fault, not mine.

What guy? Obviously I'm talking about the guy who invented wax fruit. At seven years of age, someone forget to inform me that the latest rage in home decorating was to place a basket of fake fruit on the kitchen table—some bogus bananas, an imitation apple, a phony pear or two. No one ever told me a thing about this.

As I remember it, I had vigorously entered Grandma's house one afternoon and went straight for the kitchen. I spotted a shiny red apple along with some other fruit sitting in a basket on the kitchen table. I never hesitated. I grabbed the apple and bit hard. But instead of sinking through the skin, my teeth slid across the apple, collecting wax. Immediately I thought the wax was pesticide.

In other words, *I had eaten an unwashed apple!*

Based on the reports I had heard from grown-ups, this meant I was going to die in less than five minutes. Grandma yelled at me. I mean, she *really* yelled. But it wasn't to save me from poisoning; it was to scold me for ruining the new batch of wax fruit she had just bought at Woolworth.

How was I to know? The apple looked ripe and ready to me.

Do you ever wonder what God thinks about wax fruit? You should. There are lots of it sitting in the church. And there are probably even more standing behind the pulpit. I should know; that's where I get to stand when I go to church.

Which is why I am glad there are stories like the one you're about to hear. It involves a man named Apollos. And no, Apollos wasn't an ancient Grecian weightlifter. He was a Book of Acts preacher. But more importantly, he allowed the Holy Spirit to do something about the wax fruit in his life. His journey and life message will encourage you. In essence, this is the lesson he left.

Even though you may be able to wax eloquent with your words, God still requires that the fruit of your heart be real.

Head and Shoulders Above the Rest

Blessed with an eloquent tongue, Apollos was a man of strength and stature. Mantled with movie-star qualities and saddled from birth with intuition and insight, his word-gifts were irresistible to the ear. When you heard him, you believed him. Apollos, like all gifted communicators, was naturally persuasive. Even the educated Pharisees coveted his abilities.

I could see his fellow fraternity of Book of Acts preachers having to nail their jealousies to the cross every time they heard him speak. He had the goods of greatness. Stacked against the man with ten talents, Apollos appeared to have eleven. But what made Apollos good was not the gift. It was the grace. The grace to grow.

But like all great stories of personal grace, there are others in the picture. For Apollos, those others were Priscilla and Aquila. Tentmakers by trade, they became kingdom makers by calling. Driven out of Italy by Emperor Claudius of Rome in A.D. 52, Priscilla and Aquila fled to the safety of Corinth. Word about this exceptional duo had reached Paul, who was now well into his second missionary journey. After arriving in Corinth, Paul quickly went looking for Priscilla and Aquila.

Paul would spend a tumultuous year and a half in Corinth before setting sail across the Syrian Sea to Ephesus. He invited his special friends, Priscilla and Aquila, to join him for the voyage. They happily agreed. Soon after landing in Ephesus, the two tentmakers from Italy stumbled into a local synagogue and heard a prolific preacher working his craft. That preacher was Apollos.

As they listened, they both agreed that this guy was a cut

above anything they had ever heard. They had enjoyed Paul's preaching ministry, but whoever this guy was, he was in a different category. The synagogue was abuzz about this wordsmith from Alexandria. His command of Scripture was spellbinding.

Priscilla and Aquila sat on the edge of their benches as Apollos used the Old Testament brilliantly. Toward the end of his sermon Apollos finally began speaking in New Testament terms. But Priscilla and Aquila were surprised at the emphasis he placed on John the Baptist. Hopefully Jesus was right around the corner.

But something happened. Or actually, *didn't* happen. Apollos finished his message without mentioning the redemptive gift of Jesus that comes through repentance. Priscilla and Aquila looked each other. "Sweetheart," Apollos whispered, "we have to get to that young preacher. That's way too much gift not to know about grace. He's got John the Baptist down pat. But what about Jesus?"

Apollos wasn't a false teacher; he just hadn't read the rest of the book.

The Bible lauds Apollos on several fronts. Here are the attributes found in Acts 18:24–25.

> *"An eloquent man"*–Apollos was a fluent orator. He was effortless and smooth as a public speaker.

> *"Mighty in the Scriptures"*–Apollos was able to powerfully explain Jewish Scriptures.

> *"Instructed in the way of the Lord"*–Apollos had a working, but limited, knowledge of Jesus.

> *"Fervent in spirit"*–Like boiling liquid, Apollos pleaded his cause with passion.

They Felt the Spirit's Touch

✍❤ *"Speaking and teaching accurately"*–Apollos accepted
what he knew and taught it in a straightforward way.

As they stepped away from the crowd for some private words, Priscilla and Aquila wore a smile, but not the usual smile Apollos was accustomed to seeing. Being pulled aside after a sermon was nothing new for Apollos.

Priscilla and Aquila were moved by what they heard, but beyond the words of a great orator they saw a fast-approaching wall. And unless there was a significant move toward grace, the fine young preacher would experience a painful crash. Tonight may be fine, but tomorrow would bring exhaustion—the exhaustion of trying to spell *love* with the letters L-A-W. Unless Apollos came into the fullness of grace, life as a verbal vagabond awaited. His influence would never reach beyond the synagogues of Ephesus.

> **But when Priscilla and Aquila heard him, they took him aside and explained to him the way of God more accurately.**
>
> **–ACTS 18:26**

Therein lies the best part of the story. In the previous verse, Apollos was commended for "speaking and teaching *accurately*" (emphasis added). The Greek word for *accurate* is *akribos*. It simply means "exactly." In other words, Apollos was teaching the Scriptures exactly as he knew them.

But after hearing him speak, the Bible says Priscilla and Aquila "explained to him [Apollos] the way of God *more accurately*" (v. 26, emphasis added). So what's the difference between "accurate" and "more accurate"? Good question. To be honest, it looks more like legalistic hairsplitting on the part of Priscilla and Aquila than genuine concern. The changes Apollos was being challenged to make in his ministry were so subtle they were nearly undetectable.

Which speaks to the glory of this man's heart.

Pride works like stealth. Our undetectable pride draws battle lines against our undetected flaws. When God looked at Apollos, He applauded his progress. But after applauding, He pulled out His dust rag. The preacher needed polishing. There was dust on his doctrine. More than He wanted to hear just a good message, God wanted to see *His* reflection in Apollos from any angle.

Apollos was an Alexandrian, but he's no foreigner. We all share his struggle.

- The struggle to move from gifts to growth

- The struggle to remain spiritually hungry when life is full of satisfying experiences

- The struggle to receive instruction from those outside your gifting

- The struggle to defend our subtle shortcomings

Preachers usually don't let plumbers help them become better preachers. But that's exactly what God required of Apollos. I haven't seen too many tentmakers offering seminars in better communication techniques. So I applaud Priscilla and Aquila for having the guts to step forward. But I applaud Apollos even more for his willingness to listen. He could have done what most of us do when confronted with correction. We smile, offer a polite nod and acknowledge, with appreciation, their input.

Inside, however, is an emotional traffic jam. This can include a soaring heart rate, rising temperature in the facial area and, last but not least, a countenance seizure. *Now, who are you again, and what do you do for living? Tentmakers? Well, isn't that sweet! Say, why don't you just go back to your seat now and keep your insignificant little mouth shut? Have you forgotten who the preacher is?* Of course we never say that, but behind the smile it has crossed our minds.

Correction is tough medicine. Improvement can be excruciating.

But for Apollos, the results were fabulous. More than just believing him, people could now believe *in him*. Apollos was now ready to step into an explosive future. After preaching in Ephesus, Apollos wanted out. He wasn't looking to run and hide. He was a dreamer set on expanding the gospel. "And when he [Apollos] wanted to go across to Achaia…" (v. 27). He longed to be there in person and see how God might use him. But in order to get a foot in the door, he would need the help of a forerunner. Someone to vouch for his heart. And to guarantee that his agenda was grace and nothing more.

Having preached about John the Baptist, Apollos knew the value of a good forerunner. Hedging the reputation and good name of another was the only way Achaia would open up to his ministry. But John the Baptist was dead, so who could run clearance on his behalf?

Hmm…How about two Jewish Italians with their own line of signature tents?

But why on earth would Priscilla and Aquila recommend Apollos for anything? He couldn't even preach a basic sermon on grace. According to their criteria, hadn't he fallen short? That may have been the case at one time, but now they were ready with letters of approval. Apollos had won their admiration in one sermon; now he owned their respect. But why?

Because humility trumps lip service every time.

The Story of Apollos

Humility rescued Apollos from a life sentence of irrelevance. The test for Apollos was not if he could discover the latest preaching technique, but whether or not he was willing to listen to advice. Nothing is more demanding than the process of personal refinement. And people tend to know when someone has an authentic passion for refinement or whether they are masquerading. When it comes to the soil of the human heart, people can discern between the fallow and the fertile. Because their advice was honestly valued, Priscilla and Aquila were ready to sow more than advice; they were ready to speak into the advancement of Apollos' dream. Assisting Apollos with letters of recommendation was now an honor, not a chore.

We don't know what the letters of recommendation to the churches in Achaia actually said, but I can guess what the personal one they put in Apollos' pocket said before he left for Achaia. I imagine it went something like this:

> We are proud to say that we know you, Apollos. You were good before, but now you're both good and ready. Go tear it up, Apollos; we believe in you. You have demonstrated a willingness to learn. You have allowed the Holy Spirit to refine your heart and shore up your edges. God asked for the deeper things of your heart, and you took delight in that. You have accepted the challenge to grow God's way.
>
> And another thing, Apollos; thank you for not tripping over protocol and titles. There's not a Pharisee in the world who could understand what you've just done. But who cares? Jesus is proud of you.
>
> You were teachable and submitted. God wanted to dot the i's and cross the t's in your life, and you handed Him the pen.

They Felt the Spirit's Touch

Keep exploring, son. You have realized the great secret of life: The gift is the starting block. Character is the finish line.

By the way, enjoy the new tent. It's the least we can do. We heard it gets cold this time of year in Achaia.

Chapter 2

The Story of the Ethiopian Eunuch

And behold, there was an Ethiopian eunuch, a court official of Candace, queen of the Ethiopians, who was in charge of all her treasure; and he had come to Jerusalem to worship. And he was returning and sitting in his chariot, and was reading the prophet Isaiah. And the Spirit said to Philip, "Go up and join this chariot."
—Acts 8:27–29

Confession time.

As a kid, I thought "Eunuch" was his first name. Seriously. And he had a twin brother named Enoch or something like that. A few years later I wised up and thought "Eunuch" was an official title, like "Herod" or "Pontius." So, being "Eunuch" meant you oversaw important things for the queen, which would explain the chariot. (See, I was smart as a kid.)

I found out that wasn't the case either, so I concluded it must be the name of his hometown. In other words, the Ethiopian was from a place called "Eunuchville."

Then I went to college and discovered what *eunuch* really meant.

That's when I took a deep breath and thanked God I wasn't from "Eunuchville."

If it's OK with you, I would like to change the subject for few moments. We will kind of ease our way into this one.

A few months ago, I had a Saturday afternoon battle with a pesky leak. My son's bike had a flat back tire. No problem. *Right.*

After three trips to the bicycle shop, two bloody knuckles and one frustrated little boy, I was about out of patience. For a busy boy, no wheels meant no life. For a beat dad, no wheels meant no Saturday nap.

At first, I looked for the obvious hole in the rubber tire, but I found none. So I pumped up the flat and listened for a moment to determine if I could hear a leak. I didn't hear a thing. So I declared the tire fixed and sent Spencer on his way.

Ten minutes later he was back in the house with a flat tire.

This time I took the tire off the bike and removed the inner tube. I carefully examined it to see if I could spot a hole. Aha! I found it. I grabbed Spencer, and we took a fun drive to the bicycle shop to purchase a patch. Back home we carefully placed it over the leak. Once the epoxy was dry, I stuffed the inner tube back inside the rubber tire, squeezed the tire around the rim, wrenched tightly all the nuts, reattached the greasy chain, wiped the grease off my hands, flipped the bike upright and handed it back to Spencer. With a big smile on his face, off he rode.

Ten minutes later he was back in the house with a flat tire.

Come on, Son, what are you doing? Riding your bike through a nail factory? I closely reexamined my patch. This made no sense. I took another trip to the bike shop and tried to blame them for selling me a faulty patch. They were friendly and gave me a new one. Back home I took off the old patch and put the new patch over the leak. I told Spencer the bike shop was to blame, not Dad. Off he rode.

Ten minutes later he was back at the house with a flat tire.

In disgust I flipped the bike upside down, balancing it on the seat and handlebars. I wrenched off the nuts, *again*… disengaged the chain, *again*…struggled to get the rubber tire off the rim, *again*…and inspected it all, *again*. This time, however, I remembered an old trick that would prove the bike shop was selling me faulty patches. After pumping the tube full of air, I got a big bucket of water and submerged the tube.

A steady rise of bubbles instantly darted to the surface. See! I knew it! Oops. The bubbles weren't coming from anywhere near the patch. This was another leak.

It never occurred to me there could be two leaks. The one I found led me to believe I was smart enough to find them all. Bad assumption, Scott.

I hate to tell you this, but you also have a leak. Your soul is losing air. Sin has created tiny punctures in your spiritual inner tube. Some of those holes are visible to the naked eye. Most are not.

No one needs to tell us when we're losing air. We can feel ourselves going flat a block from the house. Sometimes even a block from the church. Some of the holes are obvious. Sometimes we can even see where the nail is sticking out. But most of the holes are so tiny they can't be found with the naked eye. We may get lucky and find one hole, patch it, and say, "There, I'm all right." But give it ten minutes, and we're flat as ever.

You may be thinking, *OK, so what's your point?*

🖎 I've discovered that air tends to hide well in an atmosphere of air.

🖎 I've also discovered that sin tends to hide well in an atmosphere of sin.

🖎 If you want to find the leak, you must change the atmosphere.

🖎 No matter how tiny the hole is, the moment air meets water, it can no longer hide.

🖎 No matter how tiny the hole is, the moment sin meets grace, it can no longer hide.

Without the atmosphere of grace, everything is a guessing game. We end up frustrated instead of fixed. Well, since this chapter is about eunuchs, "getting fixed" is probably not the best choice of words.

Why couldn't God have made him a fisherman from Capernaum? Or a pigeon salesman from Bethlehem? Why did he have to be a eunuch? There is no debate over what the definition of a eunuch is. It is a castrated male.

There were three ways a male could end up in this condition.

1. He was born that way by God's design.
2. He made a personal choice to become one.
3. It was his sentence for a crime.

The Ethiopian was about to experience a sudden change of cabin pressure. God was sending a change in atmosphere.

The eunuch from Ethiopia we are about to meet made a career choice to become a eunuch. Service in the queen's court was a high privilege. To ensure purity of service, many who served in close proximity to the queen and her maidens took a vow of celibacy. Part of that vow was to become a eunuch. It was regarded as an act of dedication to God and master.

This eunuch was God fearing but Jesus illiterate. He had ventured to Jerusalem to worship God. We have no idea what he actually encountered while in Jerusalem, but something tells you it was more temple than triumph… more religious than refreshing. He came looking, but he left empty. The chariot ride home was filled with unmet curiosity and growing confusion.

In other words, he felt flat, but he couldn't find the leak.

Somewhere along the way, the Ethiopian eunuch took out the scroll of Isaiah that had captured his interest. These were the words he read: "He was led as a sheep to slaughter; and as a lamb before its shearer is silent, so He does not open His mouth. In humiliation His judgment was taken away; who shall relate His generation? For His life is removed from the earth" (Acts 8:32–33).

Who was this talking about? Was Isaiah describing himself, or was he talking about another? Being a part of City Hall himself, the eunuch knew the ropes of civil authority. Why would an innocent man remain silent and allow himself to be slaughtered? And if a man is removed from the earth, where does he go?

Here come the bubbles. The leak is about to be patched.

Philip had his own set of questions. One of the seven original deacons, he was asked without warning to head south and take the desert road from Jerusalem to Gaza. The angel gave him no future instructions. There was no "mission impossible tape" waiting for him to tell him what his next step would be. It was basically, "Start walking, pal." Philip must have thought about ancient Israel. They too stepped into a desert, but it was forty years before they found their way out.

You have to give Philip credit. He was willing to accept the extreme…to enter a desert without details of the assignment.

Along the way to "who knows where," Philip began looking for clues. He spotted a carriage. It was the official chariot of the Ethiopian finance minister. The Spirit of God said to him, "Go up and join this chariot," and Philip never asked why. The Bible says that he ran up to it. Like a parade gawker chasing the float of dignitary, Philip, who has no idea why, was running alongside the chariot of a total stranger.

If you won't say it, I will.

> *✍* Sometimes obedience looks totally ridiculous.

> *✍* And sometimes the preposterous precedes understanding our purpose.

"Hey, Philip, why are you out here running in the desert chasing the chariot of a total stranger?"

"God asked me to."

"So what happens next?"

"No clue."

Something the eunuch heard in Jerusalem deeply affected him, but he couldn't find clarity. So God created a divine encounter—but one that was still dependent upon obedience to the odd. Imagine the devastating consequence if Philip had introduced logic into the story. *Lord, I was just elected as a deacon two chapters ago. Stephen is already dead, so we are now down to six deacons. I don't have time for ridiculous trips to nowhere.*

It wasn't until he was next to the chariot that Philip began to spot the clues. He heard the driver of the chariot reading a familiar story. He recognized the words of Isaiah. In an instant the assignment made sense to Philip.

"Do you understand what you are reading?" Philip asked.

The eunuch responded, "'Well, how could I, unless someone guides me?' And he invited Philip to come up and sit with him" (Acts 8:31).

What looks like confusion and coincidence to us is often the long-range strategic planning of God. God processes His plan differently for each individual. In this case, God had to get the eunuch outside the religious atmosphere of Jerusalem in order to locate the leak. The demands of Ethiopia, the religiosity of Jerusalem—it's like trying to locate doubt in an atmosphere of doubt.

A lonely desert. Anointed scripture. A man with crazy, obedient love for Jesus running next to your chariot. And you have an atmosphere of faith.

Beginning with the words of Isaiah, Philip patched the leak. The great questions of life have all been answered for the eunuch from Ethiopia. But why stop here? The eunuch spotted a place to be baptized. Philip asked him the most important question ever asked of the human heart: "If you believe with all heart, you may [be baptized]" (Acts 8:37). And the eunuch gave the only response that matters in life: *"I believe that Jesus Christ is the Son of God."*

The fun was long from over. As Philip lifted the eunuch out of the water, God lifted Philip out of the tank and abruptly placed him sixty miles away in Azotus. The man (Philip), who was willing to walk by faith through a hot desert solely because God had asked him to, suddenly got the ride of lifetime.

For Philip, this was much more than a short assignment in

the desert. The Spirit "translated" him á la *Star Trek* some sixty miles away to Azotus. The next time we read about Philip in the Book of Acts is twenty years later. He was still near Azotus. Can you imagine the fun Philip had when the neighbors asked...

"So, what brought you to Azotus?"

Chapter 3

The Story of Ananias

And Ananias departed and entered the house, and after laying his hands on him said, "Brother Saul, the Lord Jesus, who appeared to you on the road by which you were coming, has sent me so that you may regain your sight, and be filled with the Holy Spirit." And immediately there fell from his eyes something like scales, and he regained his sight, and he arose and was baptized; and he took food and was strengthened.
—Acts 9:17–19

What bothered John most that afternoon was not the questionable company or the lousy food prepared by the women at the church. It was the ticking watch on Uncle Frederick's left wrist.

Uncle Frederick was dressed in gray flannel. His favorite hat rested on his chest. Having spent his entire working life in the lumber mill, and then as a retired handyman, Uncle Frederick would have been appalled at the makeup someone in the embalming room had put on his face.

Earlier that morning, John had privately mulled around

They Felt the Spirit's Touch

Uncle Frederick's open casket, which was suspended over a freshly dug grave at the Oak Hill Cemetery. Looking around, he took mental notes of how death is finally dealt with. There was a pile of rich brown dirt, four rolls of moist green sod, two shovels and a pine box with a few upgrades. And, of course, Uncle Frederick's motionless body.

The outdoor memorial would soon find itself competing with an unexpected fall storm. In less than an hour, the first significant rainfall of the season would hit. The dark clouds above the cemetery had diffused the late-morning sun. Countless orange and yellow leaves were falling like parade confetti. The semiordered tapestry of tombstones, many of which were displaced by the roots of old trees, was now quickly disappearing beneath the spectacular leafy hues of mid-October.

Following the brief memorial, a small crowd of shirttail relatives began moving toward their cars. Out of the corner of his eye, John spotted two mortuary staffers closing the casket lid. The muted sunlight was still bright enough to create a shadow line across Uncle Frederick's torso as the lid was slowly closed. For a melancholy life and man like Uncle Frederick, the moment was invitingly dramatic. Just as the lid was about to close, John noticed the gold watch on Uncle Frederick's left wrist. It was new.

At last month's funeral for Ed, a longtime friend and fishing buddy from the mill, Uncle Frederick had been showing off his new watch to anybody who would look and listen. He kept bragging about the lifetime battery. *How ridiculous*, John thought. *A running watch on a dead man's arm.*

Back at Aunt Mary's house the postmortem potluck was well under way. John shifted the paper plate that was balanced on his right thigh, being careful not to knock over the glass of iced tea near his foot. The plate was filled with two chicken legs, cream corn and a heap of potato salad. A thick photo album was straddled between his left knee and the knee of his younger sister Nancy.

Nancy was feeling nostalgic. John was feeling numb and disengaged. The stack of family photo albums on the coffee table meant nothing to him. Nancy knew her older brother didn't care a lick about the pictures. But still, she kept turning the pages, pointing her finger and directing comments to no one in particular. Once she finished looking at one album, she would move to the next. The pages were mostly filled with square black-and-whites. The pictures revealed a series of boxlike houses, an occasional car with big fins, and people who hadn't been told yet it was OK to smile in a picture.

Nancy had always carried the responsibility for covering up the family dysfunction as best she could. But this time, her small talk was getting her nowhere with her older brother John. A trip down memory lane was the last road John wanted to travel. Just ask him, and he would be the first to say his family tree was covered with poison bark.

At forty-eight, John viewed himself as bald, fat, alone and in debt. The only reason he had come to the house that weekend was because of the funeral. For John, family gatherings meant appearances, not relationships. A few fond boyhood memories about Uncle Frederick and duty for the dead were the only reasons he decided to stop by the house.

John had risen many times at the local AA meetings to clear his throat and acknowledge his alcoholism. That wasn't the problem. The problems began once the meetings dismissed. Now the adults from his childhood were dying off one by one. The dark conveyor belt moving toward the local morgue was moving fast—and the line ahead of him seemed to be getting shorter by the month.

He was about to call it quits and leave when his sister turned another page. He noticed a picture he had never seen. Neither had Nancy. As a kid, most of these photos were in a shoebox. He and his sister would look through them once a year when his family visited Aunt Mary's house. But this one he couldn't place. It was a grainy black-and-white, faded and forgotten by six decades. He looked again, but couldn't place the man in the picture.

Across the room, rocking in perfect time, was Grandma Alice. She lived with Aunt Mary. She was as quiet and still as a morning pond and wrinkled from head to toe. She was legacy the way it ought to be. Everyone loved her. But few family members ever conversed with her beyond the obligatory hug and hello when entering the room. She was the only one who knew the mysterious identity of the man in the photograph.

Without any prompting, Grandma Alice spoke up. She had been monitoring every page as Nancy turned them. "That's your father's father." John and Nancy were shocked. They had never seen a picture of their grandfather on Dad's side. All they knew was that he died when their father was an infant. There were rumors, but no one knew for certain how or why he died.

Grandma Alice knew. She always did. But she chose not to tell. But even Grandma knew it was time for this family secret to come out of the closet. "Helen's son found that picture in their attic and gave it to me last month at church. So I put it in the photo album. I was hoping someone would see it."

This explained why no one had ever seen the photo.

The Story of Ananias

"What happened to him?" asked someone standing in the entryway.

"He was shot to death!" Everyone within earshot of the rocker was startled to hear Grandma Alice's candid explanation.

"Why was he shot?" asked one of the young nephews sprawled on the carpet. "Did they catch the guy?"

"No, they never got him."

Grandma Alice kept right on rocking, and then added, "A United States marshal shot him." She paused for several more seconds. Even the disengaged John couldn't remain detached now. He wanted more details.

Grandma Alice leaned forward. Using her toes for brakes, she brought her rocking chair to a halt. "Twice, in the back of the head. He was shot in Pickens, Oklahoma, 1932."

With an air of self-righteousness, John demanded an explanation. "Why on earth would a U.S. marshal shoot my grandfather in the back of the head?"

"Because he was running away with illegal whiskey in his arms. You kids are old enough to know the truth." Then like a judge pronouncing the sentence, she blurted out, "Your daddy's papa was a bootlegger."

John was no longer looking at his grandmother. His eyes were fixed on the small photo at the bottom of the page. He was studying the scene that surrounded the grandfather he had just met. It was a makeshift bar located somewhere in the middle of Oklahoma.

The man in the photo had the smile of a drunk. John had seen that face a hundred times in his own mirror.

For John, the chain was now complete. His grandfather had been a drunk—executed over a bottle of whiskey. His own father, George, was also a drunk. He died of a failed liver at sixty-one. And now there was John's own twenty-two-year-old son, Clay, who was absent from the funeral because he was serving out a court-ordered work project, having been arrested for his third DUI in two years.

John got up from the couch and slipped away without saying a word to anyone. The caustic taste of bile was burning its way up his esophagus. He was fighting the sensation to vomit. Grossly distraught, he left for good. Only one person in the crowded house heard the sound of the back screen door slamming shut.

They thought it was the wind.

A Journey of Self-Awareness

So what does a man named Ananias (this is not the Ananias who was married to Sapphira) have to do with the story of an alcoholic named John? More than we care to admit. John saw a photo. Ananias heard a voice speak his name. Both had the same result. The real identity from within surfaced. A decision had to be made. And like John, Ananias had the option of running from the ugliness. Or he could allow God to dramatically change him forever.

The Lord's instruction to Ananias was unthinkable. God told him to go and touch the untouchable. To risk it all by approaching the unapproachable. Ananias' first response to God is typical of most of us. He was fearful and unwilling. The social conditions around him said that it was a mistake. The logic inside of him said that it was absurd. Recent history told him it was a setup. But God kept talking. Ananias quickly realized he was arguing with a stubborn God.

For the most part, our journey with Jesus is a journey toward self-awareness. *Who am I really? And what truly fills my heart?* Everyone confronts the issue; most, however, find the screen door and disappear.

Like the alcoholic, Ananias came face to face with his past and its powerful control over his future. And, like John, others would pay dearly unless something changed inside of Ananias.

We know from Scripture that Ananias was a disciple of Jesus and that he lived in Damascus. His love for the Lord was evident by his immediate response to His voice: "And the Lord said to him in a vision, 'Ananias.' And he said, 'Behold, here am I, Lord'" (Acts 9:10).

In many ways Ananias was like the quiet church mouse. He was a private but devout and faithful Christian. He held no public office. He had no desire to.

But life for the church mouse was now over. It was time for the mouse to loose the lion.

Ananias was the kind of Christian Saul was looking to arrest and persecute. This wasn't breaking news to Ananias. "Lord, I have heard from many about this man, how much harm he did to Thy saints at Jerusalem; and here he has authority from the chief priests to bind all who call upon Thy name" (Acts 9:13–14).

To hear the Lord say that Saul was a "chosen instrument of Mine" wasn't exactly music to Ananias' ears. Even without the aid of modern media, word spread easily about this Saul of Tarsus. The last thing Christians in Damascus wanted was for the contentions of Jerusalem to come to their city. They wanted Saul of Tarsus to just go away.

Instead, the Lord told Ananias to go find Saul and pray for him. The Lord was saying to Ananias, "Don't hesitate; I've disabled him. There is greatness in Saul's heart. He too will be a great risk taker. But I have called you to take the first risk. Quickly, Ananias, go find him and reveal yourself."

For Ananias to obey this request and touch Saul would be the greatest challenge of his life. His only guarantee of safety was the peace and assurance that God had asked him to do this. Nothing else.

Ananias was about to discover that for the lost to be reached, the saved must be willing to touch.

Like most Christians, Ananias loved the Lord, but his life was ruled by the stories around him. Let's be honest; Ananias was a mixture of faith and fear. We all are to some degree. It took this unusual circumstance for Ananias to see himself with a clear sense of self-awareness. Only then could God change him.

"I am afraid."

Afraid of what, Ananias?

"Stories."

What kind of stories, Ananias?

Ananias's fears about Saul had grown larger than life itself. Someone he had never met now paralyzed him. Yet God said to Ananias, "Go find the killer, and pray for him."

One of the more difficult tests of faith is not only to love our enemies, but also to believe God loves them, too. And that He has a plan for them. A plan that could be bigger than His plan for us. Even more faith stretching is when He asks us to risk our lives so our current enemies can prosper in His kingdom.

It is no wonder Ananias had an honest talk with God about all of this. But God handled his questions beautifully. When God sees a person's life, He sees through His own set of Alpha and Omega eyes. God sees beginnings as well as endings.

In other words, when God sees the cradle, He also sees the rocking chair.

The Story of Ananias

Ananias yielded to God's wish. And the Holy Spirit's one touch changed the world. Ananias overcame his fears and left them behind. In some way, every act of glorious faith leaves behind a destroyed set of fears.

> **And Ananias departed and entered the house, and after laying his hands on him said, "Brother Saul, the Lord Jesus, who appeared to you on the road by which you were coming, has sent me so that you may regain your sight, and be filled with the Holy Spirit."**
> —ACTS 9:17

The Bible goes on to indicate that "something" fell from his eyes (v. 18). But it was more like something fell into place for the kingdom of God.

For Paul to reach the lost, the Holy Spirit first had to reach the saved. Ananias loved the Lord, but he had no idea how passionate the Lord was about reaching this world. Or what that love would require of him personally.

Ananias finally welcomed Saul like family, referring to him as "Brother Saul," words that to him seemed foreign and impossible only hours earlier. As a resident of Damascus himself, he knew Saul's original intent for coming to Damascus. But Ananias allowed Redemption to be King, even when it came to aggressive, mean-spirited sinners who were still living on the ugly side of their miracle.

I guess you can sum it up this way. The killer named Saul became the mighty steamship known as *Paul the Apostle*. But the mighty steamship would have sat blinded and powerless in the harbor had it not been for one thing:

A willing tugboat named Ananias.

Chapter 4

The Story of Sosthenes

And they all took hold of Sosthenes, the leader of the synagogue, and began beating him in front of the judgment seat. And Gallio was not concerned about any of these things.
—Acts 18:17

Sosthenes could feel the fullness of the rage on the first strike. His mind told his body to relax and just take it. Maybe through mental techniques he could minimize the pain. It was useless. The blows were too powerful. His body resisted in the same way soft butter resists a hot knife.

A thousand bolts of electric agony pinged in all directions throughout his chest cavity. The side of his face was next. Then his legs. Then his groin. Hellish echoes of pain shot everywhere. *They are trying to kill me.* Each reverberation was as agonizing as the initial blast. Without time to think...

without time to assimilate the pain, the next set of fists, clubs and boots arrived, each jamming pain into spaces already overloaded with pain. So what did Sosthenes do to deserve this barrage in broad daylight?

Just one thing—he had stood too close to the vision. That was it.

Paul had been ministering in Corinth for nearly a year and a half. For many of the Jews in Corinth, that was a year and a half too long. Their disdain for Paul had finally reached a climax. Out of that violent storm, a mob formed like a sudden Kansas twister. Attempting to use the Roman system to their advantage, the Jews in one accord brought Paul before the leader of the Greek proconsul of Achaia. His name was Gallio. They wanted Gallio to send a strong message to future agitators.

They started by accusing Paul of trampling down the holy laws of Israel. "This man persuades men to worship God contrary to the law" (Acts 18:13). Big stuff to an orthodox mob. Sorry, but paltry peanuts to a busy Roman proconsul.

Gallio quickly decided this wasn't worth his time. It was frivolous and petty. He had no interest in meddling in the affairs of these Jewish law squabblers. He dismissed the court and drove everyone from the judgment seat area. Court closed. This infuriated the Jews. For a year and a half they had put up with Paul's garbage about grace and love, and now, in a matter of seconds, their small window for revenge slammed shut in their face. Without realizing it, Gallio had just poured rocket fuel on their fiery rage.

Standing quietly by was Sosthenes. Some historians believe this was the same Sosthenes that Paul mentioned later: "Paul, called as an apostle of Jesus Christ by the will of God, and Sosthenes our brother" (1 Cor. 1:1). If true, this meant the leader of the synagogue had covertly converted from Judaism to Christianity. Which also meant he knew several of the mob.

Sosthenes had quietly pitied their spiritual shackles ever since he came to know the joys of grace. He also knew that when law rules you, there is only one thing you can become—more lawless. The angry crowd was proving his theory true. What Sosthenes did not know, however, was that he would soon be standing in the crosshairs of that lawlessness himself.

With Gallio gone and Paul nowhere in sight, the crowd began looking for a way to vent their anger. There were no newspaper stands to trash or police cars to tip over and ignite. But there was Sosthenes. Some in the crowd had already made eye contact with him. They had noticed his indifference a few minutes earlier while they were making their appeal to Gallio. It left them wondering why a good, law-abiding Jew would be such a pacifist at a time like this.

Another in the crowd who also saw Sosthenes standing nearby suddenly remembered the rumor about Sosthenes agreeing with Paul's strange version of God—a version that renounced the Law of Moses in favor of a Carpenter. Rumor or not, it was all the crowd needed.

The revolting majority had found their outlet. Gallio had rejected their public wish, but so what? If they couldn't have Paul, then Sosthenes would serve as his replacement. Sosthenes suddenly wished he wasn't so visible. Before he could think twice…before he could offer a solid defense… he was surrounded and under assault.

Like lightning gone mad, the crowd began beating him senseless. Sosthenes was now taking another man's beating. His only mistake was being in the wrong place at the wrong time. Fun stuff.

Here's the lesson. Sometimes serving Jesus means you also get picked to be the surrogate punching bag. Which shouldn't surprise us because that's what Jesus was on the cross—the surrogate Savior. Taking the pain for something He didn't do. Crucified by a human horde for something Adam did. Actually, for something we all did. We deserved that hanging on the cross, not Jesus. But He took it in our place.

When Calvary was all said and done, the Bible continued to hint at something most of us fail to remember. It was Peter who restated what Jesus had already said in His first public sermon. Jesus said:

> **Blessed are those who have been persecuted for the sake of righteousness, for theirs is the kingdom of heaven. Blessed are you when men cast insults at you, and persecute you, and say all kinds of evil against you falsely, on account of Me.**
> **—MATTHEW 5:10–11**

Here is how Peter said it years later:

> **For you have been called for this purpose, since Christ also suffered for you, leaving you an example for you to follow in His steps.**
> **—1 PETER 2:21**

In other words, sometimes the devil takes a swing at God and ends up hitting the church in the nose. And sometimes being in the right place with God can feel like being in all the wrong places with people. And sometimes people who think their problems are with other people are really just mad at God. But since they can't figure out where God is or how to tell Him off, you and I become the next best thing.

Jesus' advice was to keep your inside smile bright by keeping your inside perspective strong. "Rejoice, and be

glad, for your reward in heaven is great, for so they persecuted the prophets who were before you" (Matt. 5:12). You
may not be facing henchmen from the palace of Pharaoh or
an angry band of law lovers who hate the grace that guides
you, but it can still hurt to be so unexpectedly selected as a
punching bag for the cause of Christ.

   ✍ A new nursery policy handed down by the church
     board suddenly means you're the one who's getting
     yelled at by an impatient parent on Sunday morning.

   ✍ The pastor transitions from a declining Sunday night
     service to a new small-group format. Your first night
     as a new small-group leader ends in disaster as every-
     body vents their frustration about the change. You
     feel blamed and on the outside.

   ✍ You volunteer to lead the youth summer missions'
     team only to return to an angry parking lot of parents
     who blame you because their kids got head lice.

   ✍ Or you volunteer to chair the building committee,
     but six months down the road you find yourself
     alienated from friends because pledges have fallen
     short and construction is half completed. Nasty let-
     ters are blaming you for the lack of foresight and
     planning.

No wonder so many in the church think, *Forget it. Who
needs this stuff? I'll just retreat back to the safety of sitting in the
church. They can yell at somebody else. In fact, yell at the pastor; he
gets paid for that, doesn't he? He can find someone else to help him
with the vision. I'll just listen to the sermon, write my check and
enjoy my quiet world of me, myself and I. After all, why get beat up?
Why serve? Why volunteer?*

When you honestly look at what's happening in many

churches, who wouldn't think like this? Well, Jesus wouldn't. And He told us not to either.

One of the most revealing lines in the story of Sosthenes is this: "And they took hold of Sosthenes...and began beating him...And Gallio was not concerned about any of these things" (Acts 18:17).

Not only was there an injustice in the making, but it also seemed seemed that nobody cared enough to step in to stop it. Don't knock Gallio; I don't see Paul, or anyone else for that matter, stepping in to defend poor Sosthenes. It was the kind of loneliness that only Jesus could understand.

Sometimes when you really love something, it might require you to move from the safety of standing by to the danger of standing up. But believing in something can also require something else.

Sometimes it requires you to stand alone and take it on the chin.

Here's a good verse to end with:

> For what credit is there if, when you sin and are harshly treated, you endure it with patience? But if when you do what is right and suffer for it you patiently endure it, this finds favor with God.
>
> —1 PETER 2:20

I told you it was a good verse.

Chapter 5

The Story of
Barsabbas

And they put forward two men, Joseph called Barsabbas (who was also called Justus), and Matthias. And they prayed, and said, "Thou, Lord, who knowest the hearts of all men, show which one of these two Thou hast chosen to occupy this ministry and apostleship from which Judas turned aside to go to his own place." And they drew lots for them, and the lot fell to Matthias . . .
—Acts 1:23–26

I t had all the trappings of a final interview. The breath mints. The posture. The etiquette. The maneuvering to make that good first impression. The arriving thirty minutes early with the look of "this is part of my normal work ethic." There were the competitive but friendly smiles exchanged between applicants as they crossed paths in the lobby. The finalists were both ready and sweaty.

The pay package? Retirement? Well, maybe these weren't the pressing issues with this particular job. But still, both men had high hopes that the job was theirs.

They Felt the Spirit's Touch

This job posting did have one oddity that needs mentioning. The last man to hold this job committed suicide. That alone should have been a warning to these final two candidates as to what the "office" job was all about. But the two stood willing. They were Matthias and Barsabbas.

The existing apostles had solicited both of them, but only one would be needed to fill the slot vacated by the departure of Judas Iscariot. The number was still twelve, not thirteen. One would end up an apostle with a signature pillar in heaven. The other would go back and take his seat as the odd man out.

It was Peter who stood up to remind those in the upper room that the current apostolic vacancy was predicted by King David long ago.

> And at this time Peter stood up in the midst of the brethren (a gathering of about one hundred and twenty persons was there together), and said, "Brethren, the Scripture had to be fulfilled, which the Holy Spirit foretold by the mouth of David concerning Judas, who became a guide to those who arrested Jesus...For it is written in the book of Psalms, 'Let his homestead be made desolate, and let no man dwell in it'; and, 'His office let another man take.'"
>
> —ACTS 1:15–16, 21

The criteria for being a replacement apostle were clear.

Applicants needed to have been among the disciples from the time of Jesus' baptism in the Jordan until His recent ascension in Jerusalem. That narrowed the list. But several were still qualified. The disciples looked around the room. The Eleven quickly caucused. Two stood out. Some among the Eleven thought it was Matthias. Others thought Barsabbas was the choice.

The Story of Barsabbas

They decided to let God have the final vote.

The decision for the next apostle wasn't going to come down to who had the right breath, the right clothes and the right moxie in front of the right people. The selection process hinged upon a simple word revealed in the apostles' prayer. "And they prayed, and said, 'Thou, Lord, who knowest the hearts of all men, show which one of these two Thou hast chosen to occupy this ministry and apostleship from which Judas turned aside to go to his own place" (vv. 24–25).

God's criteria went where no man could look. God was establishing a new set of ground rules. The stakes were too high and the church too young to risk the chance of failure through an unprepared heart. For God it came down to five letters: H-E-A-R-T.

The process of "lots" was simple. Two names were written on either two stones or two separate pieces of parchment and placed in an urn. Someone trustworthy from the congregation was then chosen to come forward and draw one of the names out of the "hat." This allowed God to direct the choice. With the upper room silent, a stone was selected. On it, the name Matthias was written.

I doubt balloons fell. I doubt music played. I doubt Matthias took a walk down the long runway with a bouquet of flowers as he waved to the crowd. No, none of that happened.

At least not on the outside.

As godly as Matthias was, he was still human. And humans get excited when they are chosen over someone else to do important stuff. Be it student council or team captain, we love to be chosen.

We also hate being rejected.

No doubt Barsabbas, the unchosen stone, hugged

Matthias and congratulated him on his selection. No doubt he remained spiritual, humble and positive.

At least on the outside.

There are some days when the lot lets you down. Just ask Barsabbas. He had just finished second in a race of two. Being a silver medalist suddenly didn't feel like such an accomplishment.

It was character that got you this far, Barsabbas, but sorry, God has picked someone else.

It was time for Matthias to move on with the Twelve. It was time for Barsabbas to go quietly back to his seat. And poor Barsabbas, not only did he not get the job, but to this day he also suffers from name confusion. Ask ten Christians who Barsabbas was, and seven of them will tell you he was the guy Pilate let go from prison in favor of Jesus.

The other three think he traveled as a missionary with Paul.

Barsabbas was learning a tough lesson. Maybe God chose him to go through it for the rest of us. As much as I would like to think that is possible, I know differently. All of us go through this moment, but at least we know we're not alone.

Maybe the real chosen one was Barsabbas, not Matthias. Maybe the assignment of modeling joy through disappointment and rejection is what God was after all along. Here are three things Barsabbas could take away from this experience.

1. The best things that happen in life are sometimes the things that do not happen.

2. The will of God is sometimes the wall of God.

3. We tend to learn far more from the word *no* than we do from the word *yes*.

The Story of Barsabbas

Our hearts are tested by disappointment. What good purpose could this experience have served in Barsabbas' life? Why bait him and then burst his bubble? Why not just have one candidate? Why take the risk of a hurt? Yes, the story teaches us that God can see where man cannot. And yes, it teaches that there are standards and qualifications for those who lead us.

But it teaches even louder through Barsabbas that we must triumph over times of personal disappointment. Over those times when we are certain God has opened a door, then after sharing our plans, the door never opens. We feel as if we have egg on our face. We are left embarrassed...sometimes even disillusioned with God.

Romans 8:28 tells us, "God causes all things to work together for good to those who love God, to those who are called according to His purpose." Imagine with me for a moment that you are looking at a beautiful painting of an outdoor landscape. It's filled with hills, a thick forest and a gentle stream. The artist has painstakingly painted the stones and rocks that line the stream.

With your mind's eye, I want you to find four stones among the landscape. And now, take everything off the canvas except for those four stones.

All you have left is a white canvas with four disconnected stones. It makes no sense. Let's say that those four stones represent your four greatest failures, disappointments and rejections in life. Events that will never be washed away from your awareness. Four stones standing alone and separated on the canvas. A painting like that would be worthless in the eyes of most.

But the Word of God promises that when we "love God," He will cause "all things to work together for good." Loving God is the equivalent to inviting a master artist to approach your canvas with permission to paint as he sees fit. When we love the Lord, Jesus, the master Artist, begins to paint between the stones, not over them. At first, it's impossible to tell what Jesus is painting. It feels more confusing than clarifying.

At least before, you could organize your stones and explain your painful but simple story. But now Jesus is painting the blank spaces with something new. The stones remain untouched.

As Jesus paints the canvas with beauty, substance and purpose, a great miracle begins to unfold. In His mercy, Jesus chooses to integrate the original stones from our past into the current and future picture of our lives. Sometimes it takes time for the work of the Artist to make sense. You wonder why He forgives the sin but leaves the stones.

Why?

Because He promised to use "all things." In other words, He takes our painful history and, through grace, incorporates it into our portrait.

When the Artist is given enough time, He will turn your life into a work of art for the world to see. No longer are you a story of disconnected stones. You are now a beautiful work of grace. The stones are included to add beauty, details and value to the portrait.

He will use "all things together" for His good. The painful things. The broken things. The rejected things. But the key is love. Not just God's love toward you, but your love toward Him.

Barsabbas will probably tell me in heaven that I made way too much out of this. That he was fine with not being chosen as Judas Iscariot's replacement. I guess I will have to believe him. But for now, he's one of my secret heroes of Acts.

And by the way, Barsabbas didn't totally disappear. He

showed up one more time in Acts 15. They needed a delegation of highly loving and sensitive individuals who could tenderly hand-deliver an important document on behalf of the early church leadership.

They chose Barsabbas (Acts 15:22).

Oh, by the way, the retirement package Matthias got for his "office" job was a killer. He was stoned by the Jews.

Chapter 6

The Story of
John Mark

*Only Luke is with me. Pick up Mark and bring him with
you, for he is useful to me for service.*
—2 Timothy 4:11

No question…Peter was a braggart. But among the
Twelve, Peter wasn't the lone tongue on parade. John,
believe it or not, also loved to brag. And nothing is worse
than two braggarts on the same team. Just ask Jesus…I'm
sure He would agree. Some of His boys loved to boast.

When Peter bragged, it usually went something like this:
"But Peter answered and said to Him, 'Even though all may
fall away because of You, I will never fall away'" (Matt.
26:33). In other words, Peter loved to brag about how much
he loved the Lord.

John, on the other hand, bragged along a different vein. John described himself as "the disciple whom Jesus loved" (John 20:2). In other words, instead of bragging about how much he loved the Lord, John bragged about how much the Lord loved him.

John the Beloved was a connoisseur of contact. Closeness was his currency. During the Last Supper, he calmly laid his head upon the breast of Jesus and conversed without fear. Everyone wanted that seat next to Jesus in heaven. Only John seemed to want it this side of the cross. Eleven others around the table that evening, including Judas, had quiet flashes of jealousy as they watched the loving interaction between Jesus and John.

Why did John feel so at ease? Maybe his sense of security was based on God's love for him and not on the shiftiness of his own love for God. Oh, yes, John loved Jesus. Everyone around that table did to some measure. But knowing he was categorically loved and accepted by Jesus first gave John the courage and capacity for loving Him in return. He used that sanctuary as a bond. John also knew that life beyond this bond was isolated and confusing.

That was Peter's world, of course.

Directing a simple question at Jesus had become an impossibility for Peter. John was the only conduit he had left. While John the Beloved was basking in God's acceptance, Peter flung more of his flimsy and unkept promises at Jesus, true signals of the uncertainty that ran abundant in his soul. For the moment, Peter thought his only way of gaining God's approval was by proving he was a death-defying superman. But his ridiculous pledges impressed no one.

This total collapse of acceptance before Jesus began nine months earlier when Peter foolishly interrupted Him. "And

Peter took Him aside and began to rebuke Him, saying, 'God forbid it, Lord! This shall never happen to you'" (Matt. 16:22). Peter then misinterpreted God's correction as God's rejection. "But he turned and said to Peter, 'Get behind Me, Satan! You are a stumbling block to Me; for you are not setting your mind on God's interests, but man's'" (Matt. 16:23). For the remainder of that year, Peter was a "pebble" without a purpose.

In nine months Christ would be dead. Then, in a matter of days, He would live again. The empty grave meant Christ would appear and then ascend. The ascension was the Holy Spirit's cue. The church, empowered by fire, was now off and running.

But the human cycle would repeat itself.

Another man, this time named John Mark, would face the rejection of a lifetime. And like Peter, he would need a conduit back to God.

Many Faces

Late in his ministry Paul would lose his ship. Early in his ministry he would lose something far worse: his shipmates. One of those first lost shipmates seemed torn between the stages of boyhood and manhood. Between a willingness to serve and an immaturity to endure. Between a commitment to the task and the downright fickleness of a no-show.

The Bible tells the story this way: "From Paphos, Paul and his companions sailed to Perga in Pamphylia, where John left them to return to Jerusalem" (Acts 13:13, NIV).

Immediately after arriving in Perga, Paul sensed something was wrong. Before Paul got to the baggage claim area, John Mark had boarded a departing flight back to Jerusalem. He never left the terminal. He never even left a note.

"Where is John Mark?" Paul demanded. By then Barnabas knew.

"He's gone."

"Gone? What do you mean, gone?"

Barnabas could only say, "Yes, gone! He must have left right after we landed in Perga and headed back."

Paul's blood boiled. Ahead was an enormous undertaking. It would take every available hand. Demons needed binding. The lost needed saving. On a practical side, Paul wasn't thrilled about losing his roadie. John was their helper. *Helper* was Greek for "godly grunt in charge of the to-do lists." In other words, John Mark was the bag carrier. The load lifter. The detail guy. No, Paul wasn't happy about this.

Paul's zeal was white hot. So hot it tended to singe even his own friends. For Paul, the calling came long before the kid. This missions trip was about results, not relationships. So without an ounce of hesitation in his heart, Paul said, "Let him go. We're moving on!"

Barnabas, the son of encouragement, was heavy laden for days. John Mark was family.

John Mark first appeared in the Scriptures in Acts 12:12. After the execution of James, Herod recognized the political advantages of exterminating Christians. So he imprisoned Peter. The "Big Fisherman" was the next "big fish" Herod was looking to fry. Knowing their friend was in grave jeopardy, the church radicals in Jerusalem called a makeshift prayer meeting at the house of Mary. This Mary (one of six mentioned in the New Testament) also happened to be John Mark's mother. "And when he [Peter] realized this, he went to the house of Mary, the mother of John who was also called Mark, where many were gathered together and were praying" (Acts 12:12). The results of that prayer meeting were immediate. Peter was freed by an angel.

Around the same time Peter was imprisoned, reports of a severe famine in the Holy City began to surface. Two men, Barnabas and Saul [Paul], were sent to the famine-stricken city of Jerusalem after spending a year in Antioch ministering to the believers. The believers in Antioch, filled with compassion, had sent a generous love offering with Paul and Barnabas to those in Jerusalem suffering from famine.

It was during that trip to Jerusalem that John Mark was introduced to Paul through his uncle Barnabas. Something about John Mark impressed Paul. Barnabas was already convinced of his value. They invited John Mark to join their ministry team. John Mark quickly accepted and went with Barnabas and Saul back to Antioch. "And Barnabas and Saul returned from Jerusalem when they had fulfilled their mission, taking along with them John, who was also called Mark" (Acts 12:25).

No one could predict what lay ahead. After arriving in Antioch, the prophets and teachers of the early church gathered for a time of prayer and fasting. Paul, Barnabas and the newest member of the team, John Mark, joined them. The Holy Spirit suddenly spoke these words to those gathered in that Antioch prayer service. "And while they were ministering to the Lord and fasting, the Holy Spirit said, 'Set apart for Me Barnabas and Saul for the work to which I have called them" (Acts 13:2).

In the blink of an eye, their bags were packed. Expectations were flying high. But so were the waves that awaited them. The first member of the "Go Ye Into All the World" team was about to go AWOL. Things went on high alert right from the start. In Acts 13 the three men landed on the beaches of Cyprus. It might as well have been the beaches of Normandy.

"And when they had gone through the whole island as far as Paphos, they found a certain magician, a Jewish false prophet whose name was Bar-Jesus, who was with the proconsul" (Acts 13:6–7). Paul and Barnabas were brought before the proconsul for cross-examination of their motives and teachings. While under examination, another member of the proconsul, a magician named Elymas, began to oppose Paul and Barnabas publicly.

Paul burnt a hole right through this guy with his glare. "You who are full of all deceit and fraud, you son of the devil, you enemy of all righteousness, will you not cease to make crooked the straight ways of the Lord?" (v. 10).

A blinding mist then fell on the man. At this point, the proconsul definitely wasn't pro-Paul.

John Mark and Barnabas just watched with their mouths open.

Maybe this was too intense for John Mark. His leader seemed more like Saul of Tarsus than Paul the Apostle. His tact looked more Old Testament than New Covenant. Barnabas, the wealthy Levite from the island of Cyprus, was a relationship guy, not a revenge guy. Paul, however, seemed ready to grab Goliath, or anyone else for that matter, by the Adam's apple and choke them to death with his bare hands if they got in his way.

Or maybe it was something totally different than Paul's actions that caused John Mark to leave. Setting sail from Paphos, John Mark laid alone in his bunk pondering the bizarre events on Cyprus. It was somewhere during that two-hundred-mile sail to Perga that John Mark made his decision to leave the team. But why?

℘ Maybe the bags got too heavy.

🖋 Maybe his unspoken expectations about ministry weren't being met.

🖋 Or maybe John Mark was still feeling offended by God.

Prior to launching their missions trip from Antioch, the Scriptures say in Acts 13:2, "And while they were ministering to the Lord and fasting, the Holy Spirit said, 'Set apart for Me Barnabas and Saul for the work to which I have called them.'"

Did you notice that the name John Mark was strangely silent? I'm sure John Mark noticed. It was the kind of silence that can sting a man's soul. Maybe God was clearing His throat. John Mark waited, but he heard nothing more from the prophets. *What am I, chopped liver? I recognize that I must decrease, and He must increase, but can't I at least get mentioned on the roll call?*

John was facing the toughest test of his life—the test of obscurity.

The invitation to obscurity will test every growing Christian at some time during his or her spiritual journey. And whether you admit it or not, it is very difficult to watch others being celebrated while you remain invisible. At some time, everyone will be overlooked. Even by God. But sometimes being overlooked is God's way of looking out. Maybe God knew there was a level of untrustworthiness still inside John Mark that needed attending. Maybe He left him out of the roll call in Antioch to protect him from the fallout He knew was coming.

At the time John Mark left, Paul felt betrayed. His wardrobe had no use for a turncoat. Later on, when discussing with Barnabas whether or not John Mark could have his starting position and locker back, Paul made his feelings about John Mark clear.

> And after some days Paul said to Barnabas, "Let us return and visit the brethren in every city in which we proclaimed the word of the Lord, and see how they are." And Barnabas was desirous of taking John, called Mark, along with them also. But Paul kept insisting that they should not take him along who had deserted them in Pamphylia and had not gone with them to the work. And there arose such a sharp disagreement that they separated from one another, and Barnabas took Mark with him and sailed away to Cyprus. But Paul chose Silas and departed, being committed by the brethren to the grace of the Lord.
>
> —ACTS 15:36–40

Yippee! The entire first missionary organization had now officially imploded.

Paul was emphatic—John Mark would have no place in his future ministry. He had his chance and blew it. Paul locked John Mark inside the prison house of lost potential and threw away the key. Paul's use of the word *aphistemi* ["deserted"] sums up his interpretation of John Mark's actions. The word means "to instigate a revolt." In other words, Paul saw John Mark's actions as mutiny against the kingdom. He would just as soon have had him court-martialed than have him back on his boat.

End of discussion.

In many ways, John Mark became a pawn pulled between Paul's rejection and Barnabas's affirmation. Neither man was going to budge. Paul felt conviction. Barnabas felt compassion. These two trial-tested companions and friends were about to part ways. Each loved the same God, but each served a different passion. Paul was driven by cause. Barnabas was driven by community.

Barnabas took his emotionally beaten nephew and said, "You can ride me piggyback for a season." That loving gesture speaks volumes about God's view of us when we disappoint Him. As long as there is breath in us, restoration remains His priority. A bad first experience in ministry is like deadly toxin. Only the surgery of loving relationship can remove it. But the real test for John Mark still lay ahead.

Would he allow his hurt to last a lifetime?

There is an obscure text found in 2 Timothy 4:11, where Paul writes, "Only Luke is with me. Pick up Mark and bring him with you, for he is useful for me." John was his Hebrew name; Mark was his Roman surname. The Roman surname Mark meant "the hammer."

Interestingly, when John Mark originally deserted Paul and Barnabas, he displayed anything but the strength of a hammer. Maybe that explains why he was referred to only by his Hebrew name: "…and they also had John as their helper…and John left them and returned to Jerusalem" (Acts 13:5, 13). Paul was leading them to the front lines of Gentile ministry. But John retreated back to his Jewish comforts in Jerusalem.

Over the next several years, we do not read of John Mark preaching a single sermon or performing a single miracle. Yet he won back his apostolic esteem. Even from Paul. And did you now notice what Paul called him later in life? "Pick up Mark…" The "hammer" had risen to live above his comfort zones. And, to his own credit, Paul had a softened heart and finally admitted that God can still use the people we have written off as worthless. When I follow the lifelong story of John Mark, I am left with three thoughts. I leave them with you.

- ✐ We must allow God to heal our hurts.

- ✐ We must allow God to heal the relationships with those who hurt us.

- ✐ The way things start does not necessarily determine how things will end.

For the guy Paul once considered a mama's boy, John left quite a "Mark."

Chapter 7

The Story of the Grumblers

Now at this time while the disciples were increasing in number, a complaint arose on the part of the Hellenistic Jews against the native Hebrews, because their widows were being overlooked in the daily serving of food.
—Acts 6:1

When it comes to relationships, have you noticed that upset folks are a lot like a strange dog? They both like to begin the conversation with a cold nose and a loose tongue.

Speaking of loose tongues, should a son be held accountable for breaking the news about a naked boozer named "Dad"?

OK, let's just say it and get it out in the open. Old man Noah was boat savvy but leisure stupid. Finding the most famous boat captain in the Bible naked and drunk is quite a shock to the senses. Especially for a son. But regardless of what he saw, Ham handled the news poorly. Actually, he handled the news like most of us. He ran outside and told the first person he saw what he had just seen. "And Ham, the father of Canaan, saw the nakedness of his father, and told his two brothers *outside*" (Gen. 9:22, emphasis added).

There are two kinds of people in this world—those who tell and those who don't. Ham's two brothers, Shem and Japheth, had a much different reaction. They saw it as their responsibility to cover the failure, not expose it further with their words. "But Shem and Japheth took a garment and laid it upon both their shoulders and walked backward and covered the nakedness of their father; and their faces were turned away, so that they did not see their father's nakedness" (v. 23).

Who do you think was guiltier on that day? The intoxicated father or the loud-mouthed informant?

The Old Testament seemed to bring out the worst in people. When it comes to the New Testament, things improved a bit. Actually, more than a bit. But some folks, even in the New Testament, still insisted on the Law while others used their lips, instead of their character, to do the talking.

Things could not have been going better for the church by the sixth chapter of Acts. Except for a few beatings along the way, the early church was increasing. God's power was more real than ever. His sovereignty was at work solving complex details. The Bible says, "Now at this time while the disciples were increasing in number…" (Acts 6:1).

But why can't the sentence ever end there? You know it never does.

"…a complaint arose on the part of the Hellenistic Jews against the native Hebrews, because their widows were being overlooked in the daily serving of the food." You can take it to the bank; blessing is usually followed by bellyaching. One of the natural by-products of growth is the grind of trying to organize the results.

Now before we are too hard on the grumblers, I will say their concern was good. If you are going to have someone complain in the church, it should be over issues of care. In this case, a certain group of widows was being overlooked. Their advocates were the Hellenistic Jews.

Notice that the Hellenistic Jews were not the ones with the problem. They were the police. The watchdogs. It was their job to inform anybody and everybody about their observations.

In the case of the widows, they accused the native Hebrews of deliberate neglect. They accused the apostles of doing nothing. Maybe there was hint of racism in their voice. The Hellenists were always on edge about how the native Hebrews viewed their importance.

Dealing with grumblers is a complicated cross to bear. If we're honest, we'd all love to put a week's worth of leprosy on the real bad ones and teach them a lesson like the one God taught Miriam. But since using leprosy is not an option, we had better figure out the right way to handle grumbling people because grumbling is here to stay.

The Scriptures are clear about controlling our tongue.

- "The lips of the righteous bring forth what is acceptable, but the mouth of the wicked, what is perverted" (Prov. 10:32).

- "With his mouth the godless man destroys his neighbor, but through knowledge the righteous will be delivered" (Prov. 11:9).

- "There is one who speaks rashly like the thrusts of a

sword, but the tongue of the wise brings healing"
(Prov. 12:18).

✐ "The heart of the righteous ponders how to answer,
but the mouth of the wicked pours out evil things"
(Prov. 15:28).

So how did the apostles handle it?

Masterfully.

If they ever had license to brush someone off, it was now.
The church was growing. Couldn't they see it? Why were they
so focused on what was missing? No one said, "Hey, all you
apostles! You guys are doing a great job. Your preaching is
great. Your prayers are powerful. I also want you to know that
everybody in the church was really impressed by your attitudes after getting flogged by the Council. You are role
models to all of us. Thank you!"

Instead, all they got was a letter with a long list of issues.
At least it was signed. But instead of becoming defensive…
instead of rationalizing the complaint away…instead of
listing the faults of the accusers, the disciples remained
humble and prayerful. They emerged with clear priorities
and set their course.

✐ I tend to get defensive, not prayerful.

✐ I tend to lose my focus and abandon key priorities.

✐ I tend to accuse those who criticize and dismiss their
concerns.

All of which tells me that grumblers are good. No, grumbling myself is not good. But the grumblers around me keep
me humble and keep me focused on the priorities that count
most. For the apostles, the grumblers renewed their prayer and
Word life.

The Story of the Grumblers

Not only do grumblers keep you humble, but also God uses them to reveal new ideas. Nowhere in the Gospels did Jesus talk about deacons or church government. Nowhere did He talk about seven guys assisting with the needs of the church. Where did this idea come from? It was genius. Was the Lord keeping it in His back pocket? Just when was He going to tell the apostles about this breakthrough new strategy for care?

Only when they were ready to listen.

The idea for the *diaconate* was like a time-released capsule. God waited until the apostles were cornered by the grumblers to reveal His care-saving idea for the early church.

Out of a hidden and unmet care issue, God raised up a new generation of leaders like Philip and Stephen—and a new life-giving structure. Had the disciples allowed themselves to be wounded by the frustration of others…had they allowed defensiveness to shield them…then key gateways for the New Testament church would have been missed.

I hate the taste of negative words in my mouth, and I certainly don't rejoice when they surface in my ministry through others. But I have found a redemptive purpose for the grumblers when they come my way. It usually signals that a new idea is on the way from Jesus.

I'm reminded of Paul's encounter with a grumbler. He had just returned from his third missionary journey and was met at the door by a grumbler. "You see, brother, how many thousands there are among the Jews of those who have believed, and they are all zealous for the Law; and they have been told about you, that you are teaching all the Jews who are among the Gentiles to forsake Moses, telling them not to circumcise their children nor to walk according to the customs" (Acts 21:20–21).

Paul teaching against Moses was no more true than saying

the apostolic community of Peter and John was uncaring toward the widows. Paul's pessimistic counselor went on to recommend that Paul shave his head in order to soothe the Orthodox community. They also asked him—in love—to enter the temple and act like a good Jew.

Though Paul had the greater results on his side, he followed their orders without question. Paul was a man whose ministry had become worldwide in every sense. How easy it would have been for Paul to push aside the wisdom of an organization he had outgrown according to human standards.

But Paul heeded their wisdom and went bald. He understood that God was going to use less-than-successful grumblers to shape his circumstances. The disciples could have fought to maintain a five-star image. But behind closed doors they probably knew they were a "greasy spoon" kitchen when it came to caring for people the way Jesus did. They were out of ideas.

When I feel negative toward others, I dip my tongue in water. James 3:6 states, "And the tongue is a fire, the very world of iniquity; the tongue is set among our members as that which defiles the entire body, and sets on fire the course of our life, and is set on fire by hell." Like I said, I dip my tongue in water.

When others are negative toward me, I again dip my tongue in water. I then remind myself that *grumble* rhymes with *humble*.

Then I wait for another one of God's great ideas.

Who knows? Maybe a Stephen or a Philip is waiting to meet me on the other side of that complaint.

Chapter 8

The Story of the Judaizers

For prior to the coming of certain men from James, he used to eat with Gentiles; but when they came, he began to withdraw and hold himself aloof, fearing the party of the circumcision. And the rest of the Jews joined him in hypocrisy, with the result that even Barnabas was carried away by their hypocrisy.
—Galatians 2:12–13

I have a late-breaking bulletin. Please pass this on to as many Christians as you can. Here it is.

The blood of Jesus is not like paint.

That's right. It doesn't take three coats to cover, and it doesn't fade with time. One coat is more than enough, and it's also guaranteed to last an eternity. And no, it doesn't come in different shades. Crimson works fine in any setting. As a matter of fact, when it is applied to scarlet, you get a lovely shade of snow white.

And since we're talking about blood, I would like your

permission to vent for just a moment about my white cuff. Here's what happened.

Somewhere before the final worship song...the straightening of my suit...the adjusting of my Bible notes...the quick check of the clock...and the frantic sucking and crunching on a breath mint...it happened. It was the "mother" of all Communion stains.

Yes, I confess. I had been reckless with the cup of remembrance.

Somehow during our congregational observance of the Lord's Supper, I had trickled some Communion juice on my sleeve. I thought, *I'm the pastor! What are these people going to think? That when it comes to the Messiah, I have no manners?*

Thankfully, with the aid of my Bible and an unusually tall floral arrangement that week, I was able to conceal my faux pas for the remainder of the service. On the drive home from church, I rested my wrist over the top of the steering wheel. I had about ten minutes to stare at the red spot. I blamed the poor design of the plastic cup. It was too small. When filled, it left no margin whatsoever for even the slightest movement of worship.

I was irritated that my shirt was ruined, but to be honest, the whole episode did get me thinking again about the cup and its contents. I thought, *Isn't it odd that a message of such eternal significance could be entrusted to disposable plastic?*

Kind of like a Creator fitting inside a Carpenter.

Some church choirs wear robes...others go casual. Some preachers wear collars and recite liturgy...other preachers sport polo shirts and project a "God is my buddy" gospel. Whether churches use lapel or hand-held microphones... offering plates or offering bags...wooden pews or folding chairs...baptismal tanks or backyard hot tubs...everyone still uses the cup. When it comes to the blood of Jesus, the cup reigns supreme. Next to the cross, the cup is the most unifying symbol of the church.

As a child growing up in the church, my hungry tummy and dry, cotton mouth would leap for joy at the sight of those brilliant metallic stacks near the pulpit. I don't know about you, but there was no hungry like Sunday hungry when you're a kid. We would still be in the car, but the smell of Sunday roast would hit you three houses from the driveway. The combination of mashed potatoes and gravy, green beans and a warm chocolate cake still baking in the oven would overtake you as you came through door.

All Communion did was get the process going earlier.

As a little fella in the pew, I wished I could swallow a whole gallon of grape juice on those hot summer Sundays. I wanted to help out in the church kitchen after service was over so I could finish off the unused cups. I confess that on many occasions, I was looking for a way to grab two cups, not one. Not because I loved Jesus twice as much that day, but because the juice tasted so good.

The message of the Lord's Table was always confusing to me as a youngster. I could never understand how something red could make something white. As I grew older, I learned that the color schemes of redemption were mostly figurative …while the forgiveness was factual.

I learned that the blood was necessary and real. It alone purchased freedom for the soul. I learned that the blood of Jesus was the liquid robe of heaven's mass choir. In other words, when we get to heaven, there won't be Armani suits or homeless rags, just white garments washed in the blood. (See Revelation 7:14.)

In my lifetime, I figure I have consumed about one cup of

Communion juice a month. Each cup holds about one-half ounce. At my current rate of celebrating the Lord's Table, I'll drink about one gallon of grape juice every ten years. If I live a full life, that means about seven gallons. Factor that by the millions of believers who have celebrated Communion for nearly two thousand years, and that's a lot of grapes.

But for some Christians, the blood of Jesus sadly has about as much meaning as a crushed grape. The history of blood and its role in salvation runs long and deep throughout Scripture. When Adam and Eve first sinned, blood flowed. An animal was quickly sacrificed to provide skins so their shamefulness could be covered. In other words, from the first moment of sin, some form of death soon followed.

But more revealing than Eden's bloodletting was Israel's blood Passover. Before Abraham's descendants began their famous passage through the desert, they had to pass through a door. A door, mind you, stained in red.

Amidst the final flurry of judgments against Pharaoh, Israel was told to pack quickly. They were given two weeks to prepare for their escape. Once the death angel was dispatched, their cruel bondage would not see another sunrise. Four hundred years of slavery would end before the morning dew had time to evaporate.

A frantic celebration ensued. Livestock and loved ones had to be organized. After being in one location for nearly half a millennium, Israel knew little about packing or what a new beginning actually felt like. But the top priority on their "to do" list was the careful preparation for the Passover.

A precise lamb would be selected and sacrificed at a precise time. The Jews were also given precise instructions on how to eat the lamb. And most importantly, a precise application of the blood on the doorposts was to be followed. Sloppiness would cost them their life. "Moreover, they shall take some of the blood and put it on the two doorposts and on the lintel of the houses in which they eat it" (Exod. 12:7).

The carnage coming upon Egypt could not be escaped, even by the Jews, without properly applying the blood to their door. The blood was to be placed exactly where God wanted it to be. Only the doorposts and header beam (lintel) were to be painted in the scrupulously selected lamb's blood.

Using the instrument of a hyssop, nothing of the blood was to be spilled on the threshold and trampled under foot. God was saying to Israel, "This Exodus is no game." He would provide the power, but they must provide the obedience.

Grace and the Blood

The grace of God is a marvelous thing. The purpose of grace is to make us comfortable with God. That feels irreverent to some. They prefer a high priest to a friendly Carpenter. In the midst of their religious blindness, they have forgotten the basic game plan God came up for saving mankind. They forget that…

- God approached us; we did not approach Him.

- He came with a gift, not a grudge.

- He paid off our fines without being asked.

- He came fully prepared with legally binding adoption papers.

- He invited us to dine and then showed us our private room at the mansion.

Sounds like a scary God to me!

Grace makes us comfortable enough to run to Him for mercy, comfortable enough to worship Him as our Father. But in that security, we must be cautious not to be disorderly or haphazard with the blood of His Son. Precious…necessary…sufficient…final…cleansing…and conquering–that is the blood of Jesus. But it must be applied exactly as God requires.

Instead of being applied to doorposts with hyssop, the blood is accurately applied through genuine repentance from sin–absolute confession of Christ's lordship–and complete faith in His resurrection. That is the New Testament door of salvation. Yes, there is much to experience beyond the door as you walk through the wilderness of discipleship, but that first step with God must be through the door painted red.

I'm a pastor, so I live with a zeal for turnouts and the occasional chaos of multiple services. Sometimes in the bedlam of a Sunday morning I get tempted to rush the salvation offer.

I have to remind myself that salvation is not just an uplifted hand anymore than it is joining the choir, passing the plates as an usher or changing a diaper in the nursery. Those things are good, but I don't think the death angel would be too impressed with those things alone. The angel wasn't looking for works; he was looking for one thing. Did they trust the blood and apply it properly?

When I see a fidgety usher give me the sanctified "evil eye" to hurry up and get the first service over because the second service crowd is overwhelming the lobby, when I feel the pressure to make the salvation appeal quick and sloppy, I have to stop and ask myself, *Are people really being saved? If this were Egypt, am I showing the people where to apply the blood? Has repentance, confession and faith been expressed?*

The Story of Judaizers

The blood of Jesus is about works—the finished work of Christ. Some have tried to take the work of the Carpenter and call it shoddy. Or they open the gift that the Carpenter has fashioned for them and ask for the receipt so they can take it back and return it for something else. Who would do such a thing? Well, actually, some folks tried to do just that.

They were called the Judaizers.

You may not be one, but don't underestimate their ability to ruin a perfectly good party. Or their ability to deceive some of God's best. Men like Peter and Barnabas found this out the hard way.

Here is how it happened.

The Judaizers were bent on putting a price tag on God's free giveaway. They couldn't spot a good thing if it hit them between the eyes. The difference between the Pharisees and the Judaizers was this. Pharisees feared that the popularity of Jesus would snatch away their prestige. They were not interested in a debate with Jesus; they wanted Him dead. The Judaizers also followed the Law, but there was something about the message of Jesus they found attractive.

Just not beautiful. For them, grace had a flaw.

They decided after hearing Jesus' message of the kingdom that with some slight reconfiguration, they could come up with something better. Maybe take a mixture of the two systems and combine them into one. Kind of law and grace Siamese twins.

The work of the Judaizers was most noticeable in the second chapter of Galatians. There we find Paul's story of a visit he made along with Barnabas and Titus to the city of Antioch. In Antioch he noticed an "about face" in Peter's actions toward the Gentiles. Paul was so utterly disgusted that he opposed Peter to his face. Peter's actions were in direct conflict with the message of Christ and His kingdom. Here is what he did.

Peter, a Jew, had been gracious in his interactions with the Gentiles, a social "no-no" within the orthodox Jewish community. The good ol' boys club wasn't looking to add new brothers to its membership. Peter was simply following the lead of Jesus. He had seen Jesus' unconditional love for people firsthand. He watched as Jesus would float between and among people groups with the utmost of ease.

He heard Jesus teach. He observed His touch. Cultural boundaries meant nothing to Jesus. Peter knew this. There could be no doubt in Peter's mind what the kingdom of God was all about.

But ugly barriers suddenly resurfaced in Peter's life. It was almost as if he had never met Christ in the first place. The guiding light of Jesus' unconditional approach to people was suddenly replaced by the guardrails of legalism.

Storming into Antioch were the Judaizers. Claiming to be buddies of James, a respected leader of the Christian church, they demanded that Peter reestablish his Jewish boundaries and quit hanging out with Gentiles.

Maybe it was the force of their request. Maybe it was the name-dropping. After all, if James knew them, then maybe he was wrong. Maybe Peter felt outnumbered. Maybe it was combination of several things. The bottom line is…Peter caved. He ashamedly pushed himself away from the table of fellowship and excused himself without explanation. After years of Spirit-filled living, Peter chose spineless, empty religion. Paul wanted to vomit when he heard about this.

The Judaizers had not only influenced Peter to abandon the ship of grace, but also the affects of his decision were felt by the entire church. Barnabas, the standard of restoration and sensitivity, was the first to be pulled under by Peter. After Barnabas, the whole church followed. Everything Jesus stood and died for was being destroyed.

Paul became desperate. There was too much at stake. "But when I saw that they were not straightforward about the truth of the gospel, I said to Cephas [Peter] in the presence of all, 'If you, being a Jew, live like the Gentiles and not like the Jews, how is it that you compel the Gentiles to live like Jews?'" (Gal. 2:14).

Paul laid his friendship with Peter on the line. He begged to Peter to remember the essentials of faith.

- 🌿 The only way to holiness is to be overcome by grace.

- 🌿 You cannot love through legislation.

- 🌿 Trying to live "outside in" will fail every time.

- 🌿 The most terrifying influence in the church is legalism, not Satan.

- 🌿 You cannot learn or earn your way to God; you can only accept what's offered you.

Legalism is an ugly amnesia.

Jesus began His public ministry with the water and the wine. He ended it three years later with the water and the towel, proving once and for all that servanthood, not the miraculous, is the checkered flag of Christian maturity.

But Peter had forgotten his own courage as a servant…

Prior to the Crucifixion there were eleven "second guessers" hiding out in Jerusalem. Moments after the Ascension there were eleven obedient soldiers ready to do exactly what Jesus had told them to do. Their orders were obscure. First pray. Then go. Somewhere along the way you'll most likely die. Each of those soldiers felt honored to serve and die if they must.

But Peter had forgotten his destiny as a martyr...

The power to accomplish this assignment was brewing just above the rooftops of Jerusalem. Neither Peter nor the others knew that the prayer meeting would last ten days. But knowing the assignment, they were determined not to leave the upper room until they were changed. So for ten days taxes went uncollected. For ten days the fish were safe. Then fire fell.

But Peter had forgotten all about the power of Pentecost...

God would only paint His portrait of wood and wonder once. There wasn't any need for a rough draft. The dress rehearsal, opening night and grand finale were all in one performance. The portrait needs no introduction. It depicts a Lion from the tribe of Judah. The Lion is adorned in a loincloth. He is suspended by the strength of the hammer and will of a nail.

Made above the angels, the Lion wasn't even given the courtesy of an angel's halo. The only circle in the portrait is the circle bearing spikes that pierced the head of the Lion. Colorful contrasts of red against brown flow down the brow of the Lion.

No Judaizer could match that picture.

> **I have been crucified with Christ; and it is not longer I who live, but Christ lives in me; and the life which I now live in the flesh I live by faith in the Son of God, who loved me, and delivered Himself up for me.**
> **—GALATIANS 2:20**

Thank goodness Peter suddenly remembered.

Chapter 9

The Story of the Loud Woman

*It happened that as we were going to the place of
prayer, a certain slave-girl having a spirit of divination
met us, who was bringing her masters much profit by
fortunetelling. Following after Paul and us, she kept
crying out, saying, "These men are bond-servants
of the Most High God, who are proclaiming to
you the way of salvation."*
—Acts 16:16–17

Littered across the outer wastelands of Egypt are the skeletal remains of an emancipated nation. They did not die *for* freedom. They died *in* freedom. Like some type of ancient Stonehenge, this ghostly pathway of shallow graves mysteriously winds through the wilderness in a circular motion before abruptly terminating at the banks of the Jordan River.

The long trail of bones, millions of them, forms a painful memorial—a reminder to all that murmuring destroys destiny. It also tells us that participating firsthand in an exodus, no matter how epic, doesn't give you a free pass for sloppy living.

They Felt the Spirit's Touch

On the other side of the river, less than one hundred feet away, lay an open pantry of promise brimming with milk and honey. A multitude of uncircumcised Israelites and their families were finally given the green light to cross. All had been babes, or at best adolescents, when they left Egypt forty years earlier. Some could still recall the vivid story of the Passover night when they watched their fathers and grandfathers free the firstborn by painting the doorposts with an unusual red.

Only two who actually painted their doorposts were still around. Now in their sixties, Joshua and Caleb had no peers to join them for the short walk across the Jordan. Their entire generation had perished for the sin of nitpicking. By letting that older generation pass away, God was saying that He would take unity over wisdom. And that the Land of Promise needed harmony more than it needed a bunch of folks who couldn't stop their griping. In other words, it was time to see if a new generation could grow old the right way.

Under the mantle of Joshua and his hearty helper Caleb, a fresh cast of Israelites was now exploring life from the other side of the river. It was a new day for Israel. Abraham's covenant had a fresh set of legs. This was God's family with God's blessing out to get God's results. Their first encounter did nothing but confirm this as the walls of Jericho turned into the walls of Jell-O with only a skip and a shout.

For Joshua, the victory at Jericho was the jump-start his career needed. "So the LORD was with Joshua, and his fame was in all the land" (Josh. 6:27). Confident but hoarse following the successful mission at Jericho, Israel rubbed its sore feet and checked the itinerary for casualty number two. "It's some powerless little town called Ai," shouted one of the captains.

The Story of the Loud Woman

What on earth is an Ai?

Good question.

It didn't take a military genius to figure out that the town of Ai was a picket fence compared to the walls of Jericho. So Joshua chose to conserve his resources by sending a mere "three thousand men" to dispose of this small flea (Josh. 7:4). But despite the favoring odds, an off-guard Joshua was about to learn a tough lesson about life in the Land of Promise. That Ai, not Israel, would land the first-round haymaker—planting Joshua and his army flat on the canvas.

Folks have laid full responsibility for the crushing failure at the feet of one man—Achan, the greedy father who got his hands filthy with the precious alloys and apparel of Babylon. His single seed of individualism rendered an entire military operation impotent. His obituary would one day read "scapegoat." Joshua was devastated by the loss. Scripture says that he ripped his shirt and wore dirt for a hat. Even his heart became like liquid. (See Joshua 7:5–6.) Joshua was stunned. He had been routed by a runt. He felt like the senior who got his lights punched out by the freshman.

Following the debacle with Ai, Joshua caught his breath and discovered with God's help the source of his Waterloo. Secret sin! Then in one fell swoop, Joshua chopped down the entire Achan family tree. It's hard to believe one man's sin could cost a family so much.

Joshua then ordered an all-nighter back to Ai. But this time he dispatched 30,000 men to engage in a battle that should have been won 27,000 men earlier. In other words, it took ten times the men to defeat an army ten times as small as Jericho.

That has a familiar ring to it, doesn't it?

✎❤ Ten more lengthy explanations
✎❤ Ten more heated board meetings

✒ Ten more gut-wrenching phone calls
✒ Ten thousand more dollars
✒ Ten more buckets of tearful regrets

Secret sin seems to cost you ten times more of everything in life.

Jericho had been a piece of cake. Ai a piece of concrete. How did a meaningless municipality become such an insurmountable metropolis? Simple. *Without God's favor during battle, every enemy becomes a giant!*

When secret sin moves in, pipsqueaks become bullies. Pea-gravel becomes meteorites. Tricycles become Harleys. Weeds become redwoods. In other words, Goliath starts small but becomes big over time. What makes Goliath the beast that he is, is often our own secret insubordination.

Thankfully, the God of a second wind gave Joshua his second chance. But deep within the private thoughts that even generals have, you know Joshua had to be wounded. Men he loved were dead. The hollow comeback against Ai was nothing to celebrate. Disappointments have a way of doing that. More often than not, the longest nights of the Christian faith are spent remapping the confusion rather than charting new roads to triumph. But Joshua was about to learn another lesson.

Things *can* get worse.

As a matter of fact, if you listen closely, you will hear the awful snap of the trap as Joshua goes for the cheese. It's the same cheese the apostle Paul was offered. But more about his trap in a moment. First, let's finish the story about Joshua and Ai.

The Trap of Flattery

In Joshua 9, we read about the inhabitants of Gibeon, a humble cartel of four small nations slightly downwind from Ai. The Gibeonites feared for their lives. To survive, they had one option: Convince Joshua and the elders they were friends from afar and live, or they would be discovered as foes from over the fence and be executed.

The Gibeonites creative war game would begin with a head game. Their weapon of choice? How about a few rounds of soothing and seductive words aimed directly at Joshua's wounded ego? So with musty sacks, threadbare shoes and cracked wineskins, the sting was on. The first shot fired was butter. "Because of your fame we have heard the report; we are your servants." Whew! It was the welcome relief Joshua had needed for weeks, an emotional balm to tranquilize the open festers of self-pity he was battling.

Flattery is an ever-changing arsenal, but the disabling consequences are always the same. And like Joshua, all of us have a hard time recognizing it. It can seduce you with the appearance of a chocolate truffle, and then strike like cyanide when you bite. Flattery is hell's perfume. It's the only compliment the devil knows how to give.

Focused on the lofty words of the Gibeonites, Joshua forgot his "baby steps" of godly character—*when you don't understand what to do next, do nothing except pray!* Deceived by their flattering words, Joshua entered into a covenant with the Gibeonites. The only problem was, he forgot to pray before signing on. Listening to flattery became his substitution for prayer.

Joshua foolishly signed a détente that obligated him to assist Gibeon during all of its future conflicts. That one prayerless agreement nearly ended up costing Joshua more lives and more fierce battles than he could ever have imagined. Battles that never should have been waged had he only prayed.

Flattery will navigate you miles off your course and lead you through confrontations you never intended to face. Flattery is no small misdemeanor to commit. Paul said, "For we *never* came with flattering speech…God is witness" (1 Thess. 2:5, emphasis added). Even more emphatically, we should never allow our lives as believers to be manipulated by someone with a flattering tongue. "A man who flatters his neighbor is spreading a net for his steps" (Prov. 29:5).

God in His mercy heard the cry of a distraught Joshua. Miles off course, Joshua experienced a divine intervention of mercy. God suspended the sun like a hot air balloon on a windless day so the battle could be completed. This solar slight of hand demonstrated that God's mercy runs deeper than the laws of the universe. In other words, God will sacrifice a sunrise if that's what it takes to get someone back on track toward victory.

Everyone enjoys and needs an honest kingdom-based compliment from time to time. But never forget the warning and wisdom from the right side of the river. If you bite and taste only frosting, it's time to pray, not swallow.

But as I said, Paul would face a Gibeon of his own. Let's see if he spit it out or swallowed.

She was the clever second lady of Philippi. The role of first lady belonged to Lydia, the maker of purple who had her scarlet sins made white at a riverbank revival service. "And a certain woman named Lydia…a seller of purple fabrics, a

The Story of the Loud Woman

worshiper of God, was listening; and the Lord opened her heart to respond to the things spoken by Paul" (Acts 16:14).

Lydia was the real deal. Her wholehearted conversion turned quickly into a desire to serve her Lord. Her motto was, "Find a need and fill it." And she quickly noticed an unmet need for Paul and his friends. They needed lodging. She humbly offered her home to the missionary team who had touched her life personally. Yes, the first lady of Philippi had a heart.

The second lady of Philippi, well, this story is actually about her. And nothing personal, but she had a mouth as big as the Euphrates River. Which fit her well because she was a fortuneteller. And like with most fortunetellers, the clients never found out where the fortune was. That usually ended up in the pockets of management.

While her masters managed the business side, her job was to be as boisterous, loud and confident as she could. The tongue of the fortuneteller is like rouge on the cheeks of a harlot—it helps attract business.

Recent history had been kind to Paul. The second missionary journey was a rousing success. Timothy had joined the team. Macedonia had made its call for help. And Europe had its first convert in Lydia. Yes, things were going quite smoothly.

Then she showed up!

Much as the beggar at the Beautiful Gate intercepted Peter and John, she intercepted Paul and his companions on their way to prayer. Using her mouth for muscle, she assaulted Paul and his associates from behind. Out of nowhere, Paul heard someone behind him creating a major fuss in the town square. Now, noise was nothing new to Paul; loud seemed to be his lifestyle as well.

At first this strange lady looked like a female version of

John the Baptist. "These men are bond-servants of the Most High God, who are proclaiming to you the way of salvation" (Acts 16:17). She was one giant worship service all by herself—yes, a little rude, but she was right! Paul was all of these things and more. But unlike John the Baptist or Lydia, the Bible describes this girl as "having a spirit of divination…who was bringing her masters much profit by fortune-telling" (v. 16).

So why would the devil take time to promote the apostle Paul and say things about him that were true? I thought the devil only lied. Ladies and gentlemen, welcome to the sly and sneaky world of flattery. Flattery is nothing more than truth with bad timing. Flattery is like a curve ball. It's designed to get you off balance. To get you thinking. It starts out looking like one pitch, but suddenly it takes a nasty turn. And like the guy standing in the batter's box, you have less than one second to figure it out.

She was Paul's perfect storm. Almost.

This had an eerie similarity to the experience of his counterpart Joshua. As I mentioned earlier, Paul's most recent history was pretty victorious, but the painful defeats from missionary journey number one were still fresh on his mind. Paul's failure with John Mark. The collapse of his relationship with Barnabas. Those kinds of breakdowns don't filter their way through the system easily. So when Paul heard this outburst of praise, even from a stranger, he no doubt faced the temptation to enjoy it.

If we are honest about our humanity for a moment, this had to feel good to Paul. I know it would if it were me. This kind of free press could open up all kinds of new possibilities. It was like having a built-in emcee. The woman was definitely networked. Her celebrity and influence could pay significant dividends.

The Story of the Loud Woman

The aim was to try and trap Paul, possibly trick him toward her craft of divination. Or at least distract him from his focus. Then maybe she could soften Paul's view of the occult. Or maybe she was really confused and was trying to audition, hoping the Savior could find room for a sooth-sayer in His starting lineup.

Even though flattery can be tough to spot the first time around, Paul realized after several days that the honey was vinegar all along. He had had enough. The scratch on the record...the repetition...had all but driven him crazy. "But Paul was greatly annoyed, and turned and said, 'I command you in the name of Jesus Christ to come out of her!' And it [the spirit] came out at that very moment" (Acts 16:18). Paul had passed the test.

Some men live to capitalize on moments like this. Moments when the line between encouragement and hero worship is so fine that no one has the guts to step forward and call it for what it is. But Paul knew his calling. He also knew where his security and esteem came from. And he didn't need some stranger replacing Jesus in his life.

There is a heavy price to be paid when we choose to honor God by deflecting the praise.

> But when her masters saw that their hope of profit was gone, they seized Paul and Silas and dragged them into the market place before the authorities... And the crowd rose up together against them, and the chief magistrates tore their robes off them, and proceeded to order them to be beaten with rods. And when they had inflicted many blows upon them...
> —ACTS 16:19–23

That's quite a price to pay for turning down a compliment.

They Felt the Spirit's Touch

Though Paul and Silas took an unjust beating, they were pleased that the story ended well for the loud lady from Philippi. She found spiritual freedom free of charge.

Let's just hope she used her gift for gab for the glory of God.

Chapter 10

The Story of the Beggar

And a certain man who had been lame from his mother's womb was being carried along, whom they used to set down every day at the gate of the temple which is called Beautiful, in order to beg alms of those who were entering the temple.
—Acts 3:2

By all accounts, this was turning out to be an ugly scene at a beautiful gate.

Peter and John woke up that day and went looking for two things—God's presence and human pain. And not necessarily in that order. They were prayerful and ready for both. Ready to grip the next heart in need of repentance. Ready to grip the next hand in need of healing. The proof was in their eyes.

Like most beggars, this guy was stationary. He was very lame and very loud. Each morning he was set up for business like a hot dog street vendor. The hustlers who laid him outside the temple made sure they got their cut at the end of the day. Kind of a transportation tax. A finder's fee for scouting out the best spot on the street.

This particular day held nothing significant. The holidays of Passover and Pentecost had come and gone. The religious tourist season was over. Crowds in the Holy City were returning to normal. The apostles were trying to do the same. This meant prayer at the temple.

The lame man outside the temple had been a fixture for years, a familiar piece of social wreckage. But along come two men who were more *need* centered than *temple* centered. Two men who were living with the wide-angle lens of compassion instead of the usual telephoto heart of selfishness. Two men who were full of everything Jesus wanted for His disciples. Power. Love. Authority. Courage. Faith.

But the most unexpected Jesus-like quality was their eyes. They looked at life through the lens of the Spirit—which gave them perfect vision for seeing. In other words, they were looking for eye contact. At three o'clock their moment came.

> **And Peter, along with John, fixed his gaze upon him and said, "Look at us!" And he began to give them his attention, expecting to receive something from them. But Peter said, "I do not possess silver and gold, but what I do have I give to you: In the name of Jesus Christ the Nazarene—walk!"**
>
> —Acts 3:4–6

Powerfully courageous words. Jesus smiled and blessed their faith with profound power. But Peter and John got more than the miracle they bargained for. Instead of just a healing, they got a shadow with jumping ability. "And with a leap, he stood upright and began to walk; and he entered the temple with them, walking and leaping and praising God. And all the people saw him walking and praising God" (Acts 3:8–9).

No crutches. No rehabilitation. No limp in his limbs. Just a 360-degree slam dunk on his first jump! He was ready to lead the new aerobics ministry. The crisis was over for this forty-year-old. It was time for a midlife beginning.

The author of confusion suddenly had no more chapters to write. He had just been outbid by the author of faith for the copyrights to the beggar's story. The story line had been unpleasant, but the final chapter now belonged to Jesus.

The Bible says, "And with a leap, he stood upright." The fact he could stand tells us that God had restored his physical capacity. But the fact he *leaped* tells us even more. God had restored his emotional capacity. Jesus had given the man his joy back, not just his legs.

This leap is very important to Jesus. Depression, the kind inside the beggar, is described well in the poem "Shesh Lehka" by Indian poet Rabindranath Tagore:

> Spring is past,
> Summer is gone,
> Winter is here,
> And the song I came to sing here stays
>   unsung.
> I have spent my days
> Stringing and unstringing my instrument.

Leaping seems to be one of the great by-products of Jesus' touch. As a matter of fact, few seem to remember that a "leap" was the first physical response recorded in the Bible caused directly by Jesus. Really? Consider this.

John the Baptist was the unborn second cousin of Jesus. John would become the forerunner for Jesus. Six months before the immaculate conception of Christ, the Lord provided Mary's cousin Elizabeth with one of His favorite gifts. He made a way for a barren woman to enjoy her first Mother's Day.

Far along in years, Elizabeth experienced a "Sarah miracle." Scripture says in Luke 1:39 that Mary "went with haste to the hill country" to visit Elizabeth, fresh with the knowledge of her own pregnancy and brimming with sheer joy for the news of her cousin's miracle pregnancy six months earlier.

Elizabeth had no idea why Mary was bursting through her door. But before Mary could utter a word, a jolt struck the midsection of Elizabeth. Something more than Mary had just walked through door. There was power in the house. It saturated Elizabeth. It electrified baby John still in the womb. Jesus had made His first house call.

No bigger than a cell cluster, the fullness of God's presence was now impacting earth at ground level. Elizabeth declared His lordship: "Blessed is the fruit of your womb! And how has it happened to me, that the mother of my Lord should come to me?" (vv. 42–43).

As for her unborn child, John, well, he exercised a foot-stomping, deep-knee-bending, hit-your-head-on-the-ceiling kind of leap. The joy John felt while still locked inside the womb was real. His kind of joy could not be verbalized; it had to be displayed.

So without much room, maximizing every inch, he jumped! "For behold, when the sound of your greeting reached my ears, the baby leaped in my womb for joy" (v. 44).

Maybe right now you feel like your world is closing in on you. You feel squeezed, unable to move forward in life. You might even identify with John—your world has little room, and you're left with little choice to do anything about it. But

The Story of the Beggar

John's reaction to the presence of Jesus proves there is always room to worship. There is always space for joy.

Peter and John also discovered that when you give someone Jesus, you are giving them yourself. "And while he was clinging to Peter and John..." (Acts 3:11). But the story could have been different.

Is financial poverty a prerequisite for effective ministry? What if Peter and John had left the house that morning with a pocket full of money? Would the story have ended with a handout instead of a healing? A paltry tip flipped the beggar's way to soothe a guilty conscience?

I don't think so. Here's why. "And Peter, along with John, fixed his gaze upon him..." (v. 4). This was the key that unlocked the miracle. Silver and salvation stood toe to toe. Who would flinch? The busted apostle or the bruised beggar?

The *fixed gaze* of Peter and John proved which beggar was most desperate. How many times have you and I turned our face away from the eyes of a homeless man near the stoplight, whispering words of self-righteousness as we hide our eyes behind the dark glasses of rationalization?

Later on the apostle Paul said it so clearly: "Therefore... we *beg* you on behalf of Christ, be reconciled to God" (2 Cor. 5:20, emphasis added).

The ugly scene at the Beautiful Gate was a confrontation between *pocket change* and *eternal change*. The next time you spot a beggar or a beggar spots you, ask yourself, "Who's more hungry?" The beggar who needs *pocket change?* Or the beggar offering *eternal change.*

They had been touched by *Heaven's Beggar...*

 ✍ By a Love humble enough to begin with diapers instead of a throne

💌 By a Love willing enough to wait nine months before making its appearance

💌 By a Love diligent enough to spend thirty-three years building a perfect bridge

💌 By a Love complete enough to cut the ribbon with a resurrection

[He] emptied Himself, taking the form of a bond-servant, and being made in the likeness of men...in appearance as a man.
—Philippians 2:7–8

The incarnation of Jesus was like cramming the entire solar system into a peanut shell. Anything more, and the human race would not have recognized Him. But Peter and John were changed by those contents. If God could somehow be fingerprinted, their faces would have appeared through the ink. They were God's imprint. His image. Unique as a snowflake...loved as a son.

This was their niche that afternoon on the way to prayer. The message of unconditional love filled their hearts. But it also burned in their eyes. Which, by the way, was the first place in forty years the beggar saw something better than gold. He found the kind of grace that makes you giddy.

Because real living is not about legs...it's about the leap. As a matter of fact, God has been jumping up and down over us for eternity. Angels, too. And He says there's still lots of room at the party.

Chapter 11

The Story of Stephen

And when they had driven him out of the city, they began stoning him, and the witnesses laid aside their robes at the feet of a young man named Saul. And they went on stoning Stephen as he called upon the Lord and said, "Lord Jesus, receive my spirit!" And falling on his knees, he cried out with a loud voice, "Lord, do not hold this sin again them!" And having said this, he fell asleep.
—Acts 7:58–60

God is the good potter. I am the not-so-good clay. My job is to spin and stay put in the center of the wheel. The potter's job is to dream and to design. Sometimes I don't appreciate how fast the potter spins me or how tightly He squeezes to change my shape. I forget that the good potter uses two hands and that He sometimes needs an external instrument to carve me and give me beauty. The hope of the potter is simple. He wants to transfer His heart and mind through His hands.

In order for clay to change shape, motion is essential. It's impossible for idle clay to change. The same is true for dry clay…it tends to shatter rather than be molded. So the good potter makes sure the clay remains moist throughout the process. Once the shape is formed, the good potter then finds a fire to capture the shape He has created.

Fire is the only agent that can make the shape permanent.

Just call me "the one-punch wonder." I threw one punch…and have wondered why ever since. I've never been a fighter. If you can find Danny, he'll confirm this. I was in sixth grade; Danny was a fifth grader. Danny walked past our class line after recess one day at Wilburton Elementary and decided to "flick" the basketball I was holding out of my hands.

After some brief "egging on" by the other sixth graders standing in line, I swung and landed about three of my five knuckles directly on his braces. Before he could swing back, I ran as fast as I could. My hand was killing me. Fortunately for me, not Danny, a teacher intercepted the scene.

So there you have it. My exhaustive fighting resumé.

One punch.

That's probably why violence turns my stomach. And why when I say I had to force myself to watch those thirty brief seconds of television footage, I mean that sincerely. Those thirty brief seconds were too graphic to stomach.

It was my first stoning.

The drive down Normandie Boulevard is tricky in a normal car. Try maneuvering a big rig. Driving a semitruck through Los Angeles surface streets is only for the highly trained.

It was late afternoon, April 29, 1992. It was a typical spring day in Los Angeles—warm and muggy. Fourteen stops down, three to go. Popeye's chicken on the right.

The Story of Stephen

Reginald Denny had no idea of the mayhem now under way. His city was free-falling into a mind-altering state of human anarchy. Injustice had lit the fuse. The pent-up hatred of a city separated by canyons of human misunderstanding was erupting.

With his rig suddenly blocked in the intersection at Normandie and Florence, Reginald Denny could have gunned his semi through the crowds in self-defense. But he was cautious not to harm those in the street. He pulled the truck to a stop. Suddenly his truck was engulfed in a faceless rage. A firefight of bricks—not bullets—ensues.

Scenes of inexplicable horror began unfolding over the next several seconds. Reginald Denny was pulled from his truck. Bricks were aimed and flung without remorse at his skull. His body was repeatedly and violently kicked. The crowd applauded. A single perpetrator methodically approached the fallen body of Reginald Denny, who was conscious but disabled. A final brick at close range was hurled directly at his head; it hit its target, crushing and maiming his face. The man who delivered the brick entertained himself with a short dance and a pirouette.

For the moment, depravity was king.

The scene was so gruesome, so heartless and so utterly unjust that I felt nauseated. It took several days to get the emotional reaction I had to that image under control. I questioned whether or not it was appropriate to make something like that public. And what the backlash would be. But then I remembered another stoning.

God had already set the precedent.

Stephen's only crime was godliness. His only mistake was willingness. He was more than ready to bus tables for an eternity if it would help serve the kingdom. The martyrdom

of Stephen was a classic struggle between right and righteousness...between good and godly. Stephen was a good
man doing the right thing. But Jesus suddenly asked
Stephen for something more. For something supreme. God
was asking Stephen to be the first deacon to go to heaven.

It's easy to look and sound like Jesus during an afternoon
Palm Sunday victory parade...or on a hillside with spiritually hungry people...or at an old-fashioned riverbank baptismal gathering.

But how about during a rock fight? A rock fight where only
one of the participants gets rocks. Where the person with the
rocks gets to take his or her own sweet time to aim, wind up
like a major leaguer and fire fastball after fastball at your
head. A rock fight where your only defense is Christlikeness.
Where your only comeback will be the resurrection.

Stephen had barely finished his first shift as a deacon
when an argument broke out between him and several members of the synagogue. Actually, Stephen never argued. He
preached. Apparently there were too many priests in
Jerusalem believing the gospel and switching sides. They
blamed Stephen. He, more than anyone else at the time,
seemed to embody the whole package. He possessed a servant's heart. A stellar reputation. A fullness of wisdom and
grace. "And yet they were unable to cope with the wisdom
and the Spirit with which he was speaking" (Acts 6:10).

Gnashing their teeth...grunting their hatred...their animosity toward Stephen became irrational. They attacked him
like a herd of bulls with flared nostrils.

Stephen could sense the circle closing in around him.
Tactics that hadn't been used since the trial of Jesus Christ
were dusted off. False witnesses with ludicrous accusations of
blasphemy suddenly surfaced. A large jury filled with negative

The Story of Stephen

public opinion was recruited. They even dragged Stephen into the courts of the Sanhedrin. It was "The Trial of Jesus–the Sequel."

The Scriptures say that they fixed their gaze on him (Acts 6:15). The high priest then demanded to know if the accusations were true. Stephen lifted his voice and delivered one the greatest sermons ever recorded in Scripture. So good, in fact, that the entire fifty-two verses of uncompromising truth were reprinted in Acts 7. Like a sudden sword, it pieced the conscience of the Sanhedrin. "Now when they heard this, they were cut to the quick, and they began gnashing their teeth at him" (Acts 7:54).

So what does a falsely accused man do when a furious crowd fixes their gaze of animosity on him? Simple.

He puts his gaze on somebody else.

We've all seen the picture of two heavyweights coming to the center of the ring prior to the first round of their match. As the referee goes over the rules for the fight, the two boxers stand toe to toe and scowl at one another in an effort to win the battle of intimidation.

But as the Sanhedrin glared at Stephen, Stephen put his eyes elsewhere. He was fixed on heaven. "Behold, I see the heavens opened up and the Son of Man standing at the right hand of God" (Acts 7:56).

The crowds could take no more. They drove Stephen outside the city limits and began to stone him. But the fires of persecution only made the character of Stephen more permanent. While being stoned, Stephen saw what Caleb and Joshua saw beyond the giants of Canaan. Stephen saw a God whose earth was His footstool. A God so great He made the giants look like grasshoppers.

What the people casting the stones could not see were the

rose pedals being poured over Stephen. The stones suddenly felt like feathers. He who wept over Stephen's hurts…He who bled for his sins and prayed over his weakness…was now within clear view.

For some, this appears to be the grand paradox. Jesus, the Author of Life, predicts an early death for some of His closest followers. It's hard to fathom that martyrdom was a promise. No one can accuse Jesus of not being forthright with His disciples. He told them clearly that tough times were ahead. "Blessed are those who have been persecuted for the sake of righteousness, for theirs is the kingdom of heaven" (Matt. 5:10). He told them again, just prior to His ascension, "But you shall receive power when the Holy Spirit has come upon you; and you shall be My witnesses [martyrs] both in Jerusalem, and in all Judea and Samaria, and even to the remotest part of the earth" (Acts 1:8).

We often read that verse and think of missions, not martyrdom. But Jesus was predicting two things with His words. He said there would be both death and life, and both would begin in Jerusalem. Stephen would be the first fruits of that cycle.

Permission to Plagiarize

Raising four small children at the same time is a bona fide challenge. One game that is universal among children is the game of copycat. That's where one child, usually the younger, mimics every move of the older child. It usually drives the older child crazy when a sibling copies their every move and repeats their every word.

Stephen died playing copycat. Listen to his final words on earth. You might recognize them. "'Lord, do not hold this sin against them!' And having said this, he fell asleep" (Acts

7:60). I too want to die acting like Jesus. I want to pass through this life with a memory verse on my lips. Personally I am thrilled that Jesus said, "Repeat after me."

- *"Forgive them..."* While the blood flowed, forgiveness flowed.

- *"For they know not what they do..."* He forgave them instantly and thoroughly.

Jesus was saying, "Leave the rebuttal to Me, Stephen. You must trust Me with this one. We'll debrief at a later time."

Blood and tears have a way of crystallizing our view of Jesus. Stephen saw Jesus clearly. He saw Him standing calmly. The calm of heaven was nothing like the chaos around Stephen. Jesus was motioning for Stephen to come home. To come upward and out of the range of the rocks and the other things people throw. Jesus was an expert in this stuff. He knew firsthand the pain of having things hurled at you. He also knew it's a temporary fight.

The blood they saw streaming down Stephen's face made Stephen look fragile to his enemies. They felt that they had won. But nothing could be further from reality. There was nothing fragile about Stephen. He was in absolute control to the end and beyond. His closing words were aimed directly at his killers.

Thank goodness, there was nothing original about them.

Chapter 12

The Story of Ananias and Sapphira

But a certain man named Ananias, with his wife Sapphira, sold a piece of property, and kept back some of the price for himself, with his wife's full knowledge, and bringing a portion of it, he laid it at the apostles' feet. But Peter said, "Ananias, why has Satan filled your heart to lie to the Holy Spirit, and to keep back some of the price of the land?"
—Acts 5:1–3

Does anyone know the actual weight of a secret? Ten pounds? One hundred pounds? Ask King David, and he will tell you it can weigh more than the sun itself. "When I kept silent about my sin, my body wasted away through my groaning all day long. For day and night Thy hand was heavy upon me; my vitality was drained away as with the fever heat of summer" (Ps. 32:3–4).

For one year David tried to manage his secret, but he lost his grip. The weight became more than he could bear.

It's hard to imagine that there could be a secret out

there heavier than David's secret.

But I found one. This secret was so heavy that not even two people could lift it.

At first, greed feels insignificant in the grand scheme of things. It feels tiny and personal. In fact, it feels very manageable. Which is why I was going to draw the line at wearing a grass skirt. Which meant, of course, that I had no problem with the pineapples, surfboards and the potential sunburns.

Allow me to explain.

We boarded on time. Found our aisle. Fastened our seatbelts and gave the stewardess our halfhearted ear. That's when the first announcement came. "Ladies and gentlemen, we have oversold this flight. We need ten volunteers who would be willing to get off the plane and take a later flight." There were no takers. It was time to up the ante.

"Ladies and gentlemen, for those who would be willing to take a later flight, you will be given a $100 discount off your next ticket." *Hmm…* I was responsible for about a hundred-plus kids. We were returning to San Jose, California, after an incredible youth choir tour of the East Coast. I was the youth pastor. Case closed. I needed to remain on board and be responsible.

Having made such a quality decision, I felt good about myself.

After a few more moments, another announcement was made. "Ladies and gentlemen, those who are willing to get off the plane and take a later flight will receive a one-way ticket anywhere in the continental United States. *Double hmm…* I felt a slight tug, but responsibility pulled me back.

Now I *really* felt good about myself.

There were only four takers on the last offer.

After a few more minutes, another announcement came.

The Story of Ananias and Sapphira

"Ladies and gentlemen, those passengers who are willing to take a later flight will be given round-trip airfare anywhere in the continental United States…or Hawaii!" I felt something die inside of me. I think it was the death of responsibility. I have always wanted to go to Hawaii. As a matter of fact, I *deserved* to go to Hawaii. These crummy kids could find their own way home from New York.

This must be God's way of blessing me!

I pulled Karen up, we gathered our things, and we whispered quickly to one of the responsible parents who stayed on the plane. I told them to make sure the kids behaved. They assured us it would be fine and that I deserved this blessing!

At least that's what I thought heard.

We were off the plane without looking back. After all, why be double-minded about this?

Four hours later we were told the second flight was also oversold, so we found ourselves holding four, not two, round-trip airline vouchers to Hawaii or wherever else in the continental United States we wanted to go. We would summer vacation in Hawaii and maybe "jet off" to New York for some Christmas shopping in the winter. Life was good.

Well, except for that little voice I kept hearing.

Within two days I was miserable. Now, don't think I am some type of kill-joy. I can handle a blessing. I have no trouble with God using an airline voucher to say He loves me. But I knew before I got up from my seat that the Lord wanted me to stay on that plane and fulfill my responsibility to those kids.

I just got swept up in the moment. My "hallelujah" got confused with my "Honolulu."

By the end of the day, Karen and I had torn up the vouchers. I wish I could report that I felt the brush of angels' wings as I tore those vouchers into little pieces. No, I felt crummy...crummy that I had to learn this lesson in the first place.

The next day several of my student leaders came into my office to share their disappointment that I had abandoned them in order to get a free trip. Before they could finish, I told them I was sorry and that the night before I had torn up the tickets.

There was a sudden change of countenance. Hugs were shared. Respect was regained.

Hawaii would have to wait.

When the preacher said, "And the two shall become one flesh," Ananias and Sapphira never knew just how fleshly that meant. Ananias and Sapphira never set out to die; they set out to shop. I don't know if the statement "shop until you drop" is attributed to them, but it could be.

What kind of statement was God making that day at church when both Ananias and Sapphira suddenly dropped dead after giving less than planned? Was the Law back in vogue? Would fearful giving now replace cheerful giving?

Before we dig too deep, there are some obvious lessons at work here:

- It was a case of dishonest living, not just dishonest giving.

- It's easier to sin in "twos."

- God always gives us a chance to repent in "ones."

- You can be possessed by your possessions.

96

The Story of Ananias and Sapphira

When Ananias arrived at church without Sapphira, he put on the face of excitement. His gift would be more than usual...more than the portion he usually gave out of his daily wages. This particular money was part of a land sale. It would be one of those "one-time" gifts we all enjoy giving.

At the appropriate time in the service, Ananias moved toward the front with his gift in hand. As he approached the front, he felt some apprehension. He knew the amount was less than it should be, but he wondered if those were just human thoughts.

He also kept wondering where Sapphira was. They were supposed to do this together.

Ananias caught the eye of Peter as he laid the money at his feet. He expected an affirming nod. A pastoral smile. A private thank-you. Instead he heard these chilling words:

> **Ananias, why has Satan filled your heart to lie to the Holy Spirit, and to keep back some of the price of the land?**
>
> —ACTS 5:3

The Bible doesn't indicate if Peter had his microphone on or not when he said this, but you can bet the air left the room. Peter continued, "While it remained unsold, did it not remain your own? And after it was sold, was it not under your control? Why is it that you have conceived this deed in your heart? You have not lied to men, but to God" (v. 4).

Those were the last words Ananias heard this side of eternity. He was gone. If his goal was to die a wealthy man, he made it. The young men in the congregation took his body away and buried it. I'm not quite sure what they did at church for the next three hours, but suddenly the door opened, and in walked old widow Sapphira. Of course, she had no idea that her husband had already moved from the sixth row to six feet under.

Sapphira was late to church because she was at the mall buying a new funeral outfit. Peter asked her a question. "Tell me whether you sold the land for such and such a price?" Sapphira answered him, "Yes, that was the price" (v. 8). Obviously, no one tipped her off in the parking lot. That was the canned answer, not the right answer.

> Then Peter said to her, "Why is it that you have agreed together to put the Spirit of the Lord to the test? Behold, the feet of those who have buried your husband are at the door, and they shall carry you out as well." And she fell immediately at his feet, and breathed her last; and the young men came in and found her dead, and they carried her out and buried her beside her husband.
>
> —ACTS 5:9–10

Her attempt to outwit the consequences of her actions failed miserably.

They sinned as a pair, but died solo. When the plan was hatched, one of them suggested it. The other nodded. Neither had the guts to do it alone. The conspiracy only felt comfortable as long as they remained a team. That loyalty to the ranks is what cost Sapphira her life.

The next time you pray to be a New Testament church, remember this scene. Especially around offering time. If this was the norm for every service today, I would venture to say there would be line of hearses circling the church property.

Ananias and Sapphira were established believers. This shows the deceptive grip of greed. They were part of the church who "were of one heart and soul; and not one of them claimed that anything belonging to him was his own; but all things were common property to them" (Acts 4:32). They had signed on as part of this new community. But privately, their thoughts drifted toward greed.

The thing that most hurt God was not the lack of zeros on the check. It was the lack of commitment to do what He asked. This was a significant moment for Ananias and Sapphira. I'm certain this wasn't the first test they failed. Grace was too real to just react like this.

Something that was made clear to their hearts was somehow renegotiated without including God in the negotiations. The Lord was teaching the early church that obedience to the voice of Holy Spirit was equal to the obedience Jesus demanded when He walked on the earth.

The reality of the Holy Spirit was not just for the Day of Pentecost and then forgotten. It was the real voice of guidance for the believer. His leading wasn't to be taken for granted or dismissed as trivial. It was to be followed.

The Bible finishes this story by saying, "And great fear came upon the whole church, and upon all who heard of these things" (Acts 5:11).

You don't say.

The weight of a secret? Only Jesus really knows.

Chapter 13

The Story of Cornelius

And they said, "Cornelius, a centurion, a righteous and God-fearing man well spoken of by the entire nation of the Jews, was divinely directed by a holy angel to send for you to come to his house and hear a message from you." And so he invited them in and gave them lodging.
—Acts 10:22–23

I will never forget the fidgety man. Nor his sweat. I'll tell you why he was so fidgety in a moment. But first, I want to share with you a powerful parable from nature.

Once upon a time two seeds were placed in the soil on the same day. Not dirt, mind you, but divine soil. The soil God made on day six of Creation, not day three. You see, the soil created on day three was able to grow a variety of seeds. But the divinely mastered soil created on day six could only grow one type of seed.

The seed with the soul.

They Felt the Spirit's Touch

The first seed with the soul was cautiously placed in the womb of royalty. The second seed seemed more carelessly placed in the womb of peasantry. The first seed was surrounded by fortune, crowns and nobility; the second, by destitution, thorns and squalor. Birthrights and legacy welcomed the first seed. Filth and tribulation soon belly-laughed at the second seed.

Two seeds—two worlds apart. Yet there was something very common about both seeds. No matter where each seed was planted, it still took nine months for it to reach fullness. The power of money, learning, geography and climate meant nothing to the gestation of the soul seed.

And actually, the same law holds true for all seeds.

Long ago Jesus declared that the science of His Father's kingdom would be agriculture, not technology. His Word and the patient unfolding of His ways were likened to the seed: "The seed is the word of God" (Luke 8:11, NKJV).

In essence, Jesus was giving us the "heads up" about the journey that lies ahead…that we need to prepare ourselves with patience, not just fire.

A seed, when first sown, must germinate. Next come the root, the blade and finally the head before the bearing of the fruit. And despite the scientific progress through the ages, it still takes the same amount of space and time today to grow a potato or an apple as it did in Old Testament days. God's "law of the seed" cannot be pushed. Tough medicine for today's Christian who tries to function in a world of spiritual speed.

Rushing toward visible results at the neglect of God's quiet and secret deepening of the heart is tempting for all of us. But the fact is that time is on God's side. And He uses the slow passing of time to mature us. In other words, to "finish the race" as Paul admonished, we cannot ignore the value of the "slow move" of God in our lives.

Don't fret; God is able to travel with great velocity. He can move a mountain in a millisecond. But when it comes to growing us, He prefers a different strategy. One based on patience and character—qualities that are formed far more through times of delay than through fast-paced Christian sizzle.

To keep growing, the Christian must cut loose from a deadly millstone, the one labeled "rush delivery." We often lose our perspectives about God's view of time. For example, I can casually read Acts 9 through Acts 13 in about fifteen minutes. But it took Paul fourteen years to live it.

When impatience tempts us, it's good to remember what God told Jeremiah: "Before I formed you in the womb I knew you, and before you were born I consecrated you; I have appointed you a prophet to the nations" (Jer. 1:5).

Jeremiah's only duty before God was to till the weeds of his heart so the seeds of destiny could freely develop. Jeremiah was reminded that God's life would grow in him like a flower, not arrive like e-mail. Serving as a prophet of the Most High God wasn't the kind of fruit that sprung up overnight.

There was no need for Jeremiah to manipulate his spiritual growth. There is no need for you and me to do it either. Before your mother knew she was pregnant, God knew your name. And the Lord can be trusted to bring to pass what He planted. But He needs your cooperation. His advice to you is still the same: "Relax. Take it slow. Let Me work in you. I am bigger than your nervousness. And I'm certainly not jittery about your success. I am older than your life span. And when it comes to your heart-soil and the seed of My design, I'm lovingly asking you to do one thing.

"Just weed and water. I'll grow the beauty."

He climbed a mountain and invited those he wanted with him. They climbed together. He settled on twelve, and designated them as apostles. The plan was that they would be with him...
—MARK 3:13–14, THE MESSAGE, EMPHASIS ADDED

Could it be that the secret formula used by Jesus to change the world had nothing to do with a prophecy or a promise? That instead it was all based on a *preposition*? It's not as preposterous as it sounds. The fact is, the impact of Jesus wasn't the result of *work*.

It was the result of *with*.

Even His investment in Judas bore that fact. After the grand scheme of betrayal was complete, Judas couldn't enjoy his prize winnings. His conscience was spoiled by Jesus' unbridled demonstration of relationship at the Last Supper.

Jesus' commitment to redemption and kingdom through relationship is staggering. To watch the administrator of the universe carve out time for twelve individuals is astonishing. It was that "withing" commitment that changed the world. I don't know about you, but I have a checkbook and a few kids to monitor, not a universe to run, and I still struggle for meaningful relationships.

When Jesus spoke of relationships, He meant it to include the following:

- An honest investment of time
- Genuine transparency
- Difficult vulnerability, which brings growth
- Times to laugh and cry together
- Growing up and growing old together

The Story of Cornelius

In other words, Jesus established a community of friendships that would stand the tests of time, trial and triumph. It's not easy to find those networks.

Remember the fidgety man I mentioned in my first paragraph? You see, he was in my office a few years ago sharing about his struggle with Christianity. It just wasn't working for him. He felt disconnected from the church. After letting him empty his heart, I asked him a few questions. That's what made him fidgety. I asked him, "So, who are your buddies in the church? Who are the guys you do fun stuff with? Who are the guys that point out a blind spot in your life? If you fell down, who would come looking for you to pick you up?"

He told me he had attended church for years, but he could not honestly point to one person he could call *friend*. He confessed that he had spent the last two decades of his Christian journey alone. That there was no one to check the radar to see if he was still airborne. No one to tell him if his ideas would work or fail. In other words, he had been left to grow himself.

He was a man without a preposition.

This is not the plan Jesus had in mind.

Cornelius was about two things in life: prayer and the poor. "Now there was certain man at Caesarea named Cornelius, a centurion of what was called the Italian cohort, a devout man, and one who feared God with all his household, and gave many alms to the Jewish people, and prayed to God continually" (Acts 10:1–2).

But like the fidgety man in my office, Cornelius needed a few more prepositions in his life. God wanted new things for His church, but the conduit of relationship was not yet in place.

For the first ten years of the early church, the Jews and the Gentiles tolerated each other. The problem was, the kingdom of God was based on *celebrating* people, not *tolerating* them. The Holy Spirit looked for an opening in the temple, the synagogue, but found none. So it was time to get creative.

The miracle relationship that ensued changed the course of the church for eternity. Sometimes it's difficult to grasp just how profound this event was for the church.

God took two men who were held by the grip of their upbringing. He broke that grip and forged a relationship that, apart from a supernatural beginning, never would have come to pass. God wanted His church to look like heaven. But at the rate His church was going about it, it would take half of eternity to get there. These issues were too deeply engraved. And to complicate matters, the church and secular society were in agreement over the issue: It's best to keep people separated. Neither institution seemed willing to take the lead in building the bridge.

So God got aggressive.

He gathered together His choice angels and told them of the dilemma with mankind…that they saw culture as the barrier, not the blessing. He said that the plan to change this was simple. "We are going to bypass religion and go straight for two things: the house and the heart."

Some angels were assigned to Peter. Some were sent to Cornelius. They agreed on their coordinates and were dispatched.

The first strike would be the house of Cornelius.

> **About the ninth hour of the day he clearly saw in a vision an angel of God who had just come in to him,**

and said to him, "Cornelius!" And fixing his gaze upon him and being much alarmed, he said, "What is it, Lord?" And he said to him, "Your prayers and alms have ascended as a memorial before God. And now dispatch some men to Joppa, and send for a man named Simon, who is also called Peter."
—Acts 10:3–5

The next day a second angelic strike occurred over Joppa.

And on the next day, as they were on their way, and approaching the city, Peter went up on the housetop about the sixth hour to pray. And he became hungry, and was desiring to eat; but while they were making preparations, he fell into a trance; and he beheld the sky opened up, and a certain object like a great sheet coming down, lowered by four corners to the ground, and there were in it all kinds of four-footed animals and crawling creatures of earth and birds of the air. And a voice came to him, "Arise, Peter, kill and eat!"
—Acts 10:9–13

Say what, Lord?

Three times Peter told the Lord that there was no way he could go against his upbringing and his religion. Yes, he was saved by grace, but his common sense was still deeply rooted in the Law. But the angel was persistent. While this scene was unfolding on the roof, three men knocked on the front door. The plan devised in the heavenlies was working to precision.

Peter accompanied the three men to the house of Cornelius though he had no idea why. Peter must have thought he was needed to solve a crisis. After arriving in Joppa, he entered the house of Cornelius. Things were still very cloudy for Cornelius as well. He fell at the feet of Peter, and Peter responded with one of the truest confessions of his life:

"Stand up; I too am just a man" (v. 26).

Cornelius had filled his house with loved ones. God's purposes were beginning to crystallize. Peter wasn't there to solve a crisis. He was there because God was healing a crisis inside of him. "And he said to them, 'You yourselves know how unlawful it is for a man who is a Jew to associate with a foreigner or to visit him; and yet God has shown me that I should not call any man unholy or unclean'" (v. 28).

I appreciate Peter's humility, but why did it take him ten years to realize something he had seen modeled through Jesus on a daily basis? Well, if Peter is like me, I can tell you why it took ten years.

Because we are slow learners.

Cornelius chimed in and told everyone about his encounter four days earlier with the angel. Peter then preached up a storm. The Christ and the cross were clearly explained. Resurrection and forgiveness, too. Peter was on his game. Then God interrupted and said that the sermon portion of the evening was over. It was time for a demonstration of power. The fire of Pentecost fell on everybody. Peter then baptized "whosoever will" in water. Quite a day!

Here are five takeaways from this story.

1. *Spiritual stretching is not easy.* Unconditional love for others seems like the most natural approach to life for a Christian. Yet it is one of the most difficult commitments to live out.

2. *The miracle of the house of Cornelius is that it happened in a house, not a temple.* God had to circumvent the natural gathering places of religion because His love was not welcome there. But His priority for healthy, unrestricted relationships prevailed.

3. *Even good people need God's help to live like Jesus.* Peter had raised the dead. He was a powerful bishop in the early church. He was good man. A good leader. But he hadn't caught the heart of God for people as he should have. God had to creatively get his attention.

4. *The powerful grip of upbringing must be broken.* Both Peter and Cornelius knew this new union and friendship would not be well received in either camp. This hadn't been a pressing issue for the church because no one had brought it up. But now God had brought it up. The church was yet to be what He had hoped for. The violence of the cross, the magnificence of the upper room outpouring had provided more than what the church was realizing.

5. *We must be hungry for what's on God's plate.* Peter was hungry before the vision came. That hunger was the key. At first, Peter didn't like what God was serving. We can be hungry for God, hungry for revival, but then reject God's chosen menu.

Much like Lewis and Clark, we need the mutual joy of one another as we adventure together in God's kingdom. If you are interested, here are two ways you can replace the weeds with a little more "with."

First, make it your goal to love people without limitation. That's how Jesus did it. Remember, God has no weeds. His love is perfect. I must choose by the grace that is at work in me to value and love those who are different with the same intensity that I love those with whom I share things in common.

Jesus isn't interested in having us put one person above the next. Jesus loved all people equally. The only preference

Jesus showed was to those in need of healing. And so should the church. But the inclination of the heart is to play it safe. God is saying, "Let Me do for you what I did for Cornelius and Peter. Let Me turn those barriers into blessing."

The second thing you can do is value people for who they are, not for what they can do for you. Jesus made people feel as though He was looking for them, even though they had been searching for Him.

So until Jesus comes... *till*. The weeds aren't worth it.

Chapter 14

The Story of Eutychus

Seated in a window was a young man named Eutychus, who was sinking into a deep sleep as Paul talked on and on. When he was sound asleep, he fell to the ground from the third story and was picked up dead. Paul went down, threw himself on the young man and put his arms around him. "Don't be alarmed," he said. "He's alive!"
—Acts 20:9–10, NIV

In Acts chapter 2, the church began with a bang. And it has only gotten louder from there. When you consider the six days of Creation, other than the sound of God's voice, the first two days were silent. As a matter of fact, it probably wasn't until the third day that any noise could be heard on earth. The separation of the seas and dry land produced the first sound of a crashing wave.

It wasn't until the fifth day of Creation that God created something with vocal cords. The first audible noise was the sound of a chirping bird. We're speculating, but it wasn't until the end of day six that casual conversation between two humans began.

Not so when He created the church. It began with vocal chords—120 of them to be exact. Evolutionists are correct; there was a "Big Bang" in history. It just didn't happen at the creation of the universe. Creation was silent compared to the sounds heard on the Day of Pentecost.

We tend to forget how the church began. The church didn't begin with a late-night board meeting. It didn't begin with a slogan or a fund-raising campaign. Nor was it a slick ad in the Saturday paper. There was no visitor parking. No smiles in the foyer. And no handshakes by the greeter. There was no opening hymn. No organ prelude. No quick prayer in the pastor's study. And certainly no orderly entrance by the choir or a note to the pastor that someone had left their lights on in the parking lot. As a matter of fact, the only thing present was desperation, quickly followed by noise...chaos...fire...disruption and total mass confusion.

Desperate but invigorated leaders began shooting from the hip. Camps quickly formed. Courage was a must. Former cowards like Peter opened their mouths and found their unrehearsed words were suddenly working. Nothing like this had ever been experienced on Planet Earth. For the Jewish onlooker, the Abraham and Moses paradigms of his past were suddenly wiped off the map.

God was saying, "Surprise!"

The 120 were now on their way to their first 120 million. When those outside of the upper room heard the ultrastrange sound of tongues, they figured the upper room included an open bar. If not drunk, then they were mentally ill. But 3,000 thought twice about their eternal soul after Peter spoke. They wanted in. Questions were raised, but the converts kept coming to be baptized. In other words, *awe* was back in town.

There is something to be remembered by all of this. Primarily, the church began with spontaneity not orthodoxy. And the Christian experience should include some of that same life and noise along the way.

But as wonderful as the Day of Pentecost was, God had more surprises on the way. And He didn't need an ominous unparted sea of red or a four-day-old dead body named Lazarus to make His point.

Sometimes all God needed to set up His awe was a hearty yawn.

A Word for Windows

Poor Eutychus. Maybe the young man deserves more of our sympathy. But then again, poor Paul. He had a burden to get off his soul. A big burden that became a long sermon. Nowhere in the Bible does it say that long sermons are sin. They are just long. And when people have things to do and places to be, that can be highly irritating.

But back to Eutychus. I'm afraid that among a certain fraternity of churchgoers, Eutychus committed a cardinal sin. He failed sermon-napping 101. The aim of a skilled sermon napper is to sleep without getting caught. To look spiritual while enjoying his weekly visit to dreamland. It can take years to perfect this craft. Obviously, Eutychus was a rookie.

If you've ever sat behind a sermon napper, he can be tough to spot at first. The people sitting in front of him can't see his face. The people to the side can't see his eyes. That just leaves the preacher. To him, the sermon napper looks prayerful. (Or at least that's what he tells himself.)

The best thing a sermon napper can find on a Sunday morning is someone with tall hair to sit behind so the pastor can't see. If you happen to be seated directly behind a sermon napper, he looks to be in complete harmony with the preacher, affirming each point with a forthright nod. But somewhere between the thirty- and forty-minute mark, you begin to notice the odd timing of his nods. The preacher says, "Turn with me to the Book of Philippians, chapter 3," and the sermon napper nods. The preacher then says, "Rome was a big city in Paul's day." Again, the sermon napper quickly agrees with a hearty nod. Those sitting behind him think he is a Bible scholar, and he's simply appreciative of the finer points of church history.

The preacher then reaches for his water, and the sermon napper once again nods in agreement.

But suddenly after nodding his approval at the pastor's sip from the water glass, his head never resumes an upward position. It lunges forward and sticks. The sermon napper is exposed! And he gets a double penalty for snoring. How long he's allowed to doze is determined by his wife's elbow.

I'm certain Eutychus tried every Sunday-morning trick he could muster just to remain semicomatose during Paul's message. He bit his lip. He sucked a mint. But the waves of drowsiness just kept coming. He waited for the congregation to close their eyes in prayer so he could uncork one of those megayawns that make your nose and neck disappear.

Now it required desperate measures. He placed his elbows on his knees, bowed his head in his hands and engaged in the deep massage of his eye sockets—followed closely by the slow raising of his head ever so discreetly so as to keep his spiritual mask from slipping.

As a last resort, he placed his index finger under his eyebrow and pushed upward like the center pole of a circus tent. But nothing was working. Eutychus was out. Worse yet, there was no closure in sight to Paul's endless sermon.

Personally speaking, I join with other preachers who find it quite encouraging to know that even the apostle Paul put someone to sleep with his sermon. In some fashion, whether it was fighting to stay awake while listening to someone else preach, or by the sad offering up of our own homiletical sedative, we've all been there.

The humid, thick, nighttime air of Troas, coupled with the dense, oily heat emanating from several lamps in the makeshift sanctuary, became more than Eutychus could take. Young people are natural risk-takers; Eutychus must have considered his maneuver to the window seat a "hip" place to sit.

But that decision, if not for the coming mercy of God, was nearly the last decision the boy would ever make. Without warning, the slumbering young man free-falls three stories in a deep sleep and collides with the quiet courtyard below. In that awful moment, Paul's theology moved to real-life drama. A veteran of three missionary tours, this was a first for Paul.

There was no synagogue mob to blame or demon power to bind. Paul knew the culprit—his own long-windedness. What a horrible moment for the apostle—from the heights of preaching euphoria to the depths of human panic in seconds. Imagine the guilt he must have felt. ("Oh, no! My preaching just killed this boy.")

The sight of a young life being jarred to death by a three-story fall is no laughing matter. We joke now because we know the end of the story. But when Paul fell upon the young corpse in the courtyard and pleaded for the return of his life, it didn't matter that he was a trophy apostle or that he had raised unprecedented funds for famine relief. Every consuming emotion sought to find a spiritual explanation for the lad's death. For Paul, people took precedence over preaching.

Once he noticed an empty windowsill, it was time to let someone else finish the sentence.

Does Satan possess such authority that he can storm upon holy turf and destroy an innocent life? How could Satan be allowed to do this under Paul's ministry? Or was there another reason besides blaming Satan?

When we think of God's public "spontaneity," it is usually stays within the lines of acceptable interruptions. A broken heart finding grace suddenly cries aloud. Though no one actually asked for the consent to weep aloud, it's a welcome signal to the pastor that a move of public repentance is underway. But God has other ways of showing up in church.

More and more, we hear of God's unorthodox arrivals when He seems to add shock value to His sovereign entrance. A nice, clean setup that fits the service schedule is not always God's order of the day. There are moments when God says, "Here I come in a moment of My design." Messy and unorthodox.

Dissecting this odd account of Eutychus leaves you with only one sensible rebuttal. Simply this: God's vast greatness cannot be scheduled. Though faithful and true, God's astonishing ways cannot be predicted—only enjoyed. When God comes via the extreme, we are simply left to witness it, relish in His perfect greatness and then advance forward in greater faith and exploits.

This stop in Troas was part of Paul's third and last missionary journey. Kind of a farewell tour. Maybe it went long because Paul was preaching his "greatest hits" sermon. Maybe he knew it would be his last message as a free man, and he wanted it to count.

So what's the point? And whom do we blame? The preacher for going long or the sleeper for getting caught?

The Story of Eutychus

Neither. Paul was sincere, and Eutychus was simply exhausted. In the final analysis, there is no blame; there is only awe.

As the sun rose over Troas, we don't know how Paul intended to end his message because God had another ending in mind. Paul can only be thankful it wasn't A.D. 2003. The lawyers and the litigation converging upon this mishap would have been staggering. Business cards would have been flying everywhere. This had *punitive damages* written all over it. Paul's act of divine healing was a nice way to destroy the evidence.

Chapter 15

The Story of Aeneas

And Peter said to him, "Aeneas, Jesus Christ heals you;
arise, and make your bed." And immediately he arose.
And all who lived in Lydda and Sharon saw him, and
they turned to the Lord.
—Acts 9:34–35

Two thousand, nine hundred twenty is an interesting number. You can get there by taking 365 and multiplying it by 8.

Those are great numbers if you are a football coach calculating your total offense over the last eight games. Those are also impressive numbers if you are a sixteen-year-old calculating how much money you've been able to save over the last eight months for your first car.

Those are also impressive numbers if you are bragging to Jesus about how many times a day you'll forgive your enemy. It makes Peter's offer of seven look pretty ridiculous.

But what if the number 2,920 represented something else? Something not so pleasant. What if the first number, 365, represented *days*, not yards? And what if the second number, 8, represented *years*, not games? And what if the number you get from multiplying those two numbers, 2,920, actually represented the number of consecutive days you were forced to *endure* without a single day's break in between?

Endure what? And what does this have to do with Aeneas? Everything.

When I was a child, my mom would order me to take a two-hour nap every afternoon. I would fuss and fight like any five-year-old. I viewed naptime as punishment and the bed as my cell. Now in my forties, I wonder what my reaction would be today if someone walked into my office at around two in the afternoon and ordered me to lie down for a two-hour nap.

I'm pretty sure I would lie down and call them blessed. I bet I wouldn't even need my "blankee." And I would promise not to ask for a drink of water or ask to get up to go the bathroom.

Really, folks, I wouldn't.

So how do you think poor Aeneas viewed his bedtime? I'm sure he found time to form an opinion. Remember the equation I gave at the start of this chapter? Two thousand, nine hundred twenty is the number of days Aeneas spent lying in his bed without getting up. "And there he found a certain man named Aeneas, who had been bedridden eight years, for he was paralyzed" (Acts 9:33).

The Bible doesn't say a thing about what paralyzed

The Story of Aeneas

Aeneas, only that he was paralyzed. The Greek medical term was *paraluo*. It means "to be dissolved, relaxed, loosened and enfeebled." In other words, his basic muscle functions were worthless. But through a tiny clue, we get a deeper picture into his condition. When Peter said to Aeneas, "Arise, and make your bed," it was more than a desire on Peter's part to change the sheets.

The "making of the bed" represented deliverance from the mental sinkhole that Aeneas had called home for the last eight years. I'm sure during those eight years many things crossed his mind, the least of which was getting up and walking out the door. Those kinds of thoughts had vanished years ago.

Instead he had four walls to entertain him. An oil lamp on a small table so he could see what a nightmare looks like in the dark. A doorway that must have seemed like a distant star in a faraway galaxy—a place he could never travel. Add to all of this eight straight years of bedpans, caregivers and obligated family members paying their once-a-year visit… and you can see why the buildup of metal anguish must have been uncontrollable.

- "I'm the object of pity, nothing else."
- "I'm half a man."
- "The world has forgotten me."

By the time Peter found Aeneas, the New Testament church was already older than his paralysis by about a year. The town of Lydda was twenty-five miles northwest of Jerusalem, so I'm sure something about Jesus' past healing ministry eventually worked its way to Aeneas' bedside. He would hear the tales about this Carpenter from Nazareth with supernatural powers. He would give a slight nod, but his melancholy would soon resettle. Aeneas must have pondered thoughts like these: *Those are great stories. But talk about bad timing. When this Jesus you keep talking about was around this area, well, that was ten years ago. I wasn't paralyzed ten years ago. I'm paralyzed now! And now that I need His help, He's nowhere in sight! My life is nothing but bad luck!*

The Bible doesn't tell us why Peter came by for a visit, only that he came. I'm still glad that Jesus comes by to visit. I hope you are, too. He's always on time. He only looks late. As a matter of fact, Jesus loves coming "Lazarus late" and turning hopelessness and its best friend, uselessness, on their ears. But many miss Jesus' visit because He wears the face of His church when He shows up.

He steps on our turf wearing the face of a pastor, an old friend or a stranger, but He comes bearing heaven's terms. Terms of love and grace. Terms of promise that include a chance to walk away from the pain of the past and into a new season of purpose. All He asks is that we "make the bed" after He gives us the strength to get up. That we do something more with His amazing grace than just sit up and rub our eyes. Why? Because there are better things to do in life than crawl back under the covers and wish for another life when God wants to bless the one you already have.

In other words, "Aeneas, go outside and breathe again."

Word about this healing spread quickly. Pity for the poor man who couldn't get out of bed quickly turned into applause. Those who didn't know the Lord knew Him now.

One of my favorite movie scenes as a child was from *Willy Wonka and the Chocolate Factory*. Charlie Bucket, a poor little boy, seemed confined to a hobbit's life. Because his father had died, he was forced to live in the same one-room house with both sets of his grandparents. They ate cabbage soup every day. I hated cabbage, so I always felt sorry for Charlie Bucket. I was about his age when I first saw the movie.

All four of Charlie's grandparents were bedridden and confined to the same bed. As a child, I didn't think about of the ramifications of this arrangement. I was too busy dreaming about my own golden ticket. Willy Wonka had placed five golden tickets inside the wrappers of five chocolate Wonka bars. They could be anywhere in the world. Well, Charlie finds the last golden ticket. The first four tickets were found by a TV addict…a spoiled brat…a gum chewer…and an overweight kid named Gloop.

Each bearer of a golden ticket was then invited to a free tour of the secret world of Willy Wonka's chocolate factory. They were also allowed to bring one adult with them for the tour.

Charlie asks his Grandpa Joe to go with him. The problem is, Grandpa Joe hadn't been out of that bed in over twenty-five years.

Motivated by the wishes of his grandson, Grandpa Joe flips back the covers and for the first time in years puts one foot on the floor. Even he can't believe it. The other three old-timers who have been sharing the bed with him for the last twenty-five years are astonished when Grandpa Joe gets out of bed and starts dancing and singing. Next stop is the chocolate factory.

Make it Jerusalem, not London. Warm it up by about forty degrees. Trade the chocolate factory for a temple. Replace a few Oompa Loompas with some apostles. And most of all, swap the golden ticket for the name of Jesus Christ, and basically you've got a repeat of this Bible story.

I picture Aeneas as a lot like Grandpa Joe. Here comes Peter, a "silver and gold(en ticket) have I none" kind of guy. With faith and health he comes bolting to the bedside of

They Felt the Spirit's Touch

Aeneas. But Peter has more than a warm smile and some warm muffins for the shut-in. He brings a *sentence*. Not a sentence of shame and judgment, but a sentence of optimism. Using one sentence Peter calls the man's name with profound confidence and joins it together with Jesus Christ. "Aeneas, Jesus Christ heals you; arise, and make your bed" (Acts 9:34).

From that moment on, Aeneas lost his options. No one had to tell him twice to make the bed. You wonder after eight years how well he tucked in his corners. Let's face it; many people in our society are emotionally bedridden.

- A wound from a broken relationship feels incurable.
- An invading disease is said to be inoperable.
- The years roll by without significant change.

Defeat takes up residence and adds on until it becomes a palace of mental and spiritual loss, a palace where mind and body settle into bed for the slow ride to hell. The good news is that beyond that bed is a vibrant church. Beyond that bed are stories about resurrected lives walking free for the first time in their lives.

For those who feel like an island in crowded church, Jesus may right now be making a personal visit to your home. Don't be fooled by the disguise. He may look like a pastor or just an old friend passing by. But just as He did through Peter, He is saying to you, "Jesus Christ heals you; arise, and make your bed." The devil had given Aeneas 2,920 reasons to laugh at such a suggestion. But God reversed that possibility with nine words.

And with that, Aeneas finally realized why Peter had actually come to his home. It was simple.

To get him out of the house.

Chapter 16

The Story of the Incestuous Son

Wherefore I urge you to reaffirm your love for him.
—2 Corinthians 2:8

As a child growing up during the late sixties and early seventies, one thing was clear: Our family television set wasn't very impressive. It was an old black-and-white Zenith with a carry handle on the top for portability. Our family moved twenty-seven times, so portability was a necessity.

Regardless of the house, the old Zenith would be placed precariously on a creaky stand in the corner of the living room. Cable was for the rich, so to improve reception, Mom would wrap the two bent antennas in aluminum foil she took from recycled Ho-Ho wrappers.

I would always try to do my part for the family by volunteering to eat a fresh Ho-Ho and donating the wrapper. New wrappers, I argued, gave better reception than old wrappers. No one ever believed my theory.

I can remember watching the grainy images of men landing on the moon. I also remember Walter Cronkite's nightly death tolls from the Vietnam War as we ate dinner with one eye on the Zenith.

To turn the set on, you had to pull out a small "on" button located near the channel dial. When you pulled the button, nothing would happen. But no one worried; we all understood the set needed time to warm up.

After some fuzzy crackling sounds, a small dot would appear in the middle of the screen. You knew things were OK if you saw the dot. After a few more seconds, the dot would become a line that stretched from one side of the screen to the other. Then all of a sudden the line would explode into a bright square. Then after thirty more seconds a clear picture would form.

So why am I bringing up the old family Zenith? Because the story you're about to hear also takes some time to warm up. In fact, the story starts in one New Testament book and ends up in another. Like the old Zenith, sometimes God chooses to warm up slowly. It's better for us that way. Too much grace all at once can get lost in the lights. The key is to stay patient…and no matter what…do not turn off the set.

There's Chaos in Corinth

Corinth in Paul's day was a vibrant, rich and intoxicating city. But there was more to Corinth than economic prosperity. When it came to the pursuit of Greek wisdom and philosophy, Corinth was second only to Athens. During the life of Paul, there were a total of twelve temples operating in Corinth. One of the most popular was the temple of Asclepius, where the god of healing was worshiped. Beyond that lay the temple of Apollo. Apollo was the patron god of music, poetry and the arts.

But the most notorious of all the temples was dedicated to Aphrodite, the goddess of sexual love. In other words, when it came to Corinth, knowledge and the arts played second fiddle, while sexual pleasure directed the orchestra.

Within the religious society of Corinth, prostitution was the best way to finance the operations of the temple. This solved the mystery as to why Paul wanted so desperately to reach Corinth with the message of Christ. Free-trade routes combined with widespread commercial immorality were nothing less than evangelistic destiny for a missionary like Paul.

But lost inside this decadent city was a confused son. He was the first prominent scar on the face of the local church at Corinth. He would test the early church in a way that the lame and blind could not. The early church at Corinth was about to confront an important question about grace. Mainly this: "Did grace come in limited supply? Or is it as boundless and available as Jesus portrayed it to be while He walked the earth?"

His name is not known. Maybe it was mercy that kept him shrouded. Paul may have initially thought about marking this man publicly by name. But Paul hesitated to name him openly like Achan of old or even Paul's contemporary nemesis, Alexander.

Maybe to Paul this sin seemed different. This kind of behavior was unthinkable to the early church. Or, for that matter, even among the people of secular Corinth.

They Felt the Spirit's Touch

It is actually reported that there is immorality among you, and immorality of such a kind as does not exist even among the Gentiles...

—1 CORINTHIANS 5:1

Which is amazing, because I thought Gentiles were pretty skilled sinners.

What deed could this young man from the ranks of the Corinthian church have committed that not even a Gentile would do? "...that someone has his father's wife" (1 Cor. 5:1). In other words, he was having sexual intercourse with his mother.

Sin is sin...but sometimes our sin is *scarlet.* It stands out like a ruby stain against satin white. Even if you believe sin comes in different shades, no one would disagree this was a bright red sin. A young adult's life was now in chaos. A mother's emotion was now sealed in the tombs of a ceaseless purgatory.

The woman at the well with a history of five husbands and one live-in...the half-dressed woman caught in an adultery ...they were nothing compared to the confusion happening at Corinth. Nobody knew what to do. Sin had played its Super Bowl.

Scripture does not indicate whether or not the husband was dead or alive when the wife and son began their relationship. From an Old Testament perspective, the Law of Moses was clear on God's position about such liaisons. "Cursed is he who lies with his father's wife" (Deut. 27:20).

There was no provision in the Old Testament Scriptures for a deceased man's wife to be taken in by a son. It was forbidden under any and all circumstances. Some theologians have suggested that it may have actually been a stepmother and not the man's biological mother. And while that may lessen the unpleasantness, God no less forbade it.

The Story of the Incestuous Son

Clearly something inside of him snapped. It was cata-strophic perversion. Social law and spiritual reason vanished from the son. His lust had gone mad. When Satan heard of what had happened, I'm sure even he sent an executive team of scout demons to confirm the story. If true, he would hammer the faithful of Corinth for years over this one. Corinth the city could shrug its shoulders and move on. But how could Corinth the church ever recover?

First of all, I find it remarkably freeing that the Lord placed this story in the Bible. Paul could just as easily have left this paragraph out of his letter. Not every problem or issue that arose in the church was mentioned. So why this one?

I also find it interesting that there is no mention of the mother's upbringing or her future status with the church. We are told nothing about the pains of her childhood or the possible scars dug into her youthful soul by others. The Bible is silent about any pagan rituals that may have been part of her childhood. We are only left with the saddening story of the son. Which leads us to conclude that he was the instigator and thus held to a higher accountability for what happened.

That absence of information about the mother is actually a sign that New Testament grace was operating in the church. Under the Law of Moses, you can picture the Pharisees drag-ging this woman to the city square for an old-fashioned stoning service. No trial; just assumptions and prejudice. She would have to pay the bill for the both of them.

Not only was grace *good* enough to give the son another chance at spiritual wholeness, but grace was also *just* enough to rise above the ancient shadows of cultural prejudice that were pitted against the woman.

If there were words being spoken between this mother and

her adult son, I am certain they were few. The conscience couldn't bear it. The bitterness and guilt inside of them forbade it. Her young motherly dreams of a small son growing into a valiant warrior were long gone. Sin, in the worst way imaginable, had stolen it all away. A son and mother are special soul mates. Instead, it was now soul *checkmate*. Game over.

Or was it?

Because the first half of this story is so difficult to tell, most Christians are never told the rest of the story. Or if they do stumble across the second half of the story, they fail to connect the dots.

Paul's first letter to the Corinthian church was written in A.D. 59. It was blunt, but graceful. The Old Covenant Law was set in stone. But grace was set in blood. Grace doesn't run from correction when correction is required. And in this case, the grace of God called for severe detention, not a stoning. God's correction is always with an eye toward the future, not the past. It was life, not death, that Paul was after. But most think the story ends there.

Paul explained the ramifications of the detention:

> **But actually, I wrote to you not to associate with any so-called brother if he should be an immoral person, or covetous, or an idolater, or a reviler, or a drunkard, or a swindler—not even to eat with such a one.**
> **—1 Corinthians 5:11**

Paul told the church that, by his own actions, the man had forfeited all rights to a normal life. His relationship with other believers would immediately cease to exist. Paul gave no timelines for his restoration. Paul then couched the man's future in spiritual mystery. "I have decided to deliver over such a one to Satan for the destruction of his flesh, that his soul might be saved" (1 Cor. 5:5). It was the last resort for a morally corrupt life.

He was instructing the church to give the man what he wanted until the man could stand it no more. The length of the detention would be up to the man.

But the power of grace is found in the chronology of the two letters. Paul wrote his first letter to the Corinthians in A.D. 59. One year later Paul was ready to write his second letter. In his second letter, written in A.D. 60, Paul readdressed the issue of the incestuous son on detention. His words were more shocking than the original sin.

> **Sufficient for such a one is this punishment which was inflicted by the majority, so that on the contrary you should rather forgive and comfort him, lest somehow such a one be overwhelmed by excessive sorrow.**
>
> —2 CORINTHIANS 2:6–7

It's amazing what a year alone with the devil can do for the soul.

Paul was asking them to "forgive." In other words, it was time to release this man from the reproach and shame of his deeds in the same way Christ had released each one of them.

Paul also was asking them to provide the man with "comfort." He was challenging them to consider the feelings of a man who had disregarded theirs just one year ago. First John 1:9 says, "If we confess our sins, He is faithful and righteous to forgive us our sins and to cleanse us from all unrighteousness." Once a person is forgiven, he needs the acceptance of a cleansing community. But would the church at Corinth become that cleansing community?

Paul told the people on the inside of the church that the

man he had delivered over to Satan one year ago was now outside wanting in. The son wanted to come home. He was ready to ditch Satan and reunite with his family. The guy who thought he could leap from the high-rise and fly, who thought he could flaunt the creative laws of God and remain unscathed, wanted his old family back. Dining twenty-four seven with Satan was not what it was cracked up to be.

But the only key that could unlock the door was hanging on a hook somewhere on the inside of the house; it wasn't in the pocket of the man at the front door. Most churches tend to lock their door from the inside. So it doesn't matter who tries what key from the outside; in order to get in, someone has to let them in.

When it comes to welcoming home front-page sinners, the church is often guilty of bolting the door, holding her finger to her lips and telling everyone inside to keep their voices down until whoever it is wanting in leaves. Sure, some churches do make an effort to look loving by unlocking the door, but then they proceed to hold the knob.

Paul wondered if the church would be more aghast at his suggestions for restoration than they were at the sin. Paul knew God could forgive great sin. But could the church follow suit?

In other words, the old question, "Can any good thing come out of Nazareth?" was now replaced by a new question: "Can any grace come out of Corinth?" (See John 1:46.)

Thankfully, and with the helpful nudge of a missionary who understood the depths of Calvary's grace himself, the answer was a resounding *yes*.

Chapter 17

The Story of
Aquila and Priscilla

*Greet Priscilla and Aquila, my fellow workers in
Christ Jesus, who for my life risked their own necks,
to whom not only do I give thanks, but also
all the churches of the Gentiles.*
—Romans 16:3–4

You might think its hard to find a love story in the Book
of Acts. Well, you're right. It is hard.

When you think of the Book of Acts, you think more
Rome than romance. More persecution than perfume. Yet
tucked inside the marvelous opening chapter of the first
church is a love story. It takes some reading between the
lines, but it's there.

There are only a select few married couples mentioned in
the Book of Acts. The most famous is famous for all the
wrong reasons—Ananias and Sapphira. They were the couple

133

who died from an acute case of escrow fever.

But a second couple appears in Acts chapter 18. They finished better than they started.

Aquila and Priscilla were a living compliment to one another. They capitalized on each other's strengths. Teamwork was their creed. Their home was a haven of rest. A doorway of salvation for hundreds. But their greatest achievement was this.

They are never mentioned in the Bible apart from one another.

In every aspect of life, they operated as one. But the million-dollar question remains: How do people turn out like this in marriage? The early church was primarily built by individuals, not couples. So in honor of these pioneers I would like to ask for your indulgence by allowing me to talk about how to have a healthy marriage. Aquila and Priscilla were helpful because they were healthy. They were healthy for a reason. Nothing happens by default. Their marriage was built on principles.

I want to share three principles for a healthy marriage. You might find some words of healing as well.

But to do so requires a brief trip backwards.

King Solomon's legacy was the grand contradiction of lust and art. For the duration of his royal years, he seemed forever torn between his music and his maidens. As a composer, he is credited with writing more than one thousand songs. As a preacher, he penned nearly three thousand proverbs. But he is best remembered for his polygamy—as the lover of a thousand wives and concubines. In many ways, the king of wisdom was a moral castaway.

Yet somewhere in the midst of Solomon's depravity, God's mercy allowed him and his marriage to a country girl named Shulamith to become the scriptural picture of romance and love. Why God would want someone like Solomon to represent His ways is difficult to reconcile. But the Father's fondness for illustrating eternity through redemption is what makes God ways so irresistible.

If King Solomon the polygamist doesn't strike you as a qualified family life counselor, you can select God's other choice—Paul the celibate.

In an odd twist, Solomon and Paul present a role reversal between Old and New Testaments. The Old Testament is usually considered the source of law and conduct, while the New Testament offers the safe haven of grace and intimacy. But when it comes to marriage, the New Testament teachings by Paul form the framework of sound companionship between a husband and a wife, while the Old Testament's Song of Solomon issues an erotic yet tasteful invitation to Spirit-filled romance and marital embrace.

Solomon's song emphasizes the *passions* of marital love. Paul underscores the essential *character* for a healthy partnership. A growing union must be a marriage of both.

A passion-based marriage void of godly principles will rupture and quickly end—with deep emotional heartbreak. A marriage relationship strong in character but lacking in genuine passion may take longer to erode, but it too will likely lead to the same devastating separation.

All too often a woman marries a man hoping she can change him. A man marries a woman hoping she will never change. It's easy to see why problems develop. Paul alluded to the marriage union as a "mystery" in Ephesians 5:32. But the mystery is turning out to be "misery" for thousands. Good intentions and surface sentiments can carry a marriage only a few miles farther down the road than the rented limousine leaving the reception.

Is there hope? Does God have a plan for short-term healing and long-term happiness? *Yes*! But you may not like the source. Compared with other topics in Scripture, marriage comes up short with regard to the amount of information written about it. By design, God kept it simple so we could master the basics.

Keep the Fire Glowing

Solomon and Shulamith are an intriguing example of marital love. Put Solomon in another setting, and he becomes a dirty old man—the kind of man the world has seen all too often. And poor Shulamith appears to be just another codependent woman who thinks she will tame the wanderer's heart long enough to heal the poor sap of his sexual peccadilloes.

But this is not a true picture of these biblical lovers. Solomon once had undisputed possession of his father David's great wealth. He owned the loves and hopes of the people of Israel. But he squandered his wealth through lavish spending and ultimately caused the division of the kingdom. But he found, for one moment in time, something very real with the young maiden from the country.

His oriental poem about their love is filled with exquisite word pictures. It reads like Shakespeare, portraying the purity of love's ideal between a man and a woman. The song tells of their journey of love and lovemaking.

The two were from entirely different backgrounds—he was from the palace; she was from the pasture. Yet this country girl from Lebanon accepted Solomon's proposal and moved to Jerusalem in preparation for the wedding day.

The honeymoon was spectacular. Solomon could hardly contain himself that night: "You have made my heart beat faster with a single glance of your eyes...How beautiful is your love...my bride" (Song of Sol. 4:9–10).

Shulamith, fully aroused, then pleads for Solomon to consummate their union: "Make my garden breathe out fragrance...May my beloved come into his garden and eat its choice fruits!" (v. 16).

Solomon passionately replies, "I have come into my garden...my bride" (Song of Sol. 5:1).

But like all great honeymoons, theirs soon ended, and troubles soon followed. Not long after their marriage, Shulamith and Solomon experienced pitfalls common to every married couple. One night, Shulamith was too tired to respond to Solomon, and she spurned his sexual advances. This episode of unsuccessful intimacy filled Solomon with rejection and Shulamith with insecurity. She was homesick.

The pressures and emotions nearly destroyed the new marriage. But the Song of Solomon is not a picture of destruction. It is a picture of romantic restoration. The apostle Paul's marriage theology found in the fifth chapter of Ephesians reinforces their wise decisions. The message of Solomon and Paul is simple:

In a healthy marriage, there can be no secrets, no stops and no substitutes.

No Secrets

According to Paul, the high calling of marriage is not sexual pleasure. It is *oneness* (Eph. 5:31). "Oneness" means no secrets. One of my favorite expeditions as an adolescent was exploring a nearby field for an oversized boulder. It had to be large enough to stand on but not too large to roll. I would imagine that from the time of Noah and the Flood the stone had never been moved.

I would place my fingers under the boulder, bend my back and try to budge the stone. It would be hard, but eventually I got most boulders to roll at least a couple of inches.

I would always find the same thing under every rock—a damp world void of life except a few worms and scurrying potato bugs. When the sunlight hit the bugs, they would scatter in all directions. Never once did I find a shred of plant life beneath any rock. But looking back now, I realize there was a life-giving marriage principle under all those rocks: Where there is no light, there is no life.

You see, beneath the big rocks was a secret place. No light could penetrate.

The same is true for marriage. Whenever spouses keep secrets from each other, the deception becomes the thriving ground of Satan, who loves darkness and hates light.

Marriage partners need good secrets—secrets they can *share* together. My wife and I have many mutual secrets. Our intimate moments are available to no one else. This type of secrecy bonds, but any secrets we *keep* from each other divide. Exposure is where grace begins. Sometimes a sharp moment of exposure can blind and blur like stepping from a dark room into the daylight. But when light is allowed time to perform its miracle, life will follow.

I know enough secret, negative information about my wife to thoroughly humiliate her in thirty seconds. She could do the same to me in ten. We know the physical quirks of each other's bodies and behavior. However, we have chosen to hide those secrets and never use them against each other publicly. No matter the pressure or surge of self-will, we keep them silent to the world. This commitment reinforces our oneness in Christ.

Secrets of the fantasy world will separate you and your

spouse. You may have one legal marriage, but how many secret "concubines" are living in your spirit? God calls fantasy relationships real and dangerous. You must forcefully rebuke the presence of anyone who tries to find his or her way into your fantasy world.

Rekindling your romance can start with a dream. Begin dreaming again about the one you love, but don't stop there. Take those dreams and share them openly with your spouse.

That was what stirred the passion of Solomon and Shulamith. "On my bed night after night I sought him whom my soul loves" (Song of Sol. 3:1). Their dreams of one another while separated became their experienced realities when together.

Never reveal your physical secrets. Never reveal your failure secrets. Never share your pleasure secrets. But never hide your dreams, your plans or your needs from the one you love.

No Stops

Paul declared to husbands, "Love your wives, just as Christ also loved the church and gave Himself up for her" (Eph. 5:25). To wives he said, "Be subject to your own husbands, as to the Lord" (v. 22). Dying to self and serving your mate in sacrificial communion are your callings in marriage.

God does not offer multiple choice. We cannot pick and choose which days of the week we will be obedient to these scriptures. Nor is our obedience a one-time event.

Though they stumbled, Solomon and Shulamith overcame the temptation to give up on their relationship. Their struggling love found renewed strength as they made the decision to escape busy palace life and get away on regular occasions to the countryside for a romantic retreat (Song of Sol. 8:5–14).

They Felt the Spirit's Touch

Prior to moving to Grand Rapids, we lived in Sacramento, California. Each year our family would head north to visit relatives. The drive from Sacramento, to Seattle was long but traditional. If you travel during the winter months and happen to be blessed with a clear day, you can enjoy some breathtaking visuals.

There is a special moment during the drive when just beyond a certain bend, Mount Shasta—the majestic crown jewel of northern California—suddenly appears. For about five seconds, the mountain is framed perfectly in the car's windshield like a beautiful painting.

One particular year, we caught it perfectly. The sight of a snow-covered mountain against the canvas of a brilliant blue sky filled the windshield. After enjoying the moment, we continued north past the base of the mountain.

After about thirty minutes, I glanced in my rearview mirror to check traffic, and there it was again: Mount Shasta in its entirety was clearly visible. God suddenly spoke to my heart: "How could a mountain that only moments ago filled your windshield now be small enough to fit in your rearview mirror?"

The mountain didn't shrink; my perspective had changed. Again, I perceived a principle I could apply to my marriage. Many marriages are struggling and are barren because one or both of the spouses have chosen to park before the mountains they are facing. But God has called us forward.

Mountains never change their size when you simply stop and stare. God has called your marriage to go forward just as He called Israel to plunge ahead through the Red Sea. It takes forward-thinking, wise choices to crystallize change.

No Substitutes

Paul challenged husbands to "love their own wives as their own bodies," nourishing and cherishing them (Eph. 5:28–29). Of the wife, he required that she "respect her husband" (v. 33). Paul called each mate to direct involvement.

The nurture and growth of a marriage are directly dependent on each spouse, not on outside sources. Solomon and Shulamith provide a stellar model for turning feelings into words. With conviction, they offered no substitute for their own spoken sentiments. The quality of your married life is directly connected to the words you speak.

A husband can begin to rekindle the romance of his marriage solely by restraining his tongue from anger. He is the protector of as well as the provider for his wife. When he becomes her predator through selfish and angry words, something in the heart of the wife dies toward him.

The husband likewise has a need that can be filled only by the words of his wife. She must be his primary source of encouraging words. When two marriage partners make it their primary vow to live with a self-controlled tongue and to dispense freely words of encouragement, then the joy of romance can really begin.

Each year, my children take a moment on my birthday to present me with cards. Like every parent, I quickly thumb them open with heartfelt surprise. There is no substitute for the words that come straight from their hearts to mine. The vocabulary of a dozen roses is limited. A love song written by another can express your love only so well.

If you want to rekindle your romance, start by holding hands with your spouse and declaring that this is the day you both dreamed of your whole life. That day is not tomorrow. It's not when the kids are grown. It's not years in the future. Today is the day you have both worked for your whole lives.

So there you have it. The magic behind the Aquila and Priscilla love story. No stops. No secrets. No substitutes. It's also the magic behind the Scott and Karen love story.

Chapter 18

The Story of Alexander the Coppersmith

Alexander the coppersmith did me much harm;
the Lord will repay him according to his deeds.
Be on guard against him yourself, for
he vigorously opposed our teaching.
—2 Timothy 4:14–15

Sometimes Mom and Dad got pretty lax about us kids watching television during dinner. Our various houses growing up were never big enough to have rooms to eat in and different rooms to watch TV in. You could pretty much do it all from one location.

My favorite television show during dinner was the news. And my favorite news stories were the live updates from a bank robbery in progress. The top of the hour would begin with a live helicopter shot from high above a neighborhood where a bank robber was trying to escape from police on foot.

The camera from the chopper would zoom in and show some guy dressed in black running down a back alley, jumping private fences, darting behind a big bush. He was on the run from the cops. And from the robber's point of view, it was working.

You could see a handful of confused cops going in the opposite direction from where the robber was hiding. The best part was that while the cops were trying to figure out where the robber was, we could eat our macaroni and cheese and follow the robber's every move.

I would scream, "He's hiding behind the fence!" As I said, from the robber's perspective, he was doing a good job of avoiding the cops. One day, however, I wondered about something. And I wondered if the robber who was trying to hide from the cops ever thought this thought, too. What thought was that? Well, I wondered if it ever occurred to him as he was hiding behind the dumpster... *that five million people were watching his every move and knew exactly where he was hiding!*

The fact was, he wasn't hiding from anybody. You can't hide from a helicopter. You can't hide from God very well either. He pretty much has the same view.

I wonder if Moses knew that when he tried to fool God by boxing up his sin and placing it in the basement. Speaking of basements, I hated them as a kid.

Basements were the dark underworld of ghosts, strange noises and big nasty spider webs. Spiders had a way of building their webs to match your height so that they hit you in the face.

Courage told me to turn the knob and take that first gutsy step. Common sense told me to run as fast as I could into the safety of my bedroom, pull the covers over my head and force Mom to make my older brother Doug go down into the basement to do her dirty work.

Spiders and goblins were down there plotting their next attack against the humans upstairs. I knew that, and so did everybody else. Even so, my mom ordered me to go get the box. It seemed like twice a year I was made to descend into the unknown and retrieve a needed item from a box for my mom or dad.

No matter what your parents may tell you today, I knew the reason they sent one of us kids down there. They were too scared of bumping into the big ghost with the black bat sitting on its head.

Our family basement was more dungeon than storage. Even curious kids dared not enter. I found tree houses much more warm and inviting. Once I found the courage to open the door leading to the basement, I would carefully calculate each step for my descent down the creaky uncarpeted stairwell. Halfway down the stairwell, there was one dark corner that needed turning.

Still no light. It was somewhere past that turn that you would have to start waving your hand in front of your face to try and locate the chain, and of course you were hoping not to hit the ghost with the black bat sitting on its head.

I did tell you that bats lived down there, didn't I?

Once you felt the chain, you would pull and pray that the light bulb worked. It barley illuminated through the dust that had built up on the bulb. That created even more terrifying shadows.

The unfinished basement consisted of exposed two-by-fours. Sagging insulation. Boxes. An old rolled-up rug. There were shadows everywhere. Did I tell you bats lived down there?

Basements are the perfect place for junk. Just set it down and get out. Basements get all the stuff not fit for daylight. The dusty throwaways that never get thrown away. Things for the big garage sale that never gets organized. Damp cold corners that never get dry. And mice who never get trapped.

Maybe that's why we like to put our sin in the basement just as Moses did. Or at least we try to put it there. It's the place nobody wants to look. It's the place we take our failures to box them up instead of throwing them away. Those boxes may be out of sight for everyone else, but at least I know where to find them if I need them. Yes, basements are the perfect place for sin.

But basements are also the first place God looks.

He knows how the human heart tries to organize things. That it likes to take something ugly, painful and shameful and put it out of sight, but not out of mind.

Once a year we like to sweep out the basement...then we restack the junk. It makes us feel better about ourselves. Sin without dust.

Moses was convinced his dead Egyptian was safely boxed away in the basement. If he ever needed the bones, he knew where to find them. But Moses was wrong. All of heaven saw what was going on. A terrifying moment of exposure soon followed for Moses. Painful? Yes. Helpful? Time would tell.

Moses found himself driven into the wilderness. Ultimately he would come to a burning bush. But the only reason Moses found the bush was because God loved him enough to expose his sin. For Moses, exposure was the road to greatness.

Living unforgiving means we have to find a place to put our sin. It has to go with us. So we box up our problems, our secrets, our pasts and even our enemies, and we pack that box with us.

The Story of Alexander the Coppersmith

Life would be so much simpler if we would let God have the boxes.

The devil had quite a small group going. Ironically, it was the apostle Paul who helped recruit his members. The first referral was the incestuous son from Corinth. "I have decided to deliver such a one to Satan for the destruction of his flesh, that his spirit may be saved in the day of the Lord Jesus" (1 Cor. 5:5).

Now Hymenaeus and Alexander were joining the group.

> **Among them are Hymenaeus and Alexander, whom I have delivered over to Satan, so that they may be taught not to blaspheme.**
> —1 Timothy 1:20

Paul's feelings about Alexander were stronger than usual. Unlike the sin of the incestuous son, Alexander's actions were in direct conflict with Paul. Alexander the coppersmith had become Alexander the copperhead snake. Paul was frustrated and furious at Alexander, but still spiritual in his approach.

Alexander was in many ways untimely born. We all have encountered those who make our life painfully difficult. The difference for Alexander was that he just happened to rub against the guy who was responsible for writing Scripture. Why did he have to meet Paul? Why did he get the tough love of a tender God?

Sometimes we must be caught before we can be taught.

The exposure of a secret is painful. Alexander made no bones about his disdain for Paul's teaching. What hurt most for Paul, however, was the fact that Alexander was considered at one time to be a brother. Scriptures tell us he "shipwrecked" his faith (1 Tim. 1:19). It was most likely a doctrinal shipwreck, but none the less, it offended Paul deeply that this man would cause him such harm.

Alexander first met Paul in Ephesus. Paul's message was putting a dent in local idol sales. The Greeks were incensed at both Christians and Jews because they were persuading people to turn away from the worship of the goddess Diana. The angry mob enlisted Alexander to represent the cause of the silversmiths who were losing business. Somewhere along the way Alexander softened to the gospel, but then he became harder than ever.

God must have had great thoughts toward this man. To place his correction in the store window as He did with Moses was a clue to the squandered potential going on with man.

God chose to have a garage sale and put all of Alexander's private boxes up for sale in the front yard. It was for redemption that God did this. Alexander was being held accountable for the intensity of his rebellion. The work of God in his life seemed dramatic. His flesh said that this was overkill on Paul's part. But sometimes light needs to be sudden and sharp.

Moses' exposure caught him off guard. He had no idea others had seen his deed. Or that they would be so open with it in public.

As I mentioned in an earlier chapter, when I was a kid I would explore the fields near my house until I found a small boulder. I would imagine that the boulder hadn't been moved in a hundred million years. I would imagine that the boulder had been there since the days of Noah and that I was the first human being to move the stone. I would work my fingertips under the rock, bend my knees and try with all my might to roll the boulder over one revolution. I was usually successful.

The Story of Alexander the Coppersmith

Under every boulder I found the same thing. A damp, life-less circle of dirt. Brilliant green grass or weeds grew tightly around the boulder, but never under the boulder. As soon as the sunlight hit the ground beneath the rock, a hundred bugs would scatter in a hundred directions.

Beneath the rock was a secret place where light wasn't wel-come. There are certain things that can only live in places without light. Things like disgusting bugs and worms. But when light invades their world, they scatter to find more darkness. The presence of light destroys their world. Grace is sometimes about lifting the rock so the blinding love of God can go where the darkness has been allowed to dwell. The light of God wants to scatter the things that are destructive in our lives.

Jesus showed us this with His life. He had a grave, but He didn't have a basement. He lived exposed. As matter of record, the very nature of God was light. When God said, "Let there be light," He certainly meant it. His Son lived in that light. The Incarnation was the ultimate cry for exami-nation. Jesus said:

- "Touch My garments."
- "See My tears."
- "Scrutinize My words."
- "Feel My embrace."
- "Lay upon My breast."
- "Rub My scars."
- "Get in My boat."
- "Walk in My steps."
- "Share My food."
- "Interrogate My motives."
- "Try Me in your courts."
- "Ask Me any question."

✍❤ "Hold Me."

✍❤ "Touch Me."

✍❤ "Hang Me on a tree."

✍❤ "Bury Me."

The Bible tells us nothing of how Alexander responded to his season of correction. We can only hope it was just a season. But if it was anything like the visit of incestuous son from Corinth, you can be sure his time with Satan was short.

God loves surprise parties. Just like the one He threw for the prodigal. He especially loves hiding in the basement after cleaning out the garbage and the secrets. Jesus wants us to step down those creaky stairs in the dark, pull the chain and enjoy the guests wearing party hats yelling, "Surprise!" There's no longer any need to be embarrassed; your basement is spotless.

I'm not kidding. God's grace is exactly like that.

Chapter 19

The Story of Onesimus

*I appeal to you for my child, whom I have begotten
in my imprisonment, Onesimus, who formerly was
useless to you, but now is useful both to you and to me.
And I have sent him back to you in person, that is,
sending my very heart.*
—Philemon 10–12

B y lap seventeen I was looking for a dignified way to
quit. My chest was heaving. It felt as if my lungs were
filled with Elmer's glue instead of oxygen. Both of my legs
were wobbly and burning. My gut was cramped up like a big
army knot.

With each heroic lunge forward of my legs, I told myself
that I was climbing the final peaks of Mount Everest with
frostbite. With each epic thrust of my arms, I imagined
myself to be swimming the Atlantic Ocean alone in heavy
boots.

They Felt the Spirit's Touch

OK, maybe it wasn't quite that dramatic. But it was a one-hour youth group jog-a-thon on a hot summer day in 1977. And it did hurt.

I had never run for this long. Never had to. Never wanted to. But on this day, I was forced to. I determined early on that I would never again push my body to this extreme. If it wasn't for a small band of spectators that included one ex-marine, a handful of moms and my older brother of three years who was running with me, I would have quit somewhere between Mom's Oldsmobile in the parking lot and the weedy cinder track we were using behind the old high school.

Clearly it was my brother, Doug, who inspired me to keep running. The last thing I wanted to do was quit in front of him. No, I wasn't trying to make him proud...I was trying to keep him from making fun of me. Little brothers don't quit in front of big brothers.

No, I would finish or die.

To get through this, I began playing mental games with myself. *Just get to the next turn.* Four turns made one lap. Four laps one mile. Twenty-eight laps made seven miles. Seven miles? That's right, my once-in-a-lifetime adventure was now just seven miles away.

With the amount of signed pledges I had gotten from friends, relatives and strangers, I needed to run twenty-eight laps during the one-hour time limit to reach my goal of $450.00. My parents were providers, not aristocrats. That kind of cash in 1977 wasn't just lying around so twelve-year-olds could fly around the country. Without twenty-eight laps, my dream was dead. I had to get to the next turn.

Like I said, this wasn't the Boston marathon. It was a jog-a-thon fundraiser for my church's eighth-grade basketball team. We qualified as finalists in the Word of Life national basketball tournament in Schroon Lake, New York. That's a long way from Redding, California. And for a boy who had only known U-Hauls, not airplanes, this was a journey worth dying for.

I made it around 112 turns in one hour. That's twenty-eight laps. Seven miles. I did it. So I collected my pledges in good conscience, boarded a plane and toured New York City. We took third place. I still have a small trophy and a huge memory. Those turns around the track back in 1977 actually taught me some valuable lessons about life. Mainly, that left to run on my own, without a pacesetter, without an occasional cheer along the way, I would have quit or lied.

I think the same thing is true for Christians who are running the race of faith.

Even though my degree is not in the social sciences, I have enjoyed watching people. Lots of them. An unofficial American pastime is going to the mall just to watch the people go by. They come in all shapes, sizes and colors.

But more than just watching people go by, I have tried to listen and figure out why some people live to rejoice and some people live to regret. I have unscientifically concluded that successful living is a lot like a successful lap. It comes down to endurance and making it around the tough corners of life. And without the right coaching on the sidelines and the right amount of cheering from the stands, most people, including myself, will lose heart and either quit or crash.

Such was the case for a runaway named Onesimus. Unlike the tidy oval track I ran on, his track was a zigzagging, cross-country maze of hide-and-seek. And to make matters worse, Onesimus had to run while looking back over his shoulder. Battle weary from the constant scheming, he ran with a blistered heart formed by the constant pounding of his own guilt against his own conscience.

Scum on the Run

From all outward appearances, Onesimus was nothing more than scum without a bucket to call home. But God was about to change all of that forever. Like a small jewel at the bottom of the treasure chest, his biography of ashes-turned-beauty is lost among the riches of other more "known" stories in the Bible. Each year thousands of Christians fly past this story…usually around November 3. That's typically the day when the tiny Book of Philemon shows up in their "Through the Bible in a Year" reading program. It may read quickly, but don't let that deceive you. Obeying its message is no easy assignment.

It's the story of…

- The famous embracing the shameful
- The loser being loved by the winner
- The giver confounding the taker
- A hand-off instead of a handout

In other words…it's about the panhandler who one day became the postman.

If anyone deserved a little simplicity in his aging life, it was the apostle Paul. Beaten. Stoned. Shipwrecked. Ridiculed. Abandoned. Whipped. These were his credentials after years of spiritual combat. The last thing Paul needed was a head case, especially one that had nothing to do with getting out from under his house arrest under the order of Caesar. But instead of spending his golden years perfecting his nine iron and trying to avoid the rough, Paul located a diamond in the rough named Onesimus, the slave-thief at the heart of the Philemon story.

The Story of Onesimus

Secure in heaven's Hall of Fame, Paul had nothing more to prove. Purely based on numbers, his apostolic spreadsheet was tops. His bottom line of souls, miracles and churches planted was unmatched. He was a decorated hero of spiritual warfare. Stripe after stripe of suffering was branded across his flesh.

Paul could have sipped tea in Caesar's court at this point without ever damaging his legacy. He didn't need to do this act of kindness. Especially toward a con.

Nevertheless, Paul saw in Onesimus what we usually avoid ten times a day—a difficult assignment from heaven. With nothing to prove other than his love for Jesus and the ministry with which he had been entrusted, he stopped. He acknowledged. He listened. He loved. He cared. He descended. He imparted. He defended. He trusted. He released.

In other words, Paul took time to "begat a son."

The relationship between Paul and Onesimus represents everything we hope for in the kingdom—an older believer investing in the life of someone younger.

In view of his age and imprisonment, Paul knew he would be unable to accomplish much more without the help of another. Jesus Himself had needed another kingdom carrier when He arrested Paul. He wasn't indicting the abilities of Peter and John by enlisting Paul; rather, He was acknowledging the greatness of the task.

God always needs others, no matter how significant an individual might be. And raising up another became the consuming dream and fulfillment for Paul. While in chains, Paul rejected thoughts of ease and spiritual retirement and instead used his energies to turn a useless slave into a life-giving messenger.

For Paul, the focus was now on *endings* not *beginnings*.

Sure, Onesimus had awful beginnings, and his life was only getting worse. Onesimus was floating like a cork amid an aimless ocean—no career, no character, nothing to offer anyone. He was a flop.

But Paul did not base Onesimus' potential on his pedigree. He saw the giftings within. If his offer to help had hinged on a clean background check, he would have thrown Onesimus out on his ear after ten minutes. Rather, Paul could sense the coming spring though Onesimus was still deep in the heart of his winter.

Paul had a passion for people. His weary bones rattled with the hope that every individual life could still find its God-given purpose.

Paul took this new assignment personally. He assumed Onesimus's debts and appealed to Philemon to receive him back as he would his own flesh-and-blood son.

But this did not happen before Onesimus experienced a total transformation. The thief needed spiritual grooming. Paul did not cast out a spirit of immaturity from Onesimus like a demon. Rather, he took the long route of investment, realizing that equipping begins with embracing. That leadership begins with friendship. This involved building into Onesimus a heart pattern of trustworthiness, faithfulness, prayer life and integrity. Then, when Onesimus was spiritually developed, Paul confidently gave him a newly written letter, not only to read, but also to carry. The letter Paul handed Onesimus is the same letter you and I carried into church last Sunday morning. We know it today as the Book of Colossians. The letter that has brought so much grace to millions, Colossians, passed through the hands of a redeemed thief while the ink was still wet.

With the letter to the Colossians under his arm and a

friend named Tychicus by his side, this former thief—who had abandoned his earthly master—now set out to preserve a piece of heaven. But come to think of it, it was only right for the story to end this way. It was in the spiritual genes.

Who else could be the spiritual father of the panhandler turned postman? How about the murderer who became a missionary?

Paul never indicted, ignored, neglected, demeaned, demanded, nor forgot his spiritual son Onesimus. Let's be honest…when most Christians see Onesimus, they see a headache coming their way. But Paul, seeing the future through the eyes of Jesus, saw more than what was coming at him. He saw what would one day be walking away from him. "And I have sent him back to you in person, that is, sending my very heart…" (Philem. 12).

And you thought Hallmark made that one up.

Chapter 20

The Story of Silas

And when they had inflicted many blows upon them,
they threw them into prison, commanding the jailer
to guard them securely; and he, having received such
a command, threw them into the inner prison, and
fastened their feet in the stocks.
—Acts 16:23–24

For many people, there's a silent space between the struggle and the song. The conductor looks their way, tips his baton, but no sound follows. It's that place of silence that God longs to heal. He never designed the song to lag slowly behind the struggle. They were meant to be one moment in time.

For some Christians, their "cue" to worship goes like this. At precisely the same time as he did seven days earlier, the rigid well-dressed gentleman stands up to say, "I invite you to turn with me to page 286. Please stand and join in as we sing the first and third stanzas." The gentleman behind the pulpit then inhales, lifts his right arm, and on the downward thrust everyone joins in and sings.

But let's face it; without someone pointing out the page and without that right arm being lifted, many well-meaning Christians would lose their only starting point for worship.

But God's way of teaching us the true essence of praise is quite different. When it comes to our personal worship, God is after one thing. He wants our *spontaneous* praise, not our practiced praise.

God desires faithfulness, but despises rhetoric. Yes, we need to learn the words and sing with confidence. And yes, the instrumentalists need to rehearse and play with excellence. But the real *clue* for discovering the pathway to pleasing worship is learning how to spot the cues of the conductor.

Spontaneous praise in the face of real life difficulty is *God's way* of teaching us to praise on cue. With our bow to the string…with our lips to the reed…with our eyes fixed on the maestro…suffering becomes the downward stroke of the conductor's baton. Sudden suffering is God's cue that tells the symphony of the redeemed to begin "praising" their measure. In other words, learning God's *cues* for spontaneous praise is what separates mature worship from religious repetition.

There are nineteen verses found in the sixteenth chapter of the Book of Acts that play like the abovementioned symphony. For two badly beaten friends, the space between the pain and the praise was nonexistent. The nineteen verses involved a small cast of people. The two main characters were men. One was named Silas. The other was his friend Paul.

By the way, did what you just read sound funny? The reason it sounds funny is because Silas is always the second half when it comes to himself and Paul. Silas (or Silvanus—

same guy) is mentioned seventeen times in the New Testament. Only twice is he mentioned by himself. Eleven of those times he is mentioned with Paul, and four times in connection with Timothy. In all eleven references with Paul, his name comes second.

Like the center on the football team, Silas put his hands on the ball on every play but never got the recognition for the touchdown. His role was supportive. He was the comrade who never got the credit.

Twice in the New Testament Silas is mentioned alone, once in Acts 15:34. There he felt the need to remain in Antioch to make certain a delicate relationship was strengthened. "But it seemed good to Silas to remain there." He is also mentioned in 1 Peter 5:12: "Through Silvanus, our faithful brother (for so I regard him), I have written to you briefly, exhorting and testifying that this is the true grace of God. Stand firm in it!"

Silas played a profound role in the New Testament. But it's nearly impossible to talk about Silas without mentioning someone else. Silas only piloted planes with two seats in the cockpit. The "faithful brother," as Peter described him, had the ability to push people over the top toward greatness with his mere presence. Listen to what Paul says of Silas's influence on his own life: "But when Silas...came down from Macedonia, Paul began devoting himself completely to the word, solemnly testifying to the Jews that Jesus was the Christ" (Acts 18:5).

So, in honor of the men and women who always seem to come up second in the dialogue, I am placing Silas first in my story.

It's tough for any of us to be one of the invisible strands Solomon talks about in Ecclesiastes 4:12:

And if one can overpower him who is alone, two can resist him. A cord of three stands is not quickly torn apart.

The fact was, Paul was a more celebrated strand than Silas. But instead of jealousy, Silas served out his relational assignments joyfully. Sometimes *standing out* means *standing with*. And sometimes God asks us to submit our individualism to the blur of togetherness.

Never is that commitment to camaraderie more tested then when you're facing your last night on earth. The intent of the magistrates who threw Silas and Paul in a cold, dark jail cell wasn't to send a message by beating them senseless (Acts 16:23). It was to execute Silas and Paul at sunrise. Beating up Christians was a worn-out method for silencing their testimony. Just after the birth of the church, the Pharisees threatened the disciples verbally (Acts 4:21). When that didn't work, they were beaten physically in Acts 5:40. When beating didn't stop them, the religious used their last option.

They began killing them.

Stephen died from stones in Acts 7. James met the blade in Acts 12. Now it was Silas's and Paul's turn to die. But the night of your execution is an odd time to choose a new profession. Their transition from missionary to musician, from incarceration to a sudden performance in concert was head spinning. These two musical upstarts found themselves in the middle of something very few entertainers will ever experience—that incredible thrill of bringing down the house.

But the scene goes from the sincere to the odd. Such as why were death row inmates singing praises instead of the blues? And why are rowdy cons being attentive instead of doing what rowdy cons do? Which is demoralizing people.

The Story of Silas

Especially these two midnight minstrels.

Sheer oddity then turns to complete lunacy as the lone prison warden on duty bends down to kiss the feet of the inmates with "Sir" on his lips. When is the last time you saw that in a prison setting? Faith strengthening? To be honest, it sounds more like a fairy tale than a fact.

Could God really orchestrate a prison rescue and a tent revival in one sweeping adjustment of His footstool? And can someone please go ask the engineer how stone walls stood under the same tension that decimated iron chains? Or shall we just watch the local Philippian seismologist spit and cough his way through an explanation of a fault line running precisely through doorknobs and handcuffs?

In other words, this was unparalleled power with pinpoint accuracy. A natural disaster with selective destruction. And lest we forget about our dynamic dueting duo in the dungeon, though no Simon and Garfunkel when it came to harmony, as least Silas and Paul were committed to the curtain call. They were committed to staying put until the final note of the fourth verse of the hymn was finished. Even if "exit stage left" meant an execution.

By the way, how did Silas and Paul find themselves in jail that night? We've all heard about the two buddies out drinking who end up getting into a fight at the pool hall only to find themselves sobering up in the for the night.

Silas and Paul, however, were jailed for righteous deeds. After winning their first convert from what we now know as modern Europe—Lydia—Silas and Paul openly ministered on the streets of Philippi. While ministering, they picked up a strange follower. It took several days for them to discern where this woman was coming from. Her words sounded right, but her heart was in left field. After several days they could take it no longer, and they turned and cast out of her a spirit of divination.

Instantly the woman was freed, which presented a new problem. She was now unemployed. The ability to seduce people and predict the future was what made her gainfully serviceable to her employer. Who, by the way, was quite ticked that his prized horse had just broken a leg and was now worthless.

The woman's master correctly blamed Silas and Paul and had them dragged before the town cronies. Appealing to the blatant anti-Semitism of the courts, they said, "These men are throwing our city into confusion, being Jews, and are proclaiming customs which it is not lawful for us to accept or to observe, being Romans" (Acts 16:20–21). The backhanded bigotry worked; Silas and Paul were beaten within an inch of their lives. Jewish law limited the beatings to thirty-nine stripes. But a Roman could beat a Jew until his arms got tired.

Bloody and beaten, Silas and Paul were placed in Roman stocks for security. These weren't the kind that you and I have put ourselves or the kids in at the theme park for a quick picture. They were designed to stretch the legs and the arms so the splits in the flesh caused by the flogging would not be able to close. That was the comfortable choir chair from which they would sing.

Maybe now you see why their lovely offertory motivated Planet Earth to give its own version of a standing ovation. In the case of Silas and Paul, the offering also sang the offertory. And the timing of God's Richter-ripping applause tells of His pleasure over both.

When you look at the nineteen verses of Silas and Paul's prison experience, you see the chameleon-like side of God. We called that the "omnipresence" of God in theology class.

The Story of Silas

Look closely; there is God as the choir director providing sheet music to the hearts of two new members. And before you can utter the word *camouflage*, there is God as the prison-busting commando freeing the helpless hostages. In a cloud of miraculous administration, there is God again as the suicide prevention counselor, the evangelism coach and the locksmith.

Yes, look closely, and there He is acting Almighty from every possible angle. Silas and Paul's prison break proves we serve a God who can shake your earth without messing up your hair. He even leaves you with the warmth of a thanksgiving gathering hosted by Deacon Silas and Pastor Paul.

It was God at His best, which is the only thing He can be. He alone is able to massage a planet with a tremor while gently cradling the tenderest of human conditions. God is big enough that the universe fits like a pinhead in His palm, yet small enough to gently rest within the tiny pincushion of your heart.

And the same holds true for you and your need. Do you need a spiritual breakout from the depths of a discouraging dungeon? A physical breakfast to sooth the aching of a homeless hunger? If so, then remember the two persecuted hearts who belted out their song. The sleepy inmates who became insomniacs. The earthquake that rang like a timely phone call. The iron chains that melted like ice cream. And last but not forgotten, the two missionaries who got a good hot breakfast after a long cold night in the studio recording the first live worship experience in the New Testament.

Don't let your soul forget that He alone is Almighty God. Better yet, sing. He's waiting to applaud. And sing loud enough so the other prisoners can hear. Whether it's an escape from your storm or an omelet for your stomach, your only answer is Jesus. So clutch your hymnal. Lift up your song. There is hope. Earthquakes and breakfast are being served.

Both Silas and Paul knew we are all cowards without a comrade. But even if you truly find yourself alone, you are still not alone. There are no solos with God. Sometimes God's presence is your only partner. And when there are two of you in the fire, like Silas and Paul, remember, God's presence makes it three. When there are three of you, God's presence makes it four. Factor in the guardian angels and suddenly you have a crowd.

By the way, when you get to heaven, just for the fun of it, go find Silas before you find Paul.

Study Guide

Written and Prepared by
Brenda Haggard

Chapter 1

The Story of Apollos

Grasp the Picture

Blessed with an eloquent tongue, Apollos was a man of strength and stature. Mantled with movie-star qualities and saddled from birth with intuition and insight, his word-gifts were irresistible to the ear. When you heard him, you believed him. Apollos, like all gifted communicators, was naturally persuasive. Even the educated Pharisees coveted his abilities.

> The author says that Apollos had the "goods of greatness." What really made Apollos "good"?

> Who helped Apollos reach his God-given potential?

> Do you know any modern-day Priscillas and Aquilas? Do you have any in your life?

Toward the end of his sermon Apollos finally began speaking in New Testament terms. But Priscilla and Aquila were surprised at the emphasis he placed on John the Baptist. Hopefully Jesus was right around the corner. But something happened. Or actually, *didn't* happen. Apollos finished his message without mentioning the redemptive gift of Jesus that comes through repentance.

    How did Priscilla and Aquila respond to Apollos' sermon? Was their response critical or caring? How do you respond to the shortcomings of others?

    What did they realize about Apollos' future ministry? Were they motivated by competition or by compassion? Are you willing to share insights with others in order to advance them in the kingdom?

    Where did they choose to address Apollos—in public or in private? Do you think their words were crushing or caressing? How would you handle the correction of a brother or a sister in Christ?

But why on earth would Priscilla and Aquila recommend Apollos for anything? He couldn't even preach a basic sermon on grace. According to their criteria, hadn't he fallen short? That may have been the case at one time, but now they were ready with letters of approval. Apollos had won their admiration in one sermon; now he owned their respect.

✒ Why did Apollos own the respect of Priscilla and Aquila?

✒ From what did humility rescue Apollos?

✒ Why were Priscilla and Aquila willing "to sow into the advancement of Apollos' dream"?

Embrace the Truth

Read Galatians 5:22–25.

✒ How does Paul define the "fruit of the Spirit" (Christian character)?

✒ Define the counterfeit ("wax fruit") of each of these qualities.

Read 1 Peter 5:5–6.

✒ What garment are we to put on, and why?

✒ When we humble ourselves, how does God respond?

They Felt the Spirit's Touch

❧ When we choose to exalt ourselves, how does God respond?

❧ In a practical sense, how can you cultivate humility in your life?

Chapter 2

The Story of the Ethiopian Eunuch

Grasp the Picture

I hate to tell you this, but you also have a leak. Your soul is losing air. Sin has created tiny punctures in your spiritual inner tube. Some of those holes are visible to the naked eye. Most are not.

> ✐ What does the author say must be done in order to find the leaks in our "spiritual inner tube"?

> ✐ What "atmosphere" most quickly reveals our sin?

Philip had his own set of questions. One of the seven original deacons, he was asked without warning to head south and take the desert road from Jerusalem to Gaza. The angel gave him no future instructions. There was no "mission impossible tape" waiting for him to tell him what his next step would be. It was basically, "Start walking, pal." Philip must have thought about ancient Israel. They too stepped into a desert, but it was forty years before they found their way out.

> ✐ For what does Philip deserve credit? What Old

Testament character does he resemble? How about you? Do you require the details before you hit the road?

☞ What sometimes precedes the understanding of our purpose? What then does obedience require?

Something the eunuch heard in Jerusalem deeply affected him, but he couldn't find clarity. So God created a divine encounter—but one that was still dependent upon obedience to the odd. Imagine the devastating consequence if Philip had introduced logic into the story. *Lord, I was just elected as a deacon two chapters ago. Stephen is already dead, so we are now down to six deacons. I don't have time for ridiculous trips to nowhere.*

☞ How is the long-range strategic planning of God sometimes disguised? Does God use the same strategy for every individual? Why not?

☞ What elements constituted the atmosphere of doubt in which the eunuch was living? What elements created the atmosphere of faith?

Embrace the Truth

Read 1 Corinthians 1:26–31.

    ✐ Is God looking for great ability, intellect and influence in those He chooses? What is He looking for?

    ✐ Why has He chosen to this method?

    ✐ When God asks you to do something, do you respond as Moses did in Exodus 4:13 or as Mary did in Luke 1:38?

Read Acts 16:6–10.

    ✐ How many times did God put a roadblock in the path of Paul and his team?

    ✐ Where did the Lord want Paul to go? What if Paul had not been flexible in his plans?

    ✐ What, then, should our attitude be when we encounter roadblocks?

Chapter 3

The Story of Ananias

Grasp the Picture

John saw a photo. Ananias heard a voice speak his name. Both had the same result. The real identity from within surfaced. A decision had to be made. And like John, Ananias had the option of running from the ugliness. Or he could allow God to dramatically change him forever.

   ✍ According to the author, what was Ananias' first response to God's instruction?

   ✍ How did God respond to Ananias' hesitation?

Like the alcoholic, Ananias came face to face with his past and its powerful control over his future. And, like John, others would pay dearly unless something changed inside of Ananias.

   ✍ What were the two biggest obstacles Ananias had to overcome in order to obey God's instruction?

   ✍ What obstacles keep you from obeying God?

Study Guide

✍ Besides yourself, who might be affected by your *unwillingness* to change? By your *willingness*?

Instead, the Lord told Ananias to go find Saul and pray for him. The Lord was saying to Ananias, "Don't hesitate, I've disabled him. There is greatness in Saul's heart. He too will be a great risk taker. But I have called you to take the first risk. Quickly, Ananias, go find him and reveal yourself."

✍ What guarantee of safety did Ananias have in approaching Saul of Tarsus, his greatest enemy as a Christian?

✍ What truth did God want Ananias to discover?

✍ Are you willing to risk "touching the untouchable" in order for them to be saved? What would this mean for you personally?

One of the more difficult tests of faith is not only to love our enemies, but also to believe God loves them, too. And that He has a plan for them. A plan that could be bigger than His plan for us. Even more faith stretching is when He asks us to risk our lives so our current enemies can prosper in His kingdom.

✐ What did Ananias allow God to do in his own heart? What did he allow God to give him?

✐ What was the result of Ananias' obedience?

✐ What could be the result of your obedience—yielding to God's desire for your life personally and for others?

Embrace the Truth

Read Galatians 6:3–5.

✐ What does verse 4 instruct us to do?

✐ What is the result?

✐ What results from not following these instructions?

Read Deuteronomy 31:6–8.

✐ To whom was Moses speaking in verse 6?

Study Guide

✍ To whom was he speaking in verse 8?

✍ Why was it important for God to make this promise personal?

Chapter 4

The Story of Sosthenes

Grasp the Picture

Gallio quickly decided this wasn't worth his time. It was frivolous and petty. He had no interest in meddling in the affairs of these Jewish law squabblers. He dismissed the court and drove everyone from the judgment seat area. Court closed.

> ✒ According to the author, what was the result of Gallio's indifference?

> ✒ Why do you think the people turned their rage on Sosthenes?

In other words, sometimes the devil takes a swing at God and ends up hitting the church in the nose. And sometimes being in the right place with God can feel like being in all the wrong places with people. And sometimes people who think their problems are with other people are really just mad at God. But since they can't figure out where God is or how to tell Him off, you and I become the next best thing.

> ✒ What did the apostle Peter say about suffering? What is its purpose?

Study Guide

✍ How do we keep our "outside smile" bright?

✍ Have you ever experienced the consequences of being "guilty by association"? How did you respond?

Sometimes when you really love something, it might require you to move from the safety of standing by to the danger of standing up. But believing in something can also require something else. Sometimes it requires you to stand alone and take it on the chin.

✍ Are you willing to stand up for your convictions, for your dreams?

✍ Are you willing to bear the consequences of those convictions, even when no one else is standing with you?

✍ Are you willing to stand with someone else so that they do not have to stand alone?

Embrace the Truth

Read 1 Peter 4:12–19.

They Felt the Spirit's Touch

✍ Why does Peter tell us to rejoice in the midst of suffering (v. 13)?

✍ If we are insulted because of the name of Christ, why are we blessed?

✍ What should our response be in the face of suffering for being a Christian?

✍ According to verse 19, those who suffer "according to God's will" should respond in what two ways?

Read James 1:2–12.

✍ Why should we be joyful in the face of trials?

✍ What blessing will we miss if we don't allow perseverance to finish its work?

✍ Have you ever "short-circuited" a test of your faith by finding your own solution to the problem? What was the result?

Chapter 5

The Story of Barsabbas

Grasp the Picture

The criteria for being a replacement apostle were clear. Applicants needed to have been among the disciples from the time of Jesus' baptism in the Jordan until His recent ascension in Jerusalem. That narrowed the list. But several were still qualified. The disciples looked around the room. The Eleven quickly caucused. Two stood out. Some among the Eleven thought it was Matthias. Others thought Barsabbas was the choice.

🖉 How did the disciples decide whom to choose as a replacement for Judas?

🖉 What minimum criteria were established by the disciples for candidates?

🖉 What criterion was God looking for?

Romans 8:28 tells us, "God causes all things to work together for good to those who love God, to those who are called

183

according to His purpose." Imagine with me for a moment that you are looking at a beautiful painting of an outdoor landscape. It's filled with hills, a thick forest and a gentle stream. The artist has painstakingly painted the stones and rocks that line the stream.

> ✍ Is it difficult to believe that God deliberately includes the stones and rocks in your life? Why do you think He does this?

> ✍ What do the "four stones" represent in your life?

> ✍ What have you done with those stones? Have you tried to hide them as you paint your life picture? Have you built a museum to display them and visit them regularly? Or have you laid them at the foot of the cross and let Jesus do with them as He sees fit?

As Jesus paints the canvas with beauty, substance and purpose, a great miracle begins to unfold. In His mercy, Jesus chooses to integrate the original stones from our past into the current and future picture of our lives. Sometimes it takes time for the work of the Artist to make sense. You wonder why He forgives the sin but leaves the stones.

> ✍ Why does God choose to leave the stones instead of removing them? What would happen if He removed them completely?

✍ If God is going to use those things in your life, what do you have to do with them? What is the key to God's using "all things" for your good?

✍ As you look back over your life, have you handed God the stones of disappointment, failure and rejection? How has God used them to bring beauty from their ashes?

Embrace the Truth

Read Acts 1:15–26.

✍ How did the disciples approach the decision that needed to be made to fill the vacancy left by Judas? What had they been doing immediately prior to discussing the need for a replacement? Did this make the decision easier?

✍ How do you think this approach affected the group down the road when difficulties and disagreements arose?

✍ How do you approach difficult decisions in your life? How do you discover God's will?

They Felt the Spirit's Touch

Read 2 Peter 1:5–11.

   ✍ What is the "reason" Peter gives for following these instructions (vv. 3–4)?

   ✍ What eight virtues does Peter list as the building blocks of Christian effectiveness?

   ✍ According to verses 10–11, what is the result of incorporating these virtues into your life?

Chapter 6

The Story of John Mark

Grasp the Picture

John the Beloved was a connoisseur of contact. Closeness was his currency. During the Last Supper, he calmly laid his head upon the breast of Jesus and conversed without fear. Everyone wanted that seat next to Jesus in heaven. Only John seemed to want it this side of the cross. Eleven others around the table that evening, including Judas, had quiet flashes of jealousy as they watched the loving interaction between Jesus and John.

> On what was John's security based? On what was it not based?

> What gave John the courage and capacity to love Christ freely?

> Do you have John's unshakable sense of security?

Directing a simple question at Jesus had become an impossibility for Peter. John was the only conduit he had left. While John the Beloved was basking in God's acceptance,

They Felt the Spirit's Touch

Peter flung more of his flimsy and unkept promises at Jesus, true signals of the uncertainty that ran abundant in his soul. For the moment, Peter thought his only way of gaining God's approval was by proving he was a death-defying superman. But his ridiculous pledges impressed no one.

    ℘ What triggered Peter's uncertainty? What misconception did he have?

    ℘ What was the result of Peter's uncertainty?

    ℘ Have you ever misinterpreted God's correction as rejection?

Barnabas took his emotionally beaten nephew and said, "You can ride me piggyback for a season." That loving gesture speaks volumes about God's view of us when we disappoint Him. As long as there is breath in us, restoration remains His priority. A bad first experience in ministry is like deadly toxin. Only the surgery of loving relationship can remove it. But the real test for John Mark still lay ahead.

    ℘ What is God's priority when we have disappointed Him?

    ℘ What was the "real test" for John Mark?

✍ Have you allowed God to heal your past hurts and restore broken relationships?

Embrace the Truth

Read John 15:1–5.

✍ What happens to branches that do not bear fruit?

✍ What happens to branches that do bear fruit? Why?

✍ Have you ever gone through a "pruning" season? What was the result?

Read Hosea 14:1–9.

✍ What was Israel's downfall? How were they instructed to return to the Lord?

✍ How would the Lord respond to their repentant attitude (v. 4)?

They Felt the Spirit's Touch

✍ Have you returned to the Lord with a heart of repentance? How did God respond to you? If you have not, what are your reasons?

Chapter 7

The Story of the Grumblers

Grasp the Picture

There are two kinds of people in this world—those who tell and those who don't. Ham's two brothers, Shem and Japheth, had a much different reaction. They saw it as their responsibility to cover the failure, not expose it further with their words. "But Shem and Japheth took a garment and laid it upon both their shoulders and walked backward and covered the nakedness of their father; and their faces were turned away, so that they did not see their father's nakedness" (v. 23). Who do you think was guiltier on that day? The intoxicated father or the loud-mouthed informant?

> ✒ Answer the author's question regarding the sons of Noah. Why do you feel this way?

> ✒ What is your tendency when someone fails—to expose it or to cover it? How does God's Word say we should respond? (See 1 Peter 4:8.)

Instead, all they got was a letter with a long list of issues. At least it was signed. But instead of becoming defensive...instead of rationalizing the complaint away…instead of listing the faults of the accusers, the disciples remained humble and prayerful. They emerged with clear priorities and set their course.

> ✍ What was the disciples' response to the complaint of the Hellenistic Jews? How do you respond to complaints and criticism?

> ✍ How are grumblers good for us?

I'm reminded of Paul's encounter with a grumbler. He had just returned from his third missionary journey and was met at the door by a grumbler. "You see, brother, how many thousands there are among the Jews of those who have believed, and they are all zealous for the Law; and they have been told about you, that you are teaching all the Jews who are among the Gentiles to forsake Moses, telling them not to circumcise their children nor to walk according to the customs" (Acts 21:20–21).

> ✍ Was this grumbler's complaint legitimate? What did he ask Paul to do?

> ✍ How did Paul respond? What did he understand about God and grumblers?

✍ What does the author recommend we do when we encounter negativity—either in our own heart or in others towards us? Of what should we remind ourselves, and for what should we wait?

Embrace the Truth

Read James 3:13–18.

✍ How does James instruct us to demonstrate wisdom?

✍ With what does he contrast meekness? Where does he say this kind of "wisdom" comes from? What always accompanies these two attitudes?

✍ In contrast, what seven characteristics of heavenly wisdom does James list? What results from developing these characteristics in your life?

Read Romans 12:1–8.

✍ What attitudes need to be transformed in your heart and mind? How is your mind renewed?

How does viewing ourselves with meekness change our perspective toward others?

How does an accurate perspective of others allow us to find creative solutions to problems and difficulties that arise between us and those around us?

Chapter 8

The Story of the Judaizers

Grasp the Picture

Grace makes us comfortable enough to run to Him for mercy, comfortable enough to worship Him as our Father. But in that security, we must be cautious not to be disorderly or haphazard with the blood of His Son. Precious...necessary...sufficient...final...cleansing...and conquering—that is the blood of Jesus. But it must be applied exactly as God requires.

> ✒ What does the author indicate is the purpose of grace?

> ✒ How is grace (represented by the blood of Jesus) accurately applied in our life?

The blood of Jesus is about works—the finished work of Christ. Some have tried to take the work of the Carpenter and call it shoddy. Or they open the gift that the Carpenter has fashioned for them and ask for the receipt so they can take it back and return it for something else. Who would do such a thing? Well, actually, some folks tried to do just that.

They Felt the Spirit's Touch

They were called the Judaizers.

> ✍ According to the author, what was the intent of the Judaizers? Why did they feel this way?

> ✍ Who fell into their trap? What impact did this have?

The Judaizers had not only influenced Peter to abandon the ship of grace, but also the affects of his decision were felt by the entire church. Barnabas, the standard of restoration and sensitivity, was the first to be pulled under by Peter. After Barnabas, the whole church followed. Everything Jesus stood and died for was being destroyed.

> ✍ How did Paul respond to the Judaizers and those who were being influenced by them? Why did he respond this way?

> ✍ What five essentials of the faith did Paul beg Peter to remember?

> ✍ Do you sometimes need to be reminded of these essentials, as Peter was?

Legalism is an ugly amnesia.

   ✐ According to the author, what three key princi-
      ples did Peter forget because of legalism?

   ✐ What does the author describe as the "checkered
      flag of Christian maturity"? Are you actively
      serving those around you?

   ✐ What had Jesus told the disciples to do at His
      ascension? What destiny did He indicate? Are
      you accurately following the instruction Christ
      has given you, regardless of the cost or what
      people may think of you?

Embrace the Truth

Read 1 John 1:16–20.

   ✐ Who was the supreme example of sincere love?

   ✐ What practical test of sincerity does John
      describe in verses 17–18?

   ✐ What does sincere love for others allow us to
      know? What does it allow us to do?

They Felt the Spirit's Touch

Read Acts 15:1–34.

    ✍ What was the core doctrine of the Judaizers? How did this fly in the face of Christ's death and resurrection? (See Galatians 2:20–21.)

    ✍ How did the church leaders respond to the confusion caused by the Judaizers? What did they do as a result?

    ✍ What was the outcome of the discussions held at the Jerusalem Council?

Chapter 9

The Story of the Loud Woman

Grasp the Picture

Flattery is an ever-changing arsenal, but the disabling consequences are always the same. And like Joshua, all of us have a hard time recognizing it. It can seduce you with the appearance of a chocolate truffle, and then strike like cyanide when you bite. Flattery is hell's perfume. It's the only compliment the devil knows how to give.

> ✒ What were the "baby steps" of godly character that Joshua had learned? What did he substitute?

> ✒ What should we never allow our life to be manipulated by others? Why?

> ✒ How is flattery different than a genuine compliment?

Much as the beggar at the Beautiful Gate intercepted Peter and John, she intercepted Paul and his companions on their way to prayer. Using her mouth for muscle, she assaulted

Paul and his associates from behind. Out of nowhere, Paul heard someone behind him creating a major fuss in the town square. Now, noise was nothing new to Paul; loud seemed to be his lifestyle as well.

    ✍ How did the loud woman appear at first? What was wrong with what she was doing?

    ✍ How does the author define flattery? What is it designed to do?

This had an eerie similarity to the experience of his counterpart Joshua. As I mentioned earlier, Paul's most recent history was pretty victorious, but the painful defeats from missionary journey number one were still fresh on his mind. Paul's failure with John Mark. The collapse of his relationship with Barnabas. Those kinds of breakdowns don't filter their way through the system easily. So when Paul heard this outburst of praise, even from a stranger, he no doubt faced the temptation to enjoy it.

    ✍ In the face of the woman's praise, what was the temptation? What was the motivation?

    ✍ If Paul had listened and succumbed to her flattery, what could have resulted?

Study Guide

Embrace the Truth

Read 1 Peter 2:4–10.

    🖉 To what does Peter liken us as believers? What is God doing with us? On what are we being built?

    🖉 What promise is given to those who trust the Cornerstone? What happens to those who reject Him?

    🖉 Who has chosen us, and to whom do we belong? How does this knowledge make us secure in our faith?

Read Hebrews 5:12–6:2.

    🖉 What is the source of spiritual nourishment?

    🖉 "Solid food" is for whom? What does the use of solid food do for those who consistently feed on it?

    🖉 What does the writer indicate are the "elementary teachings" about Christ? Why does he want the letter's recipients to move past these things?

Chapter 10

The Story of the Beggar

Grasp the Picture

Peter and John woke up that day and went looking for two things—God's presence and human pain. And not necessarily in that order. They were prayerful and ready for both. Ready to grip the next heart in need of repentance. Ready to grip the next hand in need of healing. The proof was in their eyes.

> ✍ What was it that caused Peter and John to look for something beyond the usual in their daily trip to the temple for prayer?

> ✍ How do you approach your everyday routines—automatic pilot or absolute purpose?

The lame man outside the temple had been a fixture for years, a familiar piece of social wreckage. But along come two men who were more *need* centered than *temple* centered. Two men who were living with the wide-angle lens of compassion instead of the usual telephoto heart of selfishness. Two men who were full of everything Jesus wanted for His disciples. Power. Love. Authority. Courage. Faith.

✍ Peter and John had to have seen this lame man before. Perhaps they had even given him money in the past. What made this day different?

✍ How did Jesus respond to the disciples' faith and courage on this day? Do you think Jesus would respond in the same way today to your faith and courage?

Leaping seems to be one of the great by-products of Jesus' touch. As a matter of fact, few seem to remember that a "leap" was the first physical response recorded in the Bible caused directly by Jesus. Really? Consider this.

✍ What example does the author use to demonstrate the response elicited by Jesus' touch?

✍ How did this response affect Elizabeth?

Embrace the Truth

Read Romans 8:28–31.

✍ What is God's ultimate, predetermined purpose for those who are His children?

✍ According to this passage, how has God enabled His children to achieve that predetermined purpose?

✍ It is said that if you don't know where you're going, any road will get you there. Given the declaration of purpose found in Romans 8:29, would you need to make any route adjustments in your life to arrive at that God-ordained destination?

Read Psalm 16:5–11.

✍ According to the psalmist, what is the source of joy?

✍ What three benefits does the psalmist list as a result of the Lord's presence in his life (v. 9)?

✍ What has been made known to the psalmist by being in the Lord's presence (v. 11)?

Chapter 11

The Story of Stephen

Grasp the Picture

God is the good potter. I am the not-so-good clay. My job is to spin and stay put in the center of the wheel. The potter's job is to dream and to design. Sometimes I don't appreciate how fast the potter spins me or how tightly He squeezes to change my shape. I forget that the good potter uses two hands and that He sometimes needs an external instrument to carve me and give me beauty. The hope of the potter is simple. He wants to transfer His heart and mind through His hands.

    ✒ What two things are essential to change the shape of the clay?

    ✒ What one thing is required to make the shape permanent?

It's easy to look and sound like Jesus during an afternoon Palm Sunday victory parade…or on a hillside with spiritually hungry people…or at an old-fashioned riverbank baptismal gathering.

🖋 In what impossible situation did Jesus ask Stephen to reflect Him to the world?

🖋 Why was Stephen singled out by the religious leaders for attack? Do you think they started out with the intention to murder Stephen? What drove them to kill him so violently?

Stephen died playing copycat. Listen to his final words on earth. You might recognize them. "'Lord, do not hold this sin against them!' And having said this, he fell asleep" (Acts 7:60). I too want to die acting like Jesus. I want to pass through this life with a memory verse on my lips. Personally I am thrilled that Jesus said, "Repeat after me."

🖋 What memory verse was on Stephen's lips as he fell asleep in Jesus' arms?

🖋 What words do you want to pass over your lips as you take your last breath? What do you want to see as you leave this world and enter heaven's gates?

Study Guide

Embrace the Truth

Read Jeremiah 18:1–6.

> ✍ What message did the Lord give to Jeremiah at the potter's house? Does this message apply to us today?

> ✍ Why does the Master Potter want to reshape us? Why do we need reshaping?

> ✍ With what does God seal His work in us? (See 1 Peter 4:12.)

Read Matthew 5:10–16.

> ✍ What does Jesus promise to those who are persecuted?

> ✍ How does He say we should we respond when this happens to us?

> ✍ Why do you think Jesus immediately goes on to talk about how we are salt and light? What happens to salt that loses its flavor? Where should we place our light? Why?

Chapter 12

The Story of Ananias and Sapphira

Grasp the Picture

What kind of statement was God making that day at church when both Ananias and Sapphira suddenly dropped dead after giving less than planned? Was the Law back in vogue? Would fearful giving now replace cheerful giving?

   ✐ To what four lessons does the author point when considering this account?

   ✐ Why do you think God responded in such a harsh way to the deception by Ananias and Sapphira? Had Ananias or Sapphira admitted the truth of what they had done, would God have "stayed their execution"?

Ananias and Sapphira were established believers. This shows the deceptive grip of greed. They were part of the church who "were of one heart and soul; and not one of them claimed that anything belonging to him was his own; but all things were common property to them" (Acts 4:32). They had signed on as part of this new community. But privately, their thoughts drifted toward greed.

> ✎ What dangerous human trait does the author point out? To what commitments does this apply?

> ✎ What is our destiny apart from the power of God?

> ✎ What does the author indicate wounded God the most in this situation? What does Ecclesiastes 5:4–7 say about the vows you make?

Something that was made clear to their hearts was somehow renegotiated without including God in the negotiations. The Lord was teaching the early church that obedience to the voice of Holy Spirit was equal to the obedience Jesus demanded when He walked on the earth.

> ✎ Is obedience to the Holy Spirit important in the life of the believer today? Why?

> ✎ What was the immediate reaction of the church and those who heard what happened to Ananias and Sapphira? What should our response be?

❧ What was God *not* trying to do through this incident? What was He attempting to do?

Embrace the Truth

Read Ephesians 4:25.

❧ Why does God place such a high premium on truthfulness?

❧ Is any untruth acceptable in God's eyes?

❧ What happens when we fail in this area in our relationships? In our work? In our ministry? Can we restore what has been destroyed?

Read 2 Corinthians 9:6–15.

❧ How does God want us to give? How does He not want us to give?

❧ What has God promised to do in response to your giving? Why has He promised to do this? What will be the result?

Study Guide

❧ How will those who benefit from your generosity respond to God? How will they respond to you?

Chapter 13

The Story of Cornelius

Grasp the Picture

Two seeds—two worlds apart. Yet there was something very common about both seeds. No matter where each seed was planted, it still took nine months for it to reach fullness. The power of money, learning, geography and climate meant nothing to the gestation of the soul seed. And actually, the same law holds true for all seeds.

> ✍ By using agriculture as the chief allegory for the kingdom of God, what did Jesus show us about our journey?

> ✍ According to the author, what is tempting for us in this world of "spiritual speed"? In contrast, what does God use to mature us? On what qualities is this strategy based?

Jesus' commitment to redemption and kingdom through relationship is staggering. To watch the administrator of the universe carve out time for twelve individuals is astonishing. It was that "withing" commitment that changed the world. I don't know about you, but I have a checkbook and a few kids to monitor, not a universe to run, and I still struggle for meaningful relationships.

    ✍ What qualities did Jesus intend to be included in our earthly relationships?

    ✍ What kinds of relationships did He establish using those principles?

For the first ten years of the early church, the Jews and the Gentiles tolerated each other. The problem was, the kingdom of God was based on *celebrating* people, not *tolerating* them. The Holy Spirit looked for an opening in the temple, the synagogue, but found none. So it was time to get creative.

    ✍ What was the dilemma faced by mankind? What was God's plan to resolve this dilemma?

    ✍ Who were the two men God chose to implement His plan to break down the barriers in His church?

    ✍ How did God set His plan in motion? (Read Acts 10:1–20.)

Embrace the Truth

Read Philippians 2:1–4.

   ✍ What did Paul say would make his joy complete? How did he appeal to the Philippian Christians?

   ✍ Do you think the church of today has practiced this scripture in its entirety—not just in letter but in spirit? Has the church successfully turned culture from a barrier to a blessing?

   ✍What are you doing personally to set an example for other believers in this area of acceptance? What could you do?

Read Philippians 3:7–14.

   ✍ What does Paul indicate is the over-arching goal of his life? What does he want to know? Why?

   ✍ Had the apostle attained this goal at the time of his writing this letter? Why does he press on?

Study Guide

🖋 Does attaining the prize require a sprint or a marathon? What does Paul say is the key to winning the prize? What is the prize?

Chapter 14

The Story of Eutychus

Grasp the Picture

The sight of a young life being jarred to death by a three-story fall is no laughing matter. We joke now because we know the end of the story. But when Paul fell upon the young corpse in the courtyard and pleaded for the return of his life, it didn't matter that he was a trophy apostle or that he had raised unprecedented funds for famine relief. Every consuming emotion sought to find a spiritual explanation for the lad's death. For Paul, people took precedence over preaching. Once he noticed an empty windowsill, it was time to let someone else finish the sentence.

> *✐* What was Paul's priority when he saw Eutychus fall—the sermon or the soul?

> *✐* What is your priority when you serve in the church—getting the job done or being the heart, hands and feet of Jesus for someone's need?

More and more, we hear of God's unorthodox arrivals when He seems to add shock value to His sovereign entrance. A nice, clean setup that fits the service schedule is not always God's order of the day. There are moments when God says, "Here I come in a moment of My design." Messy and unorthodox.

   ✍ What should our response be when God uses "messy and unorthodox" methods to grab our attention?

   ✍ What should be the result of seeing an awe-inspiring display of God's power?

      ✍ Question it? (See Luke 5:17–25.)

      ✍ Enshrine it? (See Matthew 17:1–6.)

      ✍ Proclaim it? (See Luke 7:11–17.)

Embrace the Truth

Read Psalm 19:1–6.

   ✍ When you look at the created world around you, does your spirit yawn, or are you awed by the power and wisdom of the Creator?

They Felt the Spirit's Touch

✍ Plan a day away from life's "to dos" some place where you can bask in the beauty of God's creation.

✍ Start with a sunrise breakfast with your family—get outside and watch the sun come up together. Give thanks for the new day (Ps. 92:1–2) and for God's fresh mercy (Lam. 3:22–24).

✍ At sunset, take a walk with your spouse, stopping to watch the sun sink below the horizon. Apologize if you need to (Eph. 4:26), and then offer a prayer of thanks for each other and for all the blessings in your life.

✍ After dinner, lie down on the grass with your children and star gaze—see how many stars you can count, and then share with them that God counts the stars and knows them all by name (Ps. 137:4). Remind them that they are far more precious to Him—and to you—than all the stars in the universe combined.

Study Guide

Read Psalm 145:1–21.

   ❧ In this psalm, what does the psalmist say he will do in response to God's greatness?

   ❧What does he admonish each generation to do (v. 4)? What does he say "they" will do? Why (v. 12)?

   ❧ How does the psalmist describe the Lord's character? What does the psalmist say the Lord will do?

Chapter 15

The Story of Aeneas

Grasp the Picture

The Bible doesn't say a thing about what paralyzed Aeneas, only that he was paralyzed. The Greek medical term was *paraluo*. It means "to be dissolved, relaxed, loosened and enfeebled." In other words, his basic muscle functions were worthless. But through a tiny clue, we get a deeper picture into his condition. When Peter said to Aeneas, "Arise, and make your bed," it was more than a desire on Peter's part to change the sheets.

✍ According to the author, what did the "making of the bed" represent?

✍ Why do you suppose the Bible says nothing about what paralyzed Aeneas? Could it be that the cause of Aeneas' condition was less important than his response to it?

✍ What about you? Is placing blame for yesterday's hurts more important than pressing through for tomorrow's victory?

The Bible doesn't tell us why Peter came by for a visit, only that he came. I'm still glad that Jesus comes by to visit. I hope you are, too. He's always on time. He only looks late. As a matter of fact, Jesus loves coming "Lazarus late" and turning hopelessness and its best friend, uselessness, on their ears. But many miss Jesus' visit because He wears the face of His church when He shows up.

> ✍ When Jesus makes a house call, what does He bring with Him? What does He ask us to do with His gift?

> ✍ Why do you suppose the Bible doesn't tell us why Peter came by for a visit? Could it be that supernatural visitations happen in the midst of ordinary acts of faithfulness?

Embrace the Truth

Read Hebrews 6:17–20.

> ✍ In this passage, what does the writer of Hebrews describe as "an anchor for the soul"?

> ✍ What does an anchor do?

> ✍ Have you taken hold of the hope that has been

offered to you? Or have you found yourself
tossed on the seas of circumstance—disillusioned,
discouraged and defeated?

Read Hebrews 11:1–6.

> ✍ How does the writer of Hebrews define faith in
> the opening verse of the "Great Hall of Faith"
> chapter?

> ✍ Why is faith foundational to serving God (v. 6)?

> ✍ How did God respond to the faith of the
> ancients?

Chapter 16

The Story of the Incestuous Son

Grasp the Picture

First of all, I find it remarkably freeing that the Lord placed this story in the Bible. Paul could just as easily have left this paragraph out of his letter. Not every problem or issue that arose in the church was mentioned. So why this one?

✍ How does the author describe the sin of this young man? What vanished from his mind?

✍ What is said about the woman involved in this account? What did this absence of information indicate?

✍ How would this situation have been handled in an Old Testament setting? What principle prevailed in the circumstance?

They Felt the Spirit's Touch

❧ Do you find it to be freeing to know that grace
  can flow in even the worst of sinful situations?

Because the first half of this story is so difficult to tell, most
Christians are never told the rest of the story. Or if they do
stumble across the second half of the story, they fail to connect the dots.

❧ Where does Paul first start to relate this incident?
  Where does he finally address it? How much
  time separated the beginning from the end of the
  matter?

❧ What was the punishment Paul prescribed for the
  young man's sin? What was Paul seeking to
  accomplish through this punishment?

❧ When the time of "detention" was concluded,
  what did Paul ask the Corinthian believers to do?
  Why?

But the only key that could unlock the door was hanging on
a hook somewhere on the inside of the house; it wasn't in
the pocket of the man at the front door. Most churches tend
to lock their door from the inside. So it doesn't matter who
tries what key from the outside; in order to get in, someone
has to let them in.

✍ What does a person need once he or she is forgiven?

✍ According to the author, of what is the church often guilty in regard to "front page sinners"?

✍ Is your church—are you—willing to unlock and open the door to those who have come out of "scarlet" sin? If this is difficult for you, what practical steps can you take to become more accepting of such an individual?

Embrace the Truth

Read Hebrews 12:5–11.

✍ Based on this passage, whom does God discipline?

✍ What is the twofold purpose of God's discipline in our lives (v. 10)?

✍ What is produced in our lives through God's discipline?

They Felt the Spirit's Touch

Read Ephesians 2:4–10.

> ✍ Based on this passage, why has God made us alive in Christ?

> ✍ What is the purpose of grace in our lives?

> ✍ What is produced in our lives through God's grace?

Chapter 17

The Story of Aquila
and Priscilla

Grasp the Picture

Aquila and Priscilla were a living compliment to one another. They capitalized on each other's strengths. Teamwork was their creed. Their home was a haven of rest. A doorway of salvation for hundreds. But their greatest achievement was this.

   ✍ What does the author indicate was Aquila and Priscilla's greatest achievement?

   ✍ If you are married, does your marriage reflect this same principle? What could you do as a couple do to achieve this same goal?

In an odd twist, Solomon and Paul present a role reversal between Old and New Testaments. The Old Testament is usually considered the source of law and conduct, while the New Testament offers the safe haven of grace and intimacy. But when it comes to marriage, the New Testament teachings by Paul form the framework of sound companionship between a husband and a wife, while the Old Testament's

They Felt the Spirit's Touch

Song of Solomon issues an erotic yet tasteful invitation to Spirit-filled romance and marital embrace.

    ❧ What does the Song of Solomon emphasize in the marriage relationship? What does Paul highlight?

    ❧ Can a marriage survive on one of these cornerstones alone? Why or why not?

I would always find the same thing under every rock—a damp world void of life except a few worms and scurrying potato bugs. When the sunlight hit the bugs, they would scatter in all directions. Never once did I find a shred of plant life beneath any rock. But looking back now, I realize there was a life-giving marriage principle under all those rocks: Where there is no light, there is no life.

    ❧ What kind of secrets should be kept in a marriage?

    ❧ What happens to a marriage when secrets are kept from one another?

If you are not married, please know that these principles apply equally to your relationship with Christ. He too asks you to keep nothing hidden from Him, to keep moving forward with Him in spite of life's difficulties and to actively participate in your relationship with Him through worship and trust.

Study Guide

Embrace the Truth

Read Colossians 3:8–17.

    ✐ What specific things does Paul tell us to rid ourselves of? What are we to put on in their place?

    ✐ This passage is a general instruction to "God's chosen people." Sometimes it is easier to live this way toward people outside of our family circle. How would your marriage and family life change if you decided to live in this way with those closest to you?

Read 1 Corinthians 13:1–8.

    ✐ There are at least sixteen characteristics of genuine love found in these eight verses. What are they?

    ✐ In the Colossians passage above, love was to be the "cloak" that covered all the other virtues and held them together. What is the quality of your cloak? What areas do you need to work on? Ask the Lord to reveal those areas that might be weak and to show you practical ways to strengthen the quality of your love.

Chapter 18

The Story of Alexander the Coppersmith

Grasp the Picture

Maybe that's why we like to put our sin in the basement just as Moses did. Or at least we try to put it there. It's the place nobody wants to look. It's the place we take our failures to box them up instead of throwing them away. Those boxes may be out of sight for everyone else, but at least I know where to find them if I need them. Yes, basements are the perfect place for sin.

℞ What does God know about the human heart?

℞ What would it take for you to move from merely "sweeping the basement" once a year at a retreat or seminar, to regularly emptying your basement of those things God never intended you to hold on to? Of what must you become convinced?

Moses was convinced his dead Egyptian was safely boxed away in the basement. If he ever needed the bones, he knew where to find them. But Moses was wrong. All of heaven saw what was going on. A terrifying moment of exposure soon followed for Moses. Painful? Yes. Helpful? Time would tell.

    ✍ Why did Moses find the burning bush? What was Moses' road to greatness?

    ✍ What must we do with our sin when we choose to live without confession and forgiveness? How can our lives be made simpler?

God must have had great thoughts toward this man. To place his correction in the store window as He did with Moses was a clue to the squandered potential going on with man.

    ✍ Why did God choose to have a "garage sale" of Alexander's deeds and motives? What was Alexander being held accountable for?

    ✍ Why do you think God allows people like Alexander to enter our lives?

    ✍ How does He expect us to live—hidden in dark-ness or exposed in the light of grace? Are there areas of your life that need to be exposed to God's grace?

Embrace the Truth

Read 1 Peter 3:8–11.

✍ To what standard did Peter say we are called? For what reason?

✍ Why is unity so important in the body of Christ?

✍ What should we do when a relationship with a brother or sister in the Lord has been damaged, either through our own actions or through the actions of someone else? When should we do it?

Read Genesis 3:7–13.

✍ What did Adam and Eve first do when their eyes were opened? What did they do when they heard the Lord walking in the garden?

✍ How did God respond?

✍ Why was it necessary for Adam and Eve to be exposed—called from their hiding place?

Chapter 19

The Story of Onesimus

Grasp the Picture

God always needs others, no matter how significant an individual might be. And raising up another became the consuming dream and fulfillment for Paul. While in chains, Paul rejected thoughts of ease and spiritual retirement and instead used his energies to turn a useless slave into a life-giving messenger.

> ✐ What would have been lost if Paul had not made a place in his life for Onesimus?

> ✐ How did Paul's experience on the Damascus Road affect his attitude about helping Onesimus?

But Paul did not base Onesimus' potential on his pedigree. He saw the giftings within. If his offer to help had hinged on a clean background check, he would have thrown Onesimus out on his ear after ten minutes. Rather, Paul could sense the coming spring though Onesimus was still deep in the heart of his winter.

❧ What hope had Paul learned from Jesus himself? Has Christ extended the same to us? (See Romans 5:6–8.) How then should we see the people around us?

❧ In what practical ways did Paul help Onesimus? What had to happen before Paul could ask Philemon to receive Onesimus back like a son?

Paul never indicted, ignored, neglected, demeaned, demanded, nor forgot his spiritual son Onesimus. Let's be honest…when most Christians see Onesimus, they see a headache coming their way. But Paul, seeing the future through the eyes of Jesus saw more than what was coming at him. He saw what would one day be walking away from him. "And I have sent him back to you in person, that is, sending my very heart…" (Philem. 12).

❧ How was Paul able to see something besides a "headache" in Onesimus?

❧ How do you view the challenging people in your life? What steps could you take to make a positive impact in the life of those individuals?

Study Guide

Embrace the Truth

Read Titus 2:1–8.

ℽ In this passage, Paul outlines the process of mentoring (to teach or train another from one's own experience or knowledge). What was Titus instructed to teach the older men?

ℽ What was he to teach the older women? What were they expected to do with this knowledge (vv. 4–5)?

ℽ What were the young men to be taught? What would happen as a result of this training?

Read Hebrews 12:1–11.

ℽ Early in this chapter on Onesimus, the author describes the importance of endurance and our need for solid coaching and consistent cheering. In this passage, who does the writer indicate are our cheerleaders?

ℽ Who is our coach? What qualifies Him?

They Felt the Spirit's Touch

❧ What slows us down? What are we to do with it?

❧ Why does God discipline us?

Chapter 20

The Story of Silas

Grasp the Picture

But God's way of teaching us the true essence of praise is quite different. When it comes to our personal worship, God is after one thing. He wants our *spontaneous* praise, not our practiced praise.

℘ What one thing does God desire of our worship?

℘ What is the clue for discovering the pathway to pleasing worship?

With our bow to the string…with our lips to the reed…with our eyes fixed on the maestro…suffering becomes the downward stroke of the conductor's baton. Sudden suffering is God's cue that tells the symphony of the redeemed to begin "praising" their measure.

℘ How does God teach us to praise "on cue"?

❧ What separates mature worship from "religious repetition"?

By the way, how did Silas and Paul find themselves in jail that night? We've all heard about the two buddies out drinking, who end up getting into a fight at the pool hall only to find themselves sobering up in the for the night.

❧ What led to Silas and Paul's imprisonment— lawlessness or righteousness?

❧ Who accused them?

❧ Have you ever been falsely accused and suffered because of it? How did you respond?

Embrace the Truth

Read Psalm 103:1–22.

❧ Make a list of all the reasons given in this chapter to praise the Lord.

Study Guide

✍ Do you think the psalmist's life was "perfect" in every regard when he wrote this song of praise to the Lord?

✍ Does your life have to be "perfect" before you can offer God praise?

Read Ecclesiastes 4:9–12.

✍ From this passage, how do you think God views human relationships?

✍ Who makes up the "cord of three strands"?

✍ Is there a friend of yours who needs your encouragement? Make a point to call or get together with that individual this week. Let that person know how he or she has impacted your life and encouraged you.

The Women in the Life
of the Bridegroom

A Feminist Historical-Literary Analysis
of the Female Characters in the Fourth Gospel

Adeline Fehribach, S.C.N.

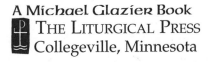

A Michael Glazier Book
THE LITURGICAL PRESS
Collegeville, Minnesota

Chapter 10

Cover design by David Manahan, O.S.B. Cover illustration: "The Marriage in Cana" by Gérard David (c. 1450–1523) Louvre, Paris.

A Michael Glazier Book published by The Liturgical Press

1   2   3   4   5   6   7   8

Library of Congress Cataloging-in-Publication Data

Fehribach, Adeline, 1950–
    The women in the life of the Bridegroom : a feminist historical-literary
analysis of the female characters in the Fourth Gospel / Adeline Fehribach.
        p.   cm.
    "A Michael Glazier book."
    Includes bibliographical references and index.
    ISBN 0-8146-5884-9 (alk. paper)
    1. Bible. N.T. John—Feminist criticism. 2. Bible. N.T. John—Socio-
rhetorical criticism. 3. Women in the Bible. I. Title.
BS2615.6.W65F44   1998
226.5'0922'082—dc21

                                                                98-7102
                                                                CIP

To Amina Bejos, S.C.N.,

faithful friend
and supportive sister

Contents

4. Mary and Martha of Bethany

5. The Mother of Jesus at the Cross

6. Mary Magdalene at the Tomb

7. Summary and Conclusion

Acknowledgements

This book would not have been possible had I not had the personal and financial support of my religious community, the Sisters of Charity of Nazareth. I am especially grateful to Amina Bejos, S.C.N. for her faithful friendship and support and to Dr. Lucy Marie Freibert, S.C.N. for her constructive input as literary critic, feminist, sister, and friend. In addition, I would like to thank Professor Mary Ann Tolbert for her direction and moral support in the writing of this book.

1

Introduction

Past Approaches to Women in the Fourth Gospel

How should the women in the Fourth Gospel[1] be regarded? On the one hand, the women in the Fourth Gospel appear at significant moments in the life of Jesus and seem to move his ministry forward. The mother of Jesus, for instance, precipitates the beginning of Jesus' ministry when she places before him the need for wine at a wedding in Cana (2:1-11); the Samaritan woman enters into a theological discussion with Jesus and her subsequent witness assists her townspeople in coming to believe in Jesus (4:1-42); the request that Mary and Martha of Bethany place before Jesus with regard to their sick brother elicits Jesus' final sign, the raising of Lazarus from the dead, which directly leads Jesus to his crucifixion (11:1-46, cf. 11:47-50; 12:9-11); Martha of Bethany makes an important profession of faith in Jesus prior to the raising of Lazarus (11:1-46) and Mary of Bethany anoints Jesus' feet prior to his passion (12:1-11); the mother of Jesus and the beloved disciple are given to each other by Jesus at the cross (19:25-28) and Mary Magdalene is the first person to whom the Risen Jesus shows himself, as well as the one to whom Jesus gives the mission of announcing his return to his Father (20:1-18).

In the face of the feminist challenge to biblical interpretation, some biblical scholars, including some feminist biblical scholars, have turned to these aspects of the treatment of women in the Fourth Gospel to try to prove that the very early Church, or at least Jesus himself, did not embrace

---

[1] I shall use "Fourth Gospel" instead of "The Gospel of John" because the author of this Gospel, like the authors of all other canonical Gospels, is unknown.

1

a patriarchal world-view.[2] For these scholars, the Fourth Gospel is seen as a window for viewing either Jesus' attitude toward women, or, more often, the Johannine community's position on women in ministry.[3]

With the assistance of the portrayal of women in the Fourth Gospel, for instance, Ben Witherington was able to conclude that Jesus' attitude toward women was quite different from the typical male attitude of his patriarchal culture.[4] For Raymond Brown and those biblical scholars who concentrated on the *Sitz-im-leben* of the text, however, the text illustrates that the Johannine community's egalitarian life-style extended to women, despite the growing patriarchal attitudes in the broader Christian community.[5]

Elisabeth Schüssler Fiorenza, who approached the topic of women in the Fourth Gospel as a feminist biblical scholar, acknowledged that the New Testament is patriarchal in nature and that women in the New Testament are often marginalized after they fulfill their function. Thus, she maintained that the New Testament does not directly or accurately describe women's historical reality and agency. For Schüssler Fiorenza, the fact that women are depicted with any agency at all in such androcentric texts indicated that they had even broader leadership roles in the early Church. For this reason she supplemented the historical critical method with a feminist sociocultural reconstruction to present a more accurate history of women in the early Church.[6] By supplementing the historical criti-

---

[2]These efforts may have been driven by a desire to salvage the reputation of the early church and/or of Jesus or by a belief that such assertions were necessary in order to argue for the full equality of women in the Church and society today. Cf. Martin Scott, *Sophia and the Johannine Jesus* (Sheffield: JSOT, 1992) 30; Elisabeth Schüssler Fiorenza, *In Memory of Her: A Feminist Theological Reconstruction of Christian Origins* (New York: Crossroad, 1983) 34; Sandra Schneiders, "Women in the Fourth Gospel and the Role of Women in the Contemporary Church," *Biblical Theological Bulletin* 12 (1982) 35.

[3]R. Alan Culpepper, *Anatomy of the Fourth Gospel: A Study in Literary Design* (Philadelphia: Fortress, 1983) 3–4. The metaphor of the literary text as a window for viewing preliterary history originates from the literary critic Murray Krieger, *A Window to Criticism: Shakespeare's Sonnets and Modern Poetics* (Princeton: Princeton University Press, 1964) 3–4.

[4]Ben Witherington III, *Women in the Ministry of Jesus* (Cambridge: Cambridge University Press, 1984) 129.

[5]Raymond Brown, "Roles of Women in the Fourth Gospel," *The Community of the Beloved Disciples* (New York: Paulist, 1979) 183. Robert Kysar, "The Women of the Gospel of John," *John: The Maverick Gospel,* revised edition (Louisville: Westminster/John Knox, 1993 [1976]) 152–4. Schneiders, "Women in the Fourth Gospel," 44; Scott, 15, 246–7, 250–2. Cf. Turid Karlsen Seim, "Roles of Women in the Gospel of John," *Aspects on the Johannine Literature,* eds. Lars Hartman and Birger Olsson (Sweden: Almqvist and Wiksell, 1987) 57 n. 4.

[6]Schüssler Fiorenza, *In Memory of Her,* 3–36.

cal work that R. Brown did on the women in the Fourth Gospel with her own sociocultural reconstructionist approach, Schüssler Fiorenza reconstructed an even more positive role for women in the early Johannine community than had Brown. She then used her reconstructed Johannine community to support her argument that the very early Church maintained a more egalitarian stance toward women than New Testament texts reflect.[7] One could say that, for Schüssler Fiorenza, the Fourth Gospel was one of the best windows for viewing the way women were treated in early Christian communities prior to the triumph of patriarchal attitudes within Christianity. Nevertheless, even this Johannine window needed to be cleansed through the process of sociocultural reconstruction where the agency of women was concerned because later patriarchal revisions had stained this window as well.

Other feminist biblical scholars who approached the topic of women in the Fourth Gospel tended to follow the lead of R. Brown and Schüssler Fiorenza by focusing on the positive aspects in the portrayal of the women in the Fourth Gospel.[8] In doing so, however, these feminist biblical scholars failed to follow the first step of Schüssler Fiorenza's four-step method of feminist biblical hermeneutics, approaching the text with a hermeneutic of suspicion.[9]

Besides the positive aspects in the portrayal of women in the Fourth Gospel mentioned above, there are other aspects in their portrayal that could be considered negative, or at least ambiguous, from the perspective of a twentieth- or twenty-first-century reader. Jesus, for example, appears to distance himself from his mother at Cana by calling her "woman" (2:4; cf. 19:26) and by using an idiom that some scholars translate as "What has this concern of yours to do with me?" (2:4).[10] Jesus also describes the

---

[7]Ibid., 323–34.

[8]Cf. Schneiders, "Women in the Fourth Gospel," 38–44; Jane Kopas, "Jesus and Women: John's Gospel," *Theology Today* 41 (1984) 201–5.

[9]Elisabeth Schüssler Fiorenza, *Bread Not Stone* (Boston: Beacon, 1984) 15–22. Schüssler Fiorenza later extended the feminist critical process to a five-dimensional hermeneutical model. Cf. Elisabeth Schüssler Fiorenza, "The Will to Choose or Reject: Continuing Our Critical Work," *Feminist Interpretation of the Bible*, ed. Letty Russell (Philadelphia: Westminster, 1985) 130–6. Schüssler Fiorenza admitted, however, that she did not use a hermeneutic of suspicion on the Fourth Gospel when she used the Fourth Gospel to reconstruct the history of Martha and Mary of Bethany. Cf. Elisabeth Schüssler Fiorenza, "A Feminist Critical Interpretation of Liberation: Martha and Mary: Lk. 10:38-42," *Religion and Intellectual Life* 3 (1986) 23–4.

[10]Cf. Jeffrey Lloyd Staley, *The Print's First Kiss: A Rhetorical Investigation of the Implied Reader of the Fourth Gospel* (Atlanta: Scholars Press, 1988) 88; Raymond Brown, *The Gospel According to John* (New York: Doubleday, 1966) 1:99; Birger Olsson,

Samaritan woman as having had five men/husbands and as currently living with one who is not her husband (4:18). In addition, at the end of the story, the Samaritan people appear to minimize the importance of the Samaritan woman by saying to her, "It is no longer because of what you said that we believe, for we have heard for ourselves, and we know that this is truly the Savior of the world" (4:42). The narrator places Mary and Martha of Bethany in the roles of servants, rather than as equal participants, at a meal held in Jesus' honor (12:2-3), and the crucifixion scene makes it obvious that the mother of Jesus needs to be placed in the care of a man (19:28). Finally, Jesus does not reciprocate Mary Magdalene's embrace when she recognizes him at the tomb, but says to her, "Do not hold onto me . . . ." (20:17). How is a reader to reconcile these aspects in the characterization of the women with what would otherwise be an affirming portrayal of women in the Fourth Gospel?

Attempts have been made to deal with the negative or ambiguous statements about the women in the Fourth Gospel. By accepting the conclusion of historical critics that the Fourth Gospel went through several revisions,[11] some biblical scholars, including some feminist biblical scholars, relegated some of the negative or ambiguous elements in the portrayal of women in the Fourth Gospel to later revisions.[12] Other negative or ambiguous elements were given theological rationales.[13] Implicit in Schüssler Fiorenza's work, however, is the understanding that those negative or ambiguous aspects in the portrayal of women in the Fourth Gospel that do not fit into one of these categories illustrate the patriarchal attitudes under which women in the early Church actually lived and against which they struggled.[14]

Structure and Meaning in the Fourth Gospel: A Text-Linguistic Analysis of John 2:1-11 and 4:1-42, trans. Jean Gray (Lund, Sweden: Greenup, 1974) 36–9; Rudolf Schnackenburg, *The Gospel According to St. John* (New York: Seabury, 1980) 1:327–9.

[11]For various theories on the stages of development of the Fourth Gospel, see Brown, *The Gospel According to John,* 1:xxxii–xl; R. Fortna, *The Fourth Gospel and its Predecessor* (Edinburgh: T. & T. Clark, 1988); Louis J. Martyn, "Source Criticism and Religionsgeschichte in the Fourth Gospel," *Jesus and Man's Hope,* ed. David Buttrick (Pittsburgh: Pittsburgh Theological Seminary, 1970) 1:247–73; R. Alan Culpepper, *The Johannine School* (Missoula, Mont.: Scholars Press, 1975) 1–37, 261–90.

[12]Cf. Brown, "Roles of Women in the Fourth Gospel," 194; Brown, *The Gospel According to John,* 1:103; Schüssler Fiorenza, *In Memory of Her,* 326–7; R. Fortna, *Gospel of Signs* (Cambridge: Cambridge University Press, 1970) 38; Raymond Brown, ed., *Mary in the New Testament* (London: Geoffrey Chapman, 1978) 182–94.

[13]Cf. Schüssler Fiorenza, *In Memory of Her,* 328; Schneiders, "Women in the Fourth Gospel," 40.

[14]Cf. Schüssler Fiorenza, *In Memory of Her,* 31–2; Schüssler Fiorenza, "The Will to Choose or Reject," 133–4.

Neither those scholars who used the historical-critical method nor Schüssler Fiorenza with her sociocultural reconstruction of the early Johannine community, however, have taken seriously the literary nature of the Fourth Gospel or the literary function of its female characters. In a literary approach to Scripture, biblical figures are analyzed, not as historical personages, but as literary characters with literary functions in the text.[15] Because a literary approach to the Fourth Gospel looks at the text as a unified and coherent whole, such an approach may more adequately explain both the positive and the negative, or ambiguous, elements in the portrayal of the women in the Fourth Gospel.

Those biblical scholars who have done a literary analysis of characterization for the Fourth Gospel, however, have tended to be interested only in the literary function of its characters, not in elements of androcentrism or patriarchy in the characterization of women. R. Alan Culpepper, for example, simply identified the female characters, like their male counterparts, as representatives of types of responses to Jesus and as plot functionaries whose purpose is to aid in the representation of Jesus.[16] Similarly, Jeffrey Staley simply concentrated on the manner in which characterization, including the characterization of the women, functions rhetorically in relationship to other narrative levels.[17] Because these male scholars have not approached the Fourth Gospel from a feminist perspective,

---

[15]Some recent publications that include a literary analysis of characterization for the Gospels: Fred Burnett, "Characterization and Reader Construction of Characters in the Gospels," *Semeia* 63 (1993) 1–28; Fred Burnett, "Characterization and Christology in Matthew: Jesus in the Gospel of Matthew," *Society of Biblical Literature: 1989 Seminar Papers,* ed. David Lull (Atlanta: Scholars Press, 1989) 588–603; C. Clifton Black, III, "Depth of Characterization and Degrees of Faith in Matthew," *Society of Biblical Literature: 1989 Seminar Papers,* ed. David Lull (Atlanta: Scholars Press, 1989) 604–23; Mary Ann Tolbert, "How the Gospel of Mark Builds Character: Characterization in the Parable of the Sower," *Interpretation* 47 (1993) 347–57; A.M. Okorie, "The Characterization of the Tax Collectors in the Gospel of Luke," *Currents in Theology and Mission* 22 (1995) 27–34; John Darr, *On Character Building: The Reader and the Rhetoric of Characterization in Luke-Acts* (Louisville: Westminster/John Knox, 1992); Marianne Meye Thompson, "'God's Voice You Have Never Heard, God's Form You Have Never Seen': The Characterization of God in the Gospel of John," *Semeia* 63 (1993) 177–204; Jeffrey Staley, "Stumbling in the Dark, Reaching for the Light: Reading Character in John 5 and 9," *Semeia* 53 (1991) 55–80; J. du Rand, "The Characterization of Jesus as Depicted in the Narrative of the Fourth Gospel," *Neotestamentica* 19 (1985) 18–36; Culpepper, "Characters," *Anatomy,* 99–148.

[16]Culpepper acknowledged, however, that some female characters may represent the ideal of female discipleship in the Gospel. Culpepper, *Anatomy,* 102, 133–4, 136–7, 140–7.

[17]Staley, *The Print's First Kiss,* 47–8, 83–4, 88–90, 96–103, 106.

they have not dealt with the androcentric or patriarchal elements inherent in the characterizations of the women.

Martin Scott, in his work *Sophia and the Johannine Jesus,* acknowledged the literary character of the Fourth Gospel,[18] dealt with the characterization of the women in greater depth than did Culpepper or Staley,[19] and identified himself as a male seeking "to take seriously the insights of feminist scholarship."[20] Scott, who recognized that the female characters in the Fourth Gospel appear at significant christological moments,[21] attempted to explain this phenomenon through the use of a heuristic methodology.[22] His research led him to conclude that Jesus in the Fourth Gospel is portrayed as Sophia incarnate and that the women of the Fourth Gospel, who support this portrayal of Jesus, are characterized as Sophia's handmaids.[23] Thus, Scott maintained that the "femaleness" of the women is very significant, for it helps to reflect the feminine side of Jesus Sophia.[24] Although Scott may have taken feminist scholarship seriously, he, like many feminist biblical scholars, concentrated on the positive aspects in the characterizations of these women, and thus failed to approach the text with a hermeneutics of suspicion.

All aspects in the portrayal of the women in the Fourth Gospel should be looked at before making any judgments about their function in the text. Also, it is my personal opinion that the literary functions of the female characters in the Fourth Gospel should be analyzed prior to any attempt at reconstructing the attitudes of the Johannine community toward women, much less Jesus' attitude toward women.

A Feminist Historical-Literary Approach

Because it is my belief that the topic of the women in the Fourth Gospel needs to be approached from both a literary perspective, in order to analyze their dynamic function in the plot, and a feminist perspective that begins with a hermeneutics of suspicion, in order to recognize the androcentric and patriarchal elements in their distinctive portrayals, I shall approach the topic from a feminist literary perspective. Because I am

---

[18]Cf. Scott, 18.

[19]Scott dedicated an entire chapter to the women in the Gospel of John. Cf. Scott, 174–240.

[20]Ibid., 16.

[21]Ibid., 12–3, 174–5.

[22]Ibid., 16–9.

[23]Ibid., 190, 196, 237–8.

[24]Ibid., 170–5, 236–9, 250.

using a literary approach, I shall focus on the text as a unity and seek to interpret the characterizations of women in light of the text as a whole.[25] This approach does not negate the possibility that the text went through several revisions at the hands of a variety of authors. What this approach does maintain, however, is that the text in its final first-century form, along with its characters, must have made sense to the author/redactor and readers of the time.[26]

Because I will be investigating how a first-century reader would have read and understood the text and the women in the text, rather than how a modern day reader could interpret the text, I call my approach a historical-literary approach. It is a Reader-response approach,[27] but with a concentration on a first-century implied reader (i.e., the reader that can be constructed from the text itself).[28] Literary critics who use Reader-response criticism on ancient texts maintain that the ancient reader was culturally determined in significant ways by the universe in which the text was written. For this reason, they attempt to explain the text in relation to the text's cultural and literary milieu. In my use of the historical-literary approach, therefore, I shall attempt to reconstruct for the reader of the twentieth or twenty-first century the cultural and literary milieu that enabled the first-century reader to interpret the Fourth Gospel.[29]

Wolfgang Iser refers to the text's cultural and literary milieu as the *repertoire* presupposed by the text.[30] According to Iser, this repertoire,

> consists of all the familiar territory within the text. This may be in the form
> of references to earlier works, or to social and historical norms, or to the

---

[25]On the literary unity of the Fourth Gospel, see G. Mlakuzhyil, "Difficulties Against the Literary Unity and Structure of the Fourth Gospel," *The Christocentric Literary Structure of the Fourth Gospel* (Roma: Editrice Pontificio Istituo Biblico, 1987) 5–16.

[26]Ibid., 13.

[27]For more information on Reader-response criticism and its use on biblical texts, see Elisabeth Freund, "Introduction: The Order of Reading," *The Return of the Reader: Reader-Response Criticism* (New York: Routedge, Chapman & Hall, 1987) 1–6; James L. Resseguie, "Reader-Response Criticism and the Synoptic Gospels," *Journal of the American Academy of Religion* 52 (1984) 307–24.

[28]Because the "implied reader" in my Reader-response approach is the first-century implied reader, unless otherwise stated, whenever I use the term "reader," I shall mean the first-century implied reader that I, as a critic, have constructed from the text itself.

[29]Cf. John Darr, "Glorified in the Presence of Kings: A Literary-Critical Study of Herod the Tetrarch in Luke-Acts" (Ph.D dissertation, Vanderbilt University, 1987) 32–3; Darr, *On Character Building,* 25–6.

[30]Cf. Wolfgang Iser, "The Repertoire," *The Act of Reading: A Theory of Aesthetic Response* (Baltimore: Johns Hopkins University Press, 1978) 53–85.

whole culture from which the text has emerged—in brief, to what the Prague structuralists have called the "extra-textual" reality.[31]

The implied author of an ancient text (i.e., the author that can be constructed from a text)[32] drew on this repertoire in the production of the text and the implied reader drew on this repertoire in the reception of the text.[33] This repertoire formed the implied reader's "horizon of expectation."[34]

Because of my own social location,[35] my historical-literary analysis of the female characters in the Fourth Gospel will be supplemented by a feminist critique. The feminist approach that I shall use in the body of this work is similar to that used by Esther Fuchs in her analysis of female characters in the Hebrew Bible. Fuchs, who uses a historical-literary approach that takes into consideration the text's literary and cultural context, supplements the approach with a hermeneutic of suspicion. Fuchs affirms, for instance, that the characterization of the mother figure in the Hebrew Bible is riddled with "patriarchal determinants,"[36] and analyzes how the Hebrew Bible "uses literary strategies to foster and perpetuate its patriarchal ideology."[37]

---

[31]Ibid., 69.

[32]The implied author, therefore, is to be distinguished from the real author(s) of the text. Even though a text may have gone through several revisions at the hands of several real authors, a reader is still able to identify one "implied author" from the text itself. Actual readers infer the implied author from the sum of the choices the implied author made in the construction of a text. The implied author of the Fourth Gospel can be inferred, for instance, from the ideology reflected in the comments of the omniscient narrator, Jesus and other reliable characters such as John the Baptist and the beloved disciple, as well as the manner in which the material was selected and organized. Cf. W. Booth, *The Rhetoric of Fiction* (Chicago: University of Chicago Press, 1961) 71–7, 151; Culpepper, *Anatomy,* 7, 15–6, 21–6, 32–49, 132–3.

[33]Darr, "Glorified," 62–8, 79–81, 125–6.

[34]For a fuller discussion of the "horizon of expectation" in reception theory, see Steven Mailloux, "Literary History and Reception Study," *Interpretive Conventions: The Reader in the Study of American Fiction* (Ithaca: Cornell University Press, 1982) 167–70.

[35]I would define my social location as that of a liberationist feminist biblical scholar and a committed Roman Catholic who is greatly concerned about the patriarchal nature of the Bible, the way in which women are treated in the Church and society today, and the manner in which the Bible is used to support or thwart feminist claims.

[36]Esther Fuchs, "The Literary Characterization of Mothers and Sexual Politics in the Hebrew Bible," *Feminist Perspectives on Biblical Scholarship,* ed. Adela Yarbro Collins (Chico, Calif.: Scholars Press, 1983) 119.

[37]Esther Fuchs, "Who is Hiding the Truth? Deceptive Women and Biblical Androcentrism," *Feminist Perspectives on Biblical Scholarship,* ed. Adela Yarbro Collins (Chico, Calif.: Scholars Press, 1983) 137.

Although the body of this work will focus on how literary strategies in the Fourth Gospel foster and perpetuate the implied author's patriarchal ideology, in the conclusion I shall present some tentative suggestions on how a reader of the twentieth or twenty-first century might interpret the female characters in a nonandrocentric manner. In this endeavor, my feminist literary approach is similar to that used by J. Cheryl Exum in her analysis of female characters in the Hebrew Bible. Although Exum also acknowledges the patriarchal context of biblical literature, she chooses to approach the biblical text from a nonandrocentric perspective. By being a resistant reader and reading against the androcentric ideology of the implied author, Exum is able to affirm female characters found within patriarchal biblical literature.[38]

The Repertoire of the Fourth Gospel

As stated above, a historical-literary analysis of the Fourth Gospel necessitates an identification of the literary and social conventions that would likely have formed the reader's "horizon of expectation." I have identified five aids for uncovering the literary and social conventions that would likely have formed the reader's "horizon of expectation" with regard to the female characters in the Fourth Gospel:

1) the Hebrew Bible;
2) Hellenistic-Jewish writings;
3) popular Greco-Roman literature;
4) the concept of "honor and shame" as used by cultural anthropologists for the study of gender relations in the Mediterranean area;
5) the history of women in the Greco-Roman world.

Information about women from these five areas will provide the twentieth- or twenty-first-century reader with the "cultural literacy" necessary to understand the text as a first-century reader might have understood it.

Historical critics have identified the Hebrew Bible as one of the most important literary resources for understanding the Fourth Gospel. R. Brown and others note that, although the Fourth Gospel has few direct citations from the Hebrew Bible, themes from the Hebrew Bible are woven

---

[38]J. Cheryl Exum, "'Mothers in Israel': A Familiar Figure Reconsidered," *Feminist Interpretation of the Bible,* ed. Letty Russell (Philadelphia: Westminster, 1985) 73–4. Cf. J. Cheryl Exum, "'You Shall Let Every Daughter Live': A Study of Exodus 1:8–2:10," *The Bible and Feminist Hermeneutics,* ed. Mary Ann Tolbert (Chico: Scholars Press, 1983) 63–82; J. Cheryl Exum, *Fragmented Women: Feminist (Sub)versions of Biblical Narratives* (Valley Forge, Pa.: Trinity, 1993) 9–15.

into the very structure of the Fourth Gospel.[39] Although the relationship between the Hebrew Bible and the Fourth Gospel is subtle, a reader who was well versed in the Hebrew Bible would have picked up on allusions to the Hebrew Bible in the reception process.

Because the implied author's use of the Hebrew Bible is generally more through allusion than direct quotations, so is the manner in which the implied author used the Hebrew Bible in the portrayal of female characters. In my historical-literary analysis of the female character of the Fourth Gospel, therefore, I shall attempt to make explicit those allusions to the Hebrew Bible that would have been readily apparent to an ancient reader, but that might not be so apparent to a reader from the twentieth or twenty-first century.

In addition to identifying the Hebrew Bible as an influence on the production of the Fourth Gospel, historical critics have also identified a Hellenistic influence. Some Hellenistic influence comes from Judaism itself, which was strongly Hellenized by the first-century C.E. Such Hellenistic-Jewish influences can be seen in the utilization of the personification of wisdom, as found in the Book of Wisdom and adapted by the Hellenistic-Jewish philosopher Philo, in the portrayal of Jesus as the "Word of God" in the prologue of the Fourth Gospel.[40] With regard to Hellenistic-Jewish portrayals of women, I shall specifically look at such Hellenistic-Jewish writings as *The Book of Aseneth, Susanna, Judith,* and *Biblical Antiquities.*

Besides this Hellenistic-Jewish influence, R. Brown identifies two other strains of Greek thought that might explain some of the peculiarities in Johannine theological expressions: popular Greek philosophy and the *Hermetica.*[41] To these three sources of Greek influences I would add a fourth—popular Greco-Roman literature.

Mary Ann Tolbert, who uses a historical-literary approach to the gospels, states that the gospels' simplicity of Greek style, unpolished rhetorical development, and relative lack of philosophical and literary pretensions seem to place the gospels on a different plane from the majority of extant works from the Greco-Roman world. She and other biblical schol-

---

[39]Cf. Brown, *The Gospel According to John,* 1:lix–lxi; Culpepper, *The Johannine School,* 274–5; C. K. Barrett, "The Old Testament in the Fourth Gospel," *Journal of Theological Studies* 48 (1947) 155–69; J. H. Bernard, *A Critical and Exegetical Commentary on the Gospel According to St. John* (Edinburgh: T & T Clark, 1928) 1:cxlvii–clvi; R. H. Lightfoot, *St. John's Gospel: A Commentary* (Oxford: Clarendon, 1956) 45–9; D. Moody Smith, *The Theology of the Gospel of John* (Cambridge: Cambridge University Press, 1995) 10, 17–20; Mark Stibbe, *John* (Sheffield: JSOT, 1993) 23–4.

[40]Brown, *The Gospel According to John,* 1:lvii–lviii.

[41]Ibid., 1:lvi–lix. Smith, 10–2. Lightfoot, 49–56.

ars maintain, therefore, that the gospels can best be compared to popular literature from the Greco-Roman world.[42] As Tolbert states,

> Popular literature . . . is related in theme and overall patterning to elite literature, but is written in an entirely different key. Its vocabulary, plot development, rhetorical strategies, and characterizations are simpler, more conventionalized, more homogenized, and often more formulaic than the cultivated and self-conscious writings of the privileged classes.[43]

The rise of popular culture and literacy among the working classes in the Hellenistic and Roman eras allowed for the development of this popular literature. The conventional and formulaic style of this writing, conducive to oral recitation, made this literature available to the illiterate masses, as well as the literate working class. Because the upper classes, who controlled the processes of preservation and transmission of literary works, preserved primarily only literature written by and for the elite, little of this literature has survived.[44] Nevertheless, extant examples of popular types of Greco-Roman literature provide sufficient evidence to illustrate that this literature may have formed part of the repertoire for the production and reception of the Fourth Gospel as a whole, and the characterization of women in particular.[45]

Within this general category of popular literature, the Fourth Gospel can best be identified as an ancient biography, because it concentrates on the person of Jesus and incorporates the literary conventions of an ancient biography.[46] One of the literary conventions of ancient biographies was

[42]Mary Ann Tolbert, *Sowing the Gospel: Mark's World in Literary-Historical Perspective* (Minneapolis: Fortress, 1989) 59–61. David Aune, *The New Testament in Its Literary Environment* (Philadelphia: Westminster, 1987) 12–13. C.W. Votaw, "Some Example of Biography in the Ancient World Comparable to the Gospels," *The Gospel and Contemporary Biographies* (Philadelphia: Fortress, 1970) 1–2, 8, reprinted from "The Gospels and Contemporary Biographies in the Greco-Roman World," *American Journal of Theology* 19 (1915) 45–73.

[43]Tolbert, *Sowing the Gospel,* 61.

[44]Ibid., 61–2, 70–2.

[45]Although I shall focus on popular Hellenistic literature as a significant part of the literary repertoire for the characterization of women in the Fourth Gospel, at times I shall compare the characterization of the women in the Fourth Gospel to the manner in which women were characterized in Greek literature in general. Cf. John Peradotto and J. P. Sullivan, eds., *Women in the Ancient World: The Arethusa Papers* (Albany: State University of New York Press, 1984); Helene Foley, ed., *Reflections of Women in Antiquity* (New York: Gordon and Breach, 1981).

[46]Fernando Segovia, "The Journey(s) of the Word of God: A Reading of the Plot of the Fourth Gospel," *Semeia* 53 (1991) 25, 32–3. Charles Talbert, *Reading John: A Literary*

that the hero was depicted as a "type" character (i.e., a character who exhibits certain distinguishing traits). Fernando Segovia identifies Jesus in the Fourth Gospel as a philosopher type and a "holy man as son of god" subtype within the philosopher type. This type embodies such identifying traits as divine parentage, miracle-working, and misunderstanding by followers and enemies alike.[47]

In identifying the Hellenistic repertoire for the Fourth Gospel, however, one cannot merely look to popular ancient biographies that depict the life of a philosopher or holy man as son of god. All genres in the first century C.E. were fluid and capable of adopting and adapting aspects of earlier genres. The Greco-Roman biography in particular was a continuously developing, complex genre with changing features.[48] Speaking of the Gospel of Mark, for instance, Frank Kermode states, "To prove that a gospel is evidently not a *chria* or an aretalogy or a *baracah* or an apocalypse is by no means to demonstrate that these genres did not contribute to the set of expectations within which Mark wrote and his audience read or listened."[49] Thus, the implied author of a gospel may have drawn on a variety of genres for the production of a gospel, and an ancient reader would have brought to the reception of that gospel literary conventions from a wide range of genres.

Like Tolbert, who sees striking stylistic similarities between the Gospel of Mark and popular Greek novels (sometimes referred to as romances or tales),[50] I see striking similarities between the Fourth Gospel

---

and Theological Commentary on the Fourth Gospel and the Johannine Epistles (New York: Crossroad, 1994) 62. Charles Talbert, "Once Again: Gospel Genre," *Semeia* 43 (1988) 53–73. Stibbe, 13. Cf. Aune, *The New Testament in Its Literary Environment*, 13, 46–74; Philip Shuler, *A Genre for the Gospels: The Biographical Character of Matthew* (Philadelphia: Fortress, 1982) 24, 34–57. For the conventions of ancient biographies, see Robert Scholes and Robert Kellogg, *The Nature of Narrative* (New York: Oxford University Press, 1966) 210–8; Patricia Cox, *A Genre for the Gospels* (Philadelphia: Fortress, 1982) 45–65; Aune, *The New Testament in Its Literary Environment*, 46–63.

[47]Segovia, "The Journey(s) of the Word of God," 32–3. Regarding the philosopher character type in ancient biographies, see Cox, 17–44; Aune, *The New Testament in Its Literary Environment*, 33–4.

[48]Cf. Tolbert, *Sowing the Gospel*, 51–2; Aune, *The New Testament in Its Literary Environment*, 27–31, 46.

[49]Frank Kermode, *The Genesis of Secrecy: On the Interpretation of Narrative* (Cambridge, Mass.: Harvard University Press, 1979) 162–3.

[50]Although Tolbert acknowledges that only ancient erotic popular novels have survived, she hypothesizes that a more historical or biographical type of popular novel may have existed, as she finds some fragmentary evidence for this. Mary Ann Tolbert,

and popular Greek novels where the portrayal of women is concerned. In my historical-literary analysis of the female characters in the Fourth Gospel, therefore, I shall attempt to make explicit those allusions to this Greco-Roman literature that would have been readily apparent to a first-century reader, but that might not be so readily apparent to today's reader who has a very different literary repertoire.

Besides analyzing the characterization of women in the Fourth Gospel in relation to that Gospel's literary repertoire, I shall also attempt to analyze the characterization of women against the cultural norms of the time in which it was written. To do this I shall draw on cultural criticism, specifically anthropological criticism,[51] and research done on the history of women in the Greco-Roman world.

Bruce Malina has attempted to reconstruct gender roles for the New Testament world by drawing on the research cultural anthropologists have done on the concept of "honor and shame" in the Mediterranean area. Cultural anthropologists have shown that, in traditional Mediterranean societies, a man's honor is directly related to the sexual purity of his mother, wife, daughters, and sisters. In order to keep the women in a man's life from hurting a man's honor by acting in a "shameless" manner, these androcentric Mediterranean societies develop behavioral expectations that are based on a gendered division of labor and space. Building on the assumption that current traditional societies in the Mediterranean area differ little from their New Testament counterparts, Malina reconstructed gender roles for the New Testament world that reflect the traditional "honor/shame" code of the Mediterranean area.[52] Although Malina's work should be used

---

"The Gospel in Greco-Roman Culture," *The Book and the Text: The Bible and Literary Theory,* ed. R. Schwartz (Cambridge: Basic Blackwell, 1990) 263–5.

[51] For the emergence of cultural criticism within biblical criticism, see Fernando Segovia, "'And They Began to Speak in Other Tongues: Competing Modes of Discourse in Contemporary Biblical Criticism," *Reading from this Place, Vol. 1: Social Location and Interpretation in the United States,* eds. Fernando Segovia and Mary Ann Tolbert (Minneapolis: Fortress, 1995) 20–8.

[52] Bruce Malina, "Honor and Shame: Pivotal Values of the First-Century Mediterranean World," *The New Testament World: Insights from Cultural Anthropology* (Louisville: John Knox, 1981) 25–50. Bruce Malina, "Dealing with Biblical (Mediterranean) Characters: A Guide to U.S. Consumers," *Biblical Theological Bulletin* 19 (1989) 127–41. Bruce Malina, *The Gospel of John in Sociolinguistic Perspectives. Forty-eighth Colloquy of the Center for Hermeneutical Studies,* ed. Herman Waetjen (Berkeley: Center for Hermeneutical Studies, 1985). Cf. Julian Pitt-Rivers, *The Fate of Shechem or the Politics of Sex: Essays in the Anthropology of the Mediterranean* (Cambridge: Cambridge University Press, 1977) 1–47; Julian Pitt-Rivers, "Honour and Social Status," *Honour and Shame: The Values of Mediterranean Society,* ed. J. G.

with caution,[53] his analysis is helpful in constructing the social and cultural repertoire on which an ancient reader would have drawn for stories involving women in the Fourth Gospel.

In order to arrive at a deeper understanding of the social and cultural repertoire of the reader of the Fourth Gospel, I shall supplement Malina's cultural anthropological findings for the New Testament world with research done in the area of the history of women in the Greco-Roman world. Suffice it to say for now that, although studies on the history of women in the Greco-Roman world indicate that the economic, legal, and cultural position of women generally improved during Hellenistic period (323–30 B.C.E.) and the era of the late republic (ca. 53 B.C.E.–96 C.E.),[54] the end of the first century saw a resurgence of patriarchal ideology especially among middle-class men.[55] In this regard, it should be noted that, on both external and internal evidence, a late first-century date is generally accepted for the Fourth Gospel.[56]

Peristiany (Chicago: University of Chicago Press, 1966) 19–77; J. G. Peristiany, "Introduction," *Honour and Shame: The Values of Mediterranean Society,* ed. J. G. Peristiany (Chicago: University of Chicago Press, 1966) 9–18.

[53]Cf. Mary Ann Tolbert, "Social, Sociological, and Anthropological Methods," *Searching the Scripture: A Feminist Introduction,* ed. Elisabeth Schüssler Fiorenza (New York: Crossroad, 1993) 264–70. In addition to the comments made by Tolbert, it should be noted that Malina drew on the work of traditional Mediterranean anthropologists such as Pitt-Rivers and Peristiany for his work on honor and shame in the New Testament world. Because the work of these traditional cultural anthropologist has subsequently been scrutinized by contemporary cultural anthropologists and feminist critics alike, I have also drawn on the work of Carol Delaney, Uni Wikan, and Fourouz Jowkar for the concept of "honor and shame" in the New Testament world. Cf. Carol Delaney, "Seeds of Honor, Fields of Shame," *Honor and Shame and the Unity of the Mediterranean,* ed. David Gilmore (Washington, D.C.: American Anthropological Association, 1987) 35–48; Uni Wikan, "Shame and Honour: A Contestable Pair," *Man* 19 (1984) 635–52; Fourouz Jowkar, "Honor and Shame: A Feminist View From Within," *Feminist Issues* 6 (Spring 1986) 45–65.

[54]Cf. Sarah Pomeroy, *Goddesses, Whores, Wives, and Slaves: Women in Classical Antiquity* (New York: Schocken Books, 1975) 120–230; Eva Cantarella, *Pandora's Daughters: The Role & Status of Women in Greek and Roman Antiquity,* trans. Maureen Fant (Baltimore: Johns Hopkins University Press, 1987).

[55]Although Schüssler Fiorenza acknowledges that this shift began as early as Augustan's rule (27 B.C.E.–14 C.E.), she sees the effects of this shift in the Church beginning in the second century. Schüssler Fiorenza, *In Memory of Her,* 77, 89–92, 286–8. Schüssler Fiorenza, *Bread Not Stone,* 77–8.

[56]Adele Reinhartz, "The Gospel of John," *Searching the Scriptures: A Feminist Commentary* ed. Elisabeth Schüssler Fiorenza (New York: Crossroad, 1994) 562. Talbert, *Reading John,* 61.

Although I am drawing on research from cultural anthropology and the history of women in the Greco-Roman world, this book is neither a sociocultural analysis nor a history of women in the early church. Rather, it is a historical-literary work that seeks to understand a literary text in relation to its cultural and historical context, as well as its literary context.

Character Analysis

Because I am approaching the Fourth Gospel from a literary perspective, I shall analyze the women in the Fourth Gospel as literary characters, even though I do not negate the possibility of their historical existence. As Culpepper states,

> Even if the figure is "real" rather than "fictional," it has to pass through the mind of the author before it can be described. It is therefore, for our present purposes, immaterial whether the literary character has its origin in historical tradition, memory, or imagination. The writer has a distinct understanding of a person and his or her role in a significant sequence of events.[57]

The freedom of a writer to portray a real or fictional figure according to the writer's own understanding of the character's function is especially evident in ancient biographies. According to Patricia Cox, ancient biographies incorporated a certain amount of "mythologizing" of a person's life in order to convey some perceived truth about that person. This "mythologizing" might include presenting, as fact, an event that *could* have taken place, given the person's character, whether the event actually happened or not.[58] Philip Shuler refers to this rhetorical technique as amplification.[59]

Although the Fourth Gospel certainly drew on tradition for the characterization of Jesus and stories involving Jesus' encounter with women, the generic conventions of the day with regard to ancient biographies allowed for amplification or mythologizing. In writing an ancient biography of Jesus, therefore, the implied author of the Fourth Gospel may have exaggerated, or even "invented," events and encounters between Jesus and other individuals so as to convince the reader about a perceived truth regarding the person of Jesus.[60] The signs of Jesus are just one area in which such amplification may have taken place. According to Robert Kysar, the

---

[57]Culpepper, *Anatomy,* 105.

[58]Cox, 8, cf. 5. Cf. Aune, *The New Testament in Its Literary Environment,* 31.

[59]Shuler, 49–50.

[60]Talbert acknowledges that all the Gospels, including the Fourth Gospel, are like ancient biographies in that they tell the story of Jesus in mythical terms. Talbert, "Once Again: Gospel Genre," 60–3.

signs of Jesus in the Fourth Gospel are fewer in number than those in the Synoptics, but "the marvelous quality of Jesus' acts are heightened."[61] The raising of Lazarus from the dead after he was in the tomb for four days is but one example mentioned by Kysar where such a heightening in the marvelous quality of Jesus' acts is evident and where female characters are involved. Thus, because I am using a literary approach that views the Fourth Gospel as an ancient biography, the characterizations of the women in the Fourth Gospel need to be seen as products of its implied author, reflecting the implied author's literary and theological purposes, as well as the implied author's ideological perspective.

As stated above, because I am using a historical-literary approach in my analysis of the female characters in the Fourth Gospel, I shall attempt to be cognizant of the literary and cultural influences that would have contributed to an ancient reader's understanding of these female characters. John Darr conveniently categorizes Iser's "extra-textual repertoire" (or "extra-text" as Darr sometimes refers to it) into four areas:

1) commonly-known historical facts and figures;
2) classical and canonical literature;
3) literary conventions such as stock characters, type scenes, topoi, etc.;
4) social norms and structures.[62]

Given the extra-textual repertoire for the Fourth Gospel outlined above, as I analyze the female characters in the Fourth Gospel, I shall pay special attention to the literary conventions, character-types, and type scenes involving women from the Hebrew Bible, Hellenistic-Jewish literature, and popular Greco-Roman literature, historical facts about women in the Greco-Roman world, and social norms and the structures for women in the New Testament world as illustrated in the honor-shame framework of the Mediterranean area.

In addition to analyzing the characterizations of the women in the Fourth Gospel according to the Fourth Gospel's "extra-text," I shall analyze the text itself for clues regarding the depiction and the function of its female characters. According to Culpepper, a character is fashioned by:

1) what the narrator says about the character,
2) what the character says and does,
3) how other characters react to the character in question."[63]

[61]Kysar, 9.

[62]Darr, "Glorified," 125–6. Cf. Iser, *The Act of Reading,* 69.

[63]Culpepper, *Anatomy,* 106. Cf. Robert Alter, *The Art of Biblical Narrative* (New York: Basic Books, 1981) 116–7.

I shall, therefore, analyze these textual components of characterization in conjunction with the "extra-text" of the Fourth Gospel in order to establish how an ancient reader would have understood the depiction and function of the women in the Fourth Gospel.

Assumptions

My analysis of the textual features of the characterizations of the women in the Fourth Gospel incorporates several assumptions. The first assumption is that characters are integrally related to the plot.[64] Because one of the functions of characters is to further the plot, an understanding of the plot is necessary for understanding the function of the characters in the text. Culpepper states that clues to the plot of the Fourth Gospel can be found in the prologue, especially 1:11-12. According to Culpepper, the plot of the Fourth Gospel revolves around the reason for Jesus' being sent to this world—that he might enable people to become "children of God."[65] Within my analysis of the female characters in the Fourth Gospel, therefore, I shall analyze how the women further this plot.

The second assumption that I bring to my textual analysis of the female characters in the Fourth Gospel is that another function characters have is that of revealing significant aspects about other characters.[66] Culpepper states that intermediary characters often reveal something about the protagonist and that this is particularly true for intermediate characters in the Fourth Gospel.[67] If the Fourth Gospel is perceived as an ancient biography of Jesus, then it would seem that one of the major functions of all intermediate characters, including female characters, is to reveal something about the person of Jesus.[68]

Jesus is presented in the Fourth Gospel in a variety of ways, as the Word of God (1:1, 14), the Son sent from the Father (1:14; 3:16-18; 5:23 etc.), the Son of Man (1:51; 3:13-14; 5:27 etc.), the one who reveals the

[64]Aristotle argued that character was subordinate to plot. According to Kermode, Henry James argued that character precedes plot in the creative process. Kermode himself, however, maintains that characters generate narrative, just as narrative generates characters. Culpepper defines one type of character, the ficelle, as a typical character who exist to serve specific plot functions. Aristotle, *The Poetics,* The Loeb Classical Library, trans. W. H. Fyfe (Cambridge: Harvard University Press, 1953) 6:19. Kermode, 75–8. Culpepper, *Anatomy,* 104. Cf. Darr, "Glorified," 91; Darr, *On Character Building,* 38–9.

[65]Culpepper, *Anatomy,* 87.

[66]Cf. Darr, "Glorified," 95–7; Darr, *On Character Building,* 41–2.

[67]Cf. Culpepper, *Anatomy,* 102–4.

[68]Cf. Kysar, 149.

Father and his glory (1:18; 2:11; 17:26), and the bridegroom (3:29), to name only a few. Different intermediary characters help to highlight different aspects of Jesus' character. Staley, for instance, illustrates how the characterization of the lame man in chapter 5 helps to portray Jesus as the charismatic healer who has authority over and above Torah authority.[69] Similarly, Nicodemus can be seen as functioning as a foil for Jesus' self-identification as the Revealer of heaven's secrets,[70] and the Jews in chapters 7 and 8 can be seen as functioning as foils for Jesus' self-identification as the Son whom the Heavenly Father sent from above to bring life.[71] This book will focus on how the women in the Fourth Gospel function to reveal Jesus as the messianic bridegroom.

The third assumption that I bring to my textual analysis is that characterization is both sequential and cumulative.[72] As any reader encounters a text, the reader can only "build" the characters according to the textual information given up to that point in the text.[73] The attitude of the reader toward a particular character, therefore, may change throughout the experience of reading a text. This is particularly important at those places in the text where the implied author leaves gaps for a reader to fill and those places where the implied author utilizes reader-victimization.[74] As I analyze the characterizations of women in the Fourth Gospel, therefore, I shall assume that the first-century reader would have understood the female characters in a sequential and cumulative manner.

The fourth assumption that I bring to my textual analysis is that characterization has a rhetorical function.[75] The rhetorical function of characterization on which Culpepper focuses for male as well as female characters in the Fourth Gospel is that of leading the reader to a particular response to Jesus. For Culpepper, "the characters represent a continuum of responses to Jesus which exemplify misunderstandings that the reader

[69]Staley, "Stumbling in the Dark," 58, 63.

[70]Cf. Stibbe, 54–5; Culpepper, *Anatomy,* 135; Scott, 145–6.

[71]Cf. Stibbe, 93–5; Culpepper, *Anatomy,* 129–30.

[72]Cf. Darr, "Glorified," 97–105; Darr, *On Character Building,* 42–3; Thomas Doherty, *Reading (Absent) Character: A Theory of Characterization in Fiction* (New York: Oxford University Press, 1983) xiii–xiv; Kermode, 77–8.

[73]For the concept of the reader as "building" characters, see Darr, *On Character Building,* 16–7, 35; Burnett, "Characterization and Reader Construction of Characters in the Gospels," 3–28.

[74]Staley states that in reader-victimization the reader is led by certain facts that are presented in a text to make erroneous judgments and later is forced to recognize his or her misjudgments. Cf. Staley, *The Print's First Kiss,* 95–118.

[75]Cf. Darr, "Glorified," 105–21; Darr, *On Character Building,* 49–50.

may share and responses one might make to the depictions of Jesus in the Gospel."[76] Reading about the encounters between intermediary characters and Jesus, Culpepper states, helps to "coax the reader" to respond to Jesus in a particular way.[77] Although I do not dispute this rhetorical function of the female characters, as well as the male characters, in the Fourth Gospel, a comparison of encounters between Jesus and male characters and Jesus and female characters has led me to wonder whether the female characters have another rhetorical function that is specific to their gender. In my character analysis, I shall seek to determine whether the implied author used the characterization of women to coax a male reader to move away from the typical male mode of relating to God and others and to appropriate a more "feminine" model of relationship.

The final assumption that I bring to my textual analysis is that the social location of the reader plays a significant role in character building. By analyzing the textual aspects of characterization in conjunction with the "extra-text" of the Fourth Gospel, I hope to be able to identify the manner in which a first-century reader would have understood, or built, the female characters. In approaching this task, however, I must concede that my chronological and cultural distance from the text and its literary and cultural milieu limits my ability to fulfill this task. Because I agree with Darr that critics "build" readers just as readers "build" characters, I must acknowledge that the reader that I, as a twentieth-century critic, construct may differ from an actual first-century reader, even though I am attempting to be sensitive to the text's own literary and cultural milieu. Similarly, the female characters my reader "builds" may differ from the female characters built by an actual first-century reader. Finally, because I acknowledge that the social location of the reader, especially the reader's gender, plays a significant role in the reading process,[78] I also acknowledge that the female characters that my reader "constructs" may differ from those constructed by other contemporary critics from other social locations who also strive to be sensitive to the text's literary and cultural milieu. A comparison of Scott's construction of the female characters as Sophia's handmaids and my construction of them as stated in the following thesis illustrates this point.

[76]Culpepper, *Anatomy,* 104.

[77]Ibid., 104.

[78]Cf. Annette Kolodny, "A Map for Reading: Or, Gender and the Interpretation of Literary Texts," *New Literary History* 11 (1980) 451–67. According to Tolbert, Kate Millett in *Sexual Politics* was the first person to raise the question of the relation of gender to reading. Cf. Mary Ann Tolbert, "Protestant Feminists and the Bible: On the Horns of a Dilemma," *Union Seminary Quarterly Review* 43 (1989) 10.

Thesis

My thesis is that the implied author of the Fourth Gospel drew on the literary and cultural conventions of the day to portray the female characters in such a way as to have them support the characterization of Jesus as the messianic bridegroom, and that the ancient reader who was familiar with the literary and cultural conventions mentioned above would have perceived the women fulfilling the role of mother of the messianic bridegroom, betrothed/bride of the messianic bridegroom, or sister of the betrothed/bride of the messianic bridegroom. Like Scott, therefore, I maintain that the gender of the women is important. Whereas Scott perceives the women as helping to portray Jesus as Sophia, I perceive the women as helping to portray Jesus as the messianic bridegroom who was sent to establish the *familia Dei*.[79]

My feminist, historical-literary analysis of the female characters of the Fourth Gospel will illustrate how such a portrayal of the women furthers the plot of Jesus' being sent to give people the power to become children of God, and how such a portrayal is, at the same time, extremely androcentric and patriarchal in nature. Such an understanding of the women helps to explain those aspects in their characterization that appear to be positive and affirming from a twentieth- or twenty-first-century perspective, as well as those aspects in their characterization that appear to be negative or ambiguous from a twentieth- or twenty-first-century perspective. It also helps to explain why the women do not appear to be dependent on husbands or other male legitimators.[80]

Procedure

Although I am approaching the Fourth Gospel as a unity, I am omitting the story of the adulterous woman (7:53–8:11) from my analysis of the female characters. Based on the fact that this story does not appear in manuscripts until the fourth century C.E. and after that time appears not only at John 7:53–8:11, but also after John 7:36, after John 21:25, and even after 21:38 in the Gospel of Luke, it has been identified by textual critics as a fourth-century addition to the Fourth Gospel.[81] Because I am

---

[79]Cf. Seim, 59–67.
[80]Cf. Schneiders, "Women in the Fourth Gospel," 44; Seim, 58.
[81]Cf. Bruce Metzger, *A Textual Commentary on the Greek New Testament* (Stuttgart: Biblia-Druck GmbH, 1975) 219–22; Brown, "Roles of Women in the Fourth Gospel," 185 n. 328; Edwyn Hoskyns, *The Fourth Gospel* (London: Faber and Faber Limited, 1940) 2:673–85; Lightfoot, 345–8.

analyzing the characterization of the women in the Fourth Gospel from the perspective of the cultural and literary milieu of the first century, this story of the adulterous woman does not belong in my analysis.[82]

The female characters and pericopae that I shall analyze within the next five chapters are as follows:

Chapter 2) the mother of Jesus at Cana (2:1-12),
Chapter 3) the Samaritan woman at the well (4:1-42),
Chapter 4) Mary and Martha of Bethany (11:1-46; 12:1-11),
Chapter 5) the mother of Jesus at the cross (19:25-28),
Chapter 6) Mary Magdalene at the tomb (20:1-18).
Chapter 7) contains my conclusions regarding the depiction and function of the women in the Fourth Gospel based on a feminist, historical-literary approach, as well as some tentative suggestions about how a reader from the twentieth or twenty-first century might acknowledge the androcentric and patriarchal aspects of the biblical text, and yet approach the women in the Fourth Gospel from a nonandrocentric perspective.

[82]Mlakuzhyil, in his argument for the literary unity of the Fourth Gospel, also prescinds from this pericope on the grounds that it is generally accepted as non-Johannine by text critics. Mlakuzhyil, 5 n. 4.

2

The Mother of Jesus at Cana

Introduction

The first female character a reader encounters as a foil for Jesus' portrayal as the messianic bridegroom is the mother of Jesus in the story of the wedding at Cana (2:1-11). Because this female character is also found at the crucifixion scene (19:25-27), because she is called "woman" by Jesus in both pericopae, and because reference is made in both pericopae to Jesus' "hour," many scholars have concluded that these two scenes form an *inclusio* for the public life of Jesus. This conclusion has led some scholars to use the crucifixion scene to interpret the significance of the mother of Jesus at Cana and thus to establish a unified meaning for her character in the Fourth Gospel.[1] R. Alan Culpepper goes so far as to say that the mother of Jesus can have no role in the life of her son until his hour comes, at which time she will be given to the ideal disciple.[2]

Generally, the role of the mother of Jesus is seen as representational, but there is no agreement on what the mother of Jesus represents. Eva Krafft, R. H. Strachan, E. F. Scott, J. Zumstein, and Rosemary Radford Reuther, for instance, view her as symbolically representing Judaism;[3]

[1] Bertrand Buby, "Mary in John's Gospel," *Mary, the Faithful Disciple* (New York: Paulist, 1985) 95. J. Zumstein, "Pourquoi s'intéresser a l'exégèse féministe?" *Foi et Vie* 88 (1989 no. 5) 5.

[2] R. Alan Culpepper, *Anatomy of the Fourth Gospel: A Study of Literary Design* (Philadelphia: Fortress, 1983) 133.

[3] Cf. Culpepper, *Anatomy,* 133; Rosemary Radford Ruether, *Mary—the Feminine Face of the Church* (Philadelphia: Westminster, 1977) 39; Zumstein, "Pourquoi s'intéresser a l'exégèse féministe?" 5.

Rudolf Bultmann, A. Loisy, S. Schulz, and John Rena view her as representing Jewish Christianity;[4] and R. J. Dillion views her as representing the remnant of Israel.[5]

Many commentators, including some from the early Church (e.g., Ambrose [d. 397 C.E.] and Ephraem [d. 373 C.E.]), perceive a symbolic connection between the mother of Jesus and the Church through the portrayal of Eve in Genesis 3, who is called "γύναι" (woman), just as the mother of Jesus is at Cana and at the Cross. Raymond Brown, Edwyn Hoskyns, F. M. Braun, and Max Thurian hold such a view. Paul Gätcher (1953) maintained a connection with both Eve and the woman of Revelation 12 (who is also called "γύναι"), and V. Anzalone, D. M. Crossan, E. J. Kilmartin, J. Leal, and M. Zerwick followed his lead in this regard. Turid Karlsen Seim, and H. Räisänen, however, reject the notion of the mother of Jesus as a New Eve. Räisänen sees such an interpretation as a heavy over-interpretation of 19:25-27 and Seim referred to the theory as a jungle growth of exegetical conjectures and catchword combination.[6]

André Feuillet rejects the connection with Gen 3:15 and instead proposes that the "woman" at Cana can be explained only by referring to "woman" at the Cross in connection with the "woman" of Revelation 12 and viewing this woman within the context of Isa 26:17 and 66:7-9. Thus, Feuillet sees her as representing the eschatological Zion/the mother of the Church. Alexander Kerrigan agrees with Feuillet and perceives the mother of Jesus as the New Jerusalem (Zion) from which the new temple arises. P. Benoit perceives her as representing the church in her role as the daughter of Zion, whereas Ignace de la Potterie sees the mother of Jesus as representing the Church in so far as the Church is the mother of believers.[7]

---

[4]Cf. Culpepper, *Anatomy,* 133; Raymond Collins, "The Representative Figures of the Fourth Gospel," *Downside Review* 94 (1976) 120; John Rena, "Women in the Gospel of John," *Église et Théogie* 17 (1986) 136.

[5]Cf. Raymond Collins, "Mary in the Fourth Gospel," *Louvain Studies* 3 (1970) 128.

[6]Cf. R. Collins, "Mary in the Fourth Gospel," 107–8, 127, 130–2; R. Collins, "The Representative Figures of the Fourth Gospel," 121–2; Culpepper, *Anatomy,* 133; Turid Karlsen Seim, "Roles of Women in the Gospel of John," *Aspects on the Johannine Literature,* eds. Lars Hartman & Birger Olsson (Sweden: Almqvist & Wiksell International, 1987) 60–2; Max Thurian, "Mary and the Church," *Mary, Mother of All Christians* (New York: Herder and Herder, 1964) 137–44.

[7]André Feuillet, "The Hour of Jesus and the Sign of Cana," *Johannine Studies* (New York: Alba, 1964) 36. André Feuillet, "The Messiah and His Mother According to Apocalypse XII," *Johannine Studies* (New York: Alba, 1964) 288, 291. Cf. R. Collins, "Mary in the Fourth Gospel," 132–4, 139.

Some scholars don't attempt to prove a connection with Old or New Testament figures. Instead, scholars such as D. Uzin, D. M. Crossan, John McHugh, and Raymond Collins simply perceive the mother of Jesus as representing the exemplar of faith.[8]

Although I agree with those scholars who perceive the wedding at Cana and the Cross pericopae as forming an *inclusio,* it is my opinion that the characterizations of the mother of Jesus in the two pericopae need to be analyzed separately in order to determine the significance of her character in each pericope. By using the historical-literary method together with relevant anthropological information, I shall show that the function of the character of the mother of Jesus in each pericope is to advance the christology of the implied author in the respective contexts. In developing her character to fulfill this function in the two pericopae, however, the implied author used different literary devices. The use of different literary devices resulted in very different characterizations of the mother of Jesus in the two pericopae. In both pericopae, however, the literary devices that are used are patriarchal and androcentric in nature.

In this chapter I shall present an analysis and feminist literary critique of the characterization of the mother of Jesus in the story of the wedding at Cana. An analysis and critique of the characterization of the mother of Jesus at the cross will be presented in chapter 5. For the character of the mother of Jesus at the wedding of Cana, I contend that the implied author used a character-type from the Hebrew Bible that I shall call the "mother of an important son."

The "Mother of an Important Son" Character-Type from the Hebrew Bible

Esther Fuchs has identified within the Hebrew Bible a "mother" character-type.[9] J. Cheryl Exum found within this broad type a more specific character-type that she calls "Mother of Israel."[10] Because previous scholars have identified the mother of Jesus in the Fourth Gospel with

---

[8]Cf. Culpepper, *Anatomy,* 134; John McHugh, "Mother of the Word Incarnate: Mary in the Theology of St. John," *The Mother of Jesus in the New Testament* (London: Darton, Longman & Todd, 1975) 388–403; R. Collins, "The Representative Figures of the Fourth Gospel," 120.

[9]Esther Fuchs, "The Literary Characterization of Mothers and Sexual Politics in the Hebrew Bible," *Feminist Perspectives on Biblical Scholarship,* ed. Adela Yarbro Collins (Chico, Calif.: Scholars Press, 1985) 117–36.

[10]J. Cheryl Exum, "'Mother in Israel': A Familiar Figure Reconsidered," *Feminist Interpretation of the Bible,* ed. Letty Russell (Philadelphia: Westminster, 1985) 73–82.

Judaism, Jewish Christianity, the New Jerusalem, and the remnant of Israel, the use of the title "Mother of Israel" for the mother of Jesus might be misleading. For this reason, I shall refer to this character-type from the Hebrew Bible as the "mother of an important son."

According to Exum, the stories of the matriarchs and patriarchs of Genesis 12–50 focus on the patriarchs, but it is the actions of the mothers at strategic points in the text that actually move the plot and insure the fulfillment of the promise made to Abraham. In some cases, the mother-character accomplishes this just by giving birth to the son of the promise. In other cases, the actions of the mother-character on behalf of her important son during his lifetime allow him to fulfill his destiny and keep alive the promise God made to Abraham regarding descendants (Gen 17:5-8).

Exum affirms that it was Sarah's actions on behalf of Isaac that guaranteed Isaac's inheritance against the threat of Ishmael (Gen 21:9-21), and Rebekah's actions on behalf of Jacob that insured Jacob's reception of the blessing instead of Esau's and then saved Jacob from Esau's wrath (Gen 27:1-46). Rebekah's advice resulted in Jacob's being sent by his father to Jacob's maternal uncle's house (Laban's house) to find a wife. This action led to Jacob's marriage to both Leah and Rachel. It was then Leah's and Rachel's actions in relation to each other and to their handmaids that resulted in the birth of Jacob's twelve sons (and one daughter). Thus, the eventual rise of the twelve tribes of Israel was accomplished through the actions of "Mothers of Israel." Similarly, the disobedience of Moses' biological mother and his surrogate mothers with regard to the Pharaoh's laws insured the survival of Moses and thus insured the future existence of the twelve tribes of Israel. All of this allows Exum to proclaim that it was these behind-the-scene actions of the "Mothers of Israel," who were rarely portrayed as major characters, that actually determined the future of Israel.[11]

The Mother of Jesus as the "Mother of an Important Son"

In the Fourth Gospel it is obvious that Jesus is connected with the promise made to Abraham. The relationship between Jesus and the promise made to Abraham is implicitly established by the narrator in the prologue to the Fourth Gospel when the narrator states that those who ac-

---

[11]Exum, "'Mother in Israel,'" 73–82. Fuchs likewise notes a "protective" role for the mother-character in the Hebrew Bible in addition to the role of giving birth. Her comments about protective actions of Sarah, Rebekah, and Bathsheba seem to indicate that this "protective" role for the mother character-type includes making sure that her son meets his destiny and fulfills his role in the text. Cf. Fuchs, "The Literary Characterization of Mothers," 135.

cept Jesus and believe in his name will be given the power of becoming
children of God (1:12). Because the Hebrew Bible portrays children of
Abraham as children of God, first-century readers with a knowledge of the
Hebrew Bible would have made the connection between giving people the
power to become children of God and fulfilling the promise made to Abraham. The connection between children of Abraham and children of God
is, in fact, made explicit in the Fourth Gospel in chapter 8. The Jews claim
Abraham as their father (8:39) and then state, "we have one Father, God
himself" (8:41). Jesus says to them, "Your ancestor Abraham rejoiced that
he would see my day" (8:56). This statement by Jesus with its surround-
ing section (8:31-59) has been interpreted by scholars not only as Jesus'
affirming his divine sonship in contrast to the sonship of the Jews, but also
as Jesus' contrasting physical descent from Abraham with true descen-
dence from Abraham.[12] Thus, 8:31-59 can be seen as connecting Jesus'
role of enabling people to become children of God with the promise made
to Abraham regarding future descendants.

The wedding feast at Cana can then be viewed as the inauguration of
Jesus' fulfillment of the promise made to Abraham because this is the first
instance in which the text actually refers to Jesus' disciples' believing in
him, a prerequisite for becoming a child of God (cf. 1:12-13). Their belief
was based on the sign that Jesus performed, turning water into wine
(2:11).

The mother of Jesus can be viewed as fulfilling her role as the
"mother of an important son" because it was her implied request, "They
have no wine" (2:3), that was the catalyst for Jesus' giving the sign that revealed his glory and resulted in his disciples' believing in him (2:11).
Thus, the action of the mother of Jesus can be viewed as occurring at a
strategic point in the text to move the plot forward and insure Jesus as
the fulfillment of the promise made to Abraham. Consequently, her
characterization fits the main elements of the "mother of an important
son" character-type from the Hebrew Bible.

The reader is not told why the mother of Jesus presented Jesus with this
problem of no wine. Rather, the implied author leaves it up to the reader to
discern the reason for her request. Although some Mariologists have asserted that the mother of Jesus in the Fourth Gospel knew of her son's ex-
traordinary abilities before the wedding at Cana, believed in him, and was

[12]According to R. Collins, S. Bartina referred to this as "applied" or "metaphorical" sonship. J. A. du Rand likewise perceives this section as establishing Jesus as the
fulfillment of Abraham's hope. R. Collins, "Mary in the Fourth Gospel," 115. J.A. du
Rand, "The Characterization of Jesus as Depicted in the Narrative of the Fourth
Gospel," *Neotestamentica* 19 (1985) 27.

asking him to perform a miracle at the wedding,[13] nothing in the text supports such an assumption.[14] Thus, it seems best to view the implied request of the mother of Jesus as a request for ordinary assistance from her son.[15]

A first-century reader who was familiar with the "mother of an important son" from the Hebrew Bible would probably have presumed that the mother of Jesus presented Jesus with the need for wine in order to further her son's importance in some way, for that is what mothers did in the Hebrew Bible. When the headwaiter takes the water changed to wine to the bridegroom to complain that the bridegroom had saved the best wine for last (2:9-10), it becomes obvious, even to a present-day reader, that the bridegroom was the one who was responsible for the wine at the wedding. According to the honor-shame code for the time period and geographic region, the bridegroom would have been indebted to Jesus if the mother of Jesus got him to provide the wine. This indebtedness would have heightened Jesus' honor in the relation to the bridegroom and would have been the basis for a dyadic relationship between Jesus and the bridegroom.[16] Based on such an honor-shame code, an increase in Jesus' honor would have heightened his mother's status in the community as well because mothers received their standing in the community on the basis of the honor bestowed on their sons.[17]

[13]For further research on those who perceive the mother of Jesus was expecting a miracle, see R. Collins, "Mary in the Fourth Gospel," 105, 122–5 and Raymond Brown, *The Gospel According to John,* The Anchor Bible (New York: Doubleday, 1966) 1:98. For a discussion of the variant of 1:13 as implying a virginal conception that would support the notion that the mother of Jesus was aware of his nature, see R. Collins, "Mary in the Fourth Gospel, 113–7; Raymond Collins, "The Mother of Jesus in the Gospel of John," *Mary in the New Testament,* ed. Raymond Brown, et. al. (Philadelphia: Fortress, 1978) 181–2; Thurian, 134; Martin Scott, *Sophia and the Johannine Jesus* (Sheffield: JSOT, 1992) 178.

[14]Cf. R. Collins, "Mary in the Fourth Gospel," 122–3; Brown, *The Gospel According to John,* 1:98–9.

[15]Charles Giblin points to the reaction of the mother of Jesus to Jesus' rebuff as an illustration that she expected only a verbal response by Jesus to the servants. Charles Giblin, "Suggestion, Negative Response and Positive Action in St. John's Portrayal of Jesus [John 2:1-11; 4:46-54; 7:2-14, 11:1-44]," *New Testament Studies* 26 (1980) 202.

[16]For explanations of the concepts of reciprocity, dyadic contracts, and honor in the first century, see Bruce Malina, "Honor and Shame: Pivotal Values of the First-Century Mediterranean World" and "The Perception of Limited Good," *The New Testament World: Insights from Cultural Anthropology* (Louisville: John Knox, 1981) 25–50, 71–93; Bruce Malina, "Game Plans and Strategies: Processes and Directions," *Christian Origins and Cultural Anthropology* (Atlanta: John Knox, 1986) 98–111.

[17]Cf. Carol Delaney, "Seeds of Honor, Fields of Shame," *Honor and Shame and the Unity of the Mediterranean,* ed. David Gilmore (Washington, D.C.: American An-

The Mother of Jesus as Mother of the Messianic Bridegroom

The Mother of Jesus Places Him in the Role of a Bridegroom

When the mother of Jesus says to Jesus, "They have no wine" (2:3), she places him in the role of the bridegroom, whose responsibility it is to provide the wine (cf. 2:9-10).[18] Jesus, however, responds to her with the words, "τί ἐμοὶ καὶ σοί, γύναι; οὔπω ἥκει ἡ ὥρα μου" ("What concern is that to you and to me? My hour has not yet come.") (2:3). Such a response by Jesus would appear to be both a recognition that the need for wine is not his responsibility and a rejection of his mother's implied request to do something about it. An ancient reader may even have perceived Jesus' rejection of his mother's request as a refusal to heighten his own honor at the expense of the bridegroom.

Jesus Acts as the Messianic Bridegroom

Jesus' response to his mother characterizes Jesus as being aloof from his mother and her "worldly" concerns. Yet, as J.A. du Rand and Charles Giblin state, when Jesus appears to be aloof and distant in his answers and exchanges with other characters in the Fourth Gospel, it is a signal that he is actually moving the discussion to "higher," non-worldly level.[19] Jesus' subsequent action in response to the need for wine, therefore, reflects his "higher" purpose in life.

When the mother of Jesus refused to take no for an answer (cf. 2:5), Jesus provided the wine, but in a way that illustrates that he acts in accord with his own purpose. Jesus turned to the six stone purification jars of water (each of which held twenty to thirty gallons), had the servants fill them with water, and then changed the water into quality wine (cf. 2:6-10). A first-century reader, familiar with the Hebrew Bible, would have known that wedding feasts in the Hebrew Bible often illustrated the relationship between Israel and its God (Exod 34:10-16; Deut 5:2-10; Isa 54:4-8; Jer 2:2; 11:15; Ezek 16:8-13; Hos 1:2-9; 2:4-25) and that quality wine in abundance sometimes functioned in the Hebrew Bible as a symbol of messianic

---

thropological Association, 1987) 42, 44–5; Farouz Jowkar, "Honor and Shame: A Feminist View From Within," *Feminist Studies Spring* (1986) 49; Malina, *The New Testament World: Insights from Cultural Anthropology,* 103–4. For examples of how the Hebrew Bible illustrates this anthropological trait for mothers, see J. Cheryl Exum, "The (M)other's Place," *Fragmented Women: Feminist (Sub)versions of Biblical Narratives* (Sheffield, JSOT, 1993) 109, 121–2, 133, 140.

[18]Cf. R. Collins, "Mary in the Fourth Gospel," 121–2.

[19]du Rand, 30. Giblin, 202.

blessings (Isa 25:6; Jer 49:11-12; Joel 4:18; Cant 1:2, 2:4).[20] Such a reader would have realized that Jesus' action of providing quality wine in abundance from the purification jars illustrated that he, in fact, accepted the role of the bridegroom, but that he was no ordinary bridegroom. As Sandra Schneiders and others have noted, the sign Jesus performed illustrated that he was accepting the role of the messianic bridegroom, and that as such he was assuming the role of Yahweh, the bridegroom of Israel.[21]

Jesus' Hour as the Hour of His Wedding

As du Rand states, the Fourth Gospel often contrasts the two ideological (evaluative) points of view, the "from above" point of view with the "from below" point of view. The "from below" point of view involves misunderstanding of Jesus, whose identity can only be grasped "from above." Although the retrospective point of view of the narrator/ implied author permits a "from above" narration, this point of view unfolds for the reader in the sequence of events.[22] Jesus uses the phrase "my hour" for the first time at Cana. Gradually, as the reader encounters more of the text, the reader comes to realize that this phrase has a deeper meaning, the hour of Jesus' death and exaltation. Yet, at this point in the text, the reader does not know that this phrase has further significance. Thus, the reader would have understood the phrase from a "below" point of view and would have perceived the mother of Jesus as understanding the phrase from a "below" point of view.[23]

One possible "below" perspective would be to view Jesus' response, "οὔπω ἥκει ἡ ὥρα μου," as an affirmation that his own wedding had not yet come.[24] Regarding the term "ὥρα," G. Delling states that the term "is defined by the context given to it and that "ὥρα" can itself stand for the

[20]Cf. R. Collins, "Mary in the Fourth Gospel," 125–6; Mark Stibbe, *John* (Sheffield: JSOT, 1993) 46.

[21]Sandra Schneider, *The Revelatory Text: Interpreting the New Testament as Sacred Scripture* (San Francisco: Harper, 1991) 187. Cf. Stibbe, 46, 61.

[22]du Rand, 20–1. Cf. Buby, 100.

[23]Cf. Mathias Rissi, "Die Hochzeit in Kana (Joh. 2:1-11)," *Oikonomia: Heilsgeschichet als Thema der Theologie,* ed. O. Cullman (Hamburg-Bergstedt: Reich, 1967) 88; Ruether, *Mary—The Feminine Face of the Church,* 39; Charles Talbert, *Reading John: A Literary and Theological Commentary on the Fourth Gospel and the Johannine Epistles* (New York: Crossroad, 1994) 85.

[24]Jeffrey Staley notes that without the word "my" (μου), "the hour" would "automatically be understood by the implied reader as having to do with some event connected with the wedding." Jeffrey Lloyd Staley, *The Print's First Kiss: A Rhetorical Investigation of the Implied Reader in the Fourth Gospel* (Atlanta: Scholars Press, 1985) 89.

content which it represents."[25] Thus, if a person uses the word "hour" out of context, then the word implies the whole context. An example of this usage can be found in John 16:21 where the phrase "ὥρα αὐτῆς" "her hour" refers to the hour in which a woman gives birth (ὅταν τίκτῃ). Delling also notes that "ὥρα" is found with the word for wedding (γάμος) in the form of γάμων ὥρα in both Philo (*De Opificio Mundi,* 103) and Josephus (*Antiq.* 12, 187), and in the form of ὥρα γάμου in *Antiq.* 4, 243-244 and 12, 186. In these cases the phrases refer to the appropriate time for a wedding.[26]

If one approaches the Gospel as literature and realizes that the reader and the mother of Jesus could not yet have interpreted Jesus' words about his "hour" from an "above" perspective, then one could perceive the mother of Jesus, as well as the reader, as interpreting Jesus' response, "τί ἐμοὶ καὶ σοί, γύναι; οὔπω ἥκει ἡ ὥρα μου," as the equivalent of, "What does this concern of yours have to do with me, woman, it's not my wedding" or "What does this have to do with you and me, woman, it's not my wedding." Read in this way, Jesus' response would have heightened the reader's perception that the request of the mother of Jesus placed Jesus in the role of a bridegroom, a role he initially rejects.

From a "below" perspective, Jesus' response gives the appearance of verbal resistance toward the implied request of his mother to supply wine for the wedding feast. The mother of Jesus does not respond to her son's apparent resistance directly. Rather, she turns to the servants. To them she says, ὅ τι ἄν λέγα ὑμῖν, ποιήσατε." Although some authors perceive possible theological implications in her response,[27] if one interprets her response from a "below" perspective, the mother of Jesus could be seen as trying to overlook her son's apparent resistance without confronting him directly. Thus, from a "below" point of view, one could perceive the mother of Jesus as reasserting her maternal role as she refuses to allow her son to miss an opportunity of increasing his honor in relation to the bridegroom. Read in this way, the passage appears to characterize Jesus as

[25]Gerhard Delling, "ὥρα," *Theological Dictionary of the New Testament,* ed. Gerhard Kittle, trans. & ed. G. Bromiley (Grand Rapids: Eerdman, 1967) 9:677.

[26]Ibid., 9:677.

[27]Rissi and R. Brown see a parallel between the mother's response (ὅ τι ἄν λέγῃ ὑμῖν, ποιήσατε) and the response of pharaoh to the servants regarding what Joseph might say to them so as to provide food during the famine (ὅ ἐὰν εἴπῃ ὑμῖν, ποιήσατε) (Gen 41:55). Birger Olsson, who prefers to see the text through the Exodus screen, points to parallels found at Exod 19:8 and 24:7 that emphasize obedience to a revelation. Rissi, 85. Brown, *The Gospel According to John,* 1:100. Birger Olsson, *Structure and Meaning in the Fourth Gospel* (Uppsala: Lund, 1974) 45–8.

distancing himself from the influence of his mother as he interprets the situation from an "above" perspective, and then to characterize the mother of Jesus as refusing to allow her son to distance himself from her as she reasserts her parental role in a situation that she interprets from a "below" perspective. Ironically, although the mother of Jesus, as well as the reader, understands Jesus as saying that it is not his wedding, that is, he is not the bridegroom responsible for providing wine, Jesus' eventual positive response to the implied request points to his acceptance of the role of the messianic bridegroom in fulfillment of the will of his Father.[28]

The importance of this bridegroom imagery for Jesus' ministry is later reinforced by John the Baptist when he states, "He who has the bride is the bridegroom. The friend of the bridegroom, who stands and hears him, rejoices greatly at the bridegroom's voice" (3:29). As will be shown in this book, it is through fulfilling his role as messianic bridegroom that Jesus gives people the power to become children of God and thus fulfills the promise made to Abraham.

Patriarchal and Androcentric Elements in the Portrayal of the Mother of Jesus at Cana

Patriarchal/Androcentric Elements in the "Mother of an Important Son" Character-Type

Both Fuchs and Exum identify patriarchal and androcentric elements in this mother character-type from the Hebrew Bible. The androcentric nature of the mother-son motif is evident in the limited literary role the mother-character is given. This female character is not significant in her own right. She is significant only to the extent that she is mother of a son, especially the mother of an important son.[29] According to Fuchs, this limited literary role often results in a degree of literary flatness for the female characters in relation to their male counterparts.[30] Another patriarchal/an-

---

[28]Such irony is characteristic of the Fourth Gospel. Cf. Paul Duke, *Irony in the Fourth Gospel* (Atlanta: John Knox, 1985); Culpepper, *Anatomy*, 149–202; Gail O'Day, "The Essence and Function of Irony," *Revelation in the Fourth Gospel* (Philadelphia: Fortress, 1986) 11–32; Staley, "Rhetorical Strategies in John 4–21: The Victimization of the Implied Reader," *The Print's First Kiss*, 95–118.

[29]Fuchs, "The Literary Characterization of Mothers," 135–6. J. Cheryl Exum, "The (M)other's Place," *Fragmented Women: Feminist (Sub)versions of Biblical Narratives* (Sheffield: JSOT, 1993) 103–4. Exum, "'Mother in Israel,'" 74.

[30]Fuchs, "The Literary Characterization of Mothers," 135–6. Exum acknowledges the secondary nature of the matriarchal characters to the patriarchal characters. She

drocentric element to this character-type can be found in the fact that the mothers of the Hebrew Bible received their status on the basis of their sons. This reflected status sometimes led to competition between mothers, as expressed in the Sarah/Hagar and Rachel/Leah/Bilhah/Zilpah stories.[31] A final element of androcentric/patriarchal ideology in this character-type, noted by both Fuchs and Exum, is that once the mother has fulfilled her androcentric role in relation to her son, she is moved offstage until such time as she might be needed to fulfill another androcentric role.[32]

Patriarchal and Androcentric Elements in the Portrayal of the Mother of Jesus

The androcentric and patriarchal elements in the character-type of the "Mother of an Important Son" are apparent in the characterization of the Mother of Jesus at Cana. When Jesus verbally responds to his mother's request with the words, "τί ἐμοὶ καὶ σοί, γύναι; οὔπω ἥκει ἡ ὥρα μου" (2:4), and then later fulfills her request in the way he did, his response indicates that the role of his mother is diminished in relation to other "mothers of an important son" from the Hebrew Bible. Jesus functions on a higher, "non-worldly" plane, not in response to earthly desires. To illustrate this diminishment in the role of the mother of Jesus in the life of her important son, all three parts of Jesus' statement need to be analyzed. The first part is Jesus' question "τί ἐμοὶ καὶ σοί;" The second part is Jesus' use of the address "γύναι" when speaking to his mother and the third part is Jesus' statement, "οὔπω ἥκει ἡ ὥρα μου." After analyzing all three segments of his statement, I shall analyze his statement as a whole.

The phrase, "τί ἐμοὶ καὶ σοί;" is a Greek rendition of a Semitic expression מַה־לִּי וָלָךְ (mah-li wālāk). The phrase can be translated in a variety of ways. How one translates it depends on the degree of distance one perceives Jesus is asserting in relation to his mother.[33] Should one translate

---

points out, however, that when matriarchs of the Hebrew Bible appear as actors, they come to life as fully developed personalities who, nonetheless, serve the interest of an androcentric agenda. Exum, "The (M)other's Place," *Fragmented Women: Feminist (Sub)versions of Biblical Narratives* (Sheffield: JSOT, 1993) 96–7. Exum, "Mother in Israel: A Familiar Figure Reconsidered," 75.

[31]Exum, "The (M)other's Place," 104, 121–4.

[32]Fuchs, "The Literary Characterization of Mothers," 135. Exum, "The (M)other's Place," 97.

[33]Rena, 133–4. R. Collins notes the usage of this formula when a person is confronted by a demonstration of hostility or an unpleasant situation (1 Kgs 17:18; 2 Kgs 3:13; 2 Sam 16:10; 19:23). He also notes that when it is used in a dialogue in the Hebrew Bible (e.g., Jos 22:24; 2 Kgs 9:18; Jer 2:18; Jos 14:9) as it is in the Fourth Gospel,

the Semitic expression as "What do I have to do with thee?" in accordance
with KJV and ASV, or as "What do you have to do with me?" in accordance
with the RSV, or as "What concern is that to you and to me?" in accordance
with the NRSV? Some early commentaries went so far as to paraphrase the
question to read "You must not tell me what to do." and "Don't try to direct me."[34]

R. Brown notes that this phrase always denotes a refusal of an inop-
portune involvement and a divergence between the views of the two persons involved. He also notes, however, that the phrase can carry with it
either a connotation of hostility or mere disengagement.[35] If one perceives
the mother of Jesus as attempting to urge him to further his honor in the
eyes of humans, then an element of rebuke may, in fact, be present.[36] Jesus
is characterized in the Fourth Gospel as hostile to this kind of glory seeking and as interested only in the glory that comes from his heavenly Father
(cf. 5:44; 7:18; 8:50-54; 12:43; 16:14; 17:1-5, 22-24).[37] This disengagement, or rebuke, is meant to support the implied author's high christology,

---

the formula is an oratorical question occasioned by the untoward action of another and
is tantamount to a refusal. A. Maynard perceives it as indicating that the two parties
have nothing to do with each other. Olsson, however, notes that the meaning of the
idiom, which is found in Greek, Latin, Hebrew and Aramaic, is dependent on the context and intonation. R. Collins, "Mary in the Fourth Gospel," 118. A. Maynard, "Ti
Emoi Kai Σοι," *New Testament Studies* 31 (1985) 583–4. Olsson, "A 'Narrative' Text,
Jn 2:1-11," *Structure and Meaning in the Fourth Gospel,* 36–40.

[34]According to Culpepper, McHugh, who maintains that the mother of Jesus believed before the sign was given at Cana, translates the question as "What is that to me
and thee, woman?" Culpepper, however, who maintains that the mother of Jesus plays
no role in the life of Jesus until his hour of glorification, perceives Jesus asking his
mother, "What have you to do with me? My hour has not yet come." Cf. Culpepper,
Anatomy, 133–4. For a discussion of the phrase, see Maynard, 582–6 and H. Buck,
"Redactions of the Fourth Gospel and the Mother of Jesus," *Studies in New Testament
and Early Christian Literature,* ed. David Aune (Leiden: E. J. Brill, 1972) 170–80. For
a discussion of the various ways in which commentaries prior to 1974 translated the
phrase, see Olsson, 36 n. 18.

[35]Brown, *The Gospel According to John,* 1:99.

[36]According to R. Collins, some Greek Fathers of the Church (e.g., Origin [d.
254] and Ephraem [d. 373]) perceived an element of fault or disordinate presumption
on the part of Jesus' mother. Rena suggests that the mother of Jesus serves as a negative example warning people not to tell God how to act. R. Collins, "Mary in the Fourth
Gospel," 105. Rena, 137.

[37]For a discussion of the male mode of behavior according to the Mediterranean
honor/shame code of the first century, see Malina, "Honor and Shame: Pivotal Values
of the First-Century Mediterranean World," *The New Testament World: Insights from
Cultural Anthropology,* 25–50.

either by directly distancing Jesus from his mother,[38] or by showing that Jesus has a point of view different from his mother with respect to the situation.[39] In either interpretation, the character of the mother of Jesus aids in the characterization of Jesus by presenting Jesus with the opportunity to show that he is disengaged from the earthly concerns of his mother. As Charles Talbert states, Jesus' words to his mother "indicates that his action to do the latter is not dictated by human initiative, even by those closest to him, but by God's timing, as illustrated by his statement, 'My hour has not yet come.'"[40] Implicitly, such a disengagement from his earthly mother's mundane concerns illustrates that his actions will be a response to his heavenly Father's sovereignty over him and not the result of any human familial agency.[41]

Increasing the disengagement involved with the question, "τί ἐμοὶ καὶ σοί;", is Jesus' use of the vocative "γύναι" for his mother. R. Brown points out that, whereas this address is a polite way of addressing a woman, it is a peculiar way for a son to address his mother.[42] Although many scholars perceive the address as establishing a connection between the mother of Jesus and Eve,[43] others interpret the address as implying that physical motherhood has no special emphasis for Jesus.[44] From this

[38]Maynard perceives the author of the Fourth Gospel to be redacting his source in order to have Jesus (instead of the demons) assert his divine nature within the context of his first miracle. According to R. Collins, Augustine, who is defending Jesus' human nature against the Manichaeans, likewise saw Jesus' response as an affirmation of his divinity. Augustine's interpretation of the passage is that it is the equivalent of, "It is not what you have generated that is the source of the miracle, for you have not generated my divinity." Maynard, 584–6. R. Collins, "Mary in the Fourth Gospel, 105.

[39]Olsson, 38–9.

[40] Talbert, 85.

[41]Cf. Brown, *The Gospel According to John,* 1:109; R. Collins, "Mary in the Fourth Gospel," 126 n. 139; Giblin, 197–211.

[42]Brown, *The Gospel According to John,* 1:99. Cf. Elisabeth Schüssler Fiorenza, *In Memory of Her: A Feminist Theological Reconstruction of Christian Origins* (New York: Crossroad, 1983) 326; R. Collins, "Mary in the Fourth Gospel," 102–6, 138.

[43]Cf. chapter 2, p. 24. Cf. Brown, "Roles of Women in the Fourth Gospel," Appendix II, *The Community of the Beloved Disciple* (New York: Paulist, 1979) 194; Brown, *The Gospel According to John,* 1:108–9; R. Collins, "The Mother of Jesus in the Gospel of John," 187–9.

[44]Brown. *The Gospel According to John,* 1:102, 109. Scott, 180. R. Collins, "Mary in the Fourth Gospel," 129. Schüssler Fiorenza accepts this interpretation, but also maintains that the address has the additional purpose of placing the mother of Jesus at the same level as the Samaritan woman (4:21) and Mary of Magdala (20:13), thus depicting her as an apostolic witness and exemplary disciple. Buby affirms that the use of the address "woman" for the mother of Jesus and other women in the Gospel

perspective the implied author can be viewed as suppressing any earthly maternal claim on Jesus in favor of a heavenly paternal one. Jesus' next statement to his mother seems to support this interpretation.

The apparent reason for Jesus' response to his mother is found in the third statement, "οὔπω ἥκει ἡ ὥρα μου."[45] Most authors assert that, even in the wedding scene at Cana, Jesus' reference to his "hour" must be understood in its technical theological sense as standing for his suffering, death, and resurrection.[46] Although I would agree with this, I must also affirm that this is the first time Jesus refers to his hour. The reader is not yet aware of the deeper significance that later passages will give to this term. The reader only progressively becomes aware of the technical theological significance that Jesus attributes to this word when he speaks from an "above" point of view, as I shall illustrate below.[47] Thus, Jesus' use of the phrase "my hour has not yet come" might refer to the sovereignty of Jesus' heavenly Father with regard to his mission in life over the wishes of Jesus' human mother, but this theological meaning for his words will not be perceived by the reader until later. At this point in the text, the reader would have searched for an "earthly" meaning to Jesus' words that would have made sense given the circumstances in which they were said, as I shall explain below.

By comparing the narrator's comments about the mother of Jesus and the actions of the mother of Jesus with Jesus' comments to his mother and his actions, one could argue that the implied author both entices the reader to interpret the pericope within the context of the "mother of an important son" type scene and eliminates any real influence this mother might have on Jesus. Aspects that would have enticed the reader to interpret the pericope within the context of the "mother of an important son" type scene include

---

could be viewed as attesting to the fact that Jesus attaches no special importance to the physical motherhood of Mary. He dismisses this interpretation, however, because the narrator refers to her as "the mother of Jesus" or "his (Jesus') mother" four times in the pericope. Buby turns to the scene at the foot of the cross for a fuller understanding of the role as mother at Cana. Schüssler Fiorenza, *In Memory of Her,* 327. Buby, 99.

[45]R. Collins notes that there is a debate regarding whether this phrase ought to be understood as a declarative statement or question that is positive in meaning (Hasn't my hour come?). He states that, although the majority of authors interpret the sentence as a declarative statement, Severin Grill argues on the basis of Syrian manuscripts for its being a question. R. Collins, "Mary in the Fourth Gospel," 119–20.

[46]Ibid., 120–1.

[47]A similar progressive awareness on the part of the implied reader has been suggested by Giblin for other literary motifs, themes, or literary devices. Giblin, 202 n. 20, 211.

1) the narrator's reference to the female character as "the mother of Jesus" after having stated the importance of Jesus in helping people become children of God—children of Abraham;

2) the mother's implied request that places Jesus in the role of a bridegroom and instigates Jesus' beginning his work of giving people the power to become children of God.

Those aspects that would have eliminated for the reader the possibility of Jesus' earthly mother having any real influence over her important son include

1) Jesus' use of a semiticism that connotes a sense of disengagement with his mother;
2) Jesus' addressing his mother as "woman;"
3) Jesus' statement that his hour had not yet come;
4) Jesus' fulfilling his mother's request in such a way as to show that he was responsive to the desires of his heavenly Father who was Bridegroom to Israel and who, in the messianic age would provide blessings in abundance.

Although the mother of Jesus acts at a strategic point in the text to move the plot forward, there is a certain flatness to her character, which is also prevalent in the "mother" characters of the Hebrew Bible. The flatness in her characterization is signaled by the narrator referring to her only in relation to Jesus and not by name.[48] R. Collins inadvertently gives evidence to the patriarchal nature of the epithet "mother of Jesus" when he states, "this epithet is a more honorable title than her own name. Even among Arabs today it is common [to] call a woman who has born a son 'the mother of (Jesus).'"[49] Such a reference to women illustrates that women were not considered important in their own right, only in so far as they were "mother of (x)." Similarly, the portrayal of the mother of Jesus

[48]Although the beloved disciple is also not referred to by name, it is evident that his anonymity is for representational purposes. He is not named so that he might represent the believing community. Although some argue that the mother of Jesus is not named for the same reason, I would argue that the primary function of the mother of Jesus in the text is not representational. Rather, the implied author is accentuating and making use of her unique relationship as mother to Jesus to further the christological portrait of Jesus as the one who fulfills the promise made to Abraham.

[49]R. Collins, "Mary in the Fourth Gospel," 100. Cf. Brown, *The Gospel According to John,* 1:98. R. Collins notes that the title is undoubtedly also consistent with the christological interest of the Fourth Gospel for the mother of Jesus appears only in relation to her Son.

as a mother who would scheme to advance her own son's standing in the community, and subsequently to heighten her own standing in the community, is also patriarchal in nature, for it further illustrates that a woman can only receive status through the actions of the men in her life.

Besides the patriarchal limitations of her character-type and the added limitations placed on her character as a result of the christology of the implied author, other patriarchal tendencies are evident in the characterization of the mother of Jesus. Such patriarchal tendencies can be found (1) within the implied request she presents her son, (2) within her response to Jesus' apparent resistance, (3) in the narrator's effort to show that she did not come alone to the wedding, and (4) in her removal from the story line at the end of the pericope.

As stated in the text, when the mother of Jesus perceives the need for wine at the wedding, she does not attempt to meet that need herself. Rather, she turns to her son to meet the need. Because she turns to her son, an ancient reader probably would have assumed that she was a widow, because otherwise she would have turned to her husband.[50] Even though the need related to food and home, which was the usual realm of women, the dependent status of the mother of Jesus would have prevented her from fulfilling the need of others herself. Thus, she would not have been able to increase her own honor or the honor of her family directly. Such a role belonged to the man of the house. In addition, when the mother of Jesus does present the need to her son, she makes an implicit, rather than an explicit, request; "They have no wine."[51] This female mode of presenting requests is also found in the message that Martha and Mary of Bethany send to Jesus regarding the illness of their brother, Lazarus. ". . . he whom you love is ill" (11:3). Because this female mode of making requests can be contrasted with the explicit request made by the royal official (4:47, 49),[52] this female mode of request may be another indication of the patriarchal culture reflected in the text.

An element of indirectness emerges also when the mother of Jesus re-asserts her motherly influence after Jesus' apparent refusal of her re-

---

[50]Talbert notes that, in the absence of a husband, a woman would depend upon the resources of her eldest son. He does not, however, explicitly state that the mother of Jesus would have been considered a widow. Cf. Talbert, 85.

[51]Giblin refers to the mother's statement as a "discreet *suggestion*" and a *suggestion* that "strongly hints" that she expects Jesus to show concern. Rudolf Schnackenburg refers to the statement of the mother of Jesus as a "silent request." Giblin, 202, 208. Rudolf Schnackenburg, *The Gospel According to St. John* (New York: Seabury, 1980) 2:323. Cf. Brown, *The Gospel According to John,* 1:98.

[52]Cf. Giblin, 202, 203, 208.

quest. Rather than address Jesus directly, she turns to address the servants. Even the words she speaks to the servants may suggest an element of patriarchy. The mother of Jesus says, "ὅ τι ἂν λέγῃ ὑμῖν, ποιήσατε," which translated literally says, "whatever he might tell you, do." Although the primary purpose of the word order of her comments may be that of refocusing attention on Jesus,[53] by placing her imperative at the end of her statement, the word order also lessens the impact of her own command to the servants. Furthermore, the use of the subjunctive λέγῃ with a relative clause produces a third class condition that implies only a probable future condition.[54] Although some scholars have emphasized the fact that her words disclose an expectation of a positive response,[55] one could also argue that, technically, her response allows Jesus the freedom to act or not act.[56] This possibility exemplifies that her authority as mother of an adult male child is more limited than would be a father's authority within the patriarchal family system of that day.[57] Whereas all of these elements of the text reflect the implied author's christology, they also expose the implied author's patriarchal and androcentric ideology. The mother's response to her son's apparent refusal is an indirect response that places the emphasis on her male son, diminishes the impact of her command to the servants, and illuminates her limited control over her adult male child.

Another aspect of androcentric/patriarchal ideology can be found in the narrator's reference to the presence of the brothers (ἀδελφοί) of Jesus at the end of the pericope. The text states, "After this he went down to Capernaum with his mother, his brothers (ἀδελφοί), and his disciples; and they remained there a few days" (2:12). Such a belated reference to the presence of the brothers of Jesus has allowed the implied author to focus

---

[53]Olsson, 46–7. Giblin, 202.

[54]On third class conditionals, see James Brooks and Carlton Winbery, *Syntax of the New Testament Greek* (Lanham, Md.: University Press of America, 1979) 121.

[55]Brown, *The Gospel According to John,* 100 n. 5.

[56]Gail O'Day and P. Gätcher note the element of freedom that the words of Jesus' mother allow Jesus. Other authors, however, emphasize an expectation of a positive response that is apparent both in her words and in the manner in which Jesus responds to her. According to R. Brown, the Greek does not really justify such a reading. Gail O'Day, "John," *The Women's Bible Commentary,* ed. Carol A. Newsom and Sharon H. Ringe (Louisville: Westminster/John Knox, 1992) 295. Cf. Brown, *The Gospel According to John,* 1:100.

[57]For a discussion of the authority that a father has over an adult son verses the respect given to the mother by an adult son within the patriarchal honor/shame code of one modern mediterranean community, see J. K. Campbell, "The Family: A System of Roles," *Honour, Family and Patronage: A Study of Institutions and Moral Values in a Greek Mountain Community* (Oxford: Clarendon, 1964) 154–72.

on the relationship between the mother and her important son (Jesus) during the scene itself, while it also communicates that Jesus' widowed mother was not at the wedding alone. The patriarchal attitude that this expresses is the notion that a widowed mother of a living son needs to be accompanied by relatives, preferably sons.[58]

A final patriarchal/androcentric element in the characterization of the mother of Jesus must be argued from the perspective of absence. Like the "mothers of important sons" in the Hebrew Bible, the mother of Jesus in the wedding scene at Cana is moved offstage after she has fulfilled her purpose in the life of her son. She will not be mentioned again until the implied author needs her to fulfill an additional patriarchal function in the crucifixion scene.

An Affirmation of the Female Mode of Relating

Although Jesus seems to reject his mother's rationale for providing assistance to others, receiving honor in the eyes of humans, it must be noted that the persistence of the mother of Jesus is portrayed as being effective. Such persistence may be seen as a character-trait of "mothers of important sons." Indeed, it results in Jesus' revealing the glory he received from his Father (cf. 1:14, 8:50-54), which in turn leads his disciples to believe in him.[59] Nevertheless, as will be shown with other female characters (the Samaritan woman, Martha of Bethany and Mary of Magdala), the persistence of these women and their willingness to remain in dialogue with Jesus result in Jesus' revealing himself to them or to others around them. This persistence on the part of the women seems to be in direct contrast with the portrayal of many of Jesus' male disciples. The male disciples are

[58]As will be shown in Chapter 5, the crucifixion scene supports this ideology because the mother of Jesus is accompanied there by her sister and is later placed into the care of the beloved disciple (19:25-27). According to the honor-shame code of the New Testament world as put forth by Malina, however, the mother of Jesus, as a widow, should have had an element of autonomy and should have been able to function more aggressively (cf. Malina, "Honor and Shame: Pivotal Values of the First-Century Mediterranean World," *The New Testament World,* 44). The implied author of the Fourth Gospel, however, portrays this widow as one who needs to be accompanied by relatives and ideally be under the protection of a son or sons.

[59]Jane Kopas notes that Jesus and his mother apparently talk past each other in the text and yet the story comes to a successful conclusion. Kopas maintains that this illustrates that a successful relationship with anyone, including God, depends upon the willingness and ability of the participants to hear more than what is spoken. Jane Kopas, "Jesus and Women: John's Gospel," *Theology Today* 41 (1984) 202.

depicted as being passively present (2:2-12),[60] as failing in persistence (e.g., they leave the tomb upon finding it empty [20:10]), and as failing to speak their mind to Jesus (4:27, 33; 6:60-61; 16:17-20).[61] This hesitancy to speak up to Jesus and be persistent may be connected to the typical male concern for honor, which is portrayed as being detrimental to belief in Jesus.[62] Where women are concerned with earthly honor (e.g., the desires of the mother of Jesus at Cana), Jesus also resists. Perhaps because women did not have much earthly honor to lose, the implied author could portray them as being able to risk being active, persistent, and vocal in their relationships with Jesus. These are attributes that the Gospel supports (cf. 15:15; 16:23). Thus, this story of the mother of Jesus at Cana may be the first story in a long line of stories that entices the reader to appropriate this aspect of the female mode of relating to Jesus.[63]

The Ambiguous Belief Status of the Mother of Jesus

At the end of the pericope—after Jesus has turned the water into wine—the reader is left to wonder about the belief status of the mother of Jesus and his ἀδελφοί. The reader is told that the disciples of Jesus saw his glory and believed in him (2:11), but nothing is said about the belief of the mother of Jesus or his ἀδελφοί. In 2:12 the reader is told that when Jesus left Cana for Capernaum after the wedding, he did so in the company of his mother, his brothers, and his disciples. Some scholars read into this statement of accompaniment an affirmation that the mother of Jesus was firmly situated as a disciple by being with the community of disciples.[64] If this is so, then the same must be said of the ἀδελφοί of Jesus at this point in the Gospel. It is my contention, however, that the implied author purposely leaves the reader to wonder about the belief status of the mother of Jesus and his ἀδελφοί. The quandary regarding the belief status of Jesus' ἀδελφοί will be clarified when the reader is informed of the lack of belief on the part of Jesus' ἀδελφοί in 7:5. The belief status of the

[60]Cf. Scott, 177, 182.

[61]Cf. Ibid., 175.

[62]Cf. The characterization of Nicodemus throughout the Fourth Gospel (3:1-21; 7:50-51; 19:38-39) and Jesus' comments in 5:44.

[63]The male appropriation of female behavior is found elsewhere in the Fourth Gospel (e.g., a male bringing forth children [1:12; 3:6]; a male body being a source of nourishment for others [6:35-59]; men experiencing the pain like that of childbirth [16:21]; and the image of a man bringing forth the children of God through an unnatural birth from his side [19:34]).

[64]Marianne Seckel, "La Mère de Jésus dans le 4ᶜ Évangile: de la Lignée des Femmes-Disciples?" *Foi et Vie* 88 (1989) 39.

mother of Jesus, however, will not be settled until the crucifixion scene (19:25-27), when Jesus gives her a new son who does believe in him—the beloved disciple.

Summary

The implied author of the Fourth Gospel characterizes the mother of Jesus at Cana along the lines of "the mother of an important son" character-type from the Hebrew Bible. As such, she is assertive and her words and actions precipitate her son's fulfilling his destiny with regard to the promise God made to Abraham. Jesus meets his destiny by eventually responding to his mother's insistence that he do something about the lack of wine. The manner in which he provides the wine (i.e., providing quality wine in abundance by changing the water from purification jars into wine) would have been perceived by a first-century reader familiar with the Hebrew Bible as a sign that Jesus was accepting the role of messianic bridegroom, the one who would provide blessings in abundance. In this way, Jesus is portrayed as the representative of his heavenly Father, the bridegroom of Israel.

Although the implied author constructs the character of the mother of Jesus along the lines of a "mother of an important son," a first-century reader would have perceived the mother of Jesus as misunderstanding her son's importance. She approaches the need for wine as a means for her son to heighten his honor, and thus her honor (a "below" point of view). When Jesus responds with the words, "Woman, what concern is that to you and me? My hour has not yet come" (2:4), a first time reader would not have understood that Jesus was raising the discussion to a higher level. Such a reader would have perceived the mother of Jesus as thinking Jesus' words meant, "Woman, what concern is that to you and me? It's not my wedding." Jesus' response would thus have been perceived as a rejection of the notion that he increase his earthly honor by providing wine for the bridegroom. Thus, a first-century reader, who was reading the Gospel for the first time, would have initially perceived the mother of Jesus as a non-believer who is simply not aware of her son's importance.

The character-type of the "mother of an important son" from the Hebrew Bible is patriarchal because the mother is only important to the extent that she furthers the role of her son. In the wedding scene at Cana, the implied author of the Fourth Gospel took an already patriarchal character-type and made it more patriarchal to fit the demands of the Father/Son christology of the Fourth Gospel. Because Jesus in the Fourth Gospel can only be responsive to his heavenly Father's desires, the mother of Jesus is denied the kind of influence that a "mother of an important son" character-type conventionally had over her son in the Hebrew Bible. Jesus' words to his mother in 2:4 distances him from his mother and makes it obvious that, what he later does, he does not do because his earthly mother asked him to do it, but because it fits his Father's plan.

After Jesus changes the water into wine, the pericope closes in such a way that a reader is left wondering about the belief status of both the mother of Jesus and Jesus' ἀδελφοί. This scenario keeps the reader involved and prepares the reader for the pericopae about the unbelief of Jesus' ἀδελφοί (7:1-9) and the mother of Jesus receiving a new son when Jesus truly fulfills his role as the messianic bridegroom at the moment of his "hour" (19:25-27).

As I shall explain in the next chapter, this characterization of Jesus as the messianic bridegroom, begun in the story of the wedding at Cana, is first implicitly reinforced by Jesus' words to Nicodemus about the need to be born "from above" (3:3-21), then explicitly reinforced by the words of John the Baptist to his disciples (3:29-36), and finally confirmed by the encounter that Jesus has with the Samaritan woman at the well. Subsequent chapters will then explain how this portrayal of Jesus as the messianic bridegroom is then continued through Jesus' encounter with other women in the Gospel.

3

The Samaritan Woman

Introduction

Prior to the second wave of feminist biblical hermeneutics in the United States, most scholars who dealt with the Samaritan woman tended to focus on her sinful and deceptive nature.[1] Since the second wave of feminist biblical hermeneutics, however, many scholars have identified the Samaritan woman as a disciple. They have come to this conclusion on the basis of one or more of the following reasons:

1) She is brought to belief by Jesus' knowledge of her (4:18, 29), just as Nathanael was (1:46-49).[2]
2) She enters into a theological discussion with Jesus.[3]
3) The disciples wonder what Jesus *seeks* (ζητεῖς) (4:27), and the text states that God *seeks* (ζητεῖ) people who worship in spirit and in truth (4:23).[4]

---

[1] Raymond Brown, *The Gospel According to John,* The Anchor Bible (New York: Doubleday, 1966, 1970) 1:177. M.-J. Lagrange, *Évangile selon saint Jean* (Paris: Gabalda, 1948) 110–1. J. H. Bernard, *A Critical and Exegetical Commentary on the Gospel According to St. John* (New York: Charles Scribner's Sons, 1929) 1:143–5.

[2] Elisabeth Schüssler Fiorenza, *In Memory of Her: A Feminist Theological Reconstruction of Christian Origins* (New York: Crossroad, 1983) 327–8. Raymond Collins, "The Representatives Figures in the Fourth Gospel," *Downside Review* 94 (1976) 38.

[3] Sandra Schneiders, "A Case Study: A Feminist Interpretation of John 4:1-42," *The Revelatory Text: Interpreting the New Testament as Sacred Scripture* (San Francisco: Harper, 1991) 188–9.

[4] Ibid., 192. Jesus does say that the Father *seeks* (ζητεῖ) those who will worship in spirit and truth (4:23). However, when the disciples see Jesus with the woman, the

45

4) She is invited to believe and is given a mission of bringing others to faith.[5]

5) She, like the disciples in the Synoptic gospels, leaves all (her jar) to take up her role as witness.[6]

6) She calls others to Jesus ("Come and see" [δεῦτε ἴδετε] [4:29]) in the same manner as Jesus invites John's disciples (ἔρχεσθε καὶ ὄψεσθε) (1:39) and Philip calls Nathanael (ἔρχουκαί ἴδε) (1:46).[7]

7) She brings others to believe through her word (λόγος/ λαλιά) (4:39, 42), and Jesus in his priestly prayer prays for those who will believe because of the disciples' word (λόγος) (17:20).[8]

8) She is viewed by some scholars as one of the sowers into whose work the disciples are entering (4:38).[9]

On the basis of this interpretation of the Samaritan woman's characterization, some scholars hypothesize that the Johannine community accepted

---

disciples wonder to themselves *what* (τί) (neuter) Jesus *seeks* (ζητεῖς) (4:27), not *whom* Jesus seeks. Thus, it seems that the implied author is not directly equating the Samaritan woman with that which the Father seeks. Rather, the implied author seems to equate the Samaritan woman with the means by which Jesus will be able to find those who worship in spirit and truth.

[5]Collins, "The Representative Figures in the Fourth Gospel," 38. Cf. Adele Reinhartz, "The Gospel of John," *Searching the Scriptures: A Feminist Commentary,* ed. Elisabeth Schüssler Fiorenza (New York: Crossroad, 1994) 573.

[6]Sandra Schneiders, "Women in the Fourth Gospel and the Role of Women in the Contemporary Church," *Biblical Theology Bulletin* 12 (1982) 40. Martin Scott, *Sophia and the Johannine Jesus* (Sheffield: JSOT, 1992) 192.

[7]R. Alan Culpepper, *Anatomy of the Fourth Gospel: A Study of Literary Design* (Philadelphia: Fortress, 1983) 137. Schüssler Fiorenza, *In Memory of Her,* 327. Gail O'Day, "John," *The Women's Bible Commentary,* ed. Carol Newsom and Sharon Ringe (Louisville: Westminster/John Knox, 1992) 296. Mark Stibbe, *John* (Sheffield: JSOT, 1993) 67. Although there is a correlation here, the Samaritan woman's "Come, see" is worded differently in the Greek, which may distinguish and diminish her "Come, see" in relation to those that went before it, as will be explained later.

[8]Raymond Brown, *The Community of the Beloved Disciple* (New York: Paulist, 1979) 187. Culpepper, *Anatomy,* 137. Schüssler Fiorenza, *In Memory of Her,* 328. Cf. O'Day, "John," 296; Schneiders, "Women in the Fourth Gospel," 40; Stibbe, 67; Scott, 193–4. The use of "λαλία" rather than "λόγος" by the townspeople may be another means of diminishing the Samaritan woman's witness in the eyes of the implied reader, as will be explained later in the chapter.

[9]Brown, *The Community of the Beloved Disciple,* 187–8. Culpepper, *Anatomy,* 137. Schüssler Fiorenza, *In Memory of Her,* 327. Cf. Schneiders, *The Revelatory Text,* 192; H. Boers, *Neither on this Mountain Nor in Jerusalem: A Study of John 4* (Atlanta: Scholars Press, 1988) 184–5.

women as equals,[10] and a few scholars go so far as to postulate that the Samaritan people may actually have been evangelized by a woman.[11]

Although this interpretation of the Samaritan woman as a disciple is certainly a valid modern interpretation, my focus will be on how a first-century reader of the Fourth Gospel would have interpreted the Samaritan woman. I shall argue, on the basis of a historical-literary approach, that a modern reader's perception of the Samaritan woman as a disciple is the result of the implied author's portrayal of the Samaritan woman as a fictive betrothed and bride of the messianic bridegroom on behalf of the Samaritan people, as a symbolic wife to Jesus who produces abundant offspring after Jesus plants the seeds of faith in her. In such a portrayal, the Samaritan woman represents the whole Samaritan people with whom Jesus desires to establish heavenly familial ties. After having established this role for the Samaritan woman, I shall present a feminist critique of her characterization.

Textual Preparations for a Symbolic Betrothal/Marriage

This characterization of the Samaritan woman as betrothed and bride of the messianic bridegroom on behalf of the Samaritan people builds on the characterization of Jesus as the messianic bridegroom at Cana (2:1-12), on Jesus' conversation with Nicodemus regarding the need to be born "from above" (3:1-21), and on John the Baptist's words to his disciples regarding the bridegroom and the one being sent from above (3:29-32). In the first instance, the mother of Jesus, as a "mother of an important son," tries to further her son's status by asking Jesus to take care of the need for wine, a responsibility of the bridegroom. Even though Jesus informs his mother that his "hour" (i.e., the appropriate time for *his* wedding) had not yet arrived, the manner in which he eventually provides the wine (changing the water in the purification jars into quality wine in abundance) would have led a first-century reader to recognize Jesus as the messianic

[10]Brown, *The Community of the Beloved Disciple*, 185 n. 328, 188–9, 197–8. Schneiders, "Women in the Fourth Gospel," 39–40, 44. David Rensberger, *Johannine Faith and Liberating Community* (Philadelphia: Westminster, 1988) 130, 148–9. Cf. Ernst Käsemann, *The Testament of Jesus: A Study of the Gospel of John in the Light of Chapter 17* (Philadelphia: Fortress, 1968) 29, 31.

[11]Rudolf Bultmann, *The Gospel of John* (Philadelphia: Westminster, 1971) 175–6. Schüssler Fiorenza, *In Memory of Her,* 327. Turid Karlsen Seim notes that this woman was honored by some church fathers as an apostle to Samaria. Turid Karlsen Seim, "Roles of Women in the Gospel of John," *Aspects on the Johannine Literature,* ed. Lars Hartman & Birger Olsson (Sweden: Alqvist & Wiksell International, 1987) 67.

bridegroom who can provide abundant messianic blessings, symbolized by the abundant wine (cf. Jer 49:11-12; Joel 4:18; Cant 1:2, 4).[12]

In the second instance, Jesus' role as the messianic bridegroom is implicitly reinforced by Jesus' dialogue with Nicodemus regarding the necessity of being born "from above." In this pericope, Jesus tells Nicodemus that a person must be born ἄνωθεν ("anew" or "from above") in order to see the reign of God (3:3). Interpreting Jesus' statement from a "below" perspective and thinking Jesus means born "anew," Nicodemus asks, "Can one enter a second time into the mother's womb and be born" (3:4). Jesus then lets Nicodemus know that he had moved the discussion to a "higher" level when he states that no one can enter into the reign of God without being born of water and the Spirit (3:5), for "What is born of flesh is flesh and what is born of the Spirit is spirit" (3:6). In this pericope, life is not the result of physical birth from a woman's womb. Rather, eternal life is the result of being born "from above" (3:11-21). My supposition is that a first-century reader would then have equated this "eternal life from above" with Jesus' giving people the power to be children of God (1:12). Just as the serpent that Moses lifted up in the wilderness was able to give life, so Jesus, as Son of Man, will give those who believe in him eternal life when he is "lifted up" above the earth (3:13-15, cf. 1:12, 51). As the reader will later recognize, Jesus is "lifted up above the earth" when he embraces his hour (the moment of his messianic wedding) at the cross. Thus, as messianic bridegroom, as well as Son of Man, Jesus will enable those who believe in him to become children of God.

In the third instance, this implicit connection between Jesus, the messianic bridegroom (2:1-11), and life "from above" (3:1-21) is made explicit in the words of John the Baptist to his disciples. John the Baptist had earlier identified Jesus as the Lamb of God who takes away the sins of the world (1:29). Now he identifies Jesus first as the bridegroom,

"the one who has the bride is the bridegroom"
(ὁ ἔχων τὴν νύμφην νυμφίος) (3:29)[13]

---

[12]Paul Duke, Jeffrey Staley and Stibbe acknowledge that the wedding at Cana places Jesus in the role of the bridegroom. Jerome Neyrey notes the fact that Jesus attended the marriage feast at Cana and provided his own superb wine, but he falls short of specifically stating that this places him in the role of the bridegroom. Paul Duke, *Irony in the Fourth Gospel* (Atlanta: John Knox, 1985) 101. Jeffrey Staley, *The Print's First Kiss: A Rhetorical Investigation of the Implied Reader in the Fourth Gospel* (Atlanta: Scholars Press, 1985) 101 n. 35. Stibbe, 46–7. Jerome Neyrey, "Jacob Traditions and the Interpretation of John 4:10-26," *Catholic Biblical Quarterly* 41 (1979) 426.

[13]Kevin Quast notes that the bridegroom language here invokes associations with

and then as the one coming "from above."

> "The one who comes from above is above all; the one who is of the earth belongs to the earth and speaks of earthly things. The one who comes from heaven is above all." (3:31)[14]

Thus, John the Baptist's words connect "the bridegroom" and the one "coming from above" with "eternal life from above," mentioned in Jesus' dialogue with Nicodemus. If Calum Carmichael is correct in his perception of a reference to prospective offspring in John the Baptist's statement that Jesus (the bridegroom) must increase (4:30),[15] then this would be another connection between the bridegroom and Nicodemus' statement about being born "from above."

Together these pericopae, the Wedding at Cana (2:1-12), the dialogue with Nicodemus about being born "from above" (3:1-21), and the words of John the Baptist to his disciples about the bridegroom from above (3:29-32), identify Jesus as the messianic bridegroom who comes "from above" and enables people to be born "from above." As Mark Stibbe notes, these pericopae lead the reader to realize that the eschatological marriage between YHWH and humanity takes place in Jesus.[16] Stibbe also indicates that the reader is encouraged to ask, "If Jesus is the messianic bridegroom, who is the bride?" This prepares the reader for a female character who will fulfill this symbolic role.[17]

Jesus' Symbolic Betrothal to the Samaritan Woman

Just as the characterization of the mother of Jesus was constructed from a character-type from the Hebrew Bible, many scripture scholars

---

the Old Testament picture of Israel as the bride of God. Kevin Quast, *Reading the Gospel of John: An Introduction* (New York: Paulist, 1991) 27.

[14]Scholars question whether 3:31-36 is a continuation of the words of John the Baptist to his disciples, an intrusion by the narrator, or Jesus' own words. Cf. Brown, *The Gospel According to John,* 1:159–60.

[15]Calum Carmichael, "Marriage and the Samaritan Woman," *New Testament Studies* 26 (1980) 333.

[16]Stibbe comments refer only to the wedding at Cana and the words of John the Baptist, and not the messianic bridegroom overtones in the Nicodemus passage. Cf. Stibbe, 44–70.

[17]Ibid., 61. Duke, Staley, Schneiders, Neyrey, and Carmichael also note that John the Baptist's designation of Jesus as the bridegroom prepares the reader for the story of the Samaritan woman at the well. Duke, 101. Staley, *The Print's First Kiss* 101 n. 35. Schneiders, *The Revelatory Text,* 189. Neyrey, "Jacob Traditions and the Interpretation of John 4:10-26," 426. Carmichael, 335.

suggest that the story of the Samaritan woman at the well was constructed along the lines of a betrothal type-scene from the Hebrew Bible.[18] According to Robert Alter, a betrothal type-scene in the Hebrew Bible occurs when the hero (the future bridegroom) or his surrogate journeys to a foreign land, encounters a girl at a well, and one of them draws water from the well. Usually the girl then rushes home to inform her family of the stranger's arrival, and a betrothal is sealed after the future bridegroom has shared a meal with her family. Alter identifies the meeting of Isaac's surrogate and Rebekah at a well (Gen 24:10-61) and the meeting of Jacob and Rachel at a well (Gen 29:1-10) as the most famous examples of this betrothal type-scene in the Hebrew Bible. Alter explains, however, that authors often communicate significant aspects of a hero's character by varying this type-scene or even suppressing it.[19]

The story of the Samaritan woman at the well contains the initial elements of a betrothal type-scene. Jesus travels to a foreign land, meets a woman at a well who has come to "draw water," asks for a drink, and later assures the woman that, if she would ask him, he could provide her with "living water." Supporting the assumption that a betrothal type-scene is implied is the astonishment (ἐθαύμαζον) of the disciples at seeing Jesus speaking with a "woman" (4:27) and their subsequent urging (ἠρώτων)[20] Jesus to eat (ραββί, φάγε) (4:31). Elsewhere in the Fourth Gospel the dis-

---

[18]Although the term betrothal type-scene may not be used by all the authors that follow, the concept of the scene as a betrothal is recognized by such authors as: Culpepper, *Anatomy,* 136–7; Duke, 101; Staley, *The Print's First Kiss,* 98–103; N. R. Bonneau, "The Woman at the Well, John 4 and Gen 24," *Bible Today* 67 (1973) 1252–9; Neyrey, "Jacob Traditions and the Interpretation of John 4:10-26," 425–6; J. Duncan Derrett, "The Samaritan Woman's Pitcher," *Downside Review* 102 (1984) 253; J. Duncan Derrett, "The Samaritan Woman's Purity (John 4:4-52)," *Evangelical Quarterly* 60 (1988) 292; J. Bligh, "Jesus in Samaria," *Heythrop Journal* 3 (1962) 332; J. E. Botha, "Reader 'Entrapment' as Literary Device in John 4:1-42," *Neotestamentica* 24 (1990) 40–5; P. J. Cahill, "Narrative Art in John IV," *Religious Studies Bulletin* 2 (1982) 41–55; Lyle Eslinger, "The Wooing of the Woman at the Well: Jesus the Reader and Reader-Response Criticism," *The Gospel of John as Literature: An Anthology of 20th Century Perspectives,* ed. Mark Stibbe (Leiden: E. J. Brill, 1993) 165–82; Carmichael, 335–6; Stibbe, 68; Schneiders, *The Revelatory Text,* 187. Cf. Quast, 29; Scott, 185–6.

[19]Robert Alter, *The Art of Biblical Narrative* (New York: Basic Books, 1981) 51–62. Cf. Robert C. Culley, *Studies in the Structure of Hebrew Narrative* (Philadelphia: Fortress, 1976) 41–3.

[20]ἐρωτάω can convey a sense of urgent request or begging. Cf. Henry G. Liddell and Robert Scott, *An Intermediate Greek-English Lexicon,* 7th ed. (Oxford: Oxford University Press, 1989) 317.

ciples are not astonished when they see Jesus talking with a woman (cf. 11:15, 17-27).[21] This discrepancy supports the argument that the reader would have interpreted the astonishment of the disciples on the basis of
. . .

Male Foreigner + Woman + Well = Betrothal.

Likewise, because betrothals in such scenes were usually completed after a meal with the woman's family, the reader may have interpreted the disciples' efforts to get Jesus to eat something as an attempt to circumvent such a betrothal.

Beyond the presence of the initial elements of the betrothal type-scene and the reactions of the disciples, the reader encounters what may be described as unconventional and ironic variations on the literary convention.[22] The drawing of water and the betrothal after a meal with the family are never narrated; the woman's marital status comes into question (4:16-18); the woman tells not her immediate family but the townspeople of the stranger's presence (4:28-30); and it is the townspeople then who invite Jesus to stay (4:39-42). These variations, however, define the future career of Jesus and provide the hermeneutical key to the female character.[23]

The fact that physical water is not drawn and a betrothal after a meal is not narrated in the pericope has led some scholars to conclude that a betrothal has not taken place.[24] Nevertheless, the Samaritan woman did, in fact,

[21]No such shock is mentioned on the part of the disciples when they perceive Jesus speaking with Martha. The text states that Martha went and met him (Jesus) (11:20). Although the text does not mention the presence of the disciple at the discussion between Jesus and Martha, the presence of the disciples can be inferred from 11:15-16.

[22]Culpepper, *Anatomy,* 136. Staley identifies this unconventional use of the type-scene as a parody that utilizes reader-victimizing irony. Botha prefers the term "reader entrapment" for the unconventional use of the type-scene. Duke identifies the irony in the type-scene as irony of identity. Staley, *The Print's First Kiss,* 98. Botha, "Reader 'Entrapment,'" 38–9. Duke, 101–3.

[23]In her analysis of betrothal type-scenes of the Hebrew Bible, Esther Fuchs states that it is the female characters who provide the hermeneutical key. Esther Fuchs, "Structure and Patriarchal Functions in the Biblical Betrothal Type-scene: Some Preliminary Notes," *Journal of Feminist Studies in Religion* 3 (1987) 7–8.

[24]Cf. Gail O'Day, *Revelation in the Fourth Gospel: Narrative Mode and Theological Claim* (Philadelphia: Fortress, 1986) 131–2 n. 49; Birger Olsson, *Structure and Meaning in the Fourth Gospel: A Text-Linguistic Analysis of John 2:1-11 and 4:1-42* (Lund: CWK Gleerup, 1974) 150–1, 133–7 169–72, 172 n. 58; Dorothy Lee, *The Symbolic Narratives of the Fourth Gospel: The Interplay of Form and Meaning* (Sheffield: JSOT, 1994) 67; Brown, *The Gospel According to John,* 1:170–1, 176; Teresa Okure,

ask for the "living water (4:15) and did come to a limited understanding of who Jesus was (4:19, 29), even though she did not fully understand that for which she was asking and who it was that she was asking. These developments, in addition to the fact that the woman left the well without her water jar, may have communicated to a first-century reader that she had, in fact, received the "living water" that Jesus said he could provide (4:10).[25] Similarly, because Jesus' need for food was satisfied by his encounter with the Samaritan woman (4:31-39), just as her need for water seems to have been satisfied by her encounter with Jesus, a first-century reader may have assumed that a metaphorical marriage had occurred and that this metaphorical marriage would eventually lead to symbolic offspring.[26] Furthermore, I hope to show that the Gospel as a whole portrays the journey of Jesus toward his messianic marriage and that the missing meal with the family is supplied later in the meal that Jesus had with Lazarus, Mary, and Martha.

Jesus' Symbolic Marriage to the Samaritan Woman

The "Hour Now Is"

One literary allusion to a symbolic marriage between Jesus and the Samaritan woman may be found in Jesus' comment about the coming of an "hour" of true worship. Jesus first says to the woman,

> "Believe me, woman, that an *hour* is coming when. . . ."
> (ἔρχεται ὥρα ὅτε) (4:21).

Later, however, he states,

> "but an *hour* is coming, *and now is,* when. . . ."
> (ἀλλὰ ἔρχεται ὥρα καὶ νῦν ἐστιν ὅτε) (4:23)

The Johannine Approach to Mission: A Contextual Study of John 4:1-42 (Tübingen: Mohr, 1988) 89–90.

[25]J. E. Botha, *Jesus and the Samaritan Woman: A Speech Act Reading of John 4:1-42* (Leiden: E. J. Brill, 1991) 163. Boers, *Neither on this Mountain nor in Jerusalem,* 182–3. Brown, *The Gospel According to John,* 1:173. For other interpretations of the leaving of the water jar, see O'Day, *Revelation in the Fourth Gospel,* 75; Stibbe, 67.

[26]Carmichael recognizes the spiritual marriage between Jesus and the Samaritan woman as a possible exegesis. Staley acknowledges that the partaking of "invisible" water and food establishes a spiritual relationship that will generate spiritual offspring. Carmichael, 333–5, 341. Staley, *The Print's First Kiss,* 102.

In the previous chapter I argued that the first-century reader would have perceived the mother of Jesus as interpreting Jesus' statement, "My hour has not yet come," as a declaration that the appropriate time for *his* wedding had not yet arrived.[27] On the basis of this interpretation of the word "hour" and the presence of a betrothal type-scene, the reader may have concluded that the "hour" of true worship was somehow connected to the "hour" of Jesus' wedding and that the appropriate time for his wedding had now arrived. In such an interpretation, Jesus' actions toward the Samaritan woman could be viewed as a foreshadowing of the "hour" when the Son of Man will be lifted up on the cross (3:14; cf. 12:23, 27, 32-34).[28]

The Consummation of Jesus' Symbolic Marriage to the Samaritan Woman

Another literary allusion to a symbolic marriage may be found in those references that imply that the symbolic marriage had been consummated. The marriage ritual, as found in the Hebrew Bible, centered on three successive incidents, the ceremonious bringing of the bride from her old house to the home of her husband, the feast, and the consummation of the marriage.[29] According to Exod 22:16-17 and Deut 22:29, however, the sexual act itself was enough to constitute a marriage and make a man responsible for paying the *mohar,* the bride-price, which would then regularize the marriage.[30] Therefore, any inference to the consummation of the marriage and/or a reference to the fruits of such a consummation may have been sufficient evidence for a first-century reader to ascertain that a symbolic marriage had occurred. If Jeremiah Jeremias and Charles Talbert are correct, the text itself may have prepared the implied reader to be ready to

[27]Cf. chapter 2, pp. 30–2.

[28]Culpepper identifies some incidents in Jesus' ministry on earth as foreshadowing his eschatological ministry as Son of Man. In these incidents, Culpepper perceives one action in narrative time being an interpretive context for another action in narrative time. I believe such an interpretive relationship also exists between Jesus' activities during his ministry and his activity on the cross. Cf. Culpepper, *Anatomy,* 107.

[29]David Mace, "Marriage Customs and Ceremonies," *Hebrew Marriage: A Sociological Study* (London: Epworth, 1953) 180. Stanley Brave, "Marriage with a History," *Marriage and the Jewish Tradition* (New York: Philosophical Library, 1951) 85, 87. Philip Goodman and Hanna Goodman, "Jewish Marriages Throughout the Ages," *The Jewish Marriage Anthology* (Philadelphia: The Jewish Publication Society of America, 1965) 73–6. Robert Bower and G. L. Knapp, "Marriage; Marry," *The International Standard Bible Encyclopedia,* gen. ed. G. W. Bromiley (Grand Rapids: Eerdmans, 1986) 3:264.

[30]Mace, 168. Goodman, 71.

perceive an act of consummation in the Fourth Gospel. Both state that the words of John the Baptist, ". . . the friend of the bridegroom, who stands and hears him, rejoices greatly at the bridegroom's voice" (3:29), refer to that function of the friend of the bridegroom whereby he stands by the door of the wedding chamber and listens for the sexual act to be completed and the virginity of the bride to be confirmed.[31]

Jesus' offer of "living water" (ὕδωρ ζῶν) to the Samaritan woman in 4:10 has been interpreted by Carmichael as just this type of a deliberate conjugal reference.[32] Such an interpretation is based on the euphemistic use of words such as "cistern," "well," "fountain," and "living water" in the Hebrew Bible and the application of such euphemistic terms in the Hebrew Bible for God's relationship with Israel. Both Carmichael and Lyle Eslinger point to a euphemistic use of these terms in the relationship between God and the people of Israel in Prov 5:15-18, Cant 4:12, and Jer 2:1-15.[33]

In Prov 5:15-18, whose larger context deals with the "loose" or "strange" woman, the author counsels,

> Drink water from your own vessels (ἀγγείων),
>> from the fountain of your own wells (ἀπὼ σῶν φρεάτων πηγῆς)
> Lest the water from your fountain (ὕδατα ἐκ τῆς σῆς πηγῆς)
>> be scattered abroad, streams of water in the streets.
> Let them be for yourself alone,
>> and not for sharing with strangers.
> Let your fountain of water (ἡ πηγή σου τοῦ ὕδατος)
>> be blessed, and rejoice in the wife of your youth.[34]

Likewise, Cant 4:12 refers to the woman as "the well (φρέαρ) of living water." This sexual imagery is then raised to a divine level when it is used for depicting God's relationship with Israel. In the book of Jeremiah, for instance, after a passage that portrays Jerusalem as the bride of God (Jer 2:2), God says,

---

[31]Jeremiah Jeremias, "νυμφη, νυμφιος," *Theological Dictionary of the New Testament,* ed. Gerhard Kittle and trans. & ed. G. Bromiley (Grand Rapids: Eerdmans, 1967) 4:1101. Charles Talbert, *Reading John: A Literary and Theological Commentary on the Fourth Gospel and the Johannine Epistles* (New York: Crossroad, 1994) 106. Cf. Mace, 181–2.

[32]Carmichael, 336.

[33]Eslinger, 168–70. Carmichael, 336, 339–40.

[34]My translation.

"They have forsaken me,
the fountain of living water (πηγὴν ὕδατος ζωῆς),
and dug out for themselves cracked reservoirs (λάκκους)
which can hold no water" (Jer 2:13).[35]

In such passages, "vessel" (ἀγγεῖον), "well" (φρέαρ) and "reservoirs" (λάκκους) always seem to connote the female element of sexual intercourse, whereas "water" (ὕδωρ) and "fountain" (ἡ πηγή) sometimes seems to connote the male element and at other times the female element.[36]

In the betrothal type-scenes of the Hebrew Bible, the "well" is identified as both a symbol of fertility and of femininity itself.[37] In John 4:1-42, Jesus is identified with the "fountain" of "living water" that "wells up to eternal life" (4:10, 14).[38] Therefore, if a first-century reader identified the Samaritan woman with any symbol in this first part of the story, the reader would have identified her as a "well" (φρέαρ) capable of receiving and containing the "living water" (ὕδωρ ζῶν) Jesus was able to provide. Although it is the satisfaction of Jesus' hunger that is emphasized in the text (4:31-38), such imagery might have led a first-century reader to conclude that, just as the Samaritan woman's need for water was met on a euphemistic and metaphorical level through her encounter with Jesus (as illustrated by her leaving the jar), so Jesus' need for a drink (4:7) was satisfied on a euphemistic and metaphorical level by his encounter with the Samaritan woman. He symbolically drank from a Samaritan "well."[39]

[35]My translation.

[36]Eslinger maintains that the words "well" or "fountain" of Prov 5:15, 18 refers to the physical features of a female, but acknowledges that the phrase "the water from your fountain" in Prov 5:16 seems to refer to male semen. Carmichael consistently connects "water" with the woman's fertility and God as the provider of this water for the woman. For him the woman's bodily responsibility in such passages is that of watering the seed. Eslinger, 169–70. Carmichael, 336, 339–40. Cf. Derrett, "The Samaritan Woman's Purity (John 4:4-52)," 295–6; W. McKane, *Proverbs* (Philadelphia: Westminster, 1970) 318–9.

[37]Fuchs, "Structure and Patriarchal Functions in the Biblical Betrothal Typescene," 7. The narrator's use of "fountain" (πηγή) rather than "well" (φρέαρ) in relation to Jacob (4:6) could be one means by which Jesus' "fountain" is contrasted with Jacob's "fountain" (cf. 4:13). The woman's consistent use of the term "well" (φρέαρ), meanwhile, should be taken literally, because she fails to understand Jesus.

[38]Cf. Staley, *The Print's First Kiss,* 100 n. 30.

[39]Schneiders maintains that Jesus' hunger *and* thirst (my emphasis) were satisfied in his encounter with the Samaritan woman, though she does not treat the symbolic significance of Jesus' thirst being satisfied. Okure, on the other hand, maintains that Jesus' thirst remained wholly unsatisfied. Schneiders, *The Revelatory Text,* 192. Okure, *The Johannine Approach to Mission,* 135.

The Offspring of the Symbolic Marriage Become Apparent

Although the Samaritan woman's acceptance of the "living water" and the satisfaction of Jesus' need for a "drink" and for "food" may only be implicit or subtle references to the consummation of a "symbolic marriage," a more obvious reference may be found in Jesus' subsequent statements about the fields being ready for the harvest (4:31-42). If the reader did interpret the "verbal intercourse" between Jesus and the Samaritan woman in a sexually symbolic and religious manner, then the reader might well have interpreted the imagery of the field in a sexually symbolic and religious manner as well. The harvest would thus represent the offspring that the Samaritan woman produced after Jesus had provided her with "living water" and had "drunk" from her "well."[40] By changing the metaphor, the implied author made the harvest the result of the seeds of faith Jesus "sowed" within her.[41]

Just as it was common in the Hebrew Bible for the male and female aspects of the sexual act to be represented by a "fountain of living water" springing up within a "well" and a man "drinking" from that "well," so too is it common in ancient cultures for a woman (or a nation characterized as female) to be symbolized as a field that a man (or God characterized as a man) plows with seed.[42] Examples of such usage may be found in Jeremiah and Hosea.

---

[40]Carmichael identifies John the Baptist's reference to joy with offspring. Lee also identifies Nicodemus' coming to Jesus when it is dark as a symbolic expression that implies that he has not yet been born into the light, but is still in the darkness of the womb. For Lee, this portrayal of Nicodemus is in contrast to the portrayal of John the Baptist, who, as a witness to the Light, functions as a midwife ushering in the new life. Carmichael, 333–4. Lee, 47, 59, 63.

[41]Cf. Carmichael, 344. Stibbe, who acknowledges the presence of a betrothal/marriage motif, also acknowledges the Samaritan woman as one who bears much fruit. He relates this to Jesus' later comments to the disciples in chapter 15 regarding their need to bear much fruit. Stibbe, however, seems to imply that the Samaritan woman is a harvester of the crop, and not the soil. Cf. Stibbe, 65, 68.

[42]In Carol Delaney's ethnographic work on Turkey, she notes that the woman is viewed as the field in which the man plants the seed. She also states that this particular way of conceptualizing the process of procreation has a long history in cultures that have been dominated by the Greco-Roman/Judeo-Christian tradition. Carol Delaney, "The Body of Knowledge," *The Seed and the Soil: Gender and Cosmology in Turkish Village Society* (Berkeley: University of California Press, 1991) 30–1. See also, Carol Delaney, "Seeds of Honor, Fields of Shame," *Honor and Shame and the Unity of the Mediterranean,* ed. David Gilmore (Washington, D.C.: American Anthropological Association, 1987) 38–9. For an example of a not so ancient culture portraying the nation as a woman that needs to be conquered by masculine power see, Annette Kolodny, *The*

Jer 3:1 specifically connects land that has been sown with an ex-wife who has been defiled through sexual contact with another man:

"If a man sends away his wife and,
after leaving him, she marries another man,
does the first husband come back to her?
Would not the land be wholly defiled" (3:1).

This image of a woman as land that a man sows is then raised to a divine level when the discussion refers to the nation of Israel and its God. In the book of Jeremiah, God tells Jeremiah to proclaim to Jerusalem,

"I remember the devotion of your youth, your love as a bride,
how you followed me in the wilderness, in a land not sown.
Israel was holy to the Lord, the first fruits of his harvest.
All who ate of it were held guilty; disaster came upon them"
(Jer 2:2-3).

This sexual allusion shows a loose connection between Jerusalem, the bride, and "a land not sown," as it equates Israel with "the first fruits of the harvest."

The book of Hosea likewise depicts God as the husband, the nation as God's wife, and Israel as the seed that God sowed in the land. After the author of Hosea characterizes the nation as an unfaithful wife (Hos 2:2), the author states that God will make her like a wilderness, a parched land, because of her harlotry (Hos 2:3). God will take "his" bride back to the desert where "she" will once again call "him" "My husband/My Baal." On that day God will "answer" and then the people will answer "Jezreel," which means "God sows" (Hos 2:14-22).[43] God then states, "and I will sow him for myself in the land" (Hos 2:23).

In all of these examples from the Hebrew Bible, the sexual act is symbolized by a man (or God portrayed as a man) sowing seed in the land. The woman or female entity (Jerusalem/the nation) is associated with or portrayed as land that is fertile and sown or arid land made to be like a desert. Israel, meanwhile, is depicted as the offspring of a divine union between God and Jerusalem/the nation that God sows in the land.

Lay of the Land: Metaphor as Experience and History in American Life and Letters (Chapel Hill, N.C.: The University of North Carolina Press, 1975).

[43]*The New Oxford Annotated Bible with the Apocrypha (New Revised Standard Version)*, ed. Bruce Metzger and Roland Murphy (New York: Oxford University Press, 1991) 1149, 1151.

For a first-century reader who was familiar with such "extratextual" material from the Hebrew Bible and who had just encountered a betrothal type-scene, the reference to the fields being ready for harvest would probably have been interpreted as an indication that the "symbolic marriage" between Jesus and the Samaritan woman was bearing fruit. In this analysis the Samaritan woman would have been identified by a first-century reader as one of the fields that Jesus had sown, one that had already produced fruit for harvest, and not as the sower of the seeds of faith in the Samaritan people, as some scholars have suggested.[44] The "others" into whose work the disciples were entering as reapers, would then be Jesus and his Father, whose sowing Jesus is in the process of completing (cf. 4:34).[45]

The Samaritan Woman as a Symbolic Representative of Her People

Besides the betrothal type-scene, Jesus' comment about "the hour now is" and the portrayal of the Samaritan woman as a "field sown with seed that produces an abundant harvest," other elements in the characterization of the Samaritan woman support her portrayal as the symbolic representative of her people who becomes the betrothed and bride of the messianic bridegroom: namely, the Samaritan woman's "we-you" mentality and her movement beyond it, her "from below" perspective and her movement beyond it, and her characterization as a woman who has had five "husbands" in the past and presently has one who is not her "husband."

The Transformation of a "We-You" Mentality

In order for the Samaritan woman to function as a symbol for her community, the implied author highlighted certain aspects of her charac-

[44]Cf. Boers, *Neither on This Mountain nor in Jerusalem*, 184–5, 190; R. H. Lightfoot, *St. John's Gospel: A Commentary*, ed. C. F. Evans (Oxford: Clarendon, 1957) 135; Bernard, 1:159; Brown, *Community of the Beloved Disciple*, 188–9; Schüssler Fiorenza, *In Memory of Her*, 327; Culpepper, *Anatomy*, 137; Quast, 37.

[45]Talbert, *Reading John*, 117. Okure, 158. For an excellent summary of the various interpretations of who the "others" may be, see Okure, *The Johannine Approach to Mission*, 157–64. See also Brown, *The Gospel According to John* 1:183–4; O'Day, *Revelation in the Fourth Gospel*, 83; Olsson, 227–8, 230; Rudolf Schnackenburg, *The Gospel According to St. John* (New York: Crossroad, 1980, 1982) 1:450; Botha, *Jesus and the Samaritan Woman*, 174–5; Boers, *Neither on this Mountain Nor in Jerusalem*, 192–3.

ter. The first is the "we-you" mentality with which she initially responds to Jesus as a Jew. In her first verbal response to Jesus, she states,

> "How is it that *you,* a Jew, ask a drink of *me,*
> a woman of Samaria?"
> (πῶς σὺ Ἰουδαῖος ὢν παρ᾽ ἐμοῦ πεῖν αἰτεῖς
> φυναικὸς Σαμαρίτιδος οὔσης;) (4:9).

Because the woman's response could have been worded in Greek without the use of the pronoun σύ, *you,* the pronoun may have been used for emphasis. This response results in emphasis being placed on the pronoun with which it is compared, ἐμοῦ, *me.* This "we-you" dichotomy supports the Jewish/Samaritan dichotomy within the statement, while it also reinforces the male/female aspect of the betrothal type-scene.

The emphatic pronoun "you" is also present in the Samaritan woman's subsequent statements to Jesus.

> "*You* are (σὺ. . .εἶ) not greater than *our* father Jacob,
> who gave us the well and who drank from it himself
> with his sons and his cattle, are you?" (4:12)[46]

> "Sir, I see that *you* are (εἶ σύ) a prophet.
> *Our* ancestors worshiped on this mountain,
> but *you* say (ὑμεῖς λέγετε) that the place
> where people must worship is in Jerusalem" (4:20).

In each of these cases, the Greek verbal ending, which includes person and number as well as tense and mode, makes the pronoun unnecessary. The Samaritan woman's consistent use of the pronoun *you,* therefore, seems to be for emphasis and results in an implied emphasis on the pronoun with which it is contrasted. This contrasting of pronouns seems to characterize the Samaritan woman as maintaining a "we-you" mentality, i.e., placing strong boundaries between herself and Jesus, Samaritans and Jews, a mentality that a first-century reader would have expected from a true Samaritan.[47]

---

[46]My translation.

[47]On the level of characters, Botha perceives the Samaritan woman as defending the status quo and protecting Jesus in 4:9. On the level of the author and reader, however, he perceives her refusal of Jesus' request in 4:9 as portraying the Samaritan woman as being a true Samaritan who clings to her beliefs and traditions. Botha, *Jesus and the Samaritan Woman,* 118–9.

At first, Jesus accepts and reinforces the boundaries drawn by the woman by responding to her "we-you" polarities with some "we-you" and "I-you" statements of his own.[48]

> "If you knew the gift of God,
> and who it is that is saying to you, 'Give me a drink,'
> *you* (σύ) would have asked *him,*
> and he would have given you living water" (4:10).

> "Everyone who drinks of *this* water will be thirsty again,
> but those who drink of the water that *I* (ἐγὼ) will give them
> will never be thirsty" (4:13-14).

Although Jesus briefly moves beyond this confrontational tone by speaking without the use of an emphatic pronoun,

> "the hour is coming when you will worship the Father
> neither on this mountain nor in Jerusalem" (4:21),

he then makes his strongest "we-you" statement of all,

> "*You* (ὑμεῖς) worship what you do not know;
> *we* (ἡμεῖς) worship what we know,
> for salvation is from the Jews" (4:22).

Nevertheless, after making such a strong "we-you" statement, Jesus returns once again to a more conciliatory tone when he emphasizes a point of "common ground," worship in spirit and in truth.

> "But the hour is coming, and now is here, when the true worshipers will worship the Father in spirit and truth, for the Father seeks such as these to worship him. God is spirit, and those who worship him must worship in spirit and truth" (4:23-24).

Jesus' movement to this "common ground" allows the Samaritan woman to move beyond her own "we-you" mentality, as evidenced by the absence of the emphatic pronoun in her response to Jesus' words about the place of true worship.

> "I know (οἶδα) that the Messiah is coming . . . .
> When he comes (ἔλθῃ ἐκεῖνος),
> he will proclaim (ἀναγγελεῖ) all things to us" (4:25).[49]

[48]Cf. O'Day, *Revelation in the Fourth Gospel,* 69–70.

[49]My translation. Boers likewise perceives a shift in her attitude at this point in the conversation. Boers, *Neither on This Mountain Nor in Jerusalem,* 176. Although

If the Samaritan woman is going to fulfill her role as betrothed/bride of the messianic bridegroom on behalf of her own community, the Samaritan woman has to move from her "we-you" mentality to an openness to Jesus. Once the Samaritan woman moves past her own "we-you" mentality, she is able to be open to Jesus' proclamation, "I am he (ἐγώ εἰμι), the one who is speaking to you" (4:26). This openness then allows her to go to her townspeople and make a tentative belief statement,

> "Come see (δεῦτε ἴδετε) a man who told (εἶπέν) me
> everything that I ever did.
> This couldn't be the Messiah, could it?"
> (μήτι οὗτός ἐστιν ὁ Χριστός) (4:29).[50]

Therefore, her change in attitude allowed her to become the vehicle by which Jesus becomes connected to her community.

A Movement beyond a "From Below" Perspective

Besides aiding in the characterization of Jesus as the messianic bridegroom by being "woman" and "Samaritan" at a well, the Samaritan woman also facilitates the characterization of Jesus by being a foil for his revelation.[51] In her initial "we-you" reply to Jesus' request for a drink (4:9), the Samaritan woman provides Jesus with the opportunity to raise the discussion to a higher level in order to reveal something about himself. He does so through his use of the term "living water."[52]

> "If you knew the gift of God,
> and who it is that is saying to you, 'Give me a drink,'
> you would have asked him,
> and he would have given you living water" (4:10).

ἐκεῖνος in this passage is used for emphasis, such emphasis is not for comparison. It is simply the implied author's way of using the adjective for the pronoun "he" to place emphasis on the person to which the text refers. Some of examples of this usage are: for Jesus (1:18; 2:21, 3:28, 30;), for John the Baptist (1:8; 5:35), for the Messiah (4:25), for God (5:19, 38; 6:29), for Moses (5:46-47) and in the generic sense (5:43).

[50]My translation.

[51]Schneiders does not think the Samaritan woman is a foil because she does more than feed him cue lines. Adele Reinhartz identifies her as a foil, but states that the content, tone and outcome of her conversation with Jesus demonstrates that she is more like a disciple than Nicodemus. Schneiders, *The Revelatory Text,* 191. Reinhartz, "The Gospel of John," 573.

[52]Cf. Culpepper, *Anatomy,* 112.

To have recognized that Jesus had raised the discussion to a higher level, the Samaritan woman, and/or the reader, would have needed to recognize that the term "living water," which can simply mean flowing water,[53] also has sexual connotations (as stated above) and that Jesus was using this sexual allusion in a religious manner, just as the implied authors of the Hebrew Bible did. Whereas the first-century reader, who was familiar with the Hebrew Bible and received privileged information about Jesus in the prologue and first three chapters of the Fourth Gospel, could be expected to recognize that Jesus was utilizing such language for the purpose of raising the discussion to a higher level, the Samaritan woman as a character in the story cannot.[54]

Johannine misunderstanding and irony are utilized as the Samaritan woman is characterized as interpreting Jesus' statement from a "below" perspective. Taking Jesus' words literally, she assumes that Jesus is speaking of physical flowing water.[55] Based on her misconception, the Samaritan woman challenges both Jesus' ability to provide this "living water"—he has no bucket and the well is deep (4:11)—and his status relative to their father Jacob, who gave them the well and drank out of it himself (4:12).[56] This ironic misunderstanding and challenge provides Jesus

[53]D. W. Wead, *The Literary Devices in John's Gospel* (Basel: Reinhardt, 1970) 87.

[54]Cf. Botha, *Jesus and the Samaritan Woman,* 127.

[55]Botha, *Jesus and the Samaritan Woman,* 125. Culpepper, *Anatomy,* 155–6. Duke, 102. Eslinger suggests that the woman believes that Jesus is responding to her own "coquetry" by offering "living water" according to its sexual connotation. Wead, who identifies the term "living water" as a metaphor rather than a double entendre, perceives a "fault" in the Samaritan woman for not being able to lift herself above the material. Eslinger, 169–70, 178. Wead, 87. For an in-depth discussion of irony in the Fourth Gospel, see Culpepper, *Anatomy,* 165–80; Duke, *Irony in the Fourth Gospel*; O'Day, "The Essence and Function of Irony," *Revelation in the Fourth Gospel,* 11–32. For a specific analysis of Johannine double entendre and misunderstanding, see Culpepper, *Anatomy,* 152–65, 181; Duke, 88–90; Wead, 30–46, 69–70; Botha, *Jesus and the Samaritan Woman,* 127–34. For a discussion of the use of metaphor in the Fourth Gospel, see Wead, 71–94; Culpepper, *Anatomy,* 151–2.

[56]In this respect, the characterization of the Samaritan woman is consistent with the characterization of women in ancient literature who defend their culture and traditions when these are threatened. Cf. Helene Foley, "'Reverse Simile' and Sex Roles in the Odyssey," *Women in the Ancient World: The Arethusa Papers,* ed. John Peradotto and J. P. Sullivan (Albany: State University of New York Press, 1984) 59–78; Helene Foley, "The Conception of Women in Athenian Drama," *Reflections of Women in Antiquity,* edited by Helene Foley (New York: Gordon and Breach Science Publishers, 1981) 162; Carol Dewald, "Women and Culture in Herodotus' *Histories,*" *Reflections of Women in Antiquity,* ed. Helene Foley (New York: Gordon and Breach Science Publishers, 1981) 96–7, 107–10.

with another opportunity to raise the discussion to a higher level in order to reveal something about himself.[57] Again he uses the topic of "water," this time to reveal that he is, in fact, greater than Jacob.

> ". . . Everyone who drinks of this water will be thirsty again, but those who drink of the water that I will give them will never be thirsty. The water that I will give will become in them a spring of water gushing up to eternal life" (4:13-14).

Again the Samaritan woman fails to realize that Jesus has raised the discussion to a higher level. Still assuming that he is speaking of ordinary flowing water, she asks for this water so that she would not have to come to draw water again (4:15). The Samaritan woman's continued misunderstanding of Jesus' statements about the type of water he is able to provide supports Jesus' negative characterization of the Samaritan woman as one who knows neither the gift of God nor the one who is speaking to her (4:10), which in turn makes her the quintessential representative for the Samaritan people who know not what they worship (cf. 4:22).[58] Her continued misunderstanding also leads Jesus to change the subject.[59]

A Woman Who Has Had Five "Men/Husbands"

Jesus changes the subject by instructing the Samaritan woman to go call her husband (ἄνδρα) and then return (4:16). This is an unconventional statement for a betrothal type-scene. Although the woman's statement that she has no husband (4:17a) appears to restore the type-scene, such restoration is short lived.[60]

Jesus' next response to the Samaritan woman appears to characterize her not as a virgin, as the reader would have expected in such a type-scene, but as a woman who has had five husbands (ἄνδρας) and is now with one who is not her husband (ἀνήρ) (4:17b-18). Depending on how the reader interpreted Jesus' statement, the Samaritan woman would have been viewed as a deceptive and evasive sinner or as someone who perceives in Jesus' comment a prophetic challenge to her community's past and present

---

[57]Botha, *Jesus and the Samaritan Woman,* 169. Boers, *Neither on this Mountain Nor in Jerusalem,* 186–7.

[58]Cf. Botha, *Jesus and the Samaritan Woman,* 123.

[59]J. E. Botha, "John 4:16: A Difficult Text—Speech Act Theoretically Revisited," *The Gospel of John as Literature: An Anthology of 20th-Century Perspectives,* ed. Mark Stibbe (Leiden: E. J. Brill, 1993) 188–9.

[60]Botha, "Reader 'Entrapment,'" 42–3. Botha, *Jesus and the Samaritan Woman,* 191–2.

religious traditions, or as a sinner whose own sexual life history reflects the apostasy of her community.

A DECEPTIVE SINNER?

Jesus' statement about the woman's marital status has been taken literally by many scholars. These scholars assume that the Samaritan woman's recognition of Jesus as a prophet (4:19) is based on his supernatural knowledge about her unsavory marital status, despite her attempt at deception (4:17-18), much the same way Nathanael's belief in Jesus is based on Jesus' knowledge of his recent history (1:48-50). Of those scholars who take the marital reference literally, some focus only on the woman's sinful and deceptive character and Jesus' ability to see through her deception.[61] Other scholars who take Jesus' statement literally, however, focus more on the implied author's use of irony in not characterizing the woman as a virgin in the betrothal type-scene than on the woman's sinful and deceptive character.[62] Among both groups who take Jesus' comments about the Samaritan woman's husbands literally, there are those who perceive her comments about the place of true worship as an attempt

[61]Ben Witherington, III, *Women in Ministry of Jesus* (Cambridge: Cambridge University Press, 1984) 59–60. Brown, *The Gospel According to John,* 1:177. Boers, *Neither on this Mountain Nor in Jerusalem,* 170–3. Lagrange, 110–11. Bernard, 1:143–5. Schnackenburg, 1:433. Although Laurence Cantwell perceives the woman as more sinned against than a sinner, both he and Boers go so far as to question whether the Samaritan woman is characterized as being married to any of the five former men in her life. Laurence Cantwell, "Immortal Longings in Sermone Humili: A Study of John 4:5-26," *Scottish Journal of Theology* 36 (1983) 78–9. Boers, *Neither on this Mountain Nor in Jerusalem,* 171.

[62]Duke, who refers to the woman as a "five-time loser," perceives irony in the fact that a reader would have expected the woman to be a virgin. He concludes on the basis of this and other elements of irony, that the implied author is presenting an ironic adaptation of the betrothal type-scene. Botha, who comments on the woman's "unsavory past," perceives the implied author as utilizing irony in these verses for the purpose of reader-entrapment. Staley, who comments on the woman's "bawdy past," likewise identifies elements of irony and identifies the story as a parody of the betrothal type-scene. In *Revelation in the Fourth Gospel,* O'Day views the woman's statement as an ironic understatement and Jesus' response as an ironic overstatement. Duke, 101–3. Botha, "Reader 'Entrapment,'" 43. Staley, *The Print's First Kiss,* 98. O'Day, *Revelation in the Fourth Gospel,* 67. O'Day's states in her later work, "John," that there are many possible reasons for the woman's many marriages, one being levirate marriages. She warns against perceiving the woman as being of dubious morals, noting that the text says she was married many times, not divorced many times, and that Jesus did not pass judgment on her moral character. O'Day, "John," 296.

to divert Jesus' attention away from her sinful past.[63] Still others state that, if the woman has had five husbands, making the one she is living with now her *de facto* sixth, Jesus is the seventh man in her life, the perfect number, the man for whom she has been waiting.[64]

AN "INNOCENT" WOMAN MOVING TOWARD A
"FROM ABOVE" PERSPECTIVE?

Although this literal interpretation is one possible interpretation, it is also possible that the first-century reader perceived Jesus' statement about the woman's marital status as yet another attempt by Jesus to raise the discussion to a higher level. To have perceived his statement in this way, the first-century reader would have perceived Jesus' reference to the *five* husbands as a symbolic reference to the foreign gods of the five groups of people brought in by the Assyrians to colonize Samaria (cf. 2 Kgs 17:13-34).[65] Although some scholars reject this notion,[66] the basic objection to the five husbands symbolizing the former gods of those who colonized Samaria is that 2 Kgs 17:13-34 actually refers to seven gods, with two groups having two gods.[67] This problem, however, could be resolved if one

[63]Bernard, 1:145. Lagrange, 110–11. Duke, 103.

[64]Stibbe, 68–9.

[65]Cf. Schneiders, *The Revelatory Text,* 190; Bligh, 336; Olsson, 186, 210–11; Edwyn Hoskyns, *The Fourth Gospel* (London: Faber and Faber Limited, 1940) 1:265; Cahill, 46–7; Carmichael, 338 n. 23.

[66]R. Brown acknowledges such an allegorical intent as possible, but states that there is no evidence in the text that it was intended and no certainty that such an allegorical jibe would be well-known at the time. Cantwell implies that one can see such symbolism in the text, but denies that it was put there by the author. Boers states that such an interpretation would be of some significance for the interpretation of the story and would be in agreement with 4:22, but he perceives serious difficulties with such an interpretation. Derrett examines such a possibility, but prefers to perceive the five husbands as representing the five senses. Bernard, Schnackenburg, Barnabas Lindars, Neyrey, and Witherington, however, reject this interpretation altogether. Cf. Brown, *The Gospel According to John,* 1:171; Cantwell, 75, 77–9; Boers, *Neither on this Mountain Nor in Jerusalem,* 172; Derrett, "The Samaritan Woman's Pitcher," 255; Bernard, 1:143–4; Schnackenburg, 1:420, 433; Barnabas Lindars, *The Gospel of John* (London: Oliphants, 1972) 185–7; Neyrey, "Jacob Traditions and the Interpretation of John 4:10-26," 426; Witherington, 57–9.

[67]Although Bernard, R. Brown, Cantwell, Derrett, and Olsson, acknowledge that Josephus seems to have simplified the number to five (*Antiq.* 9:288), Boers complicates this observation with the opinion that it is unclear in Josephus' account whether the five is meant to refer to the number of nations or gods. Cf. Bernard, 1:143–4; Brown, *The Gospel According to John,* 1:171; Cantwell, 75, 77–9; Derrett, "The

accepted Gerard Sloyan's interpretation of 2 Kgs 17:13-34. Sloyan implies that two of the seven deities are consorts. This would make the number of male gods be five, and only the male gods of the Samaritan people would have been symbolized by the woman's five former husbands.[68] In this interpretation the Samaritan woman would be interpreted as understanding that Jesus has moved the discussion to a higher level, and her comments on worship would be seen as a continuation of the discussion on that higher level.[69]

The ambiguity in this interpretation rests on the Greek word ἀνήρ. This word, which can signify man, husband, or male sexual partner, has also been used for the deity in the Hebrew Bible. In the book of Hosea, for instance, God says of the nation, "On that day . . . you will call me, 'My husband'" (Hos 2:16). This theological use of the term would have opened up for the reader the possibility that Jesus' reference to the husbands was a metaphorical challenge to the Samaritan woman as a Samaritan, and not a literal challenge of her sexual life style. Supporting this sexually-symbolic, theological interpretation for the reader is the improbability that a Samaritan woman could have had five legal husbands.[70] This realization may have led the reader to interpret Jesus' reference to the number "five" as a clue that he was again altering the level of discussion, this time for the purpose of presenting a critique of the Samaritans' past and present religious tradition in preparation for renewing a true covenant relationship with her people. This interpretation would have encouraged the reader to see the woman as mainly a symbolic figure, a cipher for her people.

Sandra Schneiders, who utilizes this interpretation, perceives the Samaritan woman as recognizing in Jesus' reference to her five husbands a critique of her people's religious heritage. Schneiders states that the Samaritan woman's acknowledgment of Jesus as a prophet is based on her

Samaritan Woman's Pitcher," 255; Olsson, 186, 210–11; Boers, *Neither on this Mountain Nor in Jerusalem,* 172.

[68]Gerard Sloyan, "The Samaritans in the New Testament," *Horizons* 10 (1983) 10. Cf. C. K. Barrett, *The Gospel According to St. John,* 2nd ed. (Philadelphia: Westminster, 1978) 235.

[69]O'Day and Schnackenburg, who interpret Jesus' statement literally, disagree that her words about the place of worship are a maneuver to steer the conversation away from a painful subject. They perceive her comments as a continuation of the religious tone of the dialogue. O'Day, *Revelation in the Fourth Gospel,* 67–8. Schnackenburg, 1:434. Cf. Cahill, 46–7.

[70]Cantwell's research shows that divorce was uncommon among the Samaritan people. However, he also maintains that the text does not necessarily imply that the woman was legally married to any of the former five men in her life. Cantwell, 78–9 n. 9.

knowledge that one of the roles of the prophet was that of criticizing idolatry. In this interpretation, the Samaritan woman's introduction of the topic of places of worship in 4:20 is not viewed as an effort to divert focus away from her sexual history. Rather, her words are viewed as a response to the realization that Jesus has moved the discussion to a higher level. She continues the discussion on the higher level as she challenges Jesus' prophetic judgment by insisting that the Samaritan tradition of worship is supported by the authority of the patriarchs.[71]

According to H. Boers and Schneiders, such a symbolic interpretation makes Jesus' statement to the woman, "the one you now have is not your husband" (4:18), a reference to YHWH. YHWH is not a true husband of the Samaritan people because Samaritan Yahwism has been tainted by the influence of the worship of false gods. Jesus' statement, "You worship what you do not know; we worship what we know. . . ." (4:22), is then viewed as being in agreement with this spiritualized interpretation of the Samaritan woman's present ἀνήρ.[72] Schneiders also perceives such an interpretation as being consistent with the implied author's unconventional adaptation of the betrothal type-scene. She states,

> . . . if the scene itself is symbolically the incorporation of Samaria into the New Israel, the bride of the new Bridegroom, which is suggested by the type scene itself, then the adultery/idolatry symbolism so prevalent in the prophetic literature for speaking of Israel's infidelity to Yahweh the Bridegroom would be a most apt vehicle for discussion of the anomalous religious situation of Samaria.[73]

A "SINFUL" WOMAN WHOSE SEXUAL LIFE SYMBOLIZES THE IDOLATRY
OF HER COMMUNITY?

Confronting this purely symbolic interpretation is the woman's emphasis on her own personal life history in her witness to the townspeople,

> "Come see a man who told me everything that *I* ever did.
> This couldn't be the Messiah, could it?" (4:29),

as well as the emphasis on her personal life history in the narrator's comments about the initial belief of the townspeople,

> Many Samaritans from that city believed in him
> because of the woman's testimony,

---

[71]Schneiders, *The Revelatory Text,* 190–1.
[72]Ibid., 190. Boers, *Neither on This Mountain Nor in Jerusalem,* 172.
[73]Schneiders, *The Revelatory Text,* 190.

"He told me everything *I* have ever done" (4:39).

If Jesus' words to her were merely a confrontation of the idolatry of the Samaritan people, one must ask why the Samaritan woman focuses on her own life history in her witness to her people.

One could perceive in these alternative interpretations an element of "reader entrapment" or "reader-victimization."[74] If the reader had assumed that the reference to the five husbands was purely a symbolic reference to the apostasy of the Samaritan people and had nothing to do with the woman's life history, at this point in the text the reader would have been forced to reevaluate that assumption, entertain some level of irregularity in the woman's marital status, and reevaluate the character of the Samaritan woman.

This need to reevaluate the woman's character would have raised several questions. Should Jesus' initial statement about the woman's marital status have been taken literally so as to imply that the woman really had five husbands in the past and was she now in an illicit relationship with a man who was not her husband? If five legal husbands is unlikely, should the passage read, "You have had five 'men' and the one you are with now is not your 'husband.'" This translation would imply that she was never legally married to any of the men in her life, a position supported by Laurence Cantwell and Boers.[75] Did Jesus, with his supernatural knowledge, simply recognize some irregularity in the woman's marital status and then use that irregularity to raise the discussion to another level through the use of the number five for the past "men" in the Samaritan woman's life? Did the Samaritan woman recognize Jesus as a prophet because he knew precisely how many men had been in her life, or because she recognized in his reference to her "five" husbands a critique of her community's religious history, or because she both recognized his awareness of her marital irregularity and realized that he had used the number "five" in a symbolic manner to present a critique of Samaritan worship? Was there then an element of deception in the Samaritan woman's response to Jesus' suggestion that she go get her husband/man and then return?

CONCLUSION TO "A WOMAN WHO HAS HAD FIVE 'MEN/HUSBANDS'"

However the first-century reader viewed the passages involved, the Samaritan woman's own words make her actual life history the focus of her witness. This focus in her witness seems to be more than simple

---

[74]For other indications of reader-entrapment or reader-victimization in this pericope, see Botha, "Reader 'Entrapment,'" 37–47; Staley, *The Print's First Kiss*, 96–103.

[75]Cantwell, 78–9. Boers, *Neither on This Mountain Nor in Jerusalem*, 171.

irony.[76] It makes her actual life history with men a symbolic representation of her people's history, just as the sexual life history of Hosea's wife, Gomer, reflects the apostasy of a nation. Thus, the Samaritan woman's own words would have confirmed the reader's assumption that this woman, with her sexual history, represents her people. As "woman," "Samaritan," and "woman who has had five men/husbands and now has one who is not her husband," the Samaritan woman enters into a metaphorical betrothal/marital relationship with the messianic bridegroom.

A Feminist Critique of the Characterization of the Samaritan Woman

Role Reversal—Son as Gift

An obvious place to begin a feminist critique of the patriarchy in this pericope is the betrothal type-scene itself because betrothal type-scenes in the Hebrew Bible are based on the patriarchal concept of the exchange of women.[77] According to Gayle Rubin, anthropologist Claude Lévi-Strauss maintains that social links in traditional cultures are created and maintained through gift-giving. Within this theory of reciprocity, Lévi-Strauss states that the exchange of women between men in marriage is the most basic form of gift exchange for it establishes not a passing reciprocal relationship between men but a permanent kinship relationship between men.[78] Rubin presents a feminist critique of this exchange of women in marriage when she states,

> If it is women who are being transacted, then it is the men who give and take them who are linked, the woman being a conduit of a relationship rather than a partner to it. . . . If women are the gifts, then it is men who are the exchange-partners. It is the partners, not the present, upon whom the reciprocal exchange confers its quasi-mystical power of social linkage. The relations of such a system are such that women are in no position to realize the benefits of their own circulation.[79]

[76]O'Day notes an elements of irony in the Samaritan woman's basing her witness on her marital status and in the manner in which she uses the word "everything." O'Day, *Revelation in the Fourth Gospel,* 76.

[77]Cf. Fuchs, "Structure and Patriarchal Functions in the Biblical Betrothal Type-scene," 7–13.

[78]Gayle Rubin, "The Traffic in Women: Notes on the 'Political Economy' of Sex," *Toward an Anthropology of Women,* ed. Rayna R. Reiter (New York: Monthly Review, 1975) 172–3.

[79]Ibid., 174.

This critique certainly applies to the betrothal type-scenes of the Hebrew Bible. The story of the Samaritan woman at the well, however, has no father or brother giving the Samaritan woman as a gift for the purpose of establishing family ties with other men. Rather, in this unconventional betrothal type-scene, one finds a reversal of roles.[80] It is not the daughter/sister who is given as gift for the purpose of re-establishing familial bonds, but the Son who is given as a gift by his heavenly Father (cf. 3:16, 4:10). For the implied author of the Fourth Gospel, Jesus, the Son, must be the exchange item because he is the one around whom the *"familia Dei"* is to be established.[81]

The Samaritan Woman as Betrothed/Bride/"Mother" in Word (Text) Only

Although one might think such a reversal of roles would mitigate the patriarchal tone of the text, in actuality the reversal of roles results in the Samaritan woman's losing status in the text, just as the mother of Jesus lost status by not being verbally recognized by her son as "mother" and by not being allowed to function fully as a mother of an important son with influence over him. Although it is patriarchal to perceive a woman as an exchange item that establishes permanent familial bonds between men, such an exchange was the means by which women received their social identity and status in the patriarchal honor-shame culture of the time.[82] Such status, however, is denied the Samaritan woman in this story. As the symbolic wife of five men in the past and present woman of a man who is not her husband, the Samaritan woman becomes the betrothed and bride

---

[80]Foley and Froma Zeitlin perceive such role reversals in Greek Literature. Both Foley and Zeitlin concentrate on women assuming male roles to restore and redefine cultural traditions by providing an avenue for corrective criticism of the status quo, but Foley does mention some occasions where the male is compared with the female. She states, for instance, that in festival and comedy the marital situation of the subordination of the female to the male is used to express, reinforce or criticize the larger range of hierarchical social and economic relations and that women functioned in literature in ways they were not allowed in real life. Foley, "'Reverse Simile,'" 59–78; Foley, "The Concept of Women in Athenian Drama," 127–68; Froma Zeitlin, "Travesties of Gender and Genre in Aristophanes," *Reflections of Women in Antiquity,* ed. Helene Foley (New York: Gordon and Breach Science Publishers, 1981) 269–318.

[81]Cf. Seim, 62–3.

[82]For an anthropological study of this concept of the woman receiving a sense of social identity by being the exchange object that unites two families, being married and becoming a mother, especially of a son, see: J. K. Campbell, *Honour, Family and Patronage* (Oxford: Claredon, 1964) 124–5, 150, 165–6 and Delaney, "Seeds of Honor, Fields of Shame," 42.

of the messianic bridegroom as the literary representative of a faith community with whom the heavenly Father desires to reestablish familial ties.[83] She is not the object of exchange that creates familial bonds between the two families; Jesus is. Also, there is no real marriage through which she could physically give birth to male children and receive status (cf. Gen 30:20). The offspring of this divine union are to be born "from above" and of the spirit, not of flesh (cf. 3:6-7). Her womb is not needed. Because the Samaritan woman only symbolically fulfills her role as betrothed, bride, and "mother," she is betrothed, bride and mother in word (text) only. As symbolic bride, she will not be the one who actually gives life; Jesus as messianic bridegroom is the one who gives eternal life. For this reason, her importance in relation to the faith of the Samaritan people will need to be minimized later, as will be shown.

Focusing on the Bridegroom—Limiting the Role of the Bride

Even though the Samaritan woman is not the object of exchange in this symbolic betrothal, androcentrism exists in this story. As in betrothal type-scenes in the Hebrew Bible,[84] in the story of the Samaritan woman at the well the focus is on the character and future career of the hero—the bridegroom, which in turn limits the role of the woman in the story. Unlike Nicodemus, the Samaritan woman is not named in the text because she is not important in her own right. She is only the literary means by which the implied author communicated to the reader that Jesus was sent as the messianic bridegroom to reestablish divine familial bonds between God and the Samaritan people, enabling them to become children of God, born not of the flesh but of the Spirit and the will of God (cf. 1:13; 3:6).

In the story of the Samaritan woman at the well, the woman's main function is that of aiding in the portrayal of Jesus as the bridegroom. She begins to fulfill this function merely by appearing at the well, for her presence there with Jesus characterizes her as a potential bride and Jesus as a potential bridegroom. For the Samaritan woman to function as the betrothed/bride of the messianic bridegroom interested in re-establishing familial relations with the Samaritan people only two elements of characterization

[83] Amy-Jill Levine notes that Judith is one of a series of female figures who represent Israel. Thus, a first-century reader familiar with the Hebrew Bible and Hellenized Jewish writings would easily have perceived the Samaritan woman as a representative of her community. Cf. Amy-Jill Levine, "Sacrifice and Salvation: Otherness and Domestication in the Book of Judith," *No One Spoke Ill of Her: Essays on Judith,* ed. James C. Vanderkam (Atlanta: Scholars Press, 1992) 17.

[84] Cf. Fuchs, "Structure and Patriarchal Functions in the Biblical Betrothal Type-scene," 7–13.

are necessary, "woman" and "Samaritan," both of which are emphasized in the text.

The narrator first introduces the female character in this story as "a woman from Samaria" (γυνὴ ἐκ τῆς Σαμαρείας) (4:7). The narrator then refers to her as "the Samaritan woman" (ἡ γυνὴ Σαμαρῖτις) and the Samaritan woman even refers to herself as "a Samaritan woman" (γυναικὸς Σαμαρίτιδος)" (4:9). Because the feminine form of the Greek word for Samaritan (ἡ Σαμαρῖτις / Σαμαρίτιδος) in 4:9 makes the Greek word "woman" (ἡ γυνὴ / γυναικὸς) unnecessary, an emphasis on the woman's female nature is especially evident in this verse. This emphasis on the woman's female nature would have reinforced the implied reader's assumption that a betrothal type-scene was being constructed. The unconventional aspect to such a betrothal is evident in the narrator's statement, "Jews have nothing to do with Samaritans" (οὐ γὰρ συγχρῶνται Ἰουδαῖοι Σαμαρίταις) (4:9). This statement by the narrator puts emphasis on the Samaritan aspect of the woman's character. Together these two elements of her characterization, "woman" and "Samaritan," enable the female character to function as the betrothed/bride of a Jewish messianic bridegroom who wants to re-establish familial relations with the Samaritan people.

Woman as Field to be Sown

A symbolic interpretation of Jesus' comments to his disciples about the fields being already white for the harvest in 4:35, which equates the Samaritan woman with the field and Jesus with the sower who sows seeds of faith within her, implies a passive role for the Samaritan woman and an active role for Jesus. Whereas the male is active in this imagery as he sows the seed, the woman is merely the passive recipient of the seed, just as the well is the passive recipient of the water. Passivity is also implied in the procreative process, for, in the ancient understanding of this procreative process, the seed that the man contributes is understood as encapsulating the essential child. The woman merely provides the nurturing "space" for the male seed to mature.[85]

One might counter that the Samaritan woman at least contributes a "nurturing" space. The woman, who is equated with land, must be recep-

---

[85]Delaney, who states this understanding of the procreation process still exists among Turkish villagers today, also mentions that this way of conceptualizing the process of procreation has a long history in cultures that have been dominated by the Greco-Roman/Judeo-Christian traditions. According to Thomas Laqueur, in the ancient understanding of procreation both the male and the female contributed semen, but the male produced the efficient cause in generation *(sperma),* as stated in Aristotle's account. Delaney, *The Seed and the Soil,* 31–2. Thomas Laqueur, "Destiny Is

tive (moist and fertile, not arid or barren), for the seed Jesus plants within her to take root.[86] Although anthropological studies have shown that women who fail to produce children (sons) for their husbands are seen to be at fault,[87] within the Hebrew Bible, God (not the woman or her husband) is seen as the one who is responsible for the fertility of women (cf. Gen 15:2; 17:15; 30:2, 22). Thus, even if the woman did provide the "nurturing" space for the seed Jesus planted, God, not the woman would have been given the praise. Nevertheless, the story of the Samaritan woman may be the Johannine equivalent of the Synoptic story of the good soil that produces much fruit, in which case the first-century reader may have at least equated the Samaritan woman with the good soil.[88]

A Necessary Positive Element in the Characterization of Women that Presents a Contrast to Some Male Characters

Although this characterization of the Samaritan woman as betrothed/bride/field to be sown/and symbol-of-her-community's-past-transgressions is certainly patriarchal, one could counter that at least the Samaritan woman is characterized as coming to some understanding of who Jesus is and acting on that limited knowledge. Her openness to remaining involved in the dialogue and her subsequent actions resulted in others' coming to Jesus—a mark of a disciple. Because this is all true and needs somehow to be connected to other aspects of her character, it must be established that such a positive outcome was necessary for the plot and especially for the positive characterization of Jesus as a successful bridegroom.

In order for the author to portray Jesus as the messianic bridegroom, the author needed a female character to be his bride.[89] The initial resistance of the woman helps to portray her as a Samaritan, whereas her eventual

---

Anatomy," *Making Sex: Body and Gender from the Greeks to Freud* (Cambridge: Harvard University Press, 1990) 35–41.

[86]Cf. Delaney, *The Seed and the Soil,* 54; Delaney, "Seeds of Honor, Fields of Shame," 38.

[87]Delaney notes that the people of Turkish villages in her ethnographic study placed some fault on the husbands for not feeding the woman properly so that she might not be barren. Delaney, *The Seed and the Soil,* 52, 55, 75.

[88]Cf. Brown, *The Gospel According to John,* 1:182; Okure, *The Johannine Approach to Mission,* 150.

[89]In a similar fashion, Mary Lefkowitz argues, ". . . Antigone must be female for the dramatic action to occur in the first place, because only a mother or sister would have felt so strongly the obligation to bury the dead." Mary Lefkowitz, "Influential Women," *Images of Women in Antiquity,* eds. Averil Cameron and Amélie Kuhrt (Detroit: Wayne State University Press, 1983) 52.

positive response helps to portray Jesus as a successful messianic bride-groom who is able to overcome that resistance. The Samaritan woman must bring to fruition what Jesus planted within her if Jesus is to be portrayed as an effective messianic bridegroom. Moreover, the Samaritan woman's apparent discipleship symbolizes the discipleship of the entire community she represents as bride.

This unnamed Samaritan woman of questionable character who bears fruit presents a contrast to certain male characters in the Fourth Gospel. First, she presents a contrast to Nicodemus, the named teacher of Israel who drops out of his conversation with Jesus and fails to act on his experience for fear of losing his status in life (3:1-2, 11; cf. 7:50; 19:39).[90] Second, she presents a contrast to the Jews, whose statement to Jesus, "You are not greater than our father Abraham, are you?" (μὴ σὺ μείζων εἶ τοῦ πατρὸς ἡμῶν Ἀβραάμ) (8:53) is a formal parallel to the Samaritan woman's statement, "You are not greater than our ancestor Jacob, are you?" (μὴ σὺ μειζων εἶ τοῦ πατρὸς ἡμῶν Ἰακώβ) (4:12).[91] Whereas the Samaritan woman's questioning of Jesus eventually moves her to ask for the water Jesus said he could give and Jesus' "I am" statement moves her to witness to her townspeople, the Jews' questioning of Jesus and Jesus' "I am" statement to them leads them to take up stones to throw at him (8:58-59). Third, this woman presents a contrast to the disciples. She freely engages in conversation with Jesus, even to the point of challenging him. The disciples are silent before Jesus and afraid to question him (4:27).[92]

In each of these instances, the positive faith and action of the Samaritan woman of questionable marital status would have heightened the negative image that the reader had of the males in the story who failed to respond to Jesus. Although these contrasts on the surface may appear to uphold the woman over the men, in actuality, an androcentric bias is ap-

[90]Mary Margaret Pazdan, "Nicodemus and the Samaritan Woman: Contrasting Models of Discipleship," *Biblical Theological Bulletin* 17 (1987) 145–8. Cantwell, 81, 85. Schneiders, *The Revelatory Text,* 187, 191. O'Day, "John," 295. Culpepper, *Anatomy,* 136. Boers, *Neither on this Mountain Nor in Jerusalem,* 182. Lee, 65–6, 72, 74. John Rena, "Women in the Gospel of John," *Église et Théologie* 17 (1986) 138, 140.

[91]Neyrey, "Jacob Traditions and the Interpretation of John 4:10-26," 420–1. Wead, 63–4.

[92]Pazdan, 148. Botha, *Jesus and the Samaritan Woman,* 161–2, 169. Cf. Scott, 187, 197. Witherington identifies a contrast on the basis of the disciples bringing Jesus physical food that does not satisfy and the Samaritan woman bringing Jesus true spiritual food by helping him to complete God's work. Witherington thus perceives the disciples as less spiritually perceptive and active in their faith than the Samaritan woman. Witherington, 62.

parent. The positive faith and actions of a negatively characterized un-named woman appears to have been provided so as to make the males in the story look bad, not to make the woman look good.[93] One knows that the men are not negatively characterized in order that the woman might be viewed positively because, in each case, the male characters continue to appear in the story, whereas the Samaritan woman drops out of the story once she has fulfilled her comparative function. She is a foil for them. They are not a foil for her.[94]

Despite this fact, the positive outcome of the Samaritan woman's en-counter with Jesus may imply that the author was urging the audience to appropriate some aspects of a "feminine" manner of responding to the Jesus experience. A woman of questionable character could risk entering into a "shameless," confrontational conversation with a Jewish male. She has little honor to protect. Supporting this assumption is the negative por-trayal of the male "honor-shame" mode of behavior that is a potential hin-drance to Jesus' ministry and a definite hindrance to others' belief in Jesus and their ability to be born "from above."[95]

The Marginalization of the Samaritan Woman

Even though the Samaritan woman is portrayed as eventually re-sponding positively to Jesus and as producing a great harvest, efforts are made in the text to limit her importance. The wording and content of her witness (4:29) is diminished in relationship to that of the disciples (1:39, 46), and the value of her witness is then diminished by the very people to whom she bore witness (4:42).

The Samaritan woman says,

[93]For betrothal type-scenes in the Hebrew Bible, Fuchs acknowledges and cri-tiques the manner in which the female characters highlight, through contrast, the fu-ture career of the potential husband, (e.g., Rachel's passivity and weakness functions as a foil for Jacob's resourcefulness and physical strength). Although she acknowl-edges a contrast between the female character and male characters who are not the bridegroom (e.g., Rebekah's positive attributes of generosity and kindness provides a contrast to the greed that forms the basis of Laban's hospitality toward potential bride-grooms or their surrogates), she does not comment on the androcentrism of such con-trasts. Fuchs, "Structure and Patriarchal Functions in the Biblical Betrothal Type-scene," 7–12.

[94]Pazdan perceives Nicodemus as the perfect foil for the Samaritan woman. Paz-dan, 148.

[95]Cf. Jane Kopas, "Jesus and Women: John's Gospel," *Theology Today* 41 (1984) 201, 203; chapter 2, pp. 40–1.

"Come see (δεῦτε ἴδετε) a man who told me
everything that I ever did. (εἶπέν μοι πάντα ἅ ἐποίησα)
This couldn't be the Messiah, could it?"
(μήτι οὗτος ἐστιν ὁ Χριστός;) (4:29).[96]

The wording of her "Come see" (δεῦτε ἴδετε) is significantly different
from Jesus' invitation to John's disciples to "Come and see" (ἔρχεσθε καὶ
ὄψεσθε) (1:39) and from Philip's call to Nathanael to "Come and see"
(ἔρχου καὶ ἴδε) (1:46). Jesus' own use of the verb ὁράω, seems to imply
a deeper sense of seeing than does Philip's use of the word ἴδε,[97] and in
this sense, the Samaritan woman's emphasis on physical seeing parallels
Philip's. Similarly, the common verb "come" (ἔρχομαι), which is sometimes used in the Fourth Gospel to imply mere physical movement, is used
at other times to convey a deeper sense of movement.[98] Although Jesus
may have used the verb ἔρχομαι in a spiritual sense and Philip in a physical sense, the wording of Philip's statement is a closer parallel to Jesus'
statement than is the wording of the Samaritan woman's statement. The
only other place in the Fourth Gospel where the verb δεῦτε is used is in
21:12, where it definitely conveys the notion of "come hither."

The content of the Samaritan woman's witness is likewise compromised. Following Jesus' words about true worship, the Samaritan
woman's statement focuses on the *Messiah's* ability to *proclaim*
(ἀναγγελεῖ) *all things to her people* (ἡμῖν ἅπαντα) (4:25). In her witness
to her townspeople, however, she focuses on a *man telling her everything
she ever did* (εἶπέν μοι πάντα ἅ ἐποίησα) (4:29). Gail O'Day perceives
elements of irony in the Samaritan woman's basing her witness on her
marital status and in the manner in which she uses the word "everything"
in her witness.[99] To these elements of irony, I would add the Samaritan
woman's basing her witness not on the Messiah's *proclaiming* (ἀναγγελεῖ)
everything to her people (ἡμῖν ἅπαντα), but on his *telling* (εἶπέν) her
everything she did (εἶπέν μοι πάντα ἅ ἐποίησα).[100]

---

[96]My translation.

[97]For an alternative view, see Brown, *The Gospel According to John,* 1:501–3.

[98]ἔρχομαι is used for such phrases as "the true light . . . was coming into the
world (1:9), "the hour is coming" (4:21, 23; 5:25), "the one who comes to me I will
not cast out" (6:37), "No one can come . . . unless the Father . . . draws" (6:44).

[99]O'Day, *Revelation in the Fourth Gospel,* 76.

[100]Cf. H. Boers, "Discourse Structure and Macro-Structure in the Interpretation of
Texts: Jn 4:1-42 as an Example," *Society of Biblical Literature 1980 Seminar Papers,*
ed. P. Achtemeier (Chico: Scholars Press, 1980) 176. For a speech act analysis of the
Samaritan woman's witness, see Botha, *Jesus and the Samaritan Woman,* 167, 186–7.

The content of the Samaritan woman's witness is further compromised by the doubt expressed in her witness. Andrew says to Peter, "We have found the Messiah" (1:41) and Philip says to Nathanael, "We have found him whom Moses in the law and also the prophets wrote . . ." (1:45). The Samaritan woman, however, states, "This couldn't be the Messiah, could it?" (μήτι οὗτος ἐστιν ὁ χριστός) (4:29). Except for the predilection of the implied author to use irony,[101] I can find no textual reason that would necessitate such a qualified ironic witness on the part of the Samaritan woman.[102] I can only conclude that the woman's witness was ironically qualified because she was a female character. We know that her statement could not have been ironically constructed because she was a Samaritan, for the Samaritan townspeople, after their own personal encounter with Jesus, supersede the Samaritan woman's tentative witness with statement that expresses certitude, ". . . we know this is truly the Savior of the world" (4:42).

Besides qualifying the significance of the Samaritan woman's witness in its wording and content, the implied author also qualifies the worth of her witness in the eyes of the Samaritan people. The narrator first states that many more townspeople believed "*because of* the word of the woman bearing testimony that . . ." (διὰ τόν λόγον τῆς γυναικὸς μαρτυρούσης ὅτι) (4:39). This statement presents a relative parallel with Jesus' prayer for those who will believe "*through* the word" of the disciples (διὰ τοῦ λόγου αὐτῶν) (17:20). In the story of the Samaritan woman, however, the narrator later states that many more townspeople believed "*because of*" Jesus' word (διὰ τόν λόγον αὐτοῦ) (4:41) and these say to the woman that they no longer believe "*because of*" her "talk" (διὰ τὴν σὴν λαλιά) (4:42). There may be some significance in the difference between believing "*because of*" the word of the woman bearing testimony" (διὰ with the accusative = Accusative of Cause) and believing "*through*" the word of the disciples (δία with the genitive = Ablative of Agency). Unlike Jesus'

[101]Staley and Duke identify elements of irony in the wording of the woman's witness, "surely (μήτι cf. 8:22; 18:35) this can't be the Christ can it?" Staley, *The Print's First Kiss,* 101. Duke, 103.

[102]Botha states on the basis of speech act theory that the Samaritan woman's witness "is formulated in such a way that the villagers are not overwhelmed by it or made incredulous by the extreme nature of the content of the utterance. She is careful not to give so much information that the villagers would reject her words out of hand . . . ." My question is, "Would such a careful formulation have been necessary if the speaker were a male Samaritan? Is the 'principle of processibility' to which Botha refers not also applicable to the witness of a male disciple to another potential male disciple?" Cf. Botha, *Jesus and the Samaritan Woman,* 164.

"word," which is not qualified, the woman's "word" is qualified and equated with "He told me everything I ever did." Later her testimony is equated with λαλιά. Although this Greek word is usually used in New Testament and other early Christian literature in a good sense, Aristophanes and others used to word in a unfavorable sense, as the equivalent to gossip.[103]

Although such wording may be meant to contrast the Samaritan woman's "talk" with Jesus' "word,"[104] such wording also diminishes the woman's importance in the progression of the townspeople's quality of faith.[105] From the perspective of the implied author's theology, such a diminishment in the role of the Samaritan woman may be considered necessary in order to connect the fullness of faith with direct self-revelation by Jesus.[106] Nevertheless, such wording would have lessened the importance of the Samaritan woman's witness in the eyes of the reader. Having the townspeople turn their backs on their "spiritual mother" in order to identify totally with the one whose "seed" they are makes Jesus the focal point for the establishment of the heavenly *pater familia*. The townspeople's words to the woman would have communicated to the reader that the woman has no real place of honor in the familial relationship that Jesus establishes between God and the Samaritan people. She was but a literary necessity and now has been returned to her proper female place. Such a reestablishment of the patriarchal norm is consistent with ancient literature.[107]

In response to those scholars who see a correlation between the diminishment in the role of the Samaritan woman and the diminishment in the role of John the Baptist (3:30),[108] I would say that such a correlation

[103]Cf. Walter Bauer, *A Greek-English Lexicon of the New Testament and Other Early Christian Literature,* 2nd ed., trans. and augmented by William Arndt and F. Wilbur Gingrich (Chicago: The University of Chicago Press, 1979 [1959]) 464.

[104]Boers perceives the use of the word (λαλιά) (v 42) as presenting a contrast with the λόγος of Jesus (v 41). He does not think the use of the term (λαλιά) is necessarily disparaging, however. O'Day perceives in the use of the two different words a difference of perception between the evangelist and the townspeople. Boers, *Neither on this Mountain Nor in Jerusalem,* 193 n. 93. O'Day, *Revelation in the Fourth Gospel,* 88.

[105]Botha, *Jesus and the Samaritan Woman,* 196. Boers, *Neither on this Mountain Nor in Jerusalem,* 197.

[106]Schüssler Fiorenza, *In Memory of Her,* 328.

[107]Cf. Zeitlin, "Travesties of Gender and Genre in Aristophanes," 196–7.

[108]Lee, 66. Rena perceives a contrast between the Samaritan woman and John the Baptist because the Samaritan woman really did decrease, whereas history shows that John the Baptist did not. Thus, Rena perceives the Samaritan woman to be a model disciple. Rena, 140.

may indeed exist. Nevertheless, it seems significant from a feminist perspective that the implied author portrayed John the Baptist as diminishing his own significance in relation to Jesus, whereas the Samaritan woman had her significance diminished by others. From a feminist perspective one might perceive this as an effort on the part of the implied author to remove the woman from her sphere of influence once she has fulfilled her literary purpose. Once the Samaritan woman has fulfilled her role as a symbol for her people, as betrothed/bride of the messianic bridegroom, and as spiritual mother, her significance is put into patriarchal perspective and she falls out of the story never to be seen or heard from again. Nicodemus, the Jews of chapter 8, and the disciples, for whom she presents a contrast, continue to appear in the gospel. The Samaritan woman does not. She has fulfilled her patriarchal, symbolic, and conventional role and is unimportant to the rest of the plot. Such a removal of women after they have fulfilled their patriarchal role in the text is common in ancient literature.[109]

This interpretation suggests that the author made use of a variety of patriarchal tendencies found in the Hebrew Bible, that of using a woman as a symbol of a nation or portraying the nation as a woman in relationship to a God who is portrayed as male,[110] that of using the sexual sin of a woman to symbolize the apostasy of a nation,[111] and possibly that of characterizing women as deceptive.[112] Although John Rena may be correct when he states that sexual discrimination does not *explicitly* loom as a major issue in this pericope,[113] because the conventions of female subordination thoroughly underlay the entire story, it certainly *implicitly* looms as a major element in this pericope, an element about which a reader from the twentieth or twenty-first century needs to be aware in order not to be influenced by it.[114]

[109]Lefkowitz and Foley note this tendency in ancient Greek history and Athenian drama; Levine notes this tendency for the Hellenized Jewish Book of Judith; and I have noted this same tendency in the Fourth Gospel for the mother of Jesus. Lefkowitz, 49, 54–6. Foley, "The Conception of Women in Athenian Drama," 135, 161–2. Levine, "Sacrifice and Salvation," 17, 27. Chapter 2, pp. 41–2.

[110]Cf. Hos 1–4 and Ezek 16 and Jer 2. For another example of female figures who symbolize the nation of Israel, see Levine, "Sacrifice and Salvation," 17.

[111]Cf. Hos 1–4; Ezek 16; and Jer 2.

[112]Cf. Esther Fuchs, "Who is Hiding the Truth? Deceptive Women and Biblical Androcentrism," *Feminist Perspectives on Biblical Scholarship,* ed. Adela Yarbro Collins (Chico, Calif.: Scholars Press, 1985) 137–44.

[113]My emphasis. Rena, 139.

[114]R. Brown and Schneiders note an element of sexual bias in the shocked response of the disciples at seeing Jesus speaking with a "woman." Brown, *The Gospel According to John,* 1:173. Schneiders, "Women in the Fourth Gospel," 40.

Summary

The decision of the implied author to portray Jesus as the messianic bridegroom suggested the presence of a woman as his betrothed/bride. As betrothed and bride of the messianic bridegroom on behalf of the Samaritan people, the Samaritan woman represents the Samaritan people with whom God desires to reestablish familial relations. The Samaritan woman is never named because she is not important in her own right. She is important only to the extent that she is "woman" and "Samaritan," the two aspects of her character that are essential for her to fulfill her role.

Assisting in her characterization as Samaritan is the "we-you" mentality with which she initially responds to Jesus as a Jew, and Jesus' portrayal of her as a woman who has had "five" husbands/men in the past and who now has one who is not truly her husband. Also supporting this symbolic characterization of the Samaritan woman is Jesus' description of her as someone who knows neither the gift of God nor the one who is talking to her, a characterization that is supported by the Samaritan woman misunderstanding of Jesus' words to her about "living water."

Like the mother of Jesus and Nicodemus before her, the Samaritan women initially interprets Jesus' statements from a "below" perspective. Unlike the mother of Jesus and Nicodemus, however, the Samaritan women, I believe, begins to move toward an "above" perspective as she recognizes within Jesus' comment about her "five" husbands a prophetic judgment of the "five" former "husbands" of the Samaritan people. Jesus' own acknowledgment of the Samaritan woman's "we-you" mentality and his subsequent movement beyond such a mentality to a point of "common ground" (true worship) allow the Samaritan woman to be open to Jesus' *"I am"* statement. Although she perceives his words to be an assertion that he *is* their Messiah and may fail to recognize the deeper significance of his "I am" statement, her openness and qualified understanding allow her to make a tentative witness to her people regarding Jesus, which then assists the Samaritan townspeople's movement toward belief in Jesus.

Although the Samaritan woman has an important part to play in the text, her importance is qualified throughout the pericope. It is first qualified by the lack of a personal name. Her significance is further qualified by her initial defensive response to Jesus. Although she enters into theological discussion with Jesus, she initially understands his words from a "below" perspective and merely functions as a foil for Jesus' self-revelations. Although she achieves partial understanding and bears witness to the townspeople on the basis of this partial understanding, the value of that witness is qualified both in its wording and in the limited worth that the Samaritan townspeople attribute to it. Once the Samaritan woman has fulfilled her patriarchal role as betrothed and bride of the messianic bridegroom on behalf of her people, her importance is diminished by her townspeople, and she then disappears from the text.

The Samaritan woman's importance continues to be diminished as the gospel portrays other women in the role of betrothed/bride of the messianic bridegroom. As I shall show in the stories involving Mary of Bethany and Mary Magdalene, the important point for this gospel is that Jesus is portrayed as the messianic bridegroom. As far as the implied author is concerned, any woman can function as the betrothed/bride of the bridegroom. The woman is not important in and of herself; she is only important to the extent that she represents some community of faith. For such a task, any woman will do.

4

Mary and Martha of Bethany

Introduction

Unlike the Samaritan woman, who appears in only one pericope in the Fourth Gospel, Mary and Martha of Bethany appear in two pericopae. They are mentioned in connection with the illness, death, and resuscitation of their brother Lazarus (11:1-54) and in connection with a supper given in honor of Jesus after he had raised Lazarus from the dead (12:1-11).

Since the second wave of feminist hermeneutics, many scholars who have dealt with Mary and Martha of Bethany in the Fourth Gospel have identified them as disciples of Jesus. Raymond Brown, for instance, identifies Mary and Martha as disciples by connecting Martha's table service (12:2) with the office of *diakonos,* Martha's confession of faith (11:27) with Peter's confession in Matthew, and Jesus' love for Mary and Martha (11:5) with Jesus' love for the beloved disciple.[1] Elisabeth Schüssler Fiorenza goes beyond R. Brown to perceive discipleship in the fact that

1) Martha calls Mary to come to Jesus (11:20), just as Andrew and Philip call Peter and Nathanael;
2) Mary is specifically called by Jesus, just as the disciples are in the Synoptic gospels;
3) Phrases such as "the Jews who were with her" (cf. 11:31, 33, 45) illustrates that Mary had many followers among the Jews who came to believe in Jesus;

[1]Raymond Brown, "The Roles of Women in the Fourth Gospel," Appendix II, *The Community of the Beloved Disciple* (New York: Paulist, 1979) 187, 190–2.

4) Mary's anointing of Jesus' feet points forward to Jesus' action of washing the disciples' feet and his command to them that they should follow his example;

5) Mary, the true disciple, is contrasted with Judas.

Schüssler Fiorenza identifies Martha as the spokeswoman for the messianic faith of the Johannine community and Mary as the one who articulates the right praxis of discipleship.[2] Some of the other scholars who identify Mary and/or Martha of Bethany as disciples are Sandra Schneiders, Adele Reinhartz, Gail O'Day, Elizabeth Platt, Turid Karlsen Seim, R. Alan Culpepper, J. Ramsey Michaels, Martin Scott, and Ben Witherington.[3]

Although this identification of Mary and Martha of Bethany as disciples, like the identification of the Samaritan woman as a disciple, is certainly a valid interpretation for a reader of the twentieth or twenty-first century, I believe that a first-century reader would not have interpreted them in exactly this way. Given the literary and cultural milieu of the first-century reader of this Gospel and the previous portrayals of women in this Gospel, I believe the first-century reader would have perceived Mary of Bethany as the betrothed/bride of the messianic bridegroom on behalf of the Jews,[4] just as the Samaritan woman would have been perceived as the

---

[2]Cf. Elisabeth Schüssler Fiorenza, *In Memory of Her: A Feminist Theological Reconstruction of Christian Origins* (New York: Crossroad, 1983) 329–31; Elisabeth Schüssler Fiorenza, "A Feminist Critical Interpretation for Liberation: Martha and Mary in Lk. 10:38-42," *Religion and Intellectual Life* 3 (1986) 31–2.

[3]Sandra Schneiders, "Women in the Fourth Gospel and the Role of Women in the Contemporary Church," *Biblical Theology Bulletin* 12 (1982) 40–3. Sandra Schneiders, "Death in the Community of Eternal Life," *Interpretation* 41 (1987) 51. Adele Reinhartz, "The Gospel of John," *Searching the Scriptures: A Feminist Commentary*, ed. Elisabeth Schüssler Fiorenza (New York: Crossroad, 1994) 583; Adele Reinhartz, "From Narrative to History: The Resurrection of Mary and Martha," *Women Like This: New Perspectives on Jewish Women in the Greco-Roman World*, ed. Amy-Jill Levine (Atlanta: Scholars Press, 1992) 160, 172–81; Gail O'Day, "John," *The Women's Bible Commentary*, eds. Carol Newsom and Sharon Ringe (Louisville: Westminster/John Knox, 1992) 294, 297–300. Elizabeth Platt, "The Ministry of Mary of Bethany," *Theology Today* 34 (1977) 35–9. Turid Karlsen Seim, "Roles of Women in the Gospel of John," *Aspects on the Johannine Literature*, eds. Lars Hartman and Birger Olsson (Sweden: Alqvist & Wiksell International, 1987) 70–3. R. Alan Culpepper, *Anatomy of the Fourth Gospel: A Study of Literary Design* (Philadelphia: Fortress, 1983) 141–2. J. Ramsey Michaels, "John 12:1-11," *Interpretation* 43 (1989) 289. Martin Scott, *Sophia and the Johannine Jesus* (Sheffield: JSOT, 1992) 199, 203–4, 207, 211–2. Ben Witherington, *Women in Ministry of Jesus* (Cambridge: Cambridge University Press, 1984) 109, 115–6.

[4]Whether Mary was perceived by a first-century reader as simply betrothed to Jesus or already married to him makes no difference because a woman who was be-

betrothed/bride of the messianic bridegroom on behalf of the Samaritan people.[5] This portrayal of Mary of Bethany as a fictive betrothed/bride of Jesus would automatically make her sister and brother members of Jesus' family within the literary structure of the story.[6]

Necessitating the portrayal of Lazarus as a member of Jesus' fictive family is the Fourth Gospel's assertion prior to chapter 11 that only those who believe in Jesus will become members of the family of God, and only these persons will see eternal life (1:12-13; cf. 3:16-18; 5:21-27, 38-40; 6:27-29, 33-40, 47-48, 53-54; 8:23, 41-47; 10:25-30). For this reason, if Jesus is to raise Lazarus from the dead as a sign that Jesus can give eternal life to those who become members of the family of God, Lazarus must somehow be characterized as a part of Jesus' family and someone in the fictive family must first give an expression of faith. Mary of Bethany is the literary means by which Lazarus is characterized as a member of the family of God, and Martha of Bethany is the person of the family who expresses the necessary faith in Jesus.[7] Such characterizations of Mary, Martha, and Lazarus indicate that, when Jesus raises Lazarus, it is not just anyone whom he raises from the dead. Jesus raises from the dead a brother of his betrothed/bride, a member of his own extended family, a member of the family of God. In this respect, Mary of Bethany, as betrothed/bride of the messianic bridegroom, represents the community of faith whose "brothers" will see eternal life and Martha of Bethany represents the community of faith in her profession of faith.

---

trothed to a man was already perceived to be his wife. She merely continued to live in her own father's house until after the wedding ceremony. Cf. S. Safrai, "Home and Family," *The Jewish People of the First Century,* eds. S. Safrai and M. Stern (Philadelphia: Fortress, 1976) 2:756; David Mace, *Hebrew Marriage: A Sociological Study* (London: Epworth, 1953) 80 n. 1.

[5]Cf. chapter 3, pp. 49–52.

[6]According to R. Brown, a comparison of the phrase "our beloved (philos) Lazarus" in 11:11 and the title "beloved" that is used for Christians in 3 John 15 seems to support the notion that Lazarus somehow represents all those whom Jesus loves. Raymond Brown, *The Gospel According to John,* The Anchor Bible Series (New York: Doubleday, 1966, 1970) 1:431.

[7]J. N. Sanders states that no theological reason can be discerned for the association of Mary, Martha and Lazarus. My interpretation provides a theological reason. Cf. J. N. Sanders, "Lazarus of Bethany," *International Dictionary of the Bible,* ed. George Arthur Buttrick (New York: Abingdon, 1962) 3:103.

Mary of Bethany—Betrothed/Bride
of the Messianic Bridegroom

As has been noted in the previous two chapters, the first-century reader was prepared to interpret Mary of Bethany as the betrothed/bride of the messianic bridegroom on behalf of the Jewish people by

1) the portrayal of Jesus as the messianic bridegroom at the wedding at Cana (2:1-11),
2) Jesus' dialogue with Nicodemus about the necessity of being born from above (3:1-21),
3) John the Baptist's identification of Jesus as the bridegroom who has the bride (3:29),
4) the portrayal of the Samaritan woman as the betrothed/ bride of the messianic bridegroom on behalf of the Samaritan people (4:1-42).

Within chapter 11, one finds a variety of internal literary clues, as well as a possible intertextual reference to the Hebrew Bible, that would have encouraged a first-century reader to interpret Mary of Bethany as the Jewish betrothed/bride of the messianic bridegroom. The internal literary clues are

1) the narrator's focus on Mary of Bethany in relation to her sister and brother in 11:1-2;
2) the social implications of Mary of Bethany's anointing Jesus with perfume (μύρῳ) and wiping his feet with her hair (11:2, cf. 12:1-3);
3) the narrator's comments about the relationship of Jesus to Martha, Mary, and Lazarus (11:3-5, 11);
4) the implied author's consistent effort to connect Mary of Bethany with the Jews (11:31, 33, 45).

The possible intertextual reference to the Hebrew Bible is a verse in Canticle of Canticles, a series of love poems or songs between a man (portrayed both as a shepherd and a king) and a woman. In addition, as I shall later illustrate, the characterizations of Mary and Martha of Bethany are consistent with a first-century reader's cultural expectations of a good betrothed/bride and her "unattached" sister. First, however, let us look at the internal literary clues.

The Relative Importance of Mary of Bethany in 11:1-2

The first two verses of chapter 11 highlight the importance of Mary of Bethany in relation to her siblings. Besides identifying the village of Bethany in relation to Mary and Martha,[8] 11:1 also identifies Martha in re-

---

[8]O'Day, "John," 298.

lation to Mary by describing Martha as Mary's sister. "Now a certain man was ill, Lazarus of Bethany, the village of Mary and her sister Martha." This passage is followed by an identification of Lazarus as a brother of Mary.[9] "It was Mary, the one who anointed the Lord with perfume (μύρῳ) and wiped his feet with her hair, whose brother Lazarus was ill" (11:2). Thus, within the first two verses of the pericope, both Martha and Lazarus are identified according to their kinship relationship to Mary.[10] The reason for highlighting Mary in relation to her siblings is implied in 11:2 itself.

The Social Implications of the Anointing Statement (11:2, cf. 12:1-3)

The second verse of chapter 11 combines an explanation of the kinship relation between Lazarus and Mary with a description of Mary's future actions in relation to Jesus. Because 11:2 is an intrusive statement and relates matters that do not occur until chapter 12, many scholars have maintained that 11:2 is a later addition.[11] Those scholars who look at the Fourth Gospel as a literary unity, however, perceive this narrative intrusion as an indication that the two stories, the raising of Lazarus and the anointing of Jesus' feet, were intended to be interpreted in relation to each other. Usually the connection between the two pericopae is identified as an interpretive correlation between Lazarus' death and resuscitation and Jesus' death and resurrection.[12] Although this connection is certainly present, I believe that the intrusive statement also has another purpose, that of informing the reader that Mary of Bethany will function as the betrothed/bride of the messianic bridegroom in these two pericopae. To understand how 11:2 would have communicated this message to a first-century reader, it will be necessary to analyze the implications of the anointing statement in light of the social customs of the day.

[9]Cf. Michaels, 287.

[10]Brendan Byrne states that 11:1, as it stands, seems to imply that Mary is the chief link with Jesus, even though Mary has a lesser role than her sister in the drama itself. Brendan Byrne, *Lazarus: A Contemporary Reading of John 11:1-46* (Collegeville: The Liturgical Press, 1991) 37.

[11]Cf. Brown, *The Gospel According to John,* 1:433; Rudolf Schnackenburg, *The Gospel According to St. John* (New York: Crossroad, 1980, 1982) 2:322; Gérard Rochais, "La résurrection de Lazare (Jn 11, 1-46)," *Les récits de résurrection des morts dans le Nouveau Testament* (Cambridge: Cambridge University Press, 1981) 125–6; Byrne, 38, 72.

[12]Cf. Byrne, 38; Schneiders, "Death in the Community of Eternal Life," 45; Platt, 35.

THE SIGNIFICANCE OF ANOINTING JESUS WITH PERFUME[13]

Witherington emphasizes that it was perfume (μύρον) and no ordinary oil that Mary used to anoint Jesus.[14] According to Witherington, perfume was reserved for burial rites, cosmetic purposes, and romantic purposes.[15] To this list I would add that perfume was also used during formal meals to make the event a more pleasant experience. The use of perfume at Greco-Roman meals is noted by many ancient writers.[16] Support for this practice is found within Judaism in the Midrash Rabbah on Eccl 7:1 that states, "The fragrance of a good perfume spreads from the bedroom to the dining room."[17]

The context for the anointing is not stated in 11:2. This literary gap would have forced the reader to speculate about the circumstances and significance of the anointing. Furthermore, as I shall soon explain, the mere comment that Mary of Bethany wiped Jesus' feet with her hair would have led the first-century reader to entertain the possibility that a romantic purpose was involved in Mary's act of anointing Jesus with perfume.

Although 11:2 does not specifically state which part of Jesus' body was anointed with perfume, the reader may have assumed from the statement that Mary wiped Jesus' feet with her hair that it was Jesus' feet that she anointed. This assumption is later confirmed in 12:3. The writings of

---

[13]For much of the material in this section, I am indebted to Emily Chaney, who shared with me her, as yet, unpublished paper on the use of perfume in the first century C.E.

[14]Witherington, 112. Although Greco-Roman philosophers spoke against respectable women using perfume (cf. Athenaeus, *Deipnosophists,* 15.686e; Plutarch, *Quaestiones Convivales,* 693b–c), it can be assumed that respectable women did indeed use perfume and that some philosophers were simply opposed to this idea. Supporting this notion is the fact that bottles of perfume were sometimes included among the wedding presents and that the somewhat later Babylonian Talmud indicates that Jewish women in Jerusalem were supposed to be provided a portion of their dowries to buy perfume (b. Ketub. 66b). Cf. Lillian Portefaix, *Sister Rejoice: Paul's Letter to the Philippians* (Stockholm: Almqvist & Wilksell International, 1988) 86.

[15]Witherington, 112.

[16]Suetonius (*Nero* 31), Plutarch (*Galb.* 19.3), and Athenaeus (*Deipn.* 12.542c–d, dated to 228 C.E. but quoting earlier works) mention perfume being sprayed on guests through pipes in the walls or ceiling and Plutarch (*Galb.* 19.3) speaks of anointing himself and then sprinkling perfume on his guest Otho. Athenaeus in *Deipn.* 14.641d also speaks of perfume being brought in between the first and second tables of food for the purpose of anointing "the whole body." In *Deipn.* 4.129d–e he mentions female servants passing out perfume to guests, and in *Deipn.* 15.686c he mentions servants smearing perfume on the face of a guest who had fallen asleep.

[17]Cf. Brown, *The Gospel According to John,* 1:453.

Petronius, Pliny, and Athenaeus assert that the anointing of feet with perfume was known in antiquity.[18] In addition, the writings of Plutarch and Athenaeus illustrate that it was not unusual for women to put perfume in their hair.[19] Putting perfume in one's hair by using one's hair to wipe the perfume off another's feet, however, might have been considered unusual.

Romantic settings are often associated with a woman's anointing a man's feet with perfume.[20] For this reason, the reader of 11:2 could have entertained the possibility of a romantic setting for Mary's anointing of Jesus' feet with perfume. Because such anointings were sometimes done by women who were not the man's wife,[21] the act of anointing Jesus' feet with perfume by itself would not necessarily have led the reader to assume that Mary's literary function was that of the betrothed/bride of the messianic bridegroom. Nevertheless, given the previous statements that portray Jesus as the messianic bridegroom, as well as subsequent statements about Mary's wiping Jesus' feet with her hair (11:2) and Jesus' love for Martha, Mary, and Lazarus (11:5), I believe that a first-century reader would have concluded that Mary of Bethany was being portrayed as another fictive betrothed/bride of Jesus.

[18]Cf. Petronius (*Satyr.* 70). Pliny in *Nat. Hist.* 13.4.22 mentions the anointing of feet with perfume, but he ridicules the act as something that could hardly be noticed or enjoyed. Athenaeus in *Deipn.* 12:553a-e states that Athenians who lived in luxury anointed feet with perfume. Although he is from a somewhat later time period, his references about the anointing of feet refer to earlier works (e.g, Cephisodorus' *Trophonius,* Eubulus' *Spinx-Cario* and *Procris,* Antiphanes' *Alcestis, The Begging Priest* and *The Man from Zante* and Anaxandrides' *Protesilaus*). In addition, Luke 7:46 refers to the anointing of Jesus' feet with perfume following a washing of his feet. According to Witherington, P. Billerbeck also cites cases where rabbis allowed their feet to be anointed. In some of these cases, the anointing was done by women. Cf. Witherington, 113, 193, n. 207.

[19]Plutarch, who was of the opinion that virtuous women ought not to use perfume (*Quaest. Conviv.* 693b–c), states that respectable women should not use perfume on their hair because doing so would suggest that they are behaving as *hetaira* (*Conj. Praec.* 2:142b). One could assume from these statements that Plutarch presumed his admonitions were necessary because respectable women were, in fact, doing that which he thought they should not. In a discussion of Antiphanes' *The Villagers of Thoricus,* Athenaeus also mentions a woman putting perfume in her hair (*Deipn.* 12.553d).

[20]See Athenaeus' references to *Sphinx-Cairo* by Eubulus and *The Man from Zante* by Antiphanes in *Deipn.* 12:553a, c–d.

[21]As quoted by Athenaeus, in Antiphanes' *The Man from Zante* mistresses anointed a man's feet, in Eubulus' *Sphinx-Cairo* luxuriant "demoiselles" rubbed a man's foot with unguents of amaracus, and in Antiphanes' *The Begging Priest* a "girl" anointed the feet of a man. Cf. Athenaeus, *Deipn.* 553a, c.

THE SIGNIFICANCE OF MARY'S WIPING JESUS' FEET WITH HER HAIR

Many scholars consider Mary's act of wiping Jesus' feet with her hair after she had anointed them with perfume to be an irrational act.[22] Its presence in the Fourth Gospel is usually explained as the result of the influence of tradition.[23] Although the implied author of the Fourth Gospel may well have drawn on tradition in the formulation of this anointing story, the story as it stands must have made sense to the implied author and the implied reader.[24] Although the full implication of Mary's actions is not apparent until chapter 12, understanding first-century social custom regarding women's hair styles will shed some light on how the reader might have understood 11:2.

First, respectable women in the first century generally wore their hair in braids.[25] For a respectable woman to let her hair down in the presence of a man to whom she was not related would have been considered scandalous behavior.[26] When Mary of Bethany lets her hair down in the presence of Jesus, however, there is no negative assessment of her action or her person. This lack of a textual censure would have encouraged the reader to construct a fictional context in which Mary's intimate action was honorable; such a context would be provided by the assumption that Mary was

[22]Cf. Herold Weiss, "Foot Washing in the Johannine Community," *Novum Testamentum* 21 (1979) 313; Brown, *The Gospel According to John,* 1:452; Schnackenburg, 2:367.

[23]Cf. Platt, 35, 37; Brown, *The Gospel According to John,* 1:433, 449–52, 454; Schnackenburg, 2:367; Witherington, 111–2.

[24]R. Brown merely states that the author of the Fourth Gospel kept the story with its confusing amalgamation of details because it fit his theological purposes. Brown, *The Gospel According to John,* 1:452.

[25]Sarah Pomeroy notes that Hellenistic Neopythagorean writing speaks about moderation in the ornamentation of the braiding. Likewise, Jerome Murphy-O'Connor states that the word περιβολαίου in 1 Cor 11:4 has to do with the practice of a woman's wrapping her long hair around her head in plaits, not with veiling, and that moderation in braiding is mentioned in 1 Tim 2:9 and 1 Pet 3:3. Sarah Pomeroy, "Hellenistic Women," *Goddess, Whores, Wives, and Slaves: Women in Classical Antiquity* (New York: Schocken, 1975) 135. Jerome Murphy-O'Connor, "Sex and Logic in 1 Corinthians 11:2-16," *Catholic Biblical Quarterly* 42 (1980) 487–90, n. 31.

[26]Witherington and R. Brown both refer to a woman letting her hair down in public as "scandalous." One example in Christian writings of a woman letting her hair down in public can be found in Luke 7:36-50. In this story, the woman is characterized as a sinner. Both Witherington and Brown state that this action was not inappropriate in the Lucan anointing story involving a sinful woman, but was out of character for the virtuous Mary of Bethany. Witherington, 111–3. Brown, *The Gospel According to John,* 1:450–1.

somehow related to Jesus. Mary's actual physical contact with Jesus would then have led the reader to assume that Mary's relationship to Jesus was that of a betrothed/ bride. This reading is supported by the description of the "love" relationship that existed between Jesus and Mary's entire family.

Jesus' Love-Relationship with Martha, Mary and Lazarus (11:3-5, 11)

Following 11:2, which both characterizes Lazarus as Mary's brother and describes Mary's future anointing of Jesus, is the statement, "Therefore (οὖν), the sisters sent word to him, saying, 'Lord, the one whom you love is ill'" (11:3). If one interprets the Greek word οὖν as an inferential particle that "introduces the result of or an inference from what preceded it,"[27] then the action of the sisters as stated in 11:3 is somehow connected with the statement in 11:2. If the reader perceived 11:2 as indicating that Mary of Bethany was being portrayed as a fictive betrothed/bride of Jesus, as well as a sister to Lazarus, then an inferential "therefore" makes these familial relationships the basis for the sisters' action of sending word to Jesus that the one whom he loved was ill. In other words, Jesus' "love" relationship with Lazarus was based on Mary's relationship to Jesus and Lazarus' relationship to her. The following explanation about marriage and dyadic alliances will illustrate this point.

In the first century, "friendship" or "love" language was often used to describe dyadic alliances between men.[28] These dyadic alliance were non-legal contractual obligations based on the principle of reciprocity and the concept of honor and shame.[29] Such dyadic alliances between men were often formed through the exchange of women in marriage.[30] In fact, Gustav Stählin notes several cases in Greek literature in which the Greek word for a member of one's household (οικειος) was used as a synonym, as an almost-synonym, or along with the Greek word for friend (φίλος) and

---

[27]Cf. Walter Bauer, *A Greek-English Lexicon of the New Testament and Other Early Christian Literature,* 2nd ed., revised and augmented by F. W. Gingrich and Frederick Danker (Chicago: University of Chicago Press, 1979 [1957]) 592–3.

[28]For a discussion of the use of friendship and love language in such alliances, see Gustav Stählin, "φιλέω," *Theological Dictionary of the New Testament,* ed. Gerhard Friedrich, trans. and ed. Geoffrey Bromiley (Grand Rapids: Eerdmans, 1974) 9:113–71.

[29]For a full discussion of dyadic alliances see: Bruce Malina, "The Perception of Limited Goods," *The New Testament World: Insights from Cultural Anthropology* (Louisville: John Knox, 1981) 71–93.

[30]For a discussion of dyadic alliances formed through marriage in the first century C.E., see Malina, "Kinship and Marriage," *The New Testament World,* 99–103.

several occasions in which φίλος occurs as a noun for "one's kin," or "nearest relative" (συγγενής). He further states that φίλος was very close to the Greek word for "one's own" (ἴδιος).[31] Thus, it is not inconceivable that a first-century reader would have assumed that the love relationship between Jesus and Lazarus was based on a fictive kinship relationship that was established by a literary, betrothal/marital relationship between Jesus and Mary of Bethany.

The assumption that the love Jesus had for Lazarus was based on a fictive kinship relationship seems to be supported by the narrator's statement, "Now Jesus loved Martha and her sister and Lazarus" (11:5).[32] For some reason, the love relationship that Jesus had with Lazarus extended to the entire family. This extended love relationship, I believe, can best be explained as the result of a fictive betrothal/marital relationship between Mary of Bethany and Jesus.[33]

The Connection Between Mary of Bethany and the Jews

Contributing to the notion that Mary of Bethany functions as the betrothed/bride of the messianic bridegroom on behalf of the Jewish people is the fact that the implied author consistently connected Mary of Bethany with the Jews (11:31, 33, 45).[34] Although Schneiders is probably correct when she says that Mary of Bethany is the literary means for the Jews' arrival on stage for the raising of Lazarus (11:31),[35] that fact does not explain Mary's repeated association with the Jews (cf. 11:33, 45). R. Brown and Brendan Byrne note that the use of the term "the Jews" in chapter 11 differs noticeably from its use in chapters 1–10. In chapter 11 the Jews are the ordinary people of Judea and Jerusalem, not hostile Jewish authorities.[36] Perceiving Mary of Bethany as betrothed/bride of the messianic bridegroom on behalf of the Jews would explain both the frequent con-

---

[31]Stählin also notes a correlation between φίλος, φιλέω, and ἴδιος in John 15:19: ὁ κόσμος ἂν τὸ ἴδιον ἐφίλει. Stählin, 114, 148, 154.

[32]In this verse, Martha's name is listed first and Mary's name is not mentioned at all. This wording may seem to present an obstacle to Mary's characterization as the fictive betrothed/bride of Jesus. This problem will be discussed later in this chapter.

[33]Jerome Neyrey perceives a similar fictive kinship circle being established in the story of the Samaritan woman at the well. Jerome Neyrey, "What's Wrong with this Picture? John 4, Cultural Stereotypes of Women, and Public and Private Space," *Biblical Theology Bulletin* 24 (1994) 77–84.

[34]Cf. John Rena, "Women in the Gospel of John," *Église et Théologie* 17 (1986) 141–2.

[35]Schneiders, "Death in the Community of Eternal Life," 53–4. Cf. Byrne, 56.

[36]Cf. Brown, *The Gospel According to John,* 1:428; Byrne, 42.

nection of Mary with the Jews and the reason the term "the Jews" is used differently in this chapter.

A Possible Intertextual Connection with the Canticle of Canticles

The full significance of Mary's act of wiping Jesus' feet with her hair after she anointed them with perfume is made known in 12:3. This verse informs the reader that the type of perfume (μύρου) Mary used to anoint Jesus' feet was pure nard (νάρδου πιστικῆς). The reader also learns that, by wiping Jesus' perfumed feet with her hair, Mary was able to fill the house with the fragrance of the perfume (ἡ δὲ οἰκία ἐπληρώθη ἐκ τῆς ὀσμῆς τοῦ μύπου) (12:3). O'Day states that the purpose for this depiction is to contrast the odor of death from Lazarus' tomb (11:39) with the odor emanating from Mary's extravagant love.[37] Although O'Day is probably correct in her analysis, there may also be an allusion here to Cant 1:12, "While the king was on his couch, my nard (νάρδος μου) gave forth its fragrance (ὀσμὴν αὐτοῦ)."[38] Although these canticles may have been used at weddings, both Jewish and Christian traditions found another level of meaning for them, for they were also perceived as expressions of the love-relationship that existed between God and God's people.[39] With the assumption that Jesus, as God's agent, is taking on the God's role in this relationship, such an intertextual reference to Canticle of Canticles would support the assumption that Mary of Bethany was functioning as the betrothed/bride of the messianic bridegroom on behalf of the Jewish people. Taken by itself, an allusion to Canticle of Canticles might not seem warranted for 12:3. If one takes into consideration, however, the possible allusion to Cant 4:12 in the story of the Samaritan woman mentioned in chapter 3 and the possible allusion to Cant 3:1-4d in the story of Mary Magdalene searching for Jesus (cf. 20:1, 13-15),[40] then the argument for an allusion to Canticle of Canticles in the story of Mary of Bethany is strengthened.

---

[37]O'Day, "John," 299.

[38]We know that Jesus was reclining at table by the narrator's statement, "Lazarus was one of those *reclining* with him" (ἀνακειμένων σὺν αὐτῷ (12:2). My translation would emphasize the concept of reclining at table. Cf. Bauer, *A Greek-English Lexicon,* 55.

[39]Cf. *The New Oxford Annotated Bible: With the Apocryphal/ Deutero-canonical Books (New Revised Standard Version),* eds. Bruce Metzger and Roland Murphy (New York: Oxford University Press, 1991) 853 OT.

[40]Cf. chapter 3, pp. 48–9, 54; chapter 6, pp. 146, 150, 157–60, 166–7.

The Function and Characterization of Mary of Bethany

Although the most significant literary function of Mary of Bethany is that of being the betrothed/bride of the messianic bridegroom on behalf of the Jewish people, her character does have other literary functions. She also functions as

1) the literary means by which the Jews are brought onto the stage for the raising of Lazarus;[41]
2) the person in Jesus' fictive family who expresses deep sorrow on the death of a loved one;[42]
3) a foil for Jesus' own emotional response and subsequent action;
4) a contrasting figure to Judas.

As Mary fulfills these functions, various aspects of her character are revealed. She is characterized as:

1) a dutiful betrothed/bride who waits to be called and then responds quickly;
2) a distraught sister and disappointed believer who takes the death of her brother personally;
3) an affectionate betrothed/bride at a meal with her beloved.

The Dutiful Betrothed/Bride of Chapter 11

In 11:20 the narrator states, "When (ὡς) Martha heard that Jesus was coming, she went out to meet him, while (δὲ) Mary sat in the house." Mary and Martha appear to be contrasted in this passage,[43] especially if one takes the δὲ of v 20 as introducing a contrasting apodosis after a temporal protasis.[44]

The implied author of the Fourth Gospel may well have drawn on tradition to construct this contrasting characterization of Martha and Mary.[45] Nevertheless, the present-day reader must remember that the implied author always used tradition in a way that furthered the narrative. One possible reason for portraying Mary as staying in the house while her sister

[41]Schneiders, "Death in the Community of Eternal Life," 53–4.
[42]Ibid., 53–4.
[43]Byrne, 48, 85.
[44]Cf. Bauer, *A Greek-English Lexicon,* 171.
[45]Cf. Luke 10:38-40; O'Day, "John," 298; Schneiders, "Death in the Community of Eternal Life," 46; Schnackenburg, 2:320–1; Reinhartz, "From Narrative to History: The Resurrection of Mary and Martha," 162, n. 7; B. McNeil, "The Raising of Lazarus," *Downside Review* 92 (1974) 274–5; Byrne, 49.

goes out to meet Jesus is that such a characterization would portray Mary as the dutiful betrothed/bride who waits until her bridegroom calls her.

Only after Martha tells Mary that the Teacher[46] is calling her, does Mary go to him quickly (ταχὺ) (11:29). As Mary goes to him quickly, she is accompanied by "the Jews who were with her" (11:31). This detail both adds to her characterization as betrothed/bride of the messianic bridegroom on behalf of the Jewish people, and allows the Jews to be brought onto the stage for the raising of Lazarus. It also illustrates that Mary of Bethany, as a betrothed/bride, acted properly according to first-century standards.

Although the text states that the Jews accompanied Mary because they thought she was going to the tomb, it should be noted that, from an anthropological point of view, a woman who was somehow connected to a man did not go out of the village alone.[47] A sensitivity to this point can be found in the literature of the period.

In her commentary on *The Book of Aseneth,* Ross Kraemer notes that the longer version of the text clarifies the point that Aseneth met her betrothed Joseph inside the courtyard. Kraemer states that this redaction illustrates a sensitivity to ancient social norms of gendered space.[48] Certainly the mother of Jesus is always accompanied by others, whether by her sons at Cana (cf. 2:12) or her sister at the cross (cf. 19:25). Martha, who is unconnected to father, husband, son, or now brother, would not have been bound by these social constraints.[49] She could freely go outside the village alone to meet Jesus without first being called (cf. 11:20, 30). Mary, as the betrothed/bride of the messianic bridegroom, however, would have been bound by these social constraints. If she went outside the village, she would need to be accompanied by someone.

[46]If these pericopae were meant to be understood within the context of a fictive family relationship, one might ask why Martha identifies Jesus as the Teacher (11:28) and not as Mary's bridegroom. The reason for such subtlety is that the bridegroom motif forms a sub-text in the Fourth Gospel. The implied author was encouraging the first-century reader to construct the sub-text, thus keeping the reader engaged in the reading process. Cf. Charles Talbert, *Reading John: A Literary and Theological Commentary on the Fourth Gospel and the Johannine Epistles* (New York: Crossroad, 1994) 103.

[47]On gendered space in the New Testament world and its implication for honor and shame, see Malina, *The New Testament World,* 42–4. For a discussion of how an understanding of gendered space can aid in an understanding of a Johannine pericope, see Neyrey, "What's Wrong with this Picture?," 79–81.

[48]Ross Kraemer, "The Book of Aseneth," *Searching the Scriptures: A Feminist Commentary,* ed. Elisabeth Schüssler Fiorenza (New York: Crossroad, 1994) 883–4.

[49]Cf. Malina, *The New Testament World,* 44.

*A Distraught Sister and Disappointed Believer Who Takes
the Death of Her Brother Personally*

As soon as Mary of Bethany arrives at the place where Jesus is, she
falls at his feet and weeps (11:32-33). This is the first of two occasions
where Mary is portrayed at Jesus' feet. The implied author of the Fourth
Gospel may well have been influenced by tradition for this aspect of
Mary's portrayal.[50] Nevertheless, in both cases in the Fourth Gospel where
Mary is portrayed at Jesus' feet, the implied author used this aspect of her
characterization to further the purposes of the text. In this first case, falling
at Jesus' feet is connected with weeping. As such, it reinforces the characterization of Mary as one who is overcome with grief at the death of her
brother.

Mary's words to Jesus basically repeat Martha's first statement to
Jesus with one notable difference. Although both say to Jesus, "Lord, if
you had been here, my brother would not have died," the placement of the
pronoun "my" in Mary's statement (οὐκ ἄν μου ἀπέθανεν ὁ ἀδελπός)
puts emphasis on this possessive pronoun, whereas the placement of the
pronoun "my" in Martha's statement (οὐκ ἄν ἀπέθανεν ὁ ἀδελπός μου)
does not (cf. 11:21, 32).[51] Thus, both women express disappointment and
belief in Jesus' ability to work miracles,[52] but Mary's statement places emphasis on the fact that it was *her* brother who died. Such an emphasis
would have been significant to a first-century reader who perceived Mary
as the betrothed/bride of the messianic bridegroom.[53] It was not just anyone who died because of Jesus' absence. It was the brother of his be-
trothed/bride who died. This emphatic use of the pronoun heightens the
understanding of Mary as the betrothed/bride of the messianic bridegroom
and supports the concept that Mary functions as a representative of the
community of faith in the text.

Unlike Martha who enters into a dialogue with Jesus about eternal
life (cf. 11:21-27), Mary makes no further comment to Jesus. Focusing
only on the past opportunity that has been missed, Mary continues to weep

[50]In Luke 10:38-42, Mary is portrayed at the feet of Jesus silently listening to his
teaching and in Luke 7:38 the woman who anoints Jesus' feet is depicted as weeping
and washing his feet with her tears. Cf. Michaels, 287; Brown, *The Gospel According
to John,* 1:433; Schüssler Fiorenza, "A Feminist Critical Interpretation for Liberation,"
32; Witherington, 104–5, 107.

[51]Giblin, 209.

[52]Cf. Giblin, 209; Schneiders, "Death in the Community of Eternal Life," 52, 54;
Reinhartz, "From Narrative to History: The Resurrection of Mary and Martha," 173.

[53]Giblin, who notes the difference in word order, attributes to Mary's response
only an emphasis in emotional tone and a sense of personal loss. Giblin, 209.

in the presence of Jesus (11:32-33). Such weeping and focusing on Jesus' failure to prevent Lazarus' death, both by Mary and by the Jews with her (11:32-33, 37), deeply moves Jesus in spirit (ἐνεβριμήσατο τῷ πνεύματι) and troubles him emotionally (ἐτάραξεν ἑαυτου) (11:33), even to the point of weeping himself (ἐδάκρυσεν ὁ Ἰησοῦς) (11:35). Jesus' emotional response seems directly connected to the emotional response of Mary and the Jews with whom she is associated.

Whether Jesus' strong emotional response is a negative commentary on Mary's character, as well as that of the Jews, is debatable.[54] If Mary is being portrayed as the betrothed/bride of the messianic bridegroom on behalf of the Jewish people, however, it is significant that the depth of her emotional response and the emotional response of the community associated with her moves Jesus to tears and action. After all, Yʜwʜ wept with Jazer over the destruction of Sibmah (Isa 16:9, cf. 14:23-24; Jer 48:32), and wept over the destruction of the people of Jerusalem, calling them to weep and mourn, and then promised that a day would come when they would not weep (Isa 22:4, 12; 30:19; Jer 8:23–9:24). Jesus, as God's agent, likewise is moved to tears and action by the deep emotion that the community of faith and the woman who represented that community of faith felt at the death of a loved one.[55]

Jesus responds to the emotion of Mary and the Jews with her by asking where they laid Lazarus (11:34). He subsequently has the stone removed, prays to his Father, and then calls Lazarus forth from the grave (11:38-43). The sign that Jesus performs by raising Lazarus from the dead causes many of the Jews "who had come with Mary" to put their faith in Jesus (11:45). Thus, Mary, like the Samaritan woman before her, facilitates

---

[54]Some scholars (e.g., Loisy, Bauer, Bultmann, Hoskyns, Davey, Wikenhauser, Lagrange, Bernard) perceive Jesus' emotional response as reflecting negatively on the mourners. Schnackenburg, however, separates Mary from the Jews with whom Jesus is angry. Other scholars also refute such a negative reflection on Mary. Noting that Jesus himself weeps, they perceive his emotional response to be based on his confrontation with realm of Satan (e.g., R. Brown, Schanz, Zahn, Schick) or the prospect of his own death (Chrysostom). Byrne, noting that the word used for Jesus' weeping is different from that used for Mary and the Jews, maintains that both aspects are present. Cf. Brown, *The Gospel According to John,* 1:425–6, 435; Edwyn Hoskyns, *The Fourth Gospel* (London: Faber and Faber Limited, 1940) 2:470–3; Schnackenburg, 2:336, 516, n. 54–6; Byrne, 57–60, 86; Talbert, 174–5.

[55]Elsewhere in Christian tradition, Jesus weeps over the spiritual loss of a community of faith (e.g., Jesus weeps over Jerusalem in Luke 19:41; cf. Heb 5:7). R. Brown acknowledges that Lazarus probably represents all those whom Jesus loves and that the raising of Lazarus was a sign of Jesus' power to give eternal life to those who believed. Cf. Brown, *The Gospel According to John,* 1:426, 430–1, 436–7.

some of her community to come to believe in Jesus. This instance strengthens her portrayal as the betrothed/bride of the messianic bridegroom with respect to her own community.

The Affectionate Betrothed/Bride at a Meal with her Bridegroom

When the reader was informed in 11:2 that Mary of Bethany is the one who anoints Jesus with perfume and wipes his feet with her hair, the reader had to speculate about the context of the anointing, as well as the significance of the action. Now in chapter 12, the reader is specifically told that Mary anointed the feet of Jesus with perfume (12:3) and that this anointing took place six days before Passover during a supper (δεῖπνον) in Bethany given in Jesus' honor (12:1-2). In terms of the immediate story line, this meal was probably understood by the reader as an act of reciprocity for Jesus' having raised Lazarus from the dead.[56] Nevertheless, at this point in my analysis, it might be helpful to look at the significance of this meal in relationship to the overall portrayal of Jesus in the Fourth Gospel as the messianic bridegroom.

In the story of the Samaritan woman at the well, it was noted that, on one level of the text, the Samaritan woman became Jesus' fictive betrothed and bride who produced a great number of offspring (a great harvest of believers). On another level of the text, however, the reader would have been aware of the fact that the betrothal dinner was missing. Interpreting the Gospel as a unity, therefore, the meal that Jesus had with the family of Mary of Bethany could have been interpreted as the betrothal meal that was missing in the story of the Samaritan woman at the well. Such an interpretation of the meal would also have prepared the reader to perceive the subsequent passion and death of Jesus as his messianic wedding.[57]

It may be especially significant for our understanding of Mary of Bethany as the betrothed/bride of the messianic bridegroom that the implied author of the Fourth Gospel chose to portray Mary's anointing Jesus' feet at a supper (δεῖπνον). Formal Greco-Roman meals, which influenced Jewish and Christian meals, generally occurred in two parts, the supper (δεῖπνον) and the drinking party or *symposium* at which conversation

[56]Cf. Michaels, 287. For an explanation of the anthropological concept of reciprocity, see Malina, *The New Testament World,* 79–82, 90.

[57]According to Mace, after the betrothal had occurred and the *mohar,* or bridal price, was handed over, the woman was at the disposal of the suitor. The wedding ceremony could happen immediately, or there could be an interim period. It was not until Talmudic times that a time interval of twelve months for a virgin and three months for a widow became obligatory. Mace, 174. Cf. Safrai, 757.

took place.[58] At these formal meals, guests' heads were often anointed with perfume at the transition between the supper (δεῖπνον) and the *symposium*.[59] The purpose for this anointing of the head with perfume was to protect the person against the ill-effects of intoxication.[60] Such anointings were usually done by servants, prostitutes or *hetaira,* because wives generally did not stay for the *symposium*.[61]

In chapter 12 of the Fourth Gospel, however, the meal is not portrayed as the symposium part of a formal meal. It is envisioned as a δεῖπνον (cf. 12:2). A wife could be present at the dinner part of such a meal, especially if the meal were considered a family supper with a limited guest list.[62] The presence of Martha and Lazarus, as well as Jesus' disciples, helps to give this meal the aura of a fictive family dinner. Because the wife would generally be portrayed as sitting at her husband's feet at these dinners,[63] the reader could very well have envisioned Mary as the

[58]Cf. Kathleen Corley, "Were The Women around Jesus Really Prostitutes? Women in the Context of Greco-Roman Meals," *Society of Biblical Literature 1989 Seminar Papers,* ed. David Lull (Atlanta: Scholars Press, 1989) 487–8, 492, 514, 519–21.

[59]Cf. Mark 14:3; Matt 26:6-7. Also see Athenaeus' comments on Plilonides' *On Perfumes and Wreaths* and Hicesius' *On Materials* in *Deipn.* 15.691f, 692b, 675, 689c and Plutarch's comments in *Quaest. Conviv.,* 711–13.

[60]Cf. Plutarch, *Quaest. Conviv.,* 647e.

[61]Corley notes that eventually the Roman matron was allowed to stay for the *symposium* in the late Republican and early Imperial periods, but not before the time of Augustus. Those who continued to follow the Greek tradition, however, generally did not allow respectable women to attend the *symposium.* Corley, 492, 494. Cf. Neyrey, "What's Wrong with this Picture," 80; David Aune, "Septem Sapientium Convivium," *Plutarch's Ethical Writings and Early Christian Literature,* ed. Hans Dieter Betz (Leiden: Brill, 1978) 70–3.

[62]According to Corley and Aune, Greco-Roman writers during the Roman period who maintained an idealistic view could accept wives being present for the supper part (δεῖπνον) of a formal meal with a limited quest list. Neyrey quotes Cornelius Nepos (*Praef.* 4–7) as stating that the Greek custom differed from that of the Romans. Greeks only allowed their wives to attend family oriented dinners with a limited guest list. Greek wives did not attend formal dinner-parties; only prostitutes did. I believe that the implied author of the Fourth Gospel would have followed the stricter Hellenistic custom, rather than the more liberal Roman custom. Either way, Mary, as betrothed/bride, could have been at the family oriented δεῖπνον. Corley, 488–90. Aune, "Septem Sapientium Convivium," 70–2. Neyrey, "What's Wrong with this Picture?," 80. Cf. Pomeroy, 189; Eva Cantarella, *Pandora's Daughters: The Role and Status of Women in Greek and Roman Antiquity,* trans. Maureen Fant (Baltimore: Johns Hopkins University Press, 1987) 134.

[63]Corley states that, according to Greek ideology, prostitutes were allowed to recline next to the men at the meal. Wives would have sat at the feet of their husbands

affectionate betrothed/bride of Jesus as she sits at his feet, anointing them with perfume.

Judas complains that the costly (πολυτίμου) perfume of pure nard should be sold for three hundred denarii and the money given to the poor (12:4-5). The narrator goes on to explain, however, that Judas said this because he was the holder of the money for the disciples (cf. 12:6). This statement by the narrator not only implies that Judas was planning on helping himself to the money generated by the selling of the perfume, but that the disciples had some right to the money that would be generated by the selling of Mary's perfume. Such an implication deepens the sense a community of faith is being depicted as a fictive family setting involving Mary.

Jesus responds to Judas' objections with the statement, "Let her alone, let her keep it (τηρήσῃ αὐτό) for the day of my burial" (12:7). Although some scholars understand Mary's anointing of Jesus' feet as a burial preparation,[64] nothing in the text of the Fourth Gospel suggests this interpretation.[65] Jesus simply defends Mary's right to "keep" the remainder of the perfume for the day of his future burial.[66] R. Brown and Rudolf Schnackenburg have a problem with this interpretation because Mary of Bethany does not actually anoint Jesus' body for burial after he dies. Joseph of Arimathea and Nicodemus are the ones who anoint and bury Jesus' body (19:38-40).[67]

---

during a meal. Roman matrons were eventually allowed to recline with their husbands during the late Republican and early Imperial periods. Prior to the time of Augustus, however, even Roman matrons would have sat at their husband's feet. Corley, 490, 492.

[64]Brown, *The Gospel According to John* 1:454. Schnackenburg, 2:369. Although R. Brown perceives Mary as being unconscious of any connection between her action and Jesus' death, Michaels, Rena and Reinhartz believe that Mary's actions were based on her own awareness of Jesus' imminent death. Schneiders perceives the anointing simply as a foreshadowing of Jesus' burial. Michaels, 288, 290. Rena, 142–3. Reinhartz, "The Gospel of John," 583. Schneiders, "Women in the Fourth Gospel," 43. Cf. O'Day, "John," 299.

[65]Although the anointings in the Gospels of Mark and Matthew are given this interpretation by Jesus (cf. Mark 14:8; Matt 26:12), in the Gospel of Luke Jesus interprets the anointing as an act that illustrates the forgiveness of sin (Luke 7:44-50).

[66]Cf. Schnackenburg, 2:368, 523, n. 22; Brown, *The Gospel According to John*, 1:449. Unlike the anointing in Mark, which presumes that the woman used all of the perfume because she "broke the jar" (cf. Mark 14:3), the Fourth Gospel says nothing about Mary's breaking a jar. Thus, the reader could have assumed that she did not use the whole pound of perfume to anoint Jesus' feet.

[67]R. Brown and Schnackenburg also state that the remainder of Mary's pound of perfume would seem insignificant in comparison with the one hundred pounds of

The implied author of the Fourth Gospel indeed may have been responding to conflicting traditions regarding the burial of Jesus.[68] If one assumes, however, that Mary did not use all the perfume and that the community of disciples in conjunction with Lazarus, Martha, and Mary constitute a fictive kinship group, then one could assume that Mary, as betrothed/bride, was to "keep" the remainder of the perfume for the men in the fictive family to use for Jesus' burial.

By portraying Mary of Bethany as an affectionate betrothed/bride willing to be extravagant with her beloved, and by having Jesus defend her, the implied author contrasts her with Judas, the male disciple who is both a self-serving thief (12:7) and the one who would betray Jesus (12:4). Again we see the positive actions of a woman providing a contrast for a negatively portrayed man (cf. Nicodemus and the Samaritan woman).[69] This contrast adds to the building assumption that the implied

---

myrrh and aloes that Joseph of Arimathea and Nicodemus used in Jesus' burial. Such problems led Barrett to suggest that the phrase "τηρήσῃ αὐτό" be translated "remember it." Cf. Brown, *The Gospel According to John,* 1:449; Schnackenburg, 2:368–9, 523, n. 22.9.

[68]In all of the Synoptic Gospels, Joseph of Arimathea asks for and buries Jesus' body (cf. Mark 15:43-46; Matt 27:57-60; Luke 23:50-53). In those Synoptic Gospels that are specifically addressed to Gentile Christians, however, the women prepared Jesus' body for burial (cf. Mark 15:47–16:1; Luke 23:54–24:3). This is in harmony with Mary Lefkowitz' statement that in Greco-Roman literature female family members usually made sure that the dead were buried properly. In the story of the women going to the tomb in the Gospel of Matthew, however, nothing is said of their intent to anoint the body. The women simply go "to inspect the tomb" (Matt 28:1). This is consistent with the implication in the Hebrew Bible and other Jewish works that a male member of the family had the religious responsibility for making sure the dead were buried (cf. *Meg.* 4:3; Tob 7:15; *Ahikar* 1:4-5).

Although women could wrap and bind the bodies of both men and women, men could wrap and bind only the bodies of men. This wrapping and binding of male bodies by men could have included anointing because men could wash the bodies of certain men and this washing of the body took place after the anointing of the body (cf. *m. Sabbath* 23:5; *b. Semahoth* 12:10). Thus, a first-century implied reader of the Gospel of Matthew with a Jewish background may have assumed that Joseph of Arimathea did the anointing when he wrapped the body with fresh linens (Matt 27:59-60). Other scholars assume that the anointing by a woman at Bethany took care of the burial preparations (cf. Matt 26:6-13). Cf. Mary Lefkowitz, "Influential Women," *Images of Women in Antiquity,* eds. Averil Cameron and Amélie Kuhrt (Detroit: Wayne State University Press, 1983) 51–2, 61; Safrai, 777; Léonie Archer, "The Role of Jewish Women in the Religion, Ritual and Cult of Graeco-Roman Palestine," *Images of Women in Antiquity,* ed. Averil Cameron and Amélie Kuhrt (Detroit: Wayne State University Press, 1983) 283.

[69]Cf. Reinhartz, "The Gospel of John," 583.

author was encouraging the first-century reader to adopt some aspects of the "feminine" approach to Jesus.

The Function and Characterization of Martha of Bethany

As is true in the story of the Samaritan woman, it is essential in the stories of Mary, Martha, and Lazarus of Bethany for someone in Jesus' fictive family to express belief in him. In the story of the Samaritan woman at the well, this belief was first tentatively expressed in the proclamation of the Samaritan woman (4:29). Her tentative belief-statement was then superseded by the townspeople's confident statement of faith (4:42). In the story of the raising of Lazarus, this role of expressing faith in Jesus is given to Martha.[70]

In chapter 11, Martha actually appears to have a four-fold function of being

1) a contrasting figure to the male disciples;
2) a foil for Jesus' teaching and self-revelation;[71]
3) that person in Jesus' fictive "Jewish" family who expresses faith in him;
4) a broker for Jesus' relationship with his betrothed/ bride.

As Martha fulfills these functions, various aspects of her character emerge. She is characterized as being

1) a sensitive woman who is aware of just how dangerous it is for Jesus to be in the area;
2) a disappointed believer in Jesus' ability to work miracles who maintains a belief in Jesus' ability to function as an intermediary with God, despite his failure to help her brother;
3) a believer who moves from a "below" perspective to an "above" perspective to make a confession of faith that embodies the theology of the implied author.

---

[70]Lazarus, who is dead at this point in the text, certainly cannot be the member of the family to express belief in Jesus. Schnackenburg questions, however, why the implied author chose Martha rather than Mary to be the one who voices a statement of belief. He hypothesizes that the implied author of the Fourth Gospel may have been using a tradition that valued the active Martha as much as the more contemplative Mary. A more probable rationale, it seems to me, is that the implied author of the Fourth Gospel was influenced by a tradition that portrayed Martha as the talkative one (cf. Luke 10:38-42). This talkative characterization would have fit the implied author's need for a dialogue with Jesus about resurrection and his relationship to eternal life better than the received tradition of a quiet Mary. Cf. Seim, 70–1; Schnackenburg, 2:329.

[71]Byrne, 50.

A Sensitive Woman Aware of Danger

Prior to Jesus' arrival at Bethany, the reader is well aware of the negative attitude some Jews have toward Jesus (cf. 5:16-18; 7:11-31, 40-44;
8:40, 57-59; 9:18-24; 10:19-21, 31-40; 11:15-16). In addition, upon Jesus'
arrival at Bethany, the reader is informed of the proximity of Jerusalem to
Bethany and the presence in the village of many Jews who had come to
console Martha and Mary (11:18-20). In the midst of these ominous statements, Martha is portrayed as going outside the village alone to meet Jesus
(11:20, 30) and then secretly or quietly (λάθρᾳ) informing Mary of Jesus'
arrival (11:28). On one level of the text, Martha's actions may indicate
that, as a woman who has no male relatives, she functions as the broker
for Jesus' relationship with her sister. On another level of the text, however, Martha's actions may indicate that she is aware of how dangerous it
would be for Jesus if certain Jews knew of his presence in the vicinity.[72]

This awareness of danger on Martha's part parallels the awareness of
the disciples who remind Jesus that the people of Judea had only recently
tried to stone him (11:8). The sensitivity with which Martha deals with
this danger, however, contrasts with the false bravado of Thomas, the male
disciple who said, "Let us also go to die with him" (11:16). This contrast,
combined with the fact that Martha is so positively portrayed, may be yet
another indication that the implied author was urging the reader to assume
a more "feminine" manner of responding to Jesus.[73] Structurally, this
awareness of danger on Martha's part allows Jesus' teaching about eternal
life and Martha's confession of faith to be made solely in the presence of
the disciples.[74] It also enables Mary to be associated with the Jews, as they
later follow her to the tomb for the raising of Lazarus.

A Disappointed Believer Who Continues to Believe in Jesus' Power

When Martha does meet Jesus, her first words to him are, "Lord, if
you had been here, my brother would not have died" (11:21). These
words, also used by her sister Mary, express both disappointment at Jesus'
failure to be present when they needed him and belief in Jesus' ability to

[72]Cf. Byrne, 55.

[73]Cheryl Brown notes similar feminine tendencies in *Biblical Antiquities* and pos-
tulates that such tendencies may be an expression of a feminine element in religious
experience. Cheryl Brown, *No Longer Be Silent: First Century Jewish Portraits of Biblical Women* (Louisville: Westminster/John Knox, 1992) 26.

[74]Byrne states that separating the two sisters enables Jesus' teaching to be given
apart from the sign. Byrne, 49.

function as a miracle worker.[75] Unlike her sister, however, Martha does not stop here. She continues, "But even now I know that God will give you whatever you ask of him" (11:22). These words imply that Martha's faith in Jesus is not centered on past possibilities that have been missed. Although she certainly is not expecting Jesus to raise her brother from the dead (cf. 11:39),[76] she does continue to believe in his ability to function as an intermediary with God, despite his failure to help in this instance.[77] Structurally, Martha's statement of continued belief in Jesus functions as an opening for Jesus to begin a theological discussion with her about the resurrection of the dead and his relationship to eternal life (11:23-27). In this sense, she functions as a foil for Jesus' teachings and self-revelations.

A Believer Who Moves from a "Below" Perspective to a Full Confession of Faith

In response to Martha's statement of continued belief in him, Jesus tells her that her brother will rise again (11:23). Interpreting Jesus' ambiguous statement from a "below" perspective, Martha understands his words within the context of the traditional Jewish belief in the resurrection on the last day (11:24).[78] As in the story of the Samaritan woman,

[75]T. E. Pollard, Reinhartz, and Byrne attribute an element of reproach to both Martha's and Mary's statements to Jesus (11:21; 11:32). Pollard, however, states that Martha's "reproach" is tempered by the faith she expresses in Jesus in 11:22. Schneiders attributes an element of reproach only to Mary's statement to Jesus (11:32), whereas Giblin perceives only a difference in the emotional tone in the regret that the sisters express. He notes that Mary's statement uses an emphatic position for the pronoun (μου), which expresses her personal loss. T. E. Pollard, "The Raising of Lazarus (John xi)," *Studia Evangelica* VI, Texte und Untersuchungen 112, ed. Elizabeth Livingstone (Berlin: Academie-Verlag, 1973) 438–40. Adele Reinhartz, "From Narrative to History: The Resurrection of Mary and Martha," 173. Byrne, 49. Schneiders, "Death in the Community of Eternal Life," 52, 54. Giblin, 209.

[76]Brown, *The Gospel According to John,* 1:433–4. Byrne, 49.

[77]R. Brown perceives her statement in v. 22 to be more of a confession of faith in Jesus' ability to function as an intermediary with God than a request for Jesus to do something about her brother's death. Brown, *The Gospel According to John,* 1:433–4. Cf. Byrne, 49–50. If God were understood as a kind of heavenly patron and humans as clients, then Martha may have perceived Jesus as an *agent* in this cosmic patron-client relationship with God. Her statement could then be understood as an expression of belief in Jesus' continued ability to function as an agent of their heavenly patron. Cf. Malina, *The New Testament World,* 80–93.

[78]O'Day, "John," 298. Brown, *The Gospel According to John,* 1:434. Reinhartz, "The Gospel of John," 581. Cf. Paul Duke, *Irony in the Fourth Gospel* (Atlanta: John Knox, 1985) 145; Byrne, 50; Scott, 201. Schnackenburg states that Jesus' initial re-

such misunderstanding provides Jesus with an opportunity for self-revelation.

Jesus first clarifies his meaning by defining resurrection and life in terms of himself. He then asks Martha if she believes what he has said to her (11:25-26). Martha begins with a simple "yes." In her elaboration on that "yes," however, she focuses on the person of Jesus, rather than on the topic of resurrection. She says, "Yes, Lord, I believe that you are the Messiah, the Son of God, the one coming into the world" (11:27).[79] This confession of faith embodies the implied author's distinctive theology.[80] Because Martha's confession of faith is made prior to Jesus' act of providing a sign, it depicts the type of faith that is not dependent on signs, an

---

mark to Martha was deliberately phrased in an ambiguous manner so as to allow a dual meaning. Although the reader could be expected to perceive the deeper meaning to Jesus' words regarding his intention to raise Lazarus from the dead (cf. 11:11), Martha, as a character, would not have been expected to perceive this level of meaning. O'Day sees a corollary between Martha's conversation with Jesus and the Samaritan woman's conversation with Jesus in that both misunderstand the present reality Jesus has to offer. Schnackenburg, 2:329–30. Gail O'Day, *Revelation in the Fourth Gospel: Narrative Mode and Theological Claim.* Philadelphia: Fortress, 1986) 72, 133, n. 64.

[79]Some scholars highlight that fact that the profession of faith, which in the Synoptics is placed in the mouth of Peter, is placed in the mouth of a woman. Cf. Scott, 202; Schüssler Fiorenza, *In Memory of Her,* 329.

[80]Schneiders, "Death in the Community of Eternal Life," 52–3. Schneiders, "Women in the Fourth Gospel," 41. Schüssler Fiorenza, "A Feminist Critical Interpretation for Liberation," 31. Schüssler Fiorenza, *In Memory of Her,* 329. Reinhartz, "The Gospel of John," 581. Reinhartz, "From Narrative to History: The Resurrection of Mary and Martha," 178–9. Brown, "Roles of Women in the Fourth Gospel," 190. Seim, 71. W. H. Cadman, "The Raising of Lazarus (John 10:40–11:53)," *Studia Evangelica* I, Texte und Untersuchungen 73, ed. S. L. Cross (Berlin: Academie-Verlag, 1959) 423–34. Raymond Collins, "The Representative Figures of the Fourth Gospel," *Downside Review* 94 (1976) 46. Rochais, 118–9, 121. Byrne, 48. Scott, 202. O'Day, however, perceives Martha's confession of faith as embodying a conventional language about Jesus that ". . . rings more of the old than it does of the radical new life offered by Jesus." Byrne agrees with this and perceives the uncertainty of Martha's level of faith as adding suspense. R. Brown, in his earlier work, *The Gospel According to John,* and Witherington state that Martha's reaction to Jesus' command to remove the stone from Lazarus' tomb (11:35) shows that her faith is inadequate, that she does not believe in Jesus' power to give life. Nevertheless, Witherington concedes that Martha's confession exceeds that of Peter in chapter 6, and therefore, believes that her confession is evidence that women are capable of being full-fledged disciples of Jesus. Pollard also entertains the possibility of inadequate faith on the part of Martha, but he prefers an interpretation in which Martha's belief in Jesus is all that matters to her. O'Day, "John," 298. Brown, *The Gospel According to John,* 1:433. Byrne, 53–4. Witherington, 105–6, 108–9. Pollard, 439–40.

important aspect of true faith in the Fourth Gospel (cf. 20:29).[81] In addition, Martha's confession expresses the type of faith that Jesus prays others will have as a result of his actions (cf. 11:42),[82] as well as the type of faith that the implied author hopes the Gospel will evoke (cf. 20:31).[83] Thus, Martha, who is also associated with the Jews (11:19), is that member of Jesus' "Jewish" family who expresses appropriate faith in him. Although some scholars perceive her confession of faith as an indication that she is entitled to eternal life,[84] it must be remembered that she, like her sister, merely represents the faith community.[85] Thus, her confession of faith indicates that all who believe in Jesus have eternal life.

By placing Johannine theology in the mouth of a woman and by having her profession of faith parallel, yet surpass, that of Peter's in 6:68-69,[86] the implied author of the Fourth Gospel followed the tendency of certain Hellenistic Jewish authors. Pseudo-Philo in *Biblical Antiquities,* for instance, portrayed Deborah both as a Wisdom figure and a counterpart to Moses and portrayed Hannah as a model of faith and piety in difficult times.[87] Similarly, Susanna is depicted as the embodiment of the sapiential principle that vengeance belongs to God, and Aseneth, after her conversion, is depicted in *The Book of Aseneth* as a Wisdom character and a counterpart to Joseph.[88] Like these other stories, the Fourth Gospel uses female characters to express the beliefs of a faith community (cf. the

[81]Reinhartz, "The Gospel of John," 581. Reinhartz, "From Narrative to History: The Resurrection of Mary and Martha," 178. Seim, 72. Rena, 142. This identification of Martha's confession of faith with the ideology of the implied author has led some scholars to raise the possibility that the author may have been a woman. Cf. Schüssler Fiorenza, *In Memory of Her,* 329–30.

[82]Schneiders, "Death in the Community of Eternal Life," 53.

[83]Ibid., 53. Schüssler Fiorenza, *In Memory of Her,* 329. McNeil, 273. Byrne, 53. Culpepper, *Anatomy,* 141.

[84]According to J. P. Martin, Bultmann interpreted the passage in this way. Cf. J. P. Martin, "History and Eschatology in the Lazarus Narrative: John 11:1-44," *Scottish Journal of Theology* 17 (1964) 340.

[85]Collins perceives Martha as a representative figure. Culpepper perceives her as representing the ideal of discerning faith and service. Martin, however, perceives her as representing the Church, and Scott perceives her as representing the confessing believer within the community. Collins, "The Representative Figures in the Fourth Gospel," 46. Culpepper, *Anatomy,* 142. Martin, 338. Scott, 203.

[86]Schüssler Fiorenza, *In Memory of Her,* 329.

[87]Cheryl Brown, 40–5, 213.

[88]Richard Pervo, "Aseneth and Her Sisters: Women in Jewish Narrative and in the Greek Novels," *Women Like This: New Perspectives on Jewish Women in the Greco-Roman World,* ed. Amy-Jill Levine (Atlanta: Scholars Press, 1992) 147–8, 153–4.

Samaritan woman), just as it uses female characters to embody faith communities themselves. Unlike these stories that feature female heroines, however, the Fourth Gospel uses female characters only for the purpose of supporting the role of a male hero.

A Critique of the Patriarchy and Androcentrism

Patriarchy and Androcentrism in the Function and Characterization of Mary of Bethany

As the text illustrates, Mary's portrayal as the betrothed/bride of Jesus on behalf of the Jewish people was constructed for the purpose of establishing a fictive, familial relationship between Jesus and Lazarus and between Jesus and those Jews who believed in him. Mary's own relationship with Jesus is not what is most important in the text. This fact can be substantiated by a closer look at the narrator's statement in 11:5, "Now, Jesus loved Martha and her sister and Lazarus." In this verse, Martha is mentioned first and Mary, who is not even mentioned by name, is listed second. This ordering does not fit the earlier pattern that highlighted Mary in relation to her sister and brother. Such a reversal of emphasis continues in 11:19, where Martha is again mentioned before Mary.[89] Part of the rationale for this reversal of names may be to prepare the reader for the upcoming dialogue between Martha and Jesus.[90] Nevertheless, one must also investigate what this reversal means for the relative importance of Mary of Bethany.

At first glance, such a reversal of emphasis and failure even to mention Mary by name in 11:5 might seem to negate the possibility that Mary functions as a betrothed/bride of the messianic bridegroom in these two pericopae. One must remember, however, the manner in which the implied author dealt with the mother of Jesus and the Samaritan woman in the previously analyzed pericopae. After the implied author established the significance of these women in relation to the messianic bridegroom, the implied author then proceeded to distance Jesus from these women,

---

[89]Many scholars (e.g., Seim, Schnackenburg, Rochais, and E. Stockton) have concluded from this ordering that the Martha strand is a Johannine expansion of a story that originally featured Mary. R. Brown perceives development within the story, but is unsure whether the Martha strand is an expansion of the Mary strand or vice versa, whereas Witherington perceives balance as the reason behind the change of order. Seim, 71. Schnackenburg, 2:317–21. Rochais, 118–9, 133. Brown, *The Gospel According to John,* 1:431, 433. Witherington, 107. Cf. Schneiders, "Death in the Community of Eternal Life," 44–5 n. 2.

[90]Cf. Byrne, 41; Schnackenburg, 2:320–2.

thereby lessening their importance in the pericopae. The same pattern can be found regarding Mary of Bethany in chapter 11. After the implied author provided sufficient material in 11:1-2 for the inference that Mary of Bethany will function as Jesus' betrothed/bride, the implied author then diminished Mary's importance in 11:5, 19. By lessening the importance of Jesus' betrothed/bride, the emphasis remains on Jesus as the messianic bridegroom. Jesus, as bridegroom, is important, not the women who are portrayed as his bride (cf. 4:41). Once again the female character is not important in and of herself. Her importance lies only in her character's ability to reveal Jesus as the messianic bridegroom and to establish a familial relationship between Jesus and those who believe in him, those whom she represents.[91]

Christian tradition regarding Mary and Martha of Bethany, together with the implied author's own ideology regarding wives, may have led the implied author to portray Mary, rather than Martha, as the betrothed/bride of Jesus. From a feminist perspective, however, it is significant that the implied author chose to depict the relatively quiet and reserved Mary, rather than the more talkative and assertive Martha, as the betrothed/bride of Jesus with respect to the Jews (11:1-54; cf. Luke 10:38-42).

Patriarchy and androcentrism is also evident in the women's request for help for their brother, in the manner in which the women inform Jesus that Lazarus is ill, in Jesus' delay in coming, and in the way in which Jesus responds to their request. First, let us look at the request itself.

The request that the women made on behalf of their brother was well within the accepted norms for women in the ancient world. As Mary Lefkowitz states, ancient women could take initiative if such actions were undertaken on behalf of a male relative.[92] In addition, like the mother of Jesus who couches her request in a statement of need ("They have no wine" [2:3]), Mary and Martha also couch their request in a statement of need ("Lord, the one whom you love is ill" [11:3]).[93] Similarly, like the mother of Jesus, Mary of Bethany is seen as not really having any influence upon Jesus.

A first-century reader would have expected a man to make an immediate response to a request for help from the family of his betrothed/bride. An immediate response from Jesus, however, was not forthcoming. He waited two days before setting out for Bethany (11:6). Such a delay is

[91]Cf. chapter 2, pp. 32–40 and chapter 3, pp. 69–79.

[92]Lefkowitz, 53, 55–6, 59, 61.

[93]Cf. Giblin, 202, 208; O'Day, "John," 298; Byrne, 92, n. 1 for ch. 3; Schnackenburg, 2:329; Brown, *The Gospel According to John,* 1:431, 433; Seim, 70; Witherington, 106; chapter 2, pp. 27, 38.

reminiscent of Jesus' delayed response to his mother's implied request in the story of the wedding at Cana.[94] This delay reinforces the point that Jesus will not be controlled by any member of his earthly family, whether biological or fictive.[95] As he would not be controlled by his mother (cf. 2:4), neither will he be by his betrothed/bride nor her sister.[96] Instead, just as at Cana, he will use this earthly situation to manifest the glory of his heavenly Father (11:4, cf. 2:5-11), thereby enabling his disciples to believe in him (11:14, cf. 2:11). Finally, just as Mary and Martha couched their request in a statement of need, they also couch their disappoint in Jesus in a statement of faith ("Lord, if you had been here, my brother would not have died" [11:21, 32]). No direct confrontation by Mary or Martha would have been acceptable, just as no direct confrontation by the mother of Jesus would have been acceptable toward Jesus in his apparent refusal to help with the need for wine.

As the mother of Jesus and the Samaritan woman were marginalized after they fulfilled their function, one can see a marginalization of Mary of Bethany as well. With Mary of Bethany the marginalization happens by a shift in emphasis from her to her sister. It is not Mary of Bethany who enters into a theological discussion with Jesus and makes a confession of faith, but her sister Martha. Although Mary does reappear at the meal in Bethany given in Jesus' honor, Mary remains the loving betrothed/bride whose whole focus is on her bridegroom as she sits at his feet anointing them with perfume and wiping his feet with her hair.

[94]Brown, *The Gospel According to John,* 1:431. Schnackenburg, 2:323. Cf. Duke, 50–1.

[95]Charles Giblin, investigates this pattern of suggestion, negative response, and positive action in the Fourth Gospel and notes that this pattern dissociates Jesus from the predominantly human concerns of those who, by merely human standards, would seem to be close to him. Although Jesus eventually does act on their request, he does so in a radical way on his own terms and in his own time. Duke refers to this phenomenon as sovereign evasion. Schneiders calls it sovereign independence. Charles Giblin, "Suggestion, Negative Response and Positive Action in St. John's Portrayal of Jesus [John 2:1-11: 4:46-54; 7:2-14; 11:1-44]," *New Testament Studies* 26 (1980) 210. Duke, 50–1. Schneiders, "Death in the Community of Eternal Life," 47. Cf. Talbert, *Reading John,* 144; Brown, *The Gospel According to John,* 1:431; Byrne, 42.

[96] Jesus, characterization here is in keeping with the sovereign prerogative of a husband. For expressions of this male sovereignty in the Greco-Roman world, see Pomeroy, 150–5. For an anthropological analysis of this phenomenon, see John Kennedy Campbell, "The Family: A System of Roles," *Honour, Family and Patronage: A Study of Institutions and Moral Values in a Greek Mountain Community* (Oxford: Clarendon, 1964) 151–3.

The Patriarchy and Androcentrism in the Function and Characterization of Martha of Bethany

If the implied author marginalized all of the other female characters in the Fourth Gospel after they had fulfilled their literary function, then one would expect the implied author to marginalize Martha as well. Martha, in fact, is marginalized in two ways. She is marginalized first by Jesus' words to her following her objection to the stone's being removed from Lazarus' tomb (11:40) and then by the narrator's statement regarding Martha's role in the dinner given in Jesus' honor (12:2).

When Jesus commands that the stone be taken away from the tomb, Martha objects on the grounds that there would be an odor by this time (11:39). Jesus rebukes Martha with the words, "Did I not tell you (σοι) that if you believed you would see the glory of God?" (11:40). In fact, such a statement by Jesus to Martha is never narrated.[97] The concept, however, is implied in Jesus' statements to the disciples prior to the journey to Bethany (cf. 11:4, 15).[98] This fact seems to support the notion that Martha, like her sister, merely represents the community of faith.[99] Jesus' rebuke of Martha, however, lessens the importance of Martha as a female character as it shifts the focus from a woman who had just made an important confession of faith back to the male hero toward whom the faith is directed.[100]

Martha's marginalization is actually not complete until chapter 12 with the story of the meal given in Jesus' honor. In this story, Martha is portrayed as a server of the meal (12:2), not as an equal participant in that meal.[101] Although the implied author may have drawn on tradition for this

[97]According to Schnackenburg, the reader is either forced to conclude that Jesus said this to Martha outside of narrative time, or that Jesus is presenting an interpretation of his earlier comment to Martha about her brother's rising again. Schnackenburg prefers the latter approach, as does Giblin. Schnackenburg, 2:338. Giblin, 210.

[98]Byrne, 62. Schnackenburg perceives Jesus' words as a prophetic fulfillment of his statement to the disciples, as well as an interpretation of his earlier comments to Martha. Schnackenburg, 2:338.

[99]If Martha does represent the community of faith and Jesus told something to his disciples, then one could infer that Jesus told it to Martha.

[100]In this respect, Jesus' rebuke of Martha is reminiscent of the rebuke that Jesus gave Peter after his confession of faith in the Synoptic gospels (cf. Matt 16:13-23). This fact illustrates that female characters are not the only ones in ancient texts to be marginalized after they have fulfilled their literary purpose.

[101]Brown, Schüssler Fiorenza, and Schneiders extrapolate from this element of characterization the possibility that Martha and/or other women in the early Christian community may have presided over Eucharist celebrations. Seim, however, notes that the concept of *diakonos,* which is significant in the Gospel of Luke, is not significant in the Fourth Gospel. For this reason, she emphasizes the subservient nature of

portrayal of Martha,[102] one must ask why the implied author of the Fourth Gospel chose to draw on this tradition to depict Martha as serving the meal. Because the expressed presence of all three family members (Lazarus, Martha, and Mary) helps to connect this story with the story of the raising of Lazarus, Martha must be present in the meal in some capacity. Nevertheless, if one looks at the reference to Martha's table service from a historical-literary perspective, the statement appears to be the means by which this significant female character is returned to her proper female place after she has completed her literary function.[103] Prior to the raising of her brother, Martha was connected to no man other than Jesus, and thus could function as an independent woman. Now that her brother is raised, however, she needs to be placed back in her feminine role. She is now the sister of a living brother, and once again needs to "act like a woman."

Summary

Given the previous Johannine passages that imply that Jesus is the messianic bridegroom, a first-century reader would have been prepared to view Mary, Martha, and Lazarus of Bethany as representatives of Jesus' fictive Jewish family. The purpose of such a portrayal would have been to illustrate that members of the family of God are those who believe in Jesus and that such people would have eternal life. Mary's primary function in the text is that of the betrothed/bride of the messianic bridegroom

---

Martha's table service. Brown, "Roles of Women in the Fourth Gospel," 187. Schüssler Fiorenza, *In Memory of Her,* 330. Schneiders, "Women in the Fourth Gospel," 42. Seim, 72–3.

[102]Martha is also portrayed as being involved with household tasks in Luke 10:38-40. Cf. Brown, *The Gospel According to John,* 1:xliv–xlvii, 433; Platt, 35; Schüssler Fiorenza, "A Feminist Critical Interpretation for Liberation," 32; Seim, 70–1, 73; Witherington, 104–5, 107, 192 n. 175; Culpepper, *Anatomy,* 140 n. 81, 141–2; Scott, 198; Schnackenburg, 2:366.

[103]Lefkowitz and Helene Foley note this tendency in ancient Greek literature and history; Amy-Jill Levine notes this tendency for the Hellenized Jewish Book of Judith; and I have noted this same tendency in the Fourth Gospel for the mother of Jesus and the Samaritan woman. Lefkowitz, 49, 54–6. Helene Foley, "The Conception of Women in Athenian Drama," *Reflections of Women in Antiquity,* ed. Helene Foley (New York: Gordon and Breach Science Publishers, 1981) 135, 161–2. Amy-Jill Levine, "Sacrifice and Salvation: Otherness and Domestication in the Book of Judith," *No One Spoke Ill of Her: Essays on Judith,* ed. James C. VanderKam (Atlanta: Scholars Press, 1992) 17, 27. Cf. chapter 2, p. 33 and chapter 3, p. 79.

on behalf of the Jewish people. Her betrothal/marital relationship with Jesus establishes the fictive kinship group. Martha's primary function is to be that member of Jesus' fictive Jewish family who expresses faith in Jesus, and Lazarus' function is simply being the member of the family who illustrates that those who are members of the family of God will have eternal life.

In the midst of fulfilling their respective literary roles, the actions of Mary and Martha of Bethany, as literary characters, would have been perceived by an ancient reader as typical behavior for women of that time. Typical female behavior is evident not only in the initiative they take for the sake of their brother, but also in the indirect manner in which they present their request of Jesus and in the indirect manner in which they express their disappoint in Jesus.

Martha may be characterized as the more assertive of the two sisters as she takes the initiative to go out and meet Jesus even before he enters the village, but such behavior would have been perceived as consistent with her portrayal as a woman whose actions would not have endangered the honor of any man. Indeed, as an independent woman and the only living relative of a betrothed sister, she would be expected to function as a broker in Jesus' relationship with her sister. Also, as an independent woman, she could be characterized as the more controlled of the two women as she stands before Jesus and voices a continued belief in him, despite his failure to help her brother. Although she is characterized as misunderstanding Jesus' words about the resurrection of her brother, she ends up making a confession of faith in the person of Jesus that reflects the implied author's understanding of true faith. Like the "officially unattached" Samaritan woman, Martha can enter into a prolonged discussion with Jesus.

Mary, as betrothed/bride, is characterized as the less assertive of the two sisters. She waits until she is called by Jesus and then quickly goes to Jesus, accompanied by the Jews. As a woman who is in relationship with a man (Jesus), she is also portrayed as the more emotional of the two sisters. Unable to rise above the immediate tragedy of her brother's death, she falls at Jesus' feet and weeps. Her role is not that of embodying the belief of the faith community, but that of embodying the emotional turmoil of the faith community as it faces the death of loved ones in the absence of Jesus. In chapter 12 Mary's role changes from that of distraught sister who is upset with her betrothed over the death of her brother to that of loving betrothed/bride who expresses both the love that the faith community has for Jesus and the effect that Jesus has on the whole faith community (οἶκος- or household/family) as she anoints his feet with perfume and carries his pleasant aroma throughout the house (οἶκος) on her hair.[104]

As has been shown in this chapter, both Mary and Martha are marginalized after they have fulfilled their respective literary roles. First, Mary is marginalized by the shift in focus to Martha, and then Martha is marginalized by Jesus' rebuke and later by the narrator's portrayal of her as one who serves the meal in Jesus' honor. In this respect, Martha is returned to her conventional, subordinate female role after her brother's resuscitation. Mary, however, as betrothed/bride, really never escapes her female function.

The primary function of Mary and Martha of Bethany in both of the pericopae in which they are found is to further the portrayal of Jesus as the messianic bridegroom who has come to enable those who believe in him to become children of God. This portrayal of Jesus was first established with the support of the mother of Jesus at Cana and then furthered by the characterization of the Samaritan woman at the well. In all four pericopae, the women function according to patriarchal and androcentric expectations and further the patriarchal ideology of the implied author. As I shall show in the stories of the mother of Jesus at the cross and Mary Magdalene at the tomb, female characters in the Fourth Gospel continue to support Jesus' role as the messianic bridegroom and consistently function in accordance with patriarchal and androcentric expectations.

[104]Culpepper perceives Mary as representing unlimited love and devotion. This representation would be consistent with a betrothed/bride. Culpepper, *Anatomy,* 142.

5

The Mother of Jesus at the Cross

Introduction

The Fourth Gospel is the only canonical Gospel in which the mother of Jesus is present at the crucifixion scene (19:25). In this scene, the mother of Jesus fulfills the same function as she did at the wedding feast at Cana, that of assisting in the characterization of Jesus as the messianic bridegroom. The pattern used to carry on that function in this scene, however, is different. For the wedding scene at Cana, the implied author used the assertive "mother of an important son" character-type from the Hebrew Bible to enable the mother of Jesus to assist in Jesus' characterization as the messianic bridegroom.[1] In the crucifixion scene, however, this assertive "mother of an important son" character-type is not used. The mother of Jesus in the crucifixion scene does not say or do anything to move the plot or to insure that her son fulfills his destiny with regard to the promise made to Abraham. She is not assertive at all, but passive, as she is merely present and acted upon by Jesus.

For the characterization of the mother of Jesus in the crucifixion scene, the implied author of the Fourth Gospel appears to have relied on a type-scene from Greco-Roman romances that I shall call the "dying king" type-scene.[2] By adapting this type-scene, the implied author of the Fourth

---

[1]Cf. chapter 2, pp. 26–32.

[2]Robert Cohn identifies a type-scene from the Hebrew Bible (1 & 2 Kings) that he refers to as the "dying monarch" type-scene. In this type-scene, the dying king sends messengers to a prophet asking whether or not he will recover. The prophet predicts death and the king dies. Robert Cohn, "Convention and Creativity in the Book of Kings: The Case of the Dying Monarch (1 Kg 14; 2 Kg 1; 8; 20)," *Catholic Biblical Quarterly* 47 (1985) 603–16. The type-scene that I refer to as the "dying-king" type-scene, however, is found in Greco-Roman literature.

Gospel was able to use Jesus' words and actions toward his mother to further the portrayal of Jesus as the messianic bridegroom.

To understand how Jesus' words and actions toward his mother support his role as the messianic bridegroom, it is first necessary to understand how a reader of the first century could have interpreted Jesus' death both as a blood sacrifice that establishes a patrilineal kinship group and as a messianic wedding. Having completed this task, I shall then explain how the implied author adapted the "dying king" type-scene so that the characterization of the mother of Jesus supported the portrayal of Jesus as the messianic bridegroom.

Jesus' Death as a Blood Sacrifice that Establishes a Patrilineal Kinship Group

To illustrate how Jesus' death could have been interpreted by a first-century reader as a blood sacrifice that establishes a patrilineal descent group, it will be necessary to explain the relationship between blood sacrifices and patrilineal descent, as established by anthropological studies of antiquity. I shall then point out where examples of this relationship between blood sacrifice and patrilineal descent can be found in Greco-Roman literature and the Hebrew Bible and demonstrate how the implied author of the Fourth Gospel used this relationship in his characterization of Jesus as the messianic bridegroom.

Blood Sacrifice as a Remedy for Having Been Born of Woman

Anthropological studies have shown that descent in matrilineal kinship groups is generally determined from maternal uncle to nephew. Moreover, membership in these matrilineal kinship groups may be determined by birth alone because sure knowledge of maternity is present. For patrilineal kinship groups, however, where descent is from father to son, sure knowledge of biological paternity is not possible. Nancy Jay notes that patrilineal kinship groups often overcome this uncertainty by a ritual that is "as powerful, definite and available to the senses as birth, blood sacrifice." As such, the ritual is an effective sign that causes what it signifies. It transforms and supersedes biological descent from woman and makes patrilineal descent a social achievement in the interest of social continuity.[3] Through this sacrificial system of establishing jural paternity (pater-

---

[3]Nancy Jay, "Sacrifice as Remedy for Having Been Born of Woman," *Immaculate and Powerful: The Female in Sacred Image and Social Reality,* ed. Clarissa Atkinson, Constance Buchanan and Margaret Miles (Boston: Beacon, 1985) 283–97.

nity in terms of rights and obligations), kinship groups can be restructured as individuals are adopted into the family through sacrifice.[4]

Blood Sacrifice in Greco-Roman Literature

According to Froma Zeitlin, the basic issue in Aeschylus' trilogy, the *Oresteia,* is the establishment of the binding nature of patriarchal marriage and patrilineal succession in the face of female resistance. In the *Oresteia,* a woman rises up against patriarchal authority, slays her husband, and chooses her own sexual partner. Shattering the social norms, she demands and usurps male power and prerogatives. The son then slays the mother in alliance with the cause of father and husband, and the mother's Erinyes (a collective female element) pursues retribution.[5] In the *Oresteia,* female dominance is expressed paradigmatically by the mother-child relationship and male dominance is expressed paradigmatically by the patriarchal marriage including the primacy of the father-son bond as expressed in patrilineal succession.[6]

Howard Eilberg-Schwartz agrees with Jay, but goes beyond Jay to illustrate the connection between circumcision and sacrifice and to state that, like blood sacrifice, circumcision creates and demonstrates patrilineal kinship ties among men. Eilberg-Schwartz, *The Savage in Judaism, An Anthropology of Israelite Religion and Ancient Judaism* (Bloomington, Ind.: University Press, 1990) 174–86. Cf. J. Cheryl Exum, "The (M)other's Place," *Fragmented Women: Feminist (Sub)versions of Biblical Narratives* (Sheffield: JSOT, 1993) 127–8. For a discussion of the male need to appropriate the child of his wife after the child's birth, see Mary O'Brien, *The Politics of Reproduction* (Boston: Routledge & Kegan Paul, 1981) 36–7, 42–3, 47, 53–62. For an anthropological discussion of this phenomenon, see Evelyn Reed, *Woman's Evolution: From Matriarchal Clan to Patriarchal Family* (New York: Pathfinder, 1975) 343–8.

[4]Jay, "Sacrifice as a Remedy for Having Been Born of Woman," 290, 293. Cf. George Thomson, *Aeschylus and Athens: A Study in the Social Origins of Drama* (London: Lawrence & Wishart, 1941) 111.

[5]Froma Zeitlin, "The Dynamics of Misogyny: Myth and Mythmaking in the *Oresteia,*" *Women in the Ancient World: The Arethusa Papers,* ed. J. Peradotto and J. P. Sullivan (Albany: State University of New York Press, 1984) 161.

[6]Zeitlin notes a frequent close correlation between myth and ritual. She states that in myth men often seize the sovereignty from women by stealing their sources of power and in rituals of initiation these sources of power are transferred to and explained to boys. The Delphic succession myth, which parallels the evolution of power in Hesiod's *Theogony,* provided a direct mythological transference of power from female to male. Aeschylus revised this myth by placing positive matriarchy in the primordial past and presenting the Erinyes as daughters of Night, as representatives of negative matriarchy that must be overcome. Zeitlin, "The Dynamics of Misogyny," 169–73.

Salvation in the *Oresteia* is contingent upon the boy's successful separation from his mother. This is illustrated by Orestes' matricide and his subsequent sitting at Delphi's *omphalos,* the navel of the world, holding white wool and the purifying blood of a pig. As artistic representations make clear, this ritual included holding a pig (which in Greek and Latin have correlations with words for female genitals) over the head of the subject who sat "like a new born under the bloody organ that gave him birth."[7] Having successfully rejected his mother by killing her, Orestes is ritually reborn at the *omphalos* of Delphi. Zeitlin connects Orestes's killing of his mother with a rejection of matrilineage and his rebirth through a blood sacrifice at the "male-centered" *omphalos* at Delphi as an affirmation of patrilineage.[8]

Zeitlin and others also see a rebirth motif in the *Odyssey*. After being presumed dead, Odysseus returns to Ithaca and must reclaim his adult status. Eurykleia, his nurse, who "took him in her own hands when his mother first bore him" (19.355), washes his feet, recalls his naming by his maternal grandfather and recognizes the scar he received in his initiatory ritual at puberty, a ritual that included the killing of a boar (19.399–409) (19.410–5).[9] This example not only documents his maternal connection at birth with his being named by his maternal grandfather and a blood ritual that included self-mutilation and boar killing when he reached the age of puberty and began to associate his existence with males, but it documents also his rebirth after an apparent death.[10]

Blood Sacrifice in the Hebrew Bible

In her study of the different traditions in the Hebrew Bible, Jay affirms that the northern, Elohist tradition utilized this concept of establishing patrilineal kinship groups through blood sacrifices.[11] Her argument

---

[7]Zeitlin, "The Dynamics of Misogyny," 176, 188 n. 18. Cf. Thomson, 93.

[8]According to Zeitlin, the *omphalos,* the navel of the earth, was originally a female symbol that was located in the center of Delphi, a place whose name means "womb." It became male-centered when it was given to Zeus as a birthday present. Zeitlin, "The Dynamics of Misogyny," 175–6, 182.

[9]Cf. Zeitlin, "The Dynamics of Misogyny," 118–9 n. 18.

[10]Cf. C. P. Segal, "Transition and Ritual in Odysseus' Return," *La Parola del Passato* 116 (1967) 321–42.

[11]According to Jay, the Priestly tradition, which recognizes only priestly sacrifice, defends patrilineal decent simply by denying any matrilineal threat as it presents a patrilineal descent of unchallenged continuity. The Yahwist tradition, however, veils the matrilineal threat through patrilineal endogamous marriages (i.e., marriage between members of the same patrilineage). By having men take wives from the house of their

regarding Jacob's use of a blood sacrifice in his covenant with Laban best illustrates her point.

According to Jay, the text of Gen 31:44-54 portrays Laban, Leah, and Rachel as upholding matrilineal descent, which maintains the maternal uncle as the authoritative figure. Laban's insistence on the principle of descent through women is asserted in his expressed claim to Jacob's sons, "the sons are my sons" (Gen 31:43). During the sacrifice that accompanied the covenant between Jacob and Laban, Jacob's patrilineal claim, which was compromised when he went to live with his mother's brother, is restored. In that blood sacrifice Jacob and Laban appeal to the God of Abraham, the God of Nahor, the God of their father. This is an appeal to the God of Terah, their common patrilineal great-grandfather. By means of a blood sacrifice to the God of their common patrilineal great-grandfather, the two men become reclassified as "brothers" within the same patrilineal kinship group. Such a change in status explains why the Elohist author could state that the "brothers" of Jacob took part in the sacrifice (Gen 31:53-54), even though none of Jacob's biological brothers were actually present.[12] It also explains why Laban's "sons" become reclassified as his grandsons (Gen 31:55).

Jesus' Crucifixion as a Blood Sacrifice

Because scholars have noted "northern" tendencies in the christology of the Fourth Gospel,[13] the use of a northern, Elohist concept of establishing

---

father, the offspring's patrilineage membership is assured even if the lineage is figured through the mother. Only in the northern, Elohist tradition does Jay find the concept of sacrifice establishing a patrilineal kinship group. Within the Elohist tradition, Jay notes Abraham's near sacrifice of Isaac, Isaac's loss of patrilineal descent with respect to his sons because he did not engage in blood sacrifice, Rachel's attempt to claim matrilineal descent through stealing of her father's gods, Jacob's recovery of patrilineal descent through the blood sacrifice that accompanied the covenant he made with Laban, and Jacob's renaming of Benjamin after the death of his mother as an indication that patrilineal descent had been restored. Nancy Jay, "Sacrifice, Descent and the Patriarchs," *Vetus Testamentum* 38 (1988) 52–70. Cf. Jay, "Sacrifice as Remedy for Having Been Born of Woman," 298–9; Exum, "The (M)other's Place," 118–20.

[12]Jay, "Sacrifice, Descent and Patriarchs," 63–7. Cf. Jay, "Sacrifice as Remedy for Having Been Born of Woman," 297–300; Exum, "The (M)other's Place," 119.

[13]Although the sociological approach of Wayne Meeks merely notes a Samaritan strain in the early Moses prophet-king christology of the Fourth Gospel, Charles Scobie goes beyond him in viewing the Fourth Gospel as an intra-Israelite document produced by Galilean and Samaritan Christian communities. Gerard Sloyan, likewise, views the Fourth Gospel as rooted in North-South tension and as portraying Jesus as a northerner who was trying to teach wisdom to the learned South. George Buchanan

a patrilineal kinship group through blood sacrifice would be consistent with the implied author's other christological tendencies. Such a usage would also explain the "blood letting" that is unique to the crucifixion scene of the Fourth Gospel. Only through such a "blood letting" could the Christian community be made members of the *familia Dei*. Several internal literary clues point to the portrayal of the crucifixion scene in the Fourth Gospel as a blood sacrifice that establishes a patrilineal kinship group.

Prior to the crucifixion scene, Jesus is connected with a sacrificial lamb through John the Baptist's reference to him as "the Lamb of God who takes away the sin of the world" (1:29, cf. 1:36). Details of Jesus' suffering and death then highlight his portrayal as the Paschal Lamb:

1) Jesus is condemned to death at noon on the day before Passover (19:14), the very time when priests began to slay paschal lambs in the Temple;
2) Hyssop was used both to smear the Paschal Lamb's blood on the doorpost (Exod 12:22) and to assist in giving Jesus wine from a sponge (19:29);
3) None of the bones of the Paschal Lamb were to be broken (Exod 12:46) and none of Jesus' bones are broken (19:31).[14]

The Fourth Gospel is the only canonical gospel to make these literary allusions to Jesus as a sacrificial paschal lamb.[15]

---

bases his argument that the Fourth Gospel originated with the Samaritans on the emphasis in the Gospel on Jacob, Jesus' refusal to deny that he was a Samaritan, the Gospel's claim that Jesus is a son of Joseph (of a Northern tribe), and the reference to Jesus as the King of Israel (North).

Although one might not want to accept all the points made by these authors, their arguments do seem to point to a northern perspective for the Fourth Gospel. Wayne Meeks, *The Prophet-King: Moses Tradition and the Johannine Christology* (Leiden: Brill, 1967) 216–57, 318. Scobie, "The Origins and Development of Samaritan Christianity," *New Testament Studies* 19 (1972–1973) 390–414. Sloyan, "The Samaritans in the New Testament," *Horizons* 10 (1983) 7–21. Buchanan, "The Samaritan Origin of the Gospel of John," *Religions in Antiquity: Essays in Memory of Erwin Ramsdell Goodenough,* ed. Jacob Neusner (Leiden: Brill, 1968) 149–75.

[14]Raymond Brown, *The Gospel According to John,* The Anchor Bible Series (New York: Doubleday, 1966, 1970) 1:62. Cf. Brown, "The Passion According to John: Chapters 18–19," *Worship* 49 (1975) 133–4; Mark Stibbe, *John* (Sheffield: JSOT, 1993) 196–7. Max Thurian goes further to see a parallel between Jesus' seamless robe (19:23) and the seamless robe of the High Priest. Thus, he perceives Jesus both as the sacrificial Paschal Lamb and the High Priest. Thurian, "Mary and the Church," *Mary, Mother of All Christians* (New York: Herder & Herder, 1964) 154.

[15]Brown notes that, although Jewish thought does not view the paschal lamb as a sacrificial victim, in Jesus' time the sacrificial aspect had begun to infiltrate the con-

In addition to these literary allusions, one also finds another unique Johannine detail that allows Jesus' death to be viewed as a blood sacrifice. The Fourth Gospel is the only canonical Gospel in which Jesus' side is pierced, causing blood and water to flow therefrom (19:34). In conjunction with those details in the Fourth Gospel that connect Jesus with a sacrificial Paschal lamb, such a reference symbolically places Jesus in the role of a sacrificial victim whose death can be viewed as a blood sacrifice.[16]

Jesus' post-resurrection statement to Mary Magdalene, ". . . go to my brothers (ἀδελπούς μου) and say to them, 'I am ascending to my Father and your Father, to my God and your God'" (20:17), illustrates that the implied author of the Fourth Gospel portrayed Jesus' blood sacrifice as establishing a patrilineal descent group. This is the first time in the Fourth Gospel that Jesus refers to the disciples as "brothers." This reference indicates that Jesus' death and resurrection enabled the disciples to become "brothers" of Jesus, just as Jacob's blood sacrifice reclassified Laban as a "brother" to Jacob. Jesus' words, "my Father and your Father," indicate that Jesus' fraternal relationship with his disciples is based on a common heavenly Father, a common patrilineal descent established through his blood sacrifice.[17]

The matrilineal threat to patrilineal descent, which had been resolved in the Elohist tradition through blood sacrifice, is resolved in the Fourth Gospel through the blood sacrifice of Jesus. The promise made to Abraham has been fulfilled. Descendants for Abraham, who constitute the *familia Dei,* have been "socially achieved" by Jesus' blood sacrifice. Commenting on the book of Hebrews in the New Testament, Jay notes that Jesus, as the perfect sacrifice who is offered once for all time, achieves the perfect Father-Son continuity for all time.[18] The crucifixion scene in the Fourth Gospel communicates the same message.

Jesus' Passion and Death as the Messianic Wedding with Subsequent Conception/Birth of the Children of God

Blood sacrifice could be interpreted as establishing patrilineal descent because such spilling of blood by men was viewed as rebirth, birth

---

cept of the paschal lamb because the priests had appropriated to themselves the act of slaying the lambs. Brown, *The Gospel According to John,* 1:62.

[16]Thurian, 158.

[17]The importance of having God as Father is emphasized elsewhere in the Gospel (cf. 8:39-45; 20:17).

[18]Jay, "Sacrifice as Remedy for Having Been Born of Woman," 301.

done on purpose and on a more spiritual, exalted level than mothers do it.[19] Mary O'Brien identifies the practice of male ritual rebirths in many of the mystery religions of antiquity as marriages followed by mock pregnancies and the male giving a second birth to himself. She bases this interpretation on the presence in these rituals of a "period of seclusion," a "trial of endurance," which sometimes includes scourging, and the "spilling of blood."[20]

To illustrate how Jesus' own passion and blood sacrifice could have been interpreted as the completion of a messianic marriage followed by giving birth to the children of God, I shall first highlight possible intertextual references in the Fourth Gospel to a messianic wedding. I shall then show how the piercing of Jesus' side could have been viewed by a first-century reader as the culmination of Jesus' messianic marriage followed by his giving birth.

Intertextual References to a Messianic Wedding

In analyzing the wedding scene at Cana, I argued that the mother of Jesus, as well as the reader, could have interpreted Jesus' statement "My hour has not yet come" as an affirmation that it was not his wedding feast. Subsequently, when Jesus' mother refused to accept that response, Jesus did respond to her request that he do something about the lack of wine, but in such a way as to assert that he was the messianic bridegroom.[21] Succeeding passages in the Fourth Gospel would then have led a first-century reader to realize that Jesus' imminent passion and death would constitute his messianic marriage.

In his "Priestly Prayer," Jesus says to his heavenly Father, "I have made your name known to them, and I shall continue to make it known" (17:26, cf. 17:6). This statement may be a veiled reference to Ps 45:17, "I will cause your name to be celebrated in all generations."[22] Because Psalm

[19]Jay points to Vedic blood sacrifices as dramatic re-enactments of being born on a divine level. Jay, "Sacrifice as Remedy for Having Been Born of Woman, 294.

[20]O'Brien perceives such practices as male attempts to control and appropriate the renewal of life and identifies this male response as "womb envy." O'Brien, 146–7. Cf. Thomson, 97–9, 103–4, 121, 127–129. For a discussion of the rituals in other societies by which men claim the child of their wife through imitating the mother's bearing of the child, see Reed, 343–6.

[21]Cf. chapter 2, pp. 29–30.

[22]The Septuagint uses the plural (μνησθήσονται τοῦ ὀνόματός σου), "They (your children) shall make mention of your name . . . ." (Ps 44 [45]:17). The Hebrew Bible uses the singular (אַזְכִּירָה שִׁמְךָ) "I will make your name remembered . . . ."

45 is an ode for a royal wedding,[23] the reader may well have understood
Jesus' words as alluding to a messianic wedding celebration. As the
psalmist's words promise the bridegroom/king successful progeny and literary immortality (Ps:45:16-17),[24] so Jesus' words could have been interpreted by the reader as the messianic bridegroom's promising his heavenly
Father that he would continue to be remembered through the messianic
bridegroom's continued reminders to his own progeny.

Another possible literary allusion to a wedding ceremony can be
found in Jesus' words to his disciples regarding his Father's house having
many dwelling places and his going to prepare a place for them (14:2-3).
According to S. Safrai, the wedding ceremony in the first century was es-
sentially the groom's induction of the bride into his house.[25] Because Jesus
is establishing a patrilineal kinship group, he would be taking his bride
(the community of believers) into his Father's house. Thus, Jesus' words
could have been viewed within the context of the messianic bridegroom
taking his bride into his Father's house.

Looking specifically at the passion narrative, the reader also could
have seen indications that the messianic marriage was taking place. Isaiah,
for instance, speaks of a bridegroom clothing himself with special garments
and decking himself with a garland (Isa 61:10), and Canticle of Canticles
speaks of Solomon's mother "crowning" him on the day of his wedding
(Cant 3:11). Likewise, *Sotah* 9:14 in the *Mishnah* speaks of wreaths being
used by bridegrooms as well as the brides,[26] and *Pirke de Rabbi Eliezer* 16
notes that both a bridegroom and a king are clothed with glory.[27] Consequently, the crown of thorns and purple cloak, which were placed on Jesus
to mock him as king (19:2-5), might also have been interpreted by the

[23]Cf. *The New Oxford Annotated Bible,* ed. Bruce Metzger and Roland Murphy
(New York: Oxford University Press, 1991) 712 OT.

[24]Cf. *The New Oxford Annotated Bible,* 712 OT.

[25]S. Safrai, "Home and Family," *The Jewish People in the First Century,* ed S.
Safrai and M. Stern (Philadelphia: Fortress, 1976) 758.

[26]Cf. Safrai, 758 n. 2; David Mace, "Marriage Customs and Ceremonies," *Hebrew
Marriage: A Sociological Study* (London: Epworth, 1953) 179, 182; Philip and Hanna
Goodman, "Jewish Marriages Throughout the Ages," *The Jewish Marriage Anthology*
(Philadelphia: The Jewish Publication Society of America, 1965) 73; A. Büchler, "In-
duction of the Bride and the Bridegroom into the *Chuppah* in the First and Second
Centuries in Palestine," *Livre d'hommage a la memoire du Samuel Poznanski,* ed. Le
Comité de la Grande Synagogue a Varsovie (Leipzig: Varsovie, 1927) 95–6.

[27]*Pirke de Rabbi Eliezer* 16 is a piece of midrashic literature that compares a
bridegroom to a king. Although this work was not completed until the ninth century
C.E., the putative author dates to the first and second centuries C.E. This may indicate a
long tradition of comparing a bridegroom to a king. Cf. Goodman, 33–5; Mace, 182.

reader as an ironic display of proper attire for a bridegroom-king at his wedding.

As Jesus' crown of thorns and cloak of purple could be viewed within the context of a wedding motif, so could the implied author's reference to a garden. The Fourth Gospel is the only canonical Gospel to refer to both the place of Jesus' arrest and the place of Jesus' burial as a garden (18:1, 26; cf. 19:41). Some scholars maintain that the garden motif is an allusion to the garden of Eden. Yet, as Nicolas Wyatt notes, scriptural and pseudepigraphal passages, as well as inconographic evidence, equated the garden of Eden and its streams of water with Zion and the streams of water that flow from it (cf. Isa 51:3; 58:11-12; Ps 36:9-10) and ritually connected the kings of Israel to this water (cf. 1 Kgs 1:33-40, 45; Ps 36:9-10; Ps 110:7; Ezek 28). Just as Adam, the archetypal king, was buried in the garden of Paradise (Apoc. Mos. 37:5; 40:2) and the kings of Israel were buried in the garden near the water, so Jesus, as the King of the Jews was buried in a garden. Iconographic tradition illustrates two streams flowing either from vases held by deities or kings or from the persons of the deities or kings themselves as they are enthroned in a temple or on a mountain. In addition, one finds pseudepigraphal references to the two springs of the heavenly garden of paradise giving forth honey and milk, which then subdivide to provide oil and wine that water the earthly Eden before flowing out into the world (2 Enoch 8:4-6; cf. T. Dan. 5:12). Thus, the blood and water flowing from the side of the King of the Jews as he dies on the cross can easily be equated with these two streams in Eden/Zion that give life to the world.[28] When one adds to this the notion that Zion is also described as the bride of YHWH (Isa 50:1; 54:1-8), then the blood and water from the side of Jesus takes on marital/wedding overtones.

The king/garden terminology may also be a veiled allusion to the garden and marital motif found in Canticle of Canticles,[29] as the next chapter will more fully illustrate. Because songs from the Canticle of Canticles

---

[28]Nicolas Wyatt, "Supposing Him to Be the Gardener" (John 20,15): A Study of the Paradise Motif in John," *Zeitschrift für die Neutestamentliche Wissenschaft und die Kunde der Alteren Kirche* 81 (1990) 24–38. Cf. Edwyn Hoskyns, *The Fourth Gospel* (London: Faber and Faber Limited, 1940) 2:646; R. H. Lightfoot, *St. John's Gospel: A Commentary,* ed. C. F. Evans (Oxford: Oxford University Press, 1956) 322. C. K. Barrett and R. Brown disagree on this point. Barrett, *The Gospel According to St. John,* 2nd ed. (Philadelphia: Westminster, 1978) 465. Brown, *The Gospel According to John* 2:990.

[29]Cf. J. Duncan Derrett, "Miriam and the Resurrection (John 20:16)," *Downside Review* 111 (1993) 178–9, 181, 185 n. 17.

were possibly composed to be used at weddings,[30] the reader could have perceived these king/garden references as part of the Fourth Gospel's wedding sub-text for the depiction of Jesus as the messianic bridegroom.

The Piercing of Jesus' Side—The Consummation of the Messianic Marriage Followed by the Conception of New Life

Besides interpreting the piercing of Jesus' side as the fulfillment of Zech 12:10,[31] the reader may also have perceived the piercing of Jesus' side as the consummation of the messianic marriage. The subsequent issuance of blood and water could then have been seen as Jesus' conceiving the children of God, as well as the fulfillment of Zech 13:1,[32] or the fulfillment of Jesus' own prediction in 7:38-39.[33] In order for the reader to have perceived these phenomena as the consummation of the marriage and subsequent conception of the children of God, the implied reader would have to have recognized the use of sexual role reversal and the male co-optation of female generativity. Precedents for using sexual role reversal and male co-optation, however, are seen in Greco-Roman literature, the Hebrew Bible, and even in the Fourth Gospel itself. In addition, the medical literature of the period exemplifies how the first-century reader could have viewed this Johannine material as a conception/birth "from above."

MALE CO-OPTATION OF FEMALE POWERS IN LITERATURE

Examples of male co-optation of female powers in Greco-Roman literature may be found in Plato's *Symposium*,[34] as well as Aeschylus'

---

[30]*The New Oxford Annotated Bible,* 853 OT. Cf. Mace, 181; Goodman, 74.

[31]Cf. John McHugh, "The Mother of the Word Incarnate: Mary in the Theology of St. John," *The Mother of Jesus in the New Testament* (London: Darton, Longman & Todd, 1975) 371; Thurian, 151, 156–7; Brown, *The Gospel According to John,* 2:954–6; Rudolf Schnackenburg, *The Gospel According to St. John* (New York: Seabury, 1980) 3:292–4; Hoskyns, 2:635, 638.

[32]Cf. John McHugh, 371; Brown, *The Gospel According to John,* 2:955; Thurian, 156–7; Schnackenburg, 3:462 n. 80.

[33]Cf. Thurian, 157–8; Brown, *The Gospel According to John,* 2:949; Schnackenburg, 3:294; Hoskyns, 2:635.

[34]David Halperin sees male co-optation of female powers in Socrates' references to the teachings of the female Diotima in the *Symposium*. Diotima's teachings on wisdom incorporate images of men becoming pregnant, suffering birth pangs, bearing and bringing forth offspring and nourishing their young. Halperin identifies within this writing a ploy by the male author to use a female figure to disembody such female images and make them a reflection of male, spiritual labor. He, likewise, sees within this literary device a reflection of the male desire to appropriate these feminine powers.

Oresteia.[35] Male co-optation of female powers appears in the birth of Athena from the head of Zeus after his head was opened with an ax,[36] in the birth of Dionysus from the thigh of Zeus,[37] in the rebirth of Phanes after Zeus had swallowed him,[38] and in the formation of the Erinyes, a female entity, from the blood of Uranus's severed genitals as found in Hesiod's *Theogony.*[39] According to Zeitlin, such myths illustrate the male usurpation of female generative ability. Zeitlin goes on to state that the myths about the origins of Athena and the Erinyes in Aeschylus' *Oresteia* were used to argue for the binding nature of patriarchal marriage, the subordination of women, and patrilineal succession in society.[40]

Within the Hebrew Bible male appropriation of the female generative ability can be found in the creation story of Genesis 2. J. Cheryl Exum notes that the first man is portrayed as unnaturally giving birth from his side to the first woman. She identifies this passage as an expression of patriarchy's fear of women's reproductive power, as well as the need to suppress and appropriate such powers.[41] As will soon be illustrated in this chapter, this story in Genesis 2 of unnatural birth from the side of the first man may have been used as a paradigm for the story of the crucifixion in the Fourth Gospel.

Halperin, "Why is Diotima A Woman? Platonic Eros and the Figuration of Gender," *Before Sexuality: The Construction of Erotic Experience in the Ancient Greek World,* ed. David M. Halperin, John J. Winkler, and Froma I. Zeitlin (Princeton: Princeton University Press, 1990) 262, 278, 285–6. Cf. O'Brien, 130–2, 137–8, 146.

[35]Cf. this chapter, note 8.

[36]The tradition of Athena being born out of the head of Zeus is mentioned in Hesiod's *Theogony* and Aeschylus' *Oresteia.* According to the myth, Zeus swallowed his pregnant consort Methis, the principle of intelligence, whom he perceived as a threat. Consequently, Athena was born fully grown and in full armor from the head of Zeus after his head was opened with an axe to relieve him of the labor pains (headache). According to Zeitlin, Athena was no threat to Zeus because she boasted that she was motherless, a child of Zeus alone. Cf. Christine Downing, "Athena," *The Encyclopedia of Religion,* ed. Mircea Eliade (New York: Macmillan, 1987) 1:490; Zeitlin, "The Dynamics of Misogyny," 178–9.

[37]According to Thomson, the tradition of the birth of Dionysus from Thebes portrays Zeus as killing the mother of Dionysus with a thunderbolt, saving the unborn child from the flames, and then sewing the unborn child to his thigh. Dionysus was then later born of Zeus. Thomson identifies the birth of Dionysus with initiations rites. Thomson, 110–1.

[38]Thomson identifies the "rebirth" of Phanes with adoption rituals. Thomson, 110–1.

[39]Cf. Zeitlin, "The Dynamics of Misogyny," 173–4.

[40]Ibid., 179–84.

[41]Exum, "The (M)other's Place," 127.

Throughout the Fourth Gospel one sees examples of male co-optation of female powers. One need only look at Jesus' statement to Nicodemus that a person must be born "again/from above" (3:3-6), at Jesus' use of the analogy of a woman giving birth to express the pain that his disciples will experience by his absence and the joy that they will experience when they see him again (16:21-22), and at Jesus' self-portrayal as one who is able to quench people's thirst and give them nourishment through his own person (7:37-38, cf. 4:10, 13-14; 6:35), the very actions that a mother is able to do for her child. Thus, perceiving Jesus' passion, his being "lifted up" above the earth, his death on the cross, and his side being pierced by a lance as the consummation of his messianic wedding, and perceiving the issuance of blood and water from his side as the subsequent conception of the children of God "from above" (cf. 3:14; 8:28; 12:32) are supported by the consistent male co-optation of female powers in the Fourth Gospel.

THE CRUCIFIXION SCENE AS JESUS' GIVING BIRTH

The idea that the crucifixion scene in the Fourth Gospel represents Jesus' giving birth to the Church or to the family of God is certainly not a new notion. Many church Fathers, members of the Council of Vienne in 1312, as well as scholars such as A. Loisy and A. Feuillet relate the Johannine crucifixion scene to Eve being taken from the side of Adam in Gen 2:21.[42] Other scholars perceive the birth of the Church or the constituting of new family of God in the mutual exchange of the mother of Jesus and the beloved disciple,[43] and even in Jesus' breathing his Spirit upon

---

[42]Part of the basis for this argument is that the word for side, $\pi\lambda\epsilon\nu\rho\alpha$, which is in the singular in 19:34 and Gen 2:21, is more commonly found in the plural. Scholars also point to a connection between Gen 3:17 where Eve is referred to a "woman" and Jesus' referral to his mother as "woman." These interpretations, however, tend to focus on the mother of Jesus as representing the church/the new Eve, either as the spiritual bride of Christ or the spiritual mother of the Church. Schnackenburg rejects such an ecclesiastical typology for 19:34-37. Cf. Brown, *The Gospel According to John,* 2:935, 949–51; R. Collins, "Mary in the Fourth Gospel: A Decade of Johannine Studies," *Louvain Studies* 3 (1970) 106–9, 130–42; Hoskyns, 636–9; Thurian, 382–7; Schnackenburg, 3:289, 294.

[43]Cf. R. Collins, "The Representative Figures of the Fourth Gospel," 121; R. Collins, "Mary in the Fourth Gospel," 134; R. Alan Culpepper, *Anatomy of the Fourth Gospel: A Study of Literary Design* (Philadelphia: Fortress, 1983) 134; Bertrand Buby, "Mary in John's Gospel," *Mary, the Faithful Disciple* (New York: Paulist, 1985) 105–6; Turid Karlsen Seim, "Roles of Women in the Gospel of John," *Aspects on the Johannine Literature,* ed. Hartman & Birger Olsson (Sweden: Almqvist & Wiksell International, 1987) 65–6. Although Paul Minear places the fulfillment of the promise of "sonship" for the disciples at the ascension of Jesus and Jesus' breathing the spirit

those gathered at the cross.[44] Raymond Collins goes so far as to acknowledge that the Fourth Gospel shares the notion of primitive Christianity of the passion as labor.[45] Although some scholars have connected either the blood or water with the concept of new life,[46] Dorothy Lee and Mark Stibbe explicitly state that the blood *and* water from the side of the crucified Jesus in 19:34 are suggestive of birth and Lee relates this occurrence to Jesus' conversation with Nicodemus regarding the need to be born "from above."[47]

THE PIERCING OF JESUS' SIDE—THE CONSUMMATION
OF THE MESSIANIC MARRIAGE

Although many scholars have noted some element of "giving birth" in the crucifixion scene, what scholars have not recognized is that the piercing of Jesus' side could have been perceived by the reader as the consummation of Jesus' messianic marriage. Jewish tradition acknowledges the sexual act as constituting a marriage.[48] Therefore, if an ancient reader were able to perceive a sexual role reversal in the case of the piercing of

upon the disciples, he acknowledges that Jesus' words of mutual exchange to his mother and the beloved disciple and the words of the resurrected Jesus to Mary Magdalene carry this same context. Minear, "'We Don't know where. . .' John 20:2." *Interpretation* 30 (1976) 137.

[44]Thurian, 155. Thurian then connects the blood and water flowing from Jesus' side with Eucharist and Baptism respectively. Nevertheless, he does connect the water from Jesus' side with the spirit of life that Jesus hands on to the church. Thurian, 155, 161, 165.

[45]R. Collins, however, places the birth at the time of the resurrection. Collins, "Mary in the Fourth Gospel," 139.

[46]Schnackenburg connects the blood flowing from Jesus' side with Jesus' death, but he also connects the water flowing from his side with the Spirit and new life. Hoskyns, however, connects the blood with new life and the water with purification. Hoskyns then connects the blood and water with Eucharist and baptism, a connection that Schnackenburg finds less immediate. R. Brown connects the water from Jesus' side with the concept of birth by identifying it as a proleptic symbol of the giving of the Spirit. Brown then connects the water with Baptism and the blood with Eucharist as secondary sacramental symbolism, but acknowledges that the blood/Eucharist connection is less certain. Schnackenburg, 3:289, 294. Hoskyns, 631, 635. Brown, *The Gospel According to John,* 2:950–2.

[47]Dorothy Lee, *The Symbolic Narratives of the Fourth Gospel* (Sheffield: JSOT, 1994) 57. Stibbe, 197. Schnackenburg acknowledges that the issuing of blood and water supports a symbolic interpretation based on Eve's origin from the side of Adam, but he does not espouse this typological interpretation. Schnackenburg, 3:289, 294.

[48]The sex act necessitates the payment of the *mohar* (bride-price) (Exod 22:16-17; Deut 22:29). Cf. Mace, 168; Goodman, 71.

Jesus' side, this action could have been viewed as the completion of the messianic marriage. Because Mieke Bal has identified this type of sexual role reversal in the story of Jael's driving a stake into Sisera's temple (Judg 4:21-22),[49] a first-century reader of the Fourth Gospel could have perceived a sexual role reversal in the piercing of Jesus' side with a lance. Because this act of piercing Jesus' side is said to happen so that the Scriptures might be fulfilled (20:36; cf. 20:28), the reader would have perceived the soldier's act as fulfilling the will of the Father.

CONCEPTION—THE MINGLING OF BLOOD, WATER, AND SPIRIT (PNEUMA)

An alternative to understanding Jesus' crucifixion on the cross as a "birthing" would be to perceive the piercing of Jesus' side as consummation followed by conception. According to Thomas Laqueur, the ancient concept of the human body and reproduction is a "one-sex/one-flesh model." In this model male and female sexual organs were understood as variations of each other, each suitable for specific roles, but not distinct types. The phallos was viewed as the convenient vehicle for dispersing the semen, and the uterus was viewed as an inverted phallos, a convenient vessel for containing semen.[50] As Laqueur states, ". . . the female body was a less hot, less perfect, and hence less potent version of the canonical body."[51]

Within this one-sex/one-flesh model, bodily fluids were perceived as variations of each other with no sharp boundary between the sexes. According to Laqueur, a Hippocratic account states that the foam-like sperm was first refined out of the blood, passed to the brain, and then made its way through the spinal marrow, to the kidneys and testicles, and finally into the penis for dispersion.[52] Such an understanding of bodily fluids

[49]Mieke Bal identifies Sisera's death as a "rape" by Jael. She notes that, although Sisera's mother presumes that her son's tardiness was due to his having his own way with a girl (literally "womb") or two (Judg 5:28-30), his failure to return was actually due to the fact that he himself had been "raped" by a woman. Danna Nolan Fewell translates the Hebrew word *raqaq* as "parted lips" instead of temple. Such a translation would support Bal's interpretation even more. Bal, *Death and Dissymmetry: The Politics of Coherence in the Book of Judges* (Chicago: University of Chicago Press, 1988) 30-1, 214-6. Nolan Fewell, "Judges," *The Women's Bible Commentary,* ed. Carol Newsom and Sharon Ringe (Louisville: Westminster/John Knox, 1992) 69.

[50]Thomas Laqueur, "Destiny Is Anatomy," *Making Sex: Body and Gender from the Greek to Freud* (Cambridge, Mass.: Harvard University Press, 1990) 25-35.

[51]Ibid., 34-5.

[52]Ibid., 35. Cf. Iain M. Lonie, *The Hippocratic Treaties: "On Generation," "The Seed," "On the Nature of the Child," "Diseases IV"* (Berlin: Walter de Gruyer, 1981) 102-3, 124-32, 277-9. Although the physician Hippocrates lived 460-377 B.C.E., much

explains how an ancient reader could accept Athena being born from the head of Zeus. Because the male semen has a thicker, whiter, frothier quality than the female ejaculate, which was thinner, less pristinely white, more watery and still red in quality, the male semen was considered a more powerful, and more efficient cause. Menstrual flow in this one-sex economy of fluid was considered a localized, even less concocted, and more superfluous variant of the same fluid. When needed, this extra blood could even be converted into milk for a nursing child. Thus, although Aristotle maintained that only the male as genitor had enough "heat" to refine the residual secretion to pure form *(sperma),*[53] male and female reproductive fluids were considered but variations of the same bodily fluid, and were not considered sexually specific. In this one-sex/one-body model, both male and female contributed their variations of the same seminal substance and conception occurred in the blending of these germinal substances.[54]

If one looks at the Fourth Gospel for signs of conception, one is initially disappointed. From Jesus' side comes not blood and a thick, white, frothy substance, but blood and water (ὕδωρ). If one realizes, however, that in the first century the male semen was thought to be thick, white and foam-like because it was composed of water mixed with breath/spirit (πνεῦμα), the tool through which the male principle worked,[55] then the situation changes. Prior to the blood and water flowing from Jesus' pierced side, Jesus "bowed his head" and "gave over" (παρέδωκεν) his spirit/pneuma (πνεῦμα) (19:30).[56] Only blood and water could flow from Jesus' side because Jesus' pneuma, which would have made the water thick, white and frothy, had been given over prior to the piercing of his side, the symbolic consummation. One might perceive a conception occurring when Jesus' blood and water mingles with the spirit he had just given over. On the other hand, if one looks at the Fourth Gospel as a unity, one might prefer to perceive a conception occurring when Jesus, after having returned to the Father, appears to his disciples and breathes

---

was later written in his name. Because the attempt to identify the material actually written by Hippocrates did not begin until the second century C.E., this material is difficult to date. Cf. *Encyclopaedia Britannica: Knowledge in Depth,* s.v. "Hippocrates."

[53]Cf. Laqueur, 30.

[54]Ibid., 35–40.

[55]Ibid., 41.

[56]I prefer the translation "give over" to "give up" for παρέδωκεν because it carries the connotation of passing onto others. Cf. Walter Bauer, *A Greek-English Lexicon of the New Testament and Other Early Christian Literature,* 2nd ed., trans., ed. and augmented by William Arndt, R. W. Gingrich and F. W. Danker (Chicago: University of Chicago Press, 1979 [1957]) 614–5.

(ἐνεφύσησεν) on them saying, "Receive the Holy Spirit" (20:22). Perhaps this is the moment when the conception/birth "from above" is truly complete.

CONCLUSION TO THE PIERCING OF JESUS' SIDE AS CONSUMMATION
FOLLOWED BY CONCEPTION

Although other scholarly explanations for the issuance of blood and water from Jesus' side have been suggested,[57] it would be consistent with the Johannine tendency of attributing generative powers to Jesus and consistent with first-century notion of reproduction for a reader to have perceived a conception in the blood and water from Jesus' side combining either with the spirit (πνεῦμα) Jesus gave over from the cross or with the Spirit he breathes on the disciples after having returned to the Father. Such a notion of conception would also be consistent with and logically follow the piercing of Jesus' side, if it were perceived as the consummation of Jesus' messianic wedding. Just as male generative creativity is displaced from phallos to head in the story of Athena's birth form the head of Zeus,[58] so Jesus' generative creativity is moved to his side, probably because of the influence of Genesis 2.

The Characterization of the Mother of Jesus at the Cross

Having established that the implied reader of the Fourth Gospel could have perceived Jesus' passion and death as both a blood sacrifice that establishes a patrilineal kinship group and a messianic wedding culminating in his conception of/giving birth to the children of God, I shall turn to the characterization of the mother of Jesus in the crucifixion scene to illustrate how her characterization supports this portrayal of Jesus. First, however, I shall illustrate why the identification of the other characters at the foot of the cross is significant for the characterization of the mother of Jesus. I shall then illustrate how the implied author of the Fourth Gospel adapted the "dying king" type-scene from a Greco-Roman romance, analyze

---

[57]According to Schnackenburg, G. Richter argues for an anti-Docetist interpretation of both 1 John 5:6 and John 19:34b. Schnackenburg, however, does not find an anti-Docetist argument for John 19:34b based on 1 John 5:6 to be compelling. Hoskyns, likewise, perceives more than an anti-Docetist argument in the issuance of blood and water. Brown mentions other theories regarding the issuance of blood and water, e.g., it affirms Jesus' divinity and it affirms that Jesus was really dead and not just in a coma. Schnackenburg, 3:290–1, 462 n. 85. Hoskyns, 635. Brown, *The Gospel According to John,* 2:947–9.

[58]Zeitlin, "The Dynamics of Misogyny," 179.

Jesus' words and actions with regard to his mother, and comment on the significance of the narrator's concluding comments.

The Other People at the Foot of the Cross

After learning of the presence of the mother of Jesus at cross, the reader is informed that she is accompanied by other women. The implied author of the Fourth Gospel may have been influenced by Christian tradition to include other women at the scene of the cross. Each of the Synoptic Gospels mentions women in the vicinity of the cross and each of the Gospels specifically names three of these women. The identification of the three women, however, varies from gospel to gospel.[59]

Most scholars maintain that the implied author of the Fourth Gospel identified four women at the cross,

1) the mother of Jesus,
2) his mother's sister,
3) Mary, the wife of Clopas,
4) Mary Magdalene (19:25).[60]

---

[59]Matt 27:55-56 has many women looking on from afar. Among them Matthew specifically mentions Mary Magdalene, Mary the mother (ἡ μήτηρ) of James and Joseph, and the mother (ἡ μήτηρ) of the sons of Zebedee. Mark 15:40-41 also has women looking on from afar. Mark specifically mentions Mary Magdalene, Mary the mother (ἡ μήτηρ) of James the younger and of Joses, and Salome (cf. Mark 15:40). Luke 23:49 states that all Jesus' acquaintances and the women who had followed him from Galilee stood at a distance and saw what happened to him at the cross. These women saw the tomb and how his body was laid and later returned with spices and ointments (Luke 23:55–24:12). Luke specifically mentions Mary Magdalene, Joanna and Mary the mother of James (ἡ Ἰακώβου), but he states that there were the other women with them (Luke 24:10). Cf. Richard Atwood, *Mary Magdalene in the New Testament Gospels and Early Tradition* (Bern, Germany: Lang, 1993) 47–9, 53–5.

[60]This hypothesis of the presence of four women at the cross is based on the assumption that the sister of the mother of Jesus is not the same person as Mary, the wife of Clopas. This assumption is based on the argument that the implied author would not have given the sister of the mother of Jesus the same name that Christian tradition maintains for the mother of Jesus, "Mary." This identification of four women at the cross in the Fourth Gospel has led to some discussion about a possible correlation between the three women at the cross mentioned with the mother of Jesus in the Fourth Gospel and the three women mentioned in the Synoptic Gospels. Cf. Brown, *The Gospel According to John,* 2:904–6; Richard Bauckham, "Mary of Clopas (John 19:25)," *Women in the Biblical Tradition,* ed. George Brooke (Lewiston, N.Y.: Edwin Mellen, 1992) 239–40; Ben Witherington, *Women in the Ministry of Jesus* (Cambridge: Cambridge University Press, 1984) 94, 120–1, 187 n. 102; Atwood, 53–9.

Some scholars support this argument for four women by asserting the presence of a contrast between the faithful presence of the four women and the actions of the *four* soldiers at the cross (who divided the garment of Jesus into four parts, one for each soldier, and who cast lots for Jesus tunic).[61] The manner in which the implied author of the Fourth Gospel listed and identified these four women at the cross, however, has added literary importance.

By listing the mother of Jesus first, the implied author gave the mother of Jesus prominence in the scene and set the stage for her important role in the pericope. Supporting the importance of the "motherhood" of the mother of Jesus is the fact that, unlike the Gospels of Matthew, Mark and Luke, the Fourth Gospel does not identify any of the other women by the expression "mother of X."[62] This absence of a specific reference to another "mother of X" allowed the implied author of the Fourth Gospel to focus on the "maternal" role for the mother of Jesus.[63]

The presence of the sister of the mother of Jesus is of literary importance because it informs the reader that the mother of Jesus is being accompanied by a relative, just as she was at wedding scene at Cana. The sister's presence indicates that the scene is a family affair, just as was the wedding at Cana. The fact that the mother of Jesus is accompanied by her sister, rather than her other sons as she was at the wedding at Cana,

---

[61]This contrasting relationship is based on connecting the μὲν of 19:24 with the δὲ of 19:25. Stibbe, 194. Schnackenburg, 3:277. Hoskyns, 630–1. Cf. Atwood, 49–50, 52, 55. R. Brown, however, maintains that this comparison is unlikely. Brown, *The Gospel According to John,* 2:903–4.

[62]The Greek word for mother (ἡ μήτηρ) is not used in Luke, only (ἡ Ἰακώβου). Nevertheless, based on Matthew's and Mark's versions of the story, a reader familiar with Christian tradition would have assumed that the relationship here is one of mother to James. The implied author of the Fourth Gospel does use the phrase "Μαρία ἡ τοῦ Κλωπᾶ," however, most scholars translate this expression as "Mary the 'wife' of Clopas." Although this Greek phrase could be translated as "Mary the 'mother' of Clopas," the efforts of historical critics to identify a correlation between the other three women in the Fourth Gospel and the three women in the Synoptic Gospels seems to have led critics to translate this Greek phrase as "Mary the 'wife' of Clopas." Even though the Greek phrase could be translated as "mother of," I believe it is of literary significance that the implied author did not specifically use the Greek word ἡ μήτηρ for any of the other women. Cf. Bauckham, 234–40.

[63]Bauckham considers the changing of the Marys of the Synoptics to Mary of Clopas to be incomprehensible. Bauckham, 249. My literary theory explains why the implied author of the Fourth Gospel may have changed the manner in which this woman was identified, if, in fact, a correlation does exist between the Johannine women at the cross and the women in the crucifixion scenes of the Synoptics.

accentuates the absence of her other sons. Because the reader has already been informed of the lack of faith of the brothers of Jesus (7:5), their lack of faith in Jesus, combined with their absence at the foot of the cross, sets the stage for Jesus' giving his mother a new son.

The full significance of the presence of Mary Magdalene at the cross in the Fourth Gospel will not be made known until Jesus' post-resurrection appearance to her (20:14-18). At that later point in the text, the first-century reader would have recognized that Mary Magdalene was fulfilling the role of the betrothed/bride in both the crucifixion scene, as well as the post-resurrection scene.[64] Mary Magdalene is the only woman who is specifically mentioned in all canonical crucifixion scenes. Although this consensus may indicate that her presence at the scene of the cross is very strong in the tradition,[65] the fact that she is listed last in the Fourth Gospel, instead of first as in the Synoptic Gospels, or second because of the presence of the mother of Jesus in the Fourth Gospel's version, may imply that the implied author of the Fourth Gospel might have been marginalizing Mary Magdalene's historical importance, while using her character for an important literary purpose.[66]

After the reader is informed of the presence of the mother of Jesus and the other women at the cross, the reader is further informed of the presence of the beloved disciple. The physical proximity of the beloved disciple to the mother of Jesus, "standing beside her" (19:26), supports Jesus' subsequent action of establishing a new relationship between them:

> When Jesus saw his mother and the disciple whom he loved standing beside her, he said to his mother, "Woman, here is your son" (γύναι, ἴδε ὁ υἱός σου). Then he said to the disciple, "Here is your mother." And from that hour the disciple took her into his own home (19:26-27).

[64]Mary Magdalene is perhaps the only woman at the foot of the cross who could fulfill the role of bride. The mother of Jesus and his mother's sister surely could not fulfill this role. Likewise, if the first-century reader read the phrase Μαρία ἡ τοῦ Κλωπᾶ as "Mary the wife of Clopas," this character also could not fulfill the role of the bride of the messianic bridegroom.

[65]Cf. Schneiders, "Women in the Fourth Gospel and the Role of Women in the Church," 43.

[66]The silence between Jesus and Mary Magdalene at the cross would not negate Mary Magdalene functioning as the bride. In wedding ceremonies among Jews in the first century, the spoken word did not constitute the marriage. The sex act itself or the induction of the bride into the home of the bridegroom for the purpose of consummating the marriage seems to be what constituted the marriage. Cf. Büchler, 112–3; Mace, 178–83; Goodman, 73–6.

In these passages one is able to identify the adaptation of the "dying king" type-scene as found in *Alexander Romance.*

The Adaptation of the "Dying King" Type-Scene

As stated in chapter 3, the giving of a daughter in marriage is a type of gift-giving that establishes permanent kinship bonds between men.[67] This means of establishing kinship ties was especially important in the establishment of political alliances between rulers, as the incident of the nine wives of King Herod illustrates.[68] Besides the exchange of a daughter in marriage, the literature of the period also illustrates other forms of the exchange of women for the establishment of kinship ties.

In the Greco-Roman *Alexander Romance,*[69] King Darius on his deathbed gives all of the women in his family to Alexander the Great. He gives his mother, wife, daughter, and sister to Alexander the Great to be Alexander's mother, sister, wife, and sister respectively. Such an exchange appears to be for the purpose of establishing a kinship bond between the two kings, one that would insure both the welfare of the female members of the dying king's family and the dying king's remembrance in his kingdom.

As quoted by Tomas Hägg, Darius states,

> Let Darius' and Alexander's family be one! I entrust my mother to you as if she were your mother. Have pity on my wife as you would your sister! My daughter Roxana I give to you as wife, that you may leave children in ever-lasting memory of you: glory in them as we gloried in our children, and keep our memories alive, you, Philip's, Roxana that of Darius, as you grow old together (2:20.4–9).[70]

---

[67]Cf. chapter 3, pp. 69–70.

[68]Cf. Josephus, *Jewish Antiquities* in *Josephus,* vol. 8, The Loeb Classical Library Series, ed. Allen Wikgren and trans. Ralph Maracus (Cambridge, Mass.: Harvard University Press, 1963) 17.19–22.

[69]Although this romance was written about 300 C.E., Tomas Hägg argues that it was built on at least three distinct Hellenistic sources: the biography of Alexander, the putative epistolary Alexander novel, and a number of longer, separate letters. Therefore, this romance can be cited as evidence that the implied author of the Fourth Gospel may have had access to this literary variation of the exchange of women by which a dying king establishes kinship bonds with the new ruler of his kingdom. Cf. Hägg, *The Novel in Antiquity* (Berkeley: University of California Press, 1983) 125–6. Albert Wolohojian also dates the romance prior to the fourth century C.E. Wolohojian, *The Romance of Alexander the Great by Pseudo-Callisthenes: translated from the Armenian Version* (New York: Columbia University Press, 1969) 1.

[70]Hägg, 132.

Although the quotation by Hägg stops here, Albert Wolohojian's translation of the Armenian version, which he considers to be an accurate translation of the oldest manuscripts of recension α,[71] goes on to state, "Honor
my sister, Gagipharta, and consider her your own sister. . . ."[72]

The importance of women as exchange objects in forming the kinship bond between the dying king and the one who will rule his kingdom
in the future is accentuated by the fact that King Darius does not give his
brother to be Alexander's brother. Regarding his own brother, King Darius states, ". . . and respect my brother, Oxydarkes, as a true king . . . ."[73]
Thus, the women of the family—not the men—are the exchange objects
that establish kinship bonds between a dying king and the one who will
rule in his place.

Part of the responsibility of the one receiving the women is to care
for the women. Alexander writes to Darius' mother and wife, "He (Darius)
recommended you to my trust and gave his daughter, Roxiana, to be my
wife. . . ."[74] They in turn wrote back to Alexander, "We know that under
your care, we will be well off."[75]

The care of the women was not the only reason for such an exchange,
however, as Darius' statement, "keep our memories alive, you, Philip's,
Roxana that of Darius, as you grow old together" indicates. Such an exchange of women was also a means of prolonging his memory in his kingdom.[76] This interpretation of the exchange seems to be supported by
Alexander's actions at the moment of his own death.

Alexander, who is childless at the moment of his death, and thus has
no children to carry on his memory as Darius had hoped, parcels out the
pieces of his kingdom and the women in his family in such a way as to be
remembered. Alexander first makes his father's (Philip's) son, who is al-

---

[71]Wolohojian, 2–5. See also Wout van Bekkum, ed., *A Hebrew Alexander Romance According to Ms London, Jews' College no. 145* (Leuven: Peeters, 1992) 13–6.

[72]*Pseudo-Callisthenes*, #197 in Wolohojian, 104–5.

[73]Ibid., #197 in Wolohojian, 105.

[74]Ibid., #204 in Wolohojian, 109.

[75]Ibid., #205 in Wolohojian, 110.

[76]The Armenian version, as translated by Wolohojian, also shows a concern on the
part of Darius that his memory survive his death. Wolohojian's translation, however,
gives the impression that the children of the kings are to be the ones remembered and
boasted about by their kingly fathers.

> . . . I beg to entrust to you as your own parent my wretched mother, Queen Rodoqoune, and
> care for my wife as a blood relative. I give you my daughter Roxiane for a wife, for if my
> memory still survives even in death, two children shall be boasted of by their parents; you by
> your father, Philip, and my daughter, Roxiana, by Darius. Honor my sister, Gagipharta, and
> consider her your own sister. . . . (Wolohojian, 104–5)

ready married to Alexander's father's daughter, king of Macedonia. He then gives his sister as a wife to Ptolomeos, who will rule Egypt, and his wife, Roxana, as a wife to Perdikkas, who will be the governor of Babylon.[77] Such a parceling out of the kingdom and exchange of female relatives in marriage assures Alexander's remembrance in the kingdom that he leaves behind through death.

The Fourth Gospel emphasizes the kingship of Jesus in Pilate's questioning of Jesus and in Jesus' response to Pilate (18:33-38), in Pilate's words to the Jews and in the Jews' response to Pilate (18:38-39; 19:12-15, 21-22), in the treatment that Jesus received from the hands of the Roman soldiers (19:2-6), and in the words nailed to his cross (19:19).[78] As the dying king of the Jews, Jesus has no daughter or sister to give in marriage. He does, however, have a mother whom he can give. Jesus does not give his mother to the beloved disciple as a wife. Rather, he, like Darius, gives his mother to the beloved disciple as a mother. This may indicate the manner in which Jesus wanted to be remembered, as "brother," as one who shares a common heavenly Father with his disciples.

Looking at the Fourth Gospel as a unity, it is evident that the implied author was adapting the "dying king" type-scene. In the typical "dying king" type-scene, the female relative of the dying king is given to the one who will rule the kingdom in the future. In the Fourth Gospel as we have it, however, Peter, and not the beloved disciple, is given the keys to Jesus' kingdom (21:15-19). Nevertheless, because the beloved disciple is the ideal disciple, the beloved disciple does represent those with whom Jesus wants to establish a kinship relationship. Therefore, in one sense, Jesus does give his mother to the one who represents those in his kingdom in the text.

Another adaptation of the "dying king" type-scene found in the Fourth Gospel is the mutuality of the exchange. Not only is the mother of Jesus given to the beloved disciple; the beloved disciple is also given to the mother of Jesus. The manner in which the implied author adapted the type-scene indicates that the purpose of the exchange was not merely to ensure Jesus' remembrance, nor to secure care of his mother.[79] The language

---

[77]*Pseudo-Callisthenes,* #274 in Wolohojian, 155.

[78]Stibbe notes that the details in this section reinforce the sense that 19:16b-30 depicts an act of regicide. Stibbe, 197.

[79]Witherington maintains that the tradition on which the Fourth Evangelist drew merely presented Jesus as providing for the security of his mother, who eventually became a member of the faith community. He states that the Fourth Evangelist altered the received tradition to make a statement about male and female disciples. According to R. Collins, P. Gätcher realized that the manner in which Jesus gives his mother to the beloved disciple indicates that Jesus is doing something more than just providing

that Jesus uses in the exchange indicates that the kinship group, which Jesus formally establishes,[80] is of a patrilineal nature and thus negates the importance of biological motherhood. To understand fully how the exchange formalizes Jesus' establishment of a patrilineal kinship group, the following aspects in the characterization of the mother of Jesus need to be analyzed:

1) Jesus' use of the appellation "woman" for his mother;
2) Jesus' mutual act of giving the beloved disciple and his mother to each other;
3) the narrator's comments regarding the beloved disciple's taking Jesus' mother into his own home (19:27).

Jesus' Referring to his Mother as "Woman"

Regarding Aeschylus' *Oresteia,* Zeitlin states that Aeschylus affirms the primacy of the father by denying the mother's role in procreation on the biological level.[81] Although Jesus may not deny his mother in as drastic a manner as Orestes denied Clytemnestra, he does distance himself from his mother to affirm the primacy of his heavenly Father. As in the wedding scene at Cana, Jesus addresses his mother by the appellation "woman." Its use carries the same significance it did at Cana. It distances Jesus from his biological mother and his matrilineal descent in order to emphasize his relationship with his heavenly Father and his patrilineal descent.[82] This sets the stage for Jesus' subsequent words and actions that will deny the importance of matrilineal descent for all those whom the beloved disciple represents.

---

for the care of a grieving mother. He, however, thought it meant that the mother of Jesus was being intrusted with the spiritual motherhood of the Church. Witherington, 93–4. R. Collins, "Mary in the Fourth Gospel," 130–1.

[80]Charles Talbert states that the language Jesus uses is that of a binding agreement (cf. Tob 7:11-12), but Schnackenburg states that the identification of the exchange as a kind of adoption formula (cf. Ps 2:7 and Tob 7:12) is disputed. Talbert, *Reading John: A Literary and Theological Commentary on the Fourth Gospel and the Johannine Epistles* (New York: Crossroad, 1994) 244. Schnackenburg, 3:278.

[81]Aeschylus does this by having Orestes kill his mother and then seek new birth through a blood ritual at the male-centered *omphalos* at Delphi. Zeitlin identifies this rebirth of the male as a necessary condition for Orestes' passage into adulthood as son of his father. Zeitlin, "The Dynamics of Misogyny," 175–6, 178, 182.

[82]Cf. chapter 2, pp. 33, 35–6. According to R. Collins, Feuillet saw the use of this appellation in the crucifixion scene as distancing Jesus from his mother. McHugh likewise acknowledges that the use of the appellation draws attention away from Jesus' "blood ties" with his mother. R. Collins, "Mary in the Fourth Gospel," 137. McHugh, 402.

Jesus' Giving the Beloved Disciple and his Mother to Each Other

Noting that the beloved disciple is first given to the mother of Jesus as a son, many authors have concluded that the mother of Jesus is being imbued here with the spiritual motherhood of the church, represented here by the beloved disciple.[83] A. Dauer and E. Meyer, however, state that the focus of the implied author of the Fourth Gospel was on raising the status of the beloved disciple, not on raising the status of the mother of Jesus.[84] In support of the latter position is the fact that the implied author deemphasized a maternal relationship with Jesus by having Jesus call his mother "woman." If the implied author of the Fourth Gospel wanted to emphasize a spiritual motherhood for the mother of Jesus, it would seem that the implied author would have had Jesus emphasize his mother's maternal relationship to him rather than deemphasize it before he gave the beloved disciple to her as a son.

After deemphasizing his mother's "maternal" relationship to him, Jesus proceeds to devalue matrilineal descent for all who believe in him. He does this by giving his mother a "non-biological" son and by giving the beloved disciple a "non-biological" mother. Jesus' act of mutually giving the beloved disciple and his mother to each other symbolizes what he is accomplishing on a "higher," spiritual level from the cross. Those whom the beloved disciple represents do become brothers of Jesus, but not because they and Jesus have a common earthly mother.[85] Rather, the disciples' "brotherly" relationship with Jesus is based on the heavenly patrilineal kinship group that Jesus' blood sacrifice will establish, a kinship group that negates the importance of having been born of woman.

If the exchange of the beloved disciple is perceived in the manner described above, he is to be interpreted as a representative figure for the community of believers. The same, however, cannot be said of the mother of Jesus. Although her presence at the cross may illustrate that she is portrayed as a believer at this point in the story,[86] her primary role is not that

[83]For a discussion of those authors who uphold the spiritual motherhood of the mother of Jesus in the Fourth Gospel, see R. Collins, "Mary in the Fourth Gospel," 106–9, 130–41 and Buby, 104.

[84]Cf. R. Collins, "Mary in the Fourth Gospel," 135; Brown, *The Gospel According to John,* 2:923.

[85]According to Seim, the new family unity is constituted by Jesus' ascension, which establishes the universal Fatherhood of God, not by the mother of Jesus becoming the mother of all believers. Seim. 66.

[86]Adele Reinhartz considers the faith status of the mother of Jesus to be unclear at this point in the text. Other scholars, such as Elisabeth Schüssler Fiorenza, McHugh, and Witherington, perceive her as a disciple in this pericope. Reinhartz, "The Gospel

of a representative figure.[87] Rather, her primary role is being an exchange object in the implied author's adaptation of the "dying king" type-scene, and being an earthly symbol for what her son is accomplishing on a heavenly level. The earthly mother of Jesus, like the water from the Jewish purification jars at the wedding at Cana, is merely an earthly symbol for the higher reality that Jesus accomplishes as the messianic bridegroom.

The Beloved Disciple Taking the Mother of Jesus into His Home

The narrator's statement concerning the beloved disciple's taking the mother of Jesus into his home accentuates the fact that it is the beloved disciple who is raised to a higher role, not the mother of Jesus who is given a spiritual role. The mother of Jesus is placed in the care of the beloved disciple. The beloved disciple is not placed in the spiritual care of Jesus' mother.[88] The beloved disciple's act of taking the mother of Jesus into his home correlates with Alexander's taking care of the women in Darius's family after Darius's death, as found in the "dying king" type-scene in *Alexander Romance*.

A Patriarchal and Androcentric Point of View

Throughout the crucifixion scene one encounters a patriarchal point of view. It is evident in the portrayal of Jesus' death as a blood sacrifice that establishes a patrilineal kinship group and in the portrayal of his conceiving/giving birth to the children of God. Such cooptation of female powers diminishes the contribution women make through childbearing. A woman's bloody ordeal is perceived as being superseded by the bloody ritual carried out by Jesus. Any blood relationships based on being born of a woman/flesh has no meaning in the Fourth Gospel. As was first suggested in Jesus' words to Nicodemus (3:3-6), the woman's womb has been superseded. All that is necessary is to be born from "above" of the water and Spirit (i.e., to be born of the divine, male *sperma*).

Patriarchal privilege is also evident in the characterization of the mother of Jesus as a woman needing to be accompanied in public, in her portrayal as a woman needing a male relative to take care of her, and in

---

of John," *Searching the Scriptures: A Feminist Commentary,* ed. Elisabeth Schüssler Fiorenza (New York: Crossroad, 1994) 591. Elisabeth Schüssler Fiorenza, *In Memory of Her: A Feminist Theological Reconstruction of Christian Origins* (New York: Crossroad, 1989) 332. McHugh, 403. Witherington, 93–4, 122–3.

[87]For a discussion of those scholars who do perceive the mother of Jesus a representative figure, see chapter 2, pp. 23–5.

[88]Talbert, *Reading John,* 244.

her portrayal as an exchange object that merely represents the new patrilineal kinship relationship that the disciples have with Jesus as a result of his blood sacrifice. The mother of Jesus as a character is even denied the female influence generally associated with the female relatives of a dying king in ancient writings. The binding force between Jesus and those in his kingdom is not the female relative whom Jesus gives to the corporate personality who will represent those in his kingdom. Rather, the binding force between Jesus and those whom the beloved disciple represents is the faith of those in the kingdom and the common heavenly Father whom believers share with Jesus.

Rosemary Radford Ruether has stated that,

> "when these stories (Cana and the Crucifixion) are looked at in the context of John's theology, rather than through the eyes of later Christian piety and art, the impression that they exalt Mary somewhat disappears."[89]

From what has been pointed out in this chapter, as well as what was asserted earlier regarding the mother of Jesus at Cana, Ruether's comments seem an understatement. One does not merely see the "exalted" status of the mother of Jesus somewhat disappear. One sees the status of the mother of Jesus virtually erased. She becomes an empty cipher used by Jesus to symbolize his role as the messianic bridegroom and his establishment of a patriarchal familial relationship with those who believe in him.

Summary

A first-century reader was very well prepared by the Fourth Gospel to interpret the passion and death of Jesus as a blood sacrifice that established a patrilineal kinship group and as a messianic wedding culminating in Jesus' conceiving/giving birth to the children of God. Because of Jesus' blood sacrifice on the cross, kinship for the believer will no longer be based on being born of a woman. The natural family for the believer has been supplanted by a family that is based on belief in Jesus and having a common heavenly Father.

---

[89]Rosemary Radford Ruether, "Mary and the Mission of Jesus," *Mary-The Feminine Face of the Church* (Philadelphia: Westminster, 1977) 38. Ruether bases her analysis on the fact that the mother of Jesus in the Fourth Gospel belongs to the fleshly level of reality, which in the Fourth Gospel is contrasted with the spiritual level. Although I agree with her on this point, I would disagree with her notion that the mother of Jesus represents Old (fleshly) Israel, which is presented to the heir of Jesus' spiritual sonship. Cf. Ruether, "Mary and the Mission of Jesus," 38–9.

The characterization of the mother of Jesus at the cross supports the portrayal of Jesus as the messianic bridegroom. By having Jesus de-emphasize his own matrilineal descent (calling his mother "woman") and then deemphasize the beloved disciple's matrilineal descent (giving him a mother who was not his biological mother), the implied author used the characterization of the mother of Jesus to support the interpretation of Jesus' death as a blood sacrifice that establishes a patrilineal kinship group. By having Jesus give his mother to the beloved disciple, the implied author adapted the "dying king" type-scene in such a way that the characterization of the mother of Jesus supports the concept of Jesus' establishing familial bonds with all those the beloved disciple represents. The use of such patriarchal type-scenes as the "blood sacrifice" type-scene and the "dying king" type-scene results in a very passive portrayal of the mother of Jesus at the cross, which is unlike her assertive portrayal at Cana. The two portrayals have the same purpose, however, that of helping to portray Jesus as the messianic bridegroom who has come to establish the family of God.

As stated in this chapter, the role of Mary Magdalene in the crucifixion scene is not fully evident until her appearances in the scenes at Jesus' tomb. These latter scenes, which will be discussed in the next chapter, will make it evident that Mary Magdalene at the cross and at the tomb, like the Samaritan woman at the well and Mary of Bethany, functions as the bride of the messianic bridegroom for the purpose of furthering Jesus' characterization as the messianic bridegroom.

6

Mary Magdalene at the Tomb

Introduction

Mary Magdalene was first introduced in the crucifixion scene. In that pericope she is merely present at the cross, and her function there is unclear. When she appears at the tomb, however, her role at the cross would have become evident to the first-century reader.

Today many scholars who comment on Mary Magdalene at the tomb acknowledge her as a disciple. They make this assessment on the basis of one or more of the following correlations:

1) Jesus prophesies that the disciple's grief will be turned to joy (16:6, 20) and Mary Magdalene's weeping (20:11, 13, 15) is turned into the joy that is implicit in her announcement, "I have seen the Lord" (20:18);[1]

2) A connection is perceived between discipleship and the seeking motif in the Fourth Gospel (1:39; 5:44; 7:34, 36; 11:56; 12:20; 13:22; 18:4, 7, 8) and Mary Magdalene's seeking (ζητεῖς) the body of Jesus (20:15);[2]

[1]Cf. Paul Minear, "'We Don't Know Where . . .' John 20:2," *Interpretation* 30 (1976) 132; Pheme Perkins, *Resurrection: New Testament Witness and Contemporary Reflection* (Garden City, N.Y.: Doubleday, 1984) 177; Sandra Schneiders, "Women in the Fourth Gospel and the Role of Women in the Contemporary Church," *Biblical Theological Bulletin* 12 (1982) 44.

[2]Adele Reinhartz, "The Gospel of John," *Searching the Scriptures: A Feminist Commentary,* ed. Elisabeth Schüssler Fiorenza (New York: Crossroad, 1994) 592. Cf. Elisabeth Schüssler Fiorenza, *In Memory of Her: A Feminist Theological Reconstruction of Christian Origins* (New York: Crossroad, 1983) 333; Mark Stibbe, *John* (Scheffield: JSOT, 1993) 204–5; Minear, 129, 132; Teresa Okure, "The Significance

143

3) Jesus calls his sheep by name and his sheep know his voice (10:1-5) and Mary Magdalene recognizes Jesus when he calls her by name (20:16);[3]

4) Like the Samaritan woman and the male disciples before her (1:40-45; 4:28-30), Mary Magdalene bears witness about Jesus to others (20:17-18).[4]

Based on the fact that Mary Magdalene experiences a christophany and then carries the news of the resurrection to the disciples, some scholars even uphold the early Church's affirmation of Mary Magdalene as *Apostola Apostolorum,* the apostle to the apostles.[5]

Although I would not negate the assumption that Mary Magdalene functions in this pericope as a disciple, or even as an apostle, I believe that it is premature to assume that the implied author was attempting to communicate to the reader that women could be disciples, as some scholars seem to suggest.[6] Rather, I would hold that, because Mary Magdalene, like

Today of Jesus' Commission to Mary Magdalene," *International Review of Mission* 81 (1992) 180.

[3]Reinhartz, "The Gospel of John," 592. Schüssler Fiorenza, *In Memory of Her,* 333. Paul Duke, *Irony in the Fourth Gospel* (Atlanta: John Knox, 1985) 105. Raymond Brown, "Roles of Women in the Fourth Gospel," *The Community of the Beloved Disciple* (New York: Paulist, 1979) 192. Cf. John Rena, "Women in the Gospel of John," *Église et Théologie* 17 (1986) 144; Okure, "The Significance Today of Jesus' Commission to Mary Magdalene," 181.

[4]Robert Kysar, "The Women of the Gospel of John," in *John The Maverick Gospel,* revised edition (Louisville: Westminster/John Knox, 1993) 152. Perkins would add to this the fact that she experienced a christophany. Pheme Perkins, "I Have Seen the Lord (John 20:18): Women Witnesses to the Resurrection," *Interpretation* 46 (1992) 41.

[5]Turid Karlsen Seim, "Roles of Women in the Gospel of John," *Aspects on the Johannine Literature,* ed. Lars Hartman & Birger Olsson (Sweden: Alqvist & Wiksell International, 1987) 67. Brown, "Roles of Women in the Fourth Gospel," 190. Kysar, "The Women of the Gospel of John," 152. Schüssler Fiorenza, *In Memory of Her,* 332. Elisabeth Schüssler Fiorenza, "Feminist Theology as a Critical Theology of Liberation," *Churches in Struggle: Liberation Theologies and Social Change in North America,* ed. William Tabb (New York: Monthly Review Press, 1986) 60, 62. Cf. Gerald O'Collins and Daniel Kendall, "Mary Magdalene as Major Witness to Jesus' Resurrection," *Theological Studies* 48 (1987) 632; Schneiders, "Women in the Fourth Gospel and the Role of Women in the Contemporary Church," 43–4; Reinhartz, "The Gospel of John, 592; Okure, "The Significance Today of Jesus' Commission to Mary Magdalene," 178.

[6]Brown, "Roles of Women in the Fourth Gospel," 189–90. Schüssler Fiorenza, *In Memory of Her,* 322–33. Perkins, *Resurrection: New Testament Witness and Contemporary Reflection,* 177. Perkins, "I Have Seen the Lord," 41. Cf. O'Collins and Kendall, 645–6; O'Day, "John," 302; Carolyn Grassi and Joseph Grassi, "The Resurrection: The New Age Begins; Mary Magdalene as Mystical Spouse," *Mary Magdalene and the Women in Jesus' Life* (Sheed & Ward, 1986) 114–5.

the Samaritan woman and Mary of Bethany before her, functions as bride of the messianic bridegroom, she functions as a representative of the broader faith community who is called to discipleship.

Scholars have long noted that the author of the Fourth Gospel drew on earlier tradition for the stories of the empty tomb and Jesus' resurrection appearance to Mary Magdalene.[7] Nevertheless, the question remains, "Why do the Fourth Gospel's versions of these stories differ so significantly from the versions found in the Synoptic tradition?" Noting an echo of the Synoptic tradition of more than one woman at the tomb in Mary Magdalene's statement, "*We* don't know (οἴδαμεν) where they have put him" (20:2), scholars have wondered why the Fourth Gospel focuses on one woman.[8] Also, because Jesus' body had already been properly and completely prepared for burial in the Fourth Gospel by Joseph of Arimathea and Nicodemus (19:38-42), scholars have wondered why Mary Magdalene even goes to the tomb in this Gospel.[9]

Although I would agree with Raymond Brown and Rudolf Schnackenburg that the Fourth Gospel focuses on Mary Magdalene in the scenes at the tomb because the implied author has a preference for bringing a

[7]Cf. Brown, *The Gospel According to John,* 2:996–1004; Schnackenburg, 3:300–21, esp. 303; Charles Talbert, *Reading John: A Literary and Theological Commentary on the Fourth Gospel and the Johannine Epistles* (New York: Crossroad, 1994) 248; D. Moody Smith, *The Theology of the Gospel of John* (Cambridge: Cambridge University Press, 1995) 46–7; R. Collins, "The Representative Figures of the Fourth Gospel," 122–3; Frank Matera, "John 20:1-18," *Interpretation* 43 (1989) 402; C. K. Barrett, *The Gospel According to St. John,* 2nd ed. (Philadelphia: Westminster, 1978) 560; Edwyn Hoskyns, *The Fourth Gospel* (London: Faber and Faber Limited, 1940) 2:647–8; Brendan Byrne, "The Faith of the Beloved Disciple and the Community in John 20," *Journal for the Study of the New Testament* 23 (1985) 85; Perkins, *Resurrection: New Testament Witness and Contemporary Reflection,* 172, 175; Pheme Perkins, "The Gospel According to John," *New Jerome Biblical Commentary,* ed. Raymond Brown, et. al. (Englewood Cliffs, N.J.: Prentice Hall, 1990) 983; Perkins, "I Have Seen the Lord (John 20:18)," 40; J. Duncan Derrett, "Miriam and the Resurrection (John 20:16)," *Downside Review* 111 (1993) 174; Richard Atwood, *Mary Magdalene in the New Testament Gospels and Early Tradition* (Bern, Germany: Lang, 1993) 105–8.

[8]Cf. Schnackenburg, 3:302, 303–4; Brown, *The Gospel According to John,* 2:984, 999–1000; R. Collins, "The Representative Figures in the Fourth Gospel," 123; Atwood, 105, 110; Talbert, 249; Minear, 126; Okure, "The Significance Today of Jesus' Commission To Mary Magdalene," 179.

[9]Schnackenburg, 3:305. Brown, *The Gospel According to John,* 2:981–2. Kysar, 148, 152. Okure, "The Significance Today of Jesus' Commission to Mary Magdalene," 179–80. Atwood, 111–2. Cf. Barnabas Lindars, *The Gospel of John* (London: Oliphants, 1972) 599.

single person to the forefront for encounters with Jesus,[10] I maintain that the author additionally drew upon scenes from Greek love-novels,[11] as well as phrases from Canticle of Canticles, for this personal encounter between Mary Magdalene and Jesus. By drawing on scenes from Greek love-novels and phrases from Canticle of Canticles, the author was able to portray Mary Magdalene as a wife in search of the body of her husband, thereby furthering the sub-text in which Jesus is portrayed as the messianic bridegroom. As another bride-figure of the messianic bridegroom, Mary Magdalene represents the entire faith community, not only women.[12]

To support this hypothesis, I shall first describe the types of Greek love-novels in order to identify the type that can best be compared to the Fourth Gospel. I shall then analyze two type-scenes from these Greek love-novels: (1) the visitation to an empty tomb, and (2) the recognition of a spouse thought to be lost, and then compare these scenes to Mary Magdalene's visitation to Jesus' tomb and her recognition of him in the Fourth Gospel. Finally, I shall describe the function and characterization of Mary Magdalene in this pericope and illustrate how her function and characterization are patriarchal in nature.

[10]Cf. Schnackenburg, 3:305; Brown, *The Gospel According to John,* 2:999.

[11]No designation was given this genre in antiquity. The broader genre has sometimes been referred to by the designation "romance" or "tale." The term "romance" comes from the use of the term for writings done in vernacular languages (Romance languages). Because "romance" currently has a more narrow connotation, some classicists have argued for dropping "romance" for the broader term "novel." The term "erotic tale" or "erotic novel" is sometimes used for those Greek romances/novels whose basic plot details the work of the god Eros. Because "erotic" also currently has a more narrow connotation, I shall refer to this sub-genre of the ancient Greek novel by the term "ancient Greek love-novel." Cf. Mary Ann Tolbert, "The Gospel in Greco-Roman Culture," *The Book and the Text: The Bible and Literary Theory,* ed. R. Schwartz (Cambridge: Basic Blackwell, 1990) 262–83, 273–4 n. 14; Mary Ann Tolbert, *Sowing the Gospel: Mark's World in Literary-Historical Perspective* (Minneapolis: Fortress, 1989) 62 n. 46; Tomas Hägg, *The Novel of Antiquity* (Berkeley: University of California Press, 1983) 1–4; Tomas Hägg, "The Beginning of the Historical Novel,"*The Greek Novel AD 1–1985,* ed. Roderick Beaton (London: Croom Helm, 1988) 169–70; Bryan Reardon, "The Form of Ancient Greek Romance," *The Greek Novel AD 1–1985,* ed. Roderick Beaton (London: Croom Helm, 1988) 205; Roderick Beaton, "Editor's Preface," *The Greek Novel AD 1–1985,* ed. Roderick Beaton (London: Croom Helm, 1988) vii–viii.

[12]Cf. Minear, 126; O'Collins and Kendall, 632; Brown, *The Gospel According to John,* 2:1010; André Feuillet, "La recherche du Christ dan la nouvelle Alliance d'apres la Christophanie de Jo 20, 11-18," *L'homme devant Dieu,* publiées sous la direction de la faculté de Théologie S.J. de Lyon-Fourviére (Paris: Aubier, 1963) 103–7; R. Collins, "The Representative Figures in the Fourth Gospel," 123.

Greek Love-Novels

The Greek novel was a type of popular literature.[13] It can be divided into two basic types, the "pre-sophistic" type and the "sophistic" type. The "pre-sophistic" novel was written in a more popular style, whereas the "sophistic" novel, which was probably aimed at a more sophisticated class of readers, fell under the influence of the Greek cultural revival, sometimes referred to as the *Second Sophistic*. Extant examples of the "pre-sophistic" type of Greek love-novel are Chariton's *Chaereas and Callirhoe*, dated to the first century B.C.E, and Xenophon's *An Ephesian Tale*, dated to the second century C.E. Extant examples of the "sophistic" type of Greek love-novel are Heliodorus' *An Ethiopian Tale*, dated from the third to fourth century C.E., Longus' *Daphnis and Chloe*, dated to the second century C.E., and Achilles Tatius' *Leucippe and Clitophon*, dated to the second century C.E.[14]

The plot of the Greek love-novel usually is as follows: a youthful man and woman meet by chance, fall in love, encounter unexpected obstacles to their union, are separated, experience separate dangerous journeys and adventures, and are eventually reunited to live happily ever after.[15] Although the Fourth Gospel, as a whole, does not fit the outline of a Greek love-novel, similarities between certain scenes in this literature and the scenes of Mary Magdalene's visitations to Jesus' tomb and Jesus' resurrection-appearance to her in the Fourth Gospel seem to indicate that the implied author of the Fourth Gospel may have drawn on these conventional scenes from popular Greek literature. Because the Fourth Gospel falls into the category of the more popular "pre-sophistic" type of writing,[16] I shall compare the Fourth Gospel to the visitation to the empty tomb and recognition scenes of Xenophon's *An Ephesian Tale* and Chariton's *Chaereas and Callirhoe*.

Visitation to the Empty Tomb Scenes in **An Ephesian Tale** *and* **Chaereas and Callirhoe**

In the Greek love-novel *An Ephesian Tale*, Habrocomes and Anthia love each other and eventually are married. They take a dangerous voyage

---

[13]For more on popular literature, see chapter 1, pp. 10–13.

[14]Hägg, *The Greek Novel*, viii, 3, 6, 20, 35, 42, 59, 240, 257–8, 260, 264.

[15]Bryan Reardon, *The Form of Greek Romance* (Princeton: Princeton University Press, 1991) 5.

[16]Tolbert, *Sowing the Gospel*, 59–66, esp. 62, 66. Cf. David Aune, *The New Testament in Its Literary Environment* (Philadelphia: Westminster, 1987) 47.

together, are attacked by pirates, and are eventually separated. Each one faces death, and each thinks the other is dead. Believing her husband to be dead, Anthia attempts suicide by poisoning herself. The potion, however, merely puts her into a deep sleep. When she is later kidnapped from her tomb by grave robbers, she longs for her forced voyage to take her to the country where Habrocomes is buried so that she might see his tomb. When Habrocomes receives word that his wife has died, he asks an old woman to take him to Anthia's tomb so that he might see her body. Habrocomes, however, never actually visits the tomb because the old woman tells him that Anthia's body had been removed from the tomb. Habrocomes bemoans the fact that he is to be deprived of her remains, his only solace. He goes in search of her body and is determined, when he finds it, to commit suicide so that he might be buried along with her.[17]

This Greek love-novel highlights the depth of love that the male and the female characters have for each other, the pain each experiences at being separated from the other and the deep desire that each has to at least visit the tomb or see the remains of the beloved. The tomb symbolizes both an apparent death and a real separation from the beloved. The need to see the tomb/body of the beloved and the willingness to face great obstacles in the quest for the tomb/body symbolizes a love that survives death.

In the Greek love-novel *Chaereas and Callirhoe,* Chaereas and Callirhoe also love each other and are eventually married. A *baskanos daimon,* a malevolent creature, attends their wedding in the human guise of Callirhoe's rejected suitors. They succeed in making Chaereas suspect that Callirhoe has been unfaithful. In a fit of jealousy, Chaereas strikes out at Callirhoe and thinks he has killed her. After he finds out that Callirhoe was innocent, Chaereas visits her tomb, ostensibly to bring wreaths and libations. In actuality, however, he plans on committing suicide there. He can not bear being separated from Callirhoe and wants at least to share a common tomb with her.

As Chaereas arrives at the tomb, he notices that the stone at the entrance has been moved and realizes that someone has disturbed the tomb. He does not, however, enter the tomb right away. Rumor carries the news of the disturbed tomb to Hermocrates, Callirhoe's father, who orders a man to go into the tomb. This man reports that even the corpse is gone. At this point in the narrative, Chaereas himself enters the tomb. Eager to see Callirhoe one more time even though she is dead, he searches the tomb, but finds nothing.

---

[17]Cf. Xenophon, "An Ephesian Tale," *Three Greek Romances,* trans. Moses Hadas (New York: Macmillan, 1953) 102–3.

When those present discover that the funeral offerings are also missing, they realize that grave robbers have been at work. Because the presence of grave robbers does not explain the missing body, Chaereas wonders if one of the male gods took the body of Callirhoe for himself, or if he had had a goddess for a wife. After vowing to search for her body, over land and sea and even into the sky, he sets out on his search.[18] In the meantime, Callirhoe faces great dangers as a female captive and would rather die than be unfaithful to Chaereas, even after she thinks he is dead. She is able to remain faithful through the intervention of the goddess Aphrodite.

Like *An Ephesian Tale, Chaereas and Callirhoe* emphasizes the depth of love the male and female characters have for each other, although the degree of love has tragic consequences in the second example. Also like *An Ephesian Tale, Chaereas and Callirhoe* highlights the pain of separation, the ability of love to survive death (or apparent death), the desire that the spouse has at least to see the body of the dead beloved, and the willingness of the survivor even to enter into death to be reunited with the beloved. In both stories, the tombs are empty. In Chariton's love-novel, however, one sees additional parallels to New Testament accounts of the stone to Jesus' tomb having been moved.[19] Another aspect found in Chariton's love-novel that is not present in Xenophone's love-novel but does have New Testament parallels is the notion that an empty tomb signifies divine origins or divine intervention.[20]

The Johannine Adaptation of the Visitation to the Empty Tomb Scene

Mary Magdalene's First Visit to the Tomb

Like the characters in Greek love-novels, Mary Magdalene in the Fourth Gospel goes in search of the tomb and body of her beloved. Unlike the convention in Greek love-novels, however, Jesus' death was not merely an apparent death. Jesus truly died, as the narrated comments about blood and water flowing from his pierced side emphasized (19:33-

---

[18]Cf. Chariton, *Chaereas and Callirhoe,* trans. Warren Blake (Ann Arbor: University of Michigan Press, 1939) 40–1; Hägg, *The Greek Novel,* 11.

[19]Cf. Mark 16:3-4; Luke 24:2; John 20:1. In Matt 28:2, an angel descends from heaven to roll back the stone, causing a great earthquake.

[20]Cf. Mark 16:6; Matt 28:1-4; Luke 24:4. In the Fourth Gospel, Mary Magdalene is left to assume that the body has been taken away. The reader, however, is aware that the missing body is a sign of heavenly origin and divine intervention.

34).[21] Despite the fact that Mary Magdalene was present to witness Jesus' death, the piercing of his side and the blood and water flowing from it (cf. 19:25), she too searches for the tomb of her beloved.

Mary Magdalene goes to the tomb early in the morning, while it was still dark (20:1). As Brown notes, it would have been considered unusual behavior for a woman in that time period to walk about the city alone in the dark.[22] On one level of characterization, the darkness may symbolize that faith in the resurrection had not yet been awakened in Mary Magdalene (cf. 20:9).[23] Nevertheless, on another level of characterization, the darkness of the early hour helps to portray Mary Magdalene as a woman obsessed with finding the tomb and body of her beloved.[24] Some scholars perceive in this obsessive behavior an allusion to the emotive quest of the woman of Canticle of Canticles for her beloved.[25] It is just this obsessive behavior in the search for the body of Jesus, however, that would have encouraged a first-century reader to hear in this story an allusion to the conventions of Greek love-novels. Whether an ancient reader perceived an allusion to the woman of Canticle of Canticles or to conventions of Greek love-novels or to both, the ancient reader would have recognized that Mary Magdalene was being portrayed as a woman in search of the body of her husband.

The Peter-and-Beloved-Disciple Interlude

Although the women in the other New Testament accounts enter the tomb,[26] Mary Magdalene, like Chaereas at the tomb of Callirhoe, finds the stone moved away from Jesus' tomb, but apparently does not approach the

[21]Cf. chapter 5, p. 131 n.57.

[22]Brown, *The Gospel According to John,* 2:981.

[23]Schnackenburg, 3:308. Matera, 403. Brown, *The Gospel According to John,* 2:981. Duke, 107. Culpepper, *Anatomy,* 192.

[24]Minear, 129.

[25]Okure perceives the entire episode as in many ways evocative of the Canticle and Carolyn, and Joseph Grassi acknowledge Mary Magdalene as Jesus' "Mystical Spouse" on the basis of a correlation with Canticle of Canticles. Okure, "The Significance Today of Jesus' Commission to Mary Magdalene," 180–1, 188. Grassi, 104–15, esp. 109–10. Cf. Stibbe, 205; Feuillet, 103–7; Brown, *The Gospel According to John,* 2:1010.

[26]Cf. Mark 16:4-5; Luke 24:2-3. In Matt 28:5-8, the angel invites the women to enter the tomb to see the place where he lay and then go tell the disciples that Jesus has risen. Although the narrator states that the women depart quickly from the tomb, there is no actual narration of entering the tomb.

opened tomb (20:1, cf. 20:11).[27] Rather than rumor carrying the news of the disturbed tomb to others, as is the case in *Chaereas and Callirhoe,* Mary Magdalene herself goes to Peter and the disciple whom Jesus loved to report her suspicion,[28] "The Lord has been taken from the tomb! We don't know where they have put him" (20:2-3). With this report, Peter and the beloved disciple go to the tomb to see for themselves. This action by these disciples needs to be analyzed because it may embody patriarchal concepts that affect the characterization of Mary Magdalene.

The implied author of the Fourth Gospel may have included this Peter-and-beloved-disciple interlude because Jewish law demanded the witness of two men (cf. Deut 19:5).[29] Whether the implied author of the Fourth Gospel and its first-century reader would have embraced this belief themselves or whether the interlude had other apologetic purposes is not known. Either way, it is significant that the implied author of the Fourth Gospel apparently felt the need to deal with the patriarchal law of two male witnesses.

The implied author of the Fourth Gospel may also have included this Peter-and-beloved-disciple interlude because it provided an opportunity to

---

[27]Because there is no narration regarding Mary Magdalene's approaching the tomb on her first visit, a reader is left to wonder whether she looked into the tomb or not. One could assume that Mary Magdalene's observance of the empty tomb on her first visit to the tomb took place outside of the narrative. On the basis of 20:11, however, Schnackenburg and Atwood state that Mary Magdalene apparently does not look into the tomb until her second visit to the tomb. Based on the first-century imperial edict against grave robbers, an ancient reader might have reasonably assumed that Mary Magdalene did not go near the tomb for fear of being accused of participating in robbing the tomb. Talbert notes that the claim that the body of Jesus has been stolen is not surprising because the robbing of tombs was so common that it became part of the plot of ancient novels such as *Chaereas and Callirhoe.* By focusing on the historicity of such occurrences, however, Talbert fails to recognize that the implied author of the Fourth Gospel may have been drawing on scenes from Greek novels in constructing this story. Schnackenburg, 3:308. Atwood, 105, 114, 115. Talbert, *Reading John,* 249. Cf. Barrett, 561–2; Lindars, 600; Brown, *The Gospel According to John,* 2:984; Perkins, "I Have Seen the Lord," 37.

[28]Talbert states that Mary Magdalene confronts Peter and the beloved disciple with her *fears* that the body had been removed. Similarly, Perkins maintains that Mary "presumes" that the body has been removed as soon as she sees that the tomb is open. Talbert, 249. Perkins, "I Have Seen the Lord," 37 n. 37. Cf. Atwood, 105, 114, 115; Brown, *The Gospel According to John,* 2:1000; Schnackenburg, 3:308; Minear, 125–6; Matera, 403.

[29]Talbert, *Reading John,* 249. Cf. O'Collins and Kendall, 631–2, 637, 640; Perkins, "I Have Seen the Lord," 40; Okure, "The Significance Today of Jesus' Commission to Mary Magdalene," 188.

emphasize the primacy of Peter's status (20:3-8),[30] as well as primacy of the beloved disciple's faith (20:8).[31] This effort to highlight the primacy of these two men, however, has an impact on the characterization of Mary Magdalene in two ways. First, although many scholars maintain that Mary Magdalene is the first witness of the empty tomb in the Fourth Gospel,[32] it must be remembered that the narration only indicates that on Mary Magdalene's first visit to the tomb she noticed that it had been disturbed. Her observation that the tomb was, in fact, empty is not narrated. Therefore, unless a reader assumes that Mary Magdalene's observation that the tomb was empty took place outside of narrative time, a reader would assume from the Peter-beloved disciple interlude that the beloved disciple or Peter, and not Mary Magdalene, was the first to observe that the tomb was empty.[33] Secondly, although there is some discussion about what the beloved disciple believed upon entering the tomb and seeing both the linens and the *soudarion* folded in a separate place,[34] it seems likely that

[30]Although the beloved disciple outruns Peter to the tomb, he waits for Peter and allows Peter to enter the tomb first.

[31]Cf. Schnackenburg, 3:310; Brown, *The Gospel of John,* 2:985, 1004–7; Byrne, 92–3.

[32]Kysar, "The Women of the Gospel of John," 148, 152. O'Day, "John," 300. Hoskyns, 646. Schüssler Fiorenza, *In Memory of Her,* 332.

[33]Although the beloved disciple waited for Peter at the tomb and let him enter the tomb first, the beloved disciple looked into the tomb and saw the linen wrappings prior to Peter's arrival (20:4-6). On this basis, Barrett assumes that the beloved disciple was the first to observe the empty tomb. Although Byrne does not specifically say that Peter was the first to discover the empty tomb, he does highlight the fact that Peter was the first to observe the full disposition of the burial clothes. Barrett, 563, cf. 561. Byrne, 85.

[34]Did the beloved disciple believe that Jesus had risen from the dead on the basis of the presence of the linens and the orderly placement of the *soudarion,* as most scholars suggest, or does the disciples' lack of knowledge of the resurrection (20:9) and their indifference to the empty tomb (20:10) suggest that the beloved disciple simply believed the report of Mary Magdalene, as Minear and others suggest? Because the sign of the separately lying *soudarion* is polyvalent in nature, perhaps the reader is meant to decide this issue for herself or himself. Cf. Brown, *The Gospel According to John,* 2:986–7, 1004–8; Brown, "Roles of Women in the Fourth Gospel," 189; Schnackenburg, 3:311–2; Stibbe, 204–5; Matera, 403; Rena, 143; Sandra Schneiders, "The Veil: A Johannine Sign," *Biblical Theological Bulletin* 13 (1981) 94–7; Byrne, 83, 85, 88–95, n. 12; Basil Osborne, "A Folded Napkin in an Empty Tomb: John 11:44 and 20:7 Again," *Heythrop Journal* 14 (1973) 437–40; Perkins, *Resurrection,* 172; Minear, 127–8; James Baker, "The Red-Haired Saint: Is Mary Magdalene the Key to the Easter Narratives?" *The Christian Century* 94 (1977) 329; Atwood, 130; On the *semeion*-character of the face veil, see Schneiders, "The Face Veil: A Johannine Sign (John 20:1-10)," 94–7; Byrne, 87–90, 94; Basil Osborne, "A Folded Napkin in an Empty Tomb: John 11:44 and 20:7 Again," 437; Perkins, *Resurrection,* 174; Matera, 403.

a first-century reader would at least have assumed that the beloved disciple believed that Jesus had returned to the Father.[35] By the first century the mere presence of an empty tomb in literature had come to represent the idea that the person had been assumed up to heaven, as indeed Chaereas' reaction to the absence of Callirhoe's body in the tomb indicates.[36] The narrator's statement regarding the belief of the beloved disciple tends, therefore, to accentuate through contrast Mary Magdalene's inability to come to faith, despite all the signs that she experiences.[37]

The Scene with the Angels Dressed in Dazzling Clothes

According to the Fourth Gospel, after Peter and the beloved disciple visit the tomb, they simply return home (20:10).[38] Mary Magdalene, on the

[35]Schneiders maintains that the beloved disciple understood the empty tomb only as a sign of Jesus' glorious return to the Father and that he did not understand Jesus' resurrection as a glorified return to his disciples as well. She perceives this interpretation as being consistent with the Fourth Gospel's preference for describing Jesus' glorification as a return to the Father. In support of this assumption, she notes a correlation between Jesus' *soudarion* and the veil which Moses removed when he communed with God. Schneiders, "The Face Veil," 96–7. Cf. Brown, *The Gospel According to John,* 2:1013–4.

[36]Tolbert notes that, as early as 1924, Elias Bickerman argued that empty tomb stories in ancient literature were a conventional device to prove the assumption of the hero into heaven. Both Wayne Meeks and Minear state that first-century Jewish interpretations of Deuteronomy 34 indicate that the absence of Moses' tomb had become linked to the belief that he had ascended into heaven. Tolbert, *Sowing the Gospel,* 288 n. 30. Elias Bickerman, "Das leere Grab," *Zeitschrift für die Neutestamentliche Wissenschaft* 23 (1924) 281–92. Wayne Meeks, *The Prophet-King: Moses Traditions and the Johannine Christology* (Leiden: E. J. Brill, 1967) 124–5, 159, 210–1. Minear, 138. Cf. Perkins, "The Gospel According to John," 983.

[37]Cf. Schüssler Fiorenza, "Feminist Theology as a Critical Theology of Liberation," 61; Rena, 143–4; Perkins, "I Have Seen the Lord," 39; Atwood, 137; D. Moody Smith, 123–4.

[38]Based on the disciples' lack of understanding of the scriptures regarding Jesus' rising from the dead (20:9), as well as the fact that the beloved disciple and Peter simply return home (20:10) and show no signs of joy or interest in announcing the resurrection, one might connect this going back home with Jesus' earlier statement about the disciple being scattered, each one to his own home (cf. 16:32). Minear maintains that this interpretation would support the argument that beloved disciple merely believes the witness of Mary Magdalene about the tomb being empty. Brown, however, maintains that the separate housing is scarcely to be related to 16:32 and Byrne understands the beloved disciple's lack of understanding in the past tense. This would mean that prior to seeing the face veil, he did not understand that Jesus must rise from the dead. Minear, 128 n. 3, 132–3. Brown, *The Gospel According to John,* 2:983. Byrne, 86, 89.

other hand, who apparently returned to the tomb with Peter and the beloved disciple, remains at the tomb weeping (20:11).[39] Whereas Mary Magdalene's weeping emphasizes her personal grief, her inability or refusal to leave the tomb emphasizes her love for Jesus,[40] as well as her commitment to finding the body of her beloved. Because such grief and commitment to finding the body of Jesus parallels the portrayal of spouses in popular Greek love-novels, these parallels may have led the first-century reader to conclude that Mary Magdalene was being portrayed as another fictive bride of the messianic bridegroom.

When Mary Magdalene does peer inside the tomb herself (20:11), apparently for the first time,[41] she sees two angels in white (20:12). This appearance of angels in the Fourth Gospel may be due to the influence of tradition.[42] Nevertheless, the implied author of the Fourth Gospel uses these characters for the implied author's own purpose, that of creating repetitions to aid in the characterization of Mary Magdalene.[43] In the angel's question, "Woman, why are you weeping?" (20:13a), the author emphasizes both Mary Magdalene's weeping (cf. 20:11) and her gender. Emphasis on both of these aspects of her character heighten her characterization as a woman who is distraught because she is unable to find the body of her beloved husband.

In response to the angel's question, Mary Magdalene basically repeats the statement she made to the disciple. This time, however, she personalizes the statement through the use of the first person singular, "They have taken away *my* Lord, and *I* do not know where they have laid him" (20:13b; cf. 20:2b). Her repetitious response accentuates the fact that the source of her grief is the missing body of her beloved.[44] Whereas the repe-

---

[39]Kysar states that there may be a contrast here between Mary Magdalene and Peter and the beloved disciple. He does not, however, perceive the contrast as constituting a polemic. Kysar, 152.

[40]Okure, "The Significance Today of Jesus' Commission to Mary Magdalene," 179–80.

[41]Schnackenburg, 3:308. Cf. Atwood, 105, 114–5.

[42]Matera, 402. Hoskyns, 2:647–8. Cf. Minear, 128.

[43]On repetition in ancient narratives, see Robert Scholes and Robert Kellogg, *The Nature of Narrative* (London: Oxford University Press, 1966) 17–56. On repetition in biblical narratives, see Robert Alter, "The Techniques of Repetition," *The Art of Biblical Narrative* (New York: Basic Books, 1981) 88–113. On repetition in the Fourth Gospel, see Fernando Segovia, *The Farewell of the Word: The Johannine Call to Abide* (Minneapolis: Fortress, 1991) 51–3. On the function of the angels as creating repetition in the scene with Mary Magdalene in the Fourth Gospel, see Minear, 128. Cf. Rena, 144.

[44]Atwood, 130.

tition accentuates her lack of knowledge about the location of the body, the variation in the repetition emphasizes her personal relationship with Jesus and her personal commitment to finding the body of Jesus.[45] Once again, the intensity of the grief, the emphasis on her personal relationship to her beloved, and her personal commitment to finding the body parallel the characterization of the wives in the pre-sophistic, Greek love-novels mentioned above.

Although Mary Magdalene's failure to understand the significance of the presence of angels may serve to highlight her misunderstanding about the significance of the absence of the body of Jesus,[46] her failure to be surprised by the appearance of the angels also helps to characterize her as a woman who is so upset about the missing body of her beloved that even the presence of angels does not startle her out of her grief.[47] Like the spouses in Greek love-novels, her focus is on finding the body of her beloved and nothing can get in the way of her search. She will persist until she finds his body. When Mary Magdalene finally does find her beloved, the encounter is narrated in the form of a recognition scene similar to the recognition scenes between spouses in Greek love-novels.

Recognition Scenes in
An Ephesian Tale *and* Chaereas and Callirhoe

"Recognition" *(anagnorisis)* in Aristotle's *Poetics* is a shift from ignorance to knowledge, the moment at which characters understand their predicament fully for the first time, the moment that the world becomes intelligible.[48] Although *Poetics* 16 is considered a late and possibly spurious

[45]O'Day and Okure note an emphasis on the personal aspect of the relationship in Mary Magdalene's use of the word *my* with Lord and on her change to the singular, "*I* do not know." Minear, however, maintains that the use of the first person singular by Mary Magdalene in her response is due to the use of the second person singular in the angel's question, "Why are you (singular) weeping?" O'Day, "John," 301. Okure, "The Significance Today of Jesus' Commission to Mary Magdalene," 180. Minear, 128 n. 4.

[46]As Minear states, at this point in the text the reader knows more than Mary Magdalene does as a character. The reader knows that the presence of angels indicates that Jesus has risen from the dead. Mary Magdalene's failure to realize this fact, even in the presence of angels, is both humorous and ironic. Minear, 126–9. Cf. Culpepper *Anatomy,* 144, 147; Duke, 104–5; Matera, 403–4.

[47]Cf. Duke, 104–5.

[48]Terence Cave, *Recognitions: A Study in Poetics* (Oxford: Clarendon, 1988) 1. For a discussion of the effect of recognition scenes on the reader, see Terence Cave, "Recognition and the Reader," *Comparative Criticism: A Yearbook,* vol. 2, ed. Elinor Shaffer (Cambridge: Cambridge University Press, 1980) 49–69.

interpolation,[49] it provides a taxonomy of the means by which such recognition occurs. It is evident from this taxonomy that the recognition of a person was one means by which a character moved from ignorance to knowledge.[50]

In the Greek novel *anagnorisis* is reduced to a mere accident of fortune that a character experiences. It does not change a character's spiritual condition.[51] Characters simply recognize each other after a prolonged separation. Although recognition scenes in Greek love-novels can involve a variety of types of characters,[52] I shall focus my analysis on the recognition scenes between married couples as found in the two extant "pre-sophistic" Greek love-novels of *An Ephesian Tale* and *Chaereas and Callirhoe*.

In *An Ephesian Tale* (5.12.1–5.13.4), after Habrocomes and Anthia experienced a long period of separation, their servants find a dedication in a temple with their mistress' name on it. Later, they see Anthia in the temple, but do not recognize her. Gradually, however, the love that she displays at the temple, her tears, offerings, and figure, as well as her inscribed name on the dedication, assist the servants in their recognition of her. She, however, does not recognize them until they reveal their names to her. The servants inform her that her husband is safe and then they run to get him. Upon hearing that Anthia is alive, Habrocomes runs to her, "like a man bereft of his wits." He and Anthia recognize each other immediately, embrace one another, and sink to the ground.[53]

In *Chaereas and Callirhoe* (8.1.7-8), Aphrodite stages a recognition scene for Callirhoe and Chaereas on the island of Aradus. Chaereas cap-

---

[49]Cave, *Recognitions: A Study in Poetics,* 37–8.

[50]For examples of characters recognizing each other in Greek novellas of the classical period, see Sophie Trenkner, *The Greek Novella in the Classical Period* (New York: Garland, 1987) 36–9, 91–6, 99, 190.

[51]Bryan Reardon, "The Form of Ancient Greek Romance," *The Greek Novel AD 1–1985,* ed. Roderick Beaton (London: Croom Helm, 1988) 206.

[52]Recognition scenes between non-lovers can be found in the later, "sophistic" Greek novels. In *An Ethiopian Tale*, a ribbon embroidered with Ethiopian characters allows Charicleia, who had been exposed as an infant, to be recognized as the daughter of an Ethiopian royal couple. In Longus' *Daphnis and Chloe,* certain tokens, clothes, and pieces of jewelry allow the parents of Daphnis and Chloe to recognize them after they had been exposed as infants. Cf. Hägg, *The Novel in Antiquity,* 36, 68; Longus, "Daphnis and Chloe," *Three Greek Romances,* trans. Hadas, 61, 66.

[53]Xenophon, "An Ephesian Tale," *Three Greek Romances,* trans. Hadas, 123–5. Cf. Hägg, *The Novel in Antiquity,* 18–32. For other examples of the recognition/non-recognition motif in this romance, see 4.3.6; 5.9.5–9; 5.10.9–11; 5.12.3–6. Cf. Tomas Hägg, *Narrative Technique in Ancient Greek Romances: Studies of Chariton, Xenophon Ephesius and Achilles Tatius* (Uppsala: Almqvist & Wiksells, 1971) 201 n. 2.

tures the island and takes its riches onto his vessel. Callirhoe is on the island but refuses to board the vessel. She is determined to stay on shore and commit suicide rather than face the possibility of infidelity to her Chaereas, whom she assumes is dead. Chaereas opens the door to where the obstinate woman is located. When he sees her lying on the ground with her head covered, her breathing and the manner in which she holds herself causes his heart to flutter. According to the text, the only reason he fails to recognize her is that he believes Dionysius has already taken her away. As Chaereas speaks to the woman, assuring her that no harm will come to her and that she will have the husband she wants, Callirhoe recognizes his voice and uncovers her head. They simultaneously cry out each other's name, embrace, and fall to the ground in a faint.[54]

In *An Ephesian Tale,* therefore, Anthia does not recognize her servants, nor do her servants recognize her immediately. Many clues are given to the servants before they recognize Anthia and they must tell her their names before she knows them. The lovers in this Greek love-novel, however, recognized one another immediately. The recognition scene in *Chaereas and Callirhoe,* however, is somewhat different. Although an element of unconscious recognition may be present in the portrayal of Chaereas' heart fluttering upon his observance of Callirhoe's breathing and manner of holding herself, Chaereas does not consciously recognize his beloved because he thinks she has been taken away from the island. In this recognition scene it is not sight that provokes recognition, but the sound of Chaereas' voice. When Callirhoe recognizes Chaereas' voice, uncovers her head and turns around, Chaereas then recognizes her. Both recognition scenes end with the couple's falling to the ground in a mutual embrace.

The Johannine Adaptation of the Recognition Scene

In the Fourth Gospel, when Mary Magdalene turns around and sees Jesus standing there, she fails to recognize Jesus (20:14), thinking that he is the gardener (20:15). This variation of thinking Jesus is the gardener may be yet another attempt to draw on Canticle of Canticles. The "garden" motif in the Fourth Gospel has occurred previously at 18:1, 26; 19:41. Although this garden motif has led some scholars to maintain an allusion to Eden/Paradise,[55] others perceive an allusion to Canticle of

---

[54]Chariton, "Chaereas and Callirhoe," *Chaereas and Callirhoe* trans. Blake, 111–2. Cf. Hägg, *The Greek Novel,* 13–4.

[55]Cf. Nicholas Wyatt, "'Supposing Him to Be the Gardener' (John 20:15): A Study of the Paradise Motif in John," *Zeitschrift für die Neutestamentliche Wis-*

Canticles.[56] Rather than interpreting this passage in an "either/or" manner, it may be best to perceive both a creation and a marriage motif at work.

When Jesus speaks to Mary Magdalene, he repeats the angel's query, "Woman, why are you weeping?" (20:15). This is the third time the reader is informed of the depth of Mary Magdalene's distress and the second time that the appellation "woman" is used for Mary Magdalene. Again, such an emphasis would encourage an ancient audience to view Mary Magdalene as a wife in search of the body of her husband.

Jesus goes on to ask her, "Whom do you seek (ζητεῖς)."[57] The Greek word ζητεῖς is a technical term in the Fourth Gospel for a deeper type of searching.[58] Although the reader might have understood the depth of Jesus' question, Mary Magdalene as a character fails to perceive the depth of this unknown man's question. Because she perceives his questions from a "below perspective,"[59] she responds accordingly. Mary Magdalene repeats for a third time her concern for the missing body of her beloved and her commitment to finding it. "Sir, if you are the one who carried him off, tell me where you have laid him and I will take him away" (20:15). R. Alan Culpepper and Paul Duke note an element of Johannine irony in Mary Magdalene's asking the living Jesus for the body of her dead beloved.[60] This is not unlike the irony found in Chaereas' statement to Callirhoe that she would have the husband she desires.

Like Callirhoe, who recognized the voice of her beloved, Mary Magdalene recognizes Jesus through his voice,[61] but only after he calls her by

---

senschaft und die Kunde der Alteren Kirche 81 (1990) 24–38; Grassi, 106–7; Duke, 184 n. 23.

[56]Feuillet and Barrett maintain that if the implied author of the Fourth Gospel had intended an allusion to the Garden of Eden, the implied author would probably have used the LXX word παράδεισος in 19:41 instead of the word κῆπος. Feuillet, 105–7. Barrett, 560. Cf. Derrett, "Miriam and the Resurrection (John 20:16)," 176–8, 181, 185 n. 17 & 19; Hoskyns, 2:646; R. H. Lightfoot, *St. John's Gospel: A Commentary,* ed. C. F. Evans (Oxford: Oxford University Press, 1956) 321–2.

[57]My translation. I use the word "seek" to emphasize the Johannine use of this technical term for Christian searching.

[58]Reinhartz, "The Gospel of John," 592. Cf. Schüssler Fiorenza, *In Memory of Her,* 333; Stibbe, 204–5; Minear, 129, 132; Schnackenburg, 3:316.

[59]To compare Mary Magdalene's "below perspective" with that of other female characters in the Fourth Gospel, see chapter 2, pp. 30–2, 36, 42 (Mother of Jesus at Cana), chapter 3, pp. 48, 58, 61–3, 80 (Samaritan Woman), chapter 4, pp. 102, 104–7 (Martha of Bethany).

[60]Culpepper, *Anatomy,* 177; Duke, 104–5.

[61]Stibbe recognizes the use of the literary device of *anagnorisis* in the Fourth Gospel, not only in Mary Magdalene's recognition of Jesus (20:16) but also in the beloved disciple's recognition of the fact that Jesus had been raised (20:8), in the post-

name, "Mariam" (20:16a). Such a reference seems to draw on Jesus' earlier comments about the Good Shepherd calling his sheep by name and their knowing his voice (10:3, 14). Although the primary purpose of Jesus' response may be the author's desire to highlight the veracity of Jesus' earlier comments about knowing "his own" and calling them by name,[62] this passage also suggests that Mary Magdalene, as the fictive bride of the messianic bridegroom, fulfills the role of representing the community of faith.[63]

J. Duncan Derrett maintains an additional level of meaning to Jesus's calling Mary Magdalene by name. For Derrett, Jesus represents the new Moses. When Jesus calls Mary Magdalene by the name "Mariam," it is seen as a variation of the name "Miriam" and is an indication that Mary Magdalene is now a sister to Jesus. He further maintains a correlation with the male lover in Canticle of Canticles, who refers to his beloved as his "sister" and "bride" (Cant 4:9, 10, 12; 5:1, 2; 8:8).[64] If Derrett is correct, then Jesus' use of the name Mariam supports the notion that Mary Magdalene fulfills her role of bride of the messianic bridegroom.[65]

When Mary Magdalene does recognize Jesus through his calling her by name, she responds by calling out "Rabbouni," not "Rabbi" (cf. 1:38). Although English texts usually render this title "Teacher," some scholars maintain that "Rabbouni" is the equivalent of "My Master" or "My Teacher," rather than just "Master" or "Teacher." This personalization of the title makes it a term of endearment.[66] On one level of the text, the use

---

resurrection recognition of Jesus by the disciples as a group (20:20), and in the climactic recognition of Jesus by Thomas (20:28). Although Stibbe notes similarities with Canticle of Canticles, he does not comment on the similarities between this recognition scene between Jesus and Mary Magdalene and the recognition scenes between lovers in Greek, "pre-sophistic" love-novels. Stibbe, 203.

[62]Cf. Matera, 403; Rena, 144; Bultmann, 686.

[63]To the extent that Mary Magdalene is characterized as a disciple through Jesus' calling her by name, I would maintain that she represents the entire community. Cf. chapter 6, p. 144.

[64]Derrett, "Miriam and the Resurrection (John 20:16)," 176–9, 181, 185 n. 16, 17, 19. Cf. Okure, "The Significance Today of Jesus' Commission to Mary Magdalene," 180–1, 188; Grassi, "The Resurrection: The New Age Begins: Mary Magdalene as Mystical Spouse," 104–15, esp. 108–10.

[65]Brown acknowledges that an allusion to the Canticle of Canticle would indicate that Mary Magdalene is representative of the Christian community searching for Jesus. Brown, however, finds an ecclesiastical dimension dubious and prefers to perceive Mary Magdalene's search as indicative of the individual's quest for Jesus. Brown, *The Gospel According to John,* 2:1010.

[66]Hoskyns, 2:648. Stibbe, 203. Okure, "The Significance Today of Jesus' Commission to Mary Magdalene," 180–1. Cf. Brown, *The Gospel According to John,* 2:991–2, 1010; Derrett, "Miriam and the Resurrection (John 20, 16)," 175; Stibbe, 203.

of this particular title by Mary Magdalene may indicate that she does not yet understand the meaning of Jesus' resurrection.[67] On another level of the text, however, the personalization of the title makes up for the fact that the christology of the implied author would not allow Mary Magdalene to call Jesus by his given name. No one in the Fourth Gospel calls Jesus by his given name. As one who has been sent from above by the Father, Jesus' aloofness from the world would not have allowed for it. Nevertheless, combined with Jesus' calling Mary Magdalene by name, Mary Magdalene's use of a personalized title for Jesus makes the Johannine text reminiscent of Chaereas and Callirhoe who call out each other's name.

After having called out to each other, Mary Magdalene apparently embraces Jesus (20:17). Not only is this reminiscent of the woman in Canticles of Canticles who states, "I found him whom my soul loves. I held him and would not let him go until I brought him into my mother's house" (Cant 3:4),[68] it is also reminiscent of the women in the Greek love-novels. Unlike the man in Canticle of Canticles or the heroes of Greek love-novels, however, Jesus does not reciprocate Mary Magdalene's embrace. He says to her, "Stop holding onto me (μή μου ἅπτου)" (20:17).[69] According to the text, Jesus' refusal to reciprocate Mary Magdalene's embrace is based on the fact that he has not yet ascended to his Father (20:17).[70] On one level of characterization, Mary Magdalene's efforts to "hold onto" Jesus may illustrate that Mary Magdalene still does not understand the nature of Jesus' resurrected state or the manner in which his followers would remain with him.[71] With regard to the correlation between this scene and

[67]Atwood, 133–4. Cf. Okure, "The Significance Today of Jesus' Commission to Mary Magdalene," 181; Brown, *The Gospel According to John,* 2:1010; Schnackenburg, 3:317.

[68]Cf. Stibbe, 205, cf. 61; Okure, 181.

[69]My translation. Hoskyns, Barrett, and Brown suggest that the use of the present imperative in (μή μου ἅπτου) puts emphasis on the cessation of an act in progress or at least the cessation of an attempted act. Hoskyns, 2:648. Barrett, 565. Brown, *The Gospel According to John,* 2:992. Cf. Atwood, 134–5; Okure, "The Significance Today of Jesus' Commission to Mary Magdalene," 181, esp. n. 8. Bernard, however, suggests the possibility that the text originally read (μὴ πτόου) "Fear Not!" Bernard, 2:670–1.

[70]Mary Rose D'Angelo and Perkins note a curious parallel between Jesus' command to Mary Magdalene and Adam's instructions to Eve in *Apocalypse of Moses* 31:3-4 not to touch his body when he dies, but to permit the angels to dispose of it. Thus, they maintain that Jesus' words implies that he is in transitional state, between his resurrection and ascension. Mary Rose D'Angelo, "A Critical Note: John 20:17 and Apocalypse of Moses 31," *Journal of Theological Studies* 41 (1990) 529–36. Perkins, "I Have Seen the Lord," 39.

[71]Brown, *The Gospel According to John,* 2:1011–2, 1014. Matera, 405. Atwood, 135. Cf. Perkins, *Resurrection: New Testament Witness and Contemporary Reflection,*

the recognition scenes between spouses in Greek love-novels, however, Mary Magdalene's attempt to embrace Jesus suggests she is a bride who longs for her beloved.

Upsetting the conventional expectations provided by the love-novels, Jesus, the bridegroom, does not embrace his bride warmly and the two do not then live with her happily ever after. Rather, Jesus gives his bride a mission, requiring her to separate from him again. "But go to my brothers and say to them, 'I am ascending to my Father and your (ὑμῶν) Father, to my God and your (ὑμῶν) God'" (20:17). Because Mary Magdalene immediately goes to the disciples to tell them this news (20:18), the reader realizes that the disciples are now Jesus' "brothers." This is the first time in the Gospel where the disciples are referred to as Jesus' "brothers." This sequence of events would have communicated to the first-century reader that Jesus had indeed fulfilled his mission of giving people the power to become children of God (cf. 1:12).[72] Because Jesus' blood sacrifice on the cross made the disciples "sons" of his heavenly Father, the disciples are now truly "brothers" of Jesus.[73]

Just as the Samaritan woman was bride of the messianic bridegroom on behalf of the Samaritan people and Mary of Bethany was the bride of the messianic bridegroom on behalf of the Jews, now Mary Magdalene is bride of the messianic bridegroom on behalf of the entire community of faith. As "bride" she is the representative of the faith community to whom Jesus weds himself. She, like the faith community she represents, cannot

---

175–6. Although Hoskyns perceives a contrast here between Jesus' telling Mary Magdalene to stop holding on to him and Jesus' telling Thomas to touch him, because different verbs are used in the two pericopae, I would agree with Brown and Atwood that no contrast was intended between Mary Magdalene and Thomas. Cf. Hoskyns 2:543. For an alternative interpretation of this passage based on an anticipatory γαρ, see Michael McGehee, "A Less Theological Reading of John 20:17," *Journal of Biblical Literature* 108 (1986) 299–302.

[72]Okure, "The Significance Today of Jesus' Commission to Mary Magdalene," 182–6, 188. Perkins, "The Gospel According to John, 983. Schneiders, "Women in the Fourth Gospel and the Role of Women in the Contemporary Church," 43. Although Minear places the fulfillment of the promise of "sonship" at Jesus' ascension to the Father and his subsequent breathing of the Spirit upon them, he does acknowledge that Jesus' words of mutual exchange between his mother and the beloved disciple from the cross and his words to Mary Magdalene after the resurrection also carry this same context. Minear, 130, 137.

[73]Cf. chapter 5, pp. 119–21. Culpepper, *Anatomy,* 134, 144; Schneiders, "Women in the Fourth Gospel and the Role of Women in the Contemporary Church," 43; Brown, *The Gospel According to John,* 2:1015–7; Okure, "The Significance Today of Jesus' Commission to Mary Magdalene," 182–6.

rest in the embrace of her beloved. She has a mission. She is sent to the "brothers" of Jesus to give them of the good news that Jesus, having established the disciples as the *familia Dei*, is now returning to their common heavenly Father.

When Mary Magdalene encounters the disciples to tell them the good news, she begins with the announcement, "I have seen the Lord!" On one level of the text, this statement may indicate that Mary Magdalene has moved from perceiving Jesus as "my teacher" to perceiving him as "the Lord."[74] Nevertheless, on another level of the text, if one understands her statement as statement of joy, then her grief, which has been so emphasized in this pericope, has now been changed into the joy that Jesus predicted would be given to the disciples/the community of faith (16:6, 20).[75] After announcing that she has seen the Lord, Mary Magdalene then reports to Jesus' "brothers" all that Jesus told her to report (20:18). Thus, by the end of this pericope, Mary Magdalene, as the representative of the faith community, is characterized as the obedient believer.[76]

A final note may be in order here regarding Mary Magdalene's mission. It may be significant, within the levirate marriage system, that Jesus sent his bride to his "brothers" as he returns to his heavenly Father. Jesus, as "dying king," had given his mother to the beloved disciple as a symbol of the relationship that his blood sacrifice was establishing with all those whom the beloved disciple represents. Now, as Jesus sends his bride to his brothers, she too is a symbol of Jesus' desire to be "remembered." Just as Jesus kept his Father's name alive by speaking his Father's word to his disciples and making them not of the world (17:6-26), so too the disciples are now responsible for keeping his name alive. Jesus entrusted to his disciples the message his Father entrusted to him (17:8). They will now be responsible for keeping that word alive within themselves (cf. 15:9-10) and bringing others to believe in Jesus "through their word" (διὰ τοῦ λόγου αὐτῶν) (17:20). In a sense, they will not only be the ones who reap the harvest (4:38, cf. 21:1-7); once they have fully received the Spirit them-

---

[74]Brown, *The Gospel According to John*, 2:1010, cf. 2:984, 994. On Mary Magdalene's use of the title Lord for Jesus when she tells Peter and the beloved disciple that the body of the Lord had been removed (20:2), see also Bultmann, 683 n. 11, 689 n. 2. Hoskyns, in a contrasting opinion, maintains that there is probably an element of faith in Mary Magdalene's use of the title "Rabbouni." Hoskyns, 2:648.

[75]Cf. chapter 6, p. 143.

[76]Although Mary Magdalene fulfills her task, some scholars (e.g. R. Collins and Rena) maintain that in the Fourth Gospel Mary Magdalene's faith is inadequate because she misses all the clues and needs to see in order to believe. R. Collins, "The Representative Figures in the Fourth Gospel," 123–4. Rena, 143.

selves (cf. 20:22-23), they will also be the ones through whom the seeds of faith are to be disseminated.[77]

Patriarchal Overtones in Mary Magdalene's Characterization

The manner in which the implied author characterizes Mary Magdalene in the Fourth Gospel is patriarchal in several ways. First, like the other women in this Gospel and women in ancient writings in general, Mary Magdalene's primary function is that of highlighting aspects of the male hero's character.[78] Because Mary Magdalene is characterized as a wife in search of the body of her beloved, Jesus, by implication, is characterized as the messianic bridegroom who has completed his task of establishing the new family of God, a task Jesus completed on the cross and signified by sending his bride to his "brothers." Like the Samaritan woman for the Samaritan people and Mary of Bethany for the Jews, Mary Magdalene, as bride, is simply the symbolic link between Jesus and the patrilineal kinship group he establishes.

Besides developing the characterization of Mary Magdalene in such a way as to make a statement about Jesus, the Johannine versions of the empty tomb scene and the scene of Jesus' post-resurrection appearance to a woman indicate a patriarchal bias because they diminish the tradition about the women at the tomb.[79] As Brendan Byrne states regarding the first episode of the pericope, "Mary Magdalene serves only to set the story in motion."[80] Her role in this episode is simply that of informing Peter and the beloved disciple about the tomb's disturbance. The inclusion of the Peter-and-beloved-disciple interlude not only fulfills the patriarchal, Jewish law about the need for two male witnesses but also allows a reader to conclude that the first person to observe that the tomb was actually empty was the beloved disciple, or Peter, rather than Mary Magdalene. In this aspect, therefore, Mary Magdalene's role in the Fourth Gospel, in compari-

[77]For the disciples, the ablative of agency is used with *logos*. For Jesus, the accusative of cause is used with *logos*. The disciples are not the cause of faith, only the instruments of spreading the faith. Cf. chapter 3, pp. 77–8.

[78]For other examples of the female function of accentuating aspects of the male hero's role in the Fourth Gospel, see chapter 2, pp. 33–40 (Mother of Jesus at Cana), chapter 3, pp. 69–79 (Samaritan Woman), chapter 4, pp. 107–9 (Mary and Martha of Bethany), chapter 5, pp. 131–41 (Mother of Jesus at the Cross).

[79]Cf. O'Collins and Kendall, 635, 637; Brown, *The Gospel According to John*, 2:986; Brown, "Roles of Women in the Fourth Gospel," 189–90, n. 335; Seim, 67, n. 23.

[80]Byrne, 85. Cf. Atwood, 110.

son to the role of women in the Synoptic tradition, is diminished. Finally, the inclusion of a belief statement on the part of the beloved disciple diminishes by contrast Mary Magdalene's stature in her encounter with Jesus. Unlike the beloved disciple, whose belief was based on a mere sign (the *soudarion*), Mary Magdalene misunderstood all the signs she encountered (the empty tomb, the angels, Jesus as the gardener). She needed to see Jesus himself and hear him call her by name in order to believe. Thus, the need for two male witnesses, the ambiguity regarding who actually observed the empty tomb first, as well as the fact that a male disciple was the first to believe in the resurrection, all lessen the tradition about women being first to observe the empty tomb and the first to believe in the resurrection.[81]

Patriarchal tendencies continue for, although Mary Magdalene is the first person in the Fourth Gospel to whom the risen Jesus shows himself,[82] Jesus' correction of Mary Magdalene and his refusal to reciprocate her embrace effectively denies Mary Magdalene the positive affirmation that women in Greek love-novels receive from their spouses. Indeed, this failure to embrace his bride is the most striking alteration the author made on the recognition scenes from the Greek love-novels. Such a dramatic change would have caused the reader to wonder why Mary Magdalene is not embraced. I would maintain that the christology and patriarchal ideology of the author denies Mary Magdalene the embrace.

Mary Magdalene, as Jesus' bride/wife, is but a literary strategy that emphasizes Jesus' function on earth. She is not important in and of herself as a female character. She functions as a representative of the faith community to whom Jesus as the messianic bridegroom weds himself. As representative of the faith community, her function is to give the message to the Jesus' "brothers" that Jesus has completed his task on earth and is now returning to his Father and their Father. Furthermore, Jesus' correction of Mary Magdalene and his refusal to embrace her emphasize once again that no biological or figurative female relative could have influence over Jesus. The biological mother of Jesus could not have influence over him at Cana (2:3-4),[83] neither could his fictive bride Mary of Bethany nor her sister

---

[81]Cf. Bernard, 671.

[82]Because the Fourth Gospel also places its christological confession in the mouth of Martha (instead of Peter as stated in Matthew), Brown maintains that Jesus' appearance first to Mary Magdalene (instead of to Peter as stated in Paul's writings and the Gospel of Luke) may well be a deliberate emphasis on the part of the implied author of the Fourth Gospel. Brown, "Roles of Women in the Fourth Gospel," 190–1.

[83]Cf. chapter 2, pp. 33–6.

Martha (11:1-7).[84] Once again Jesus demonstrates that, as the son sent by
the Father in heaven, he remains aloof from the earthly concerns of others, especially the women in his life. Thus, Jesus' correction of Mary Magdalene and his refusal to embrace her, both of which are based on the fact
that he had not yet ascended to the Father, is yet another indication that the
christology of the implied author of the Fourth Gospel denies any earthly
female relative influence over Jesus. The only one who could have influence over him is his heavenly Father.

Jesus' correction of Mary Magdalene and his refusal to reciprocate
her embrace has also led scholars to negative perceptions of Mary Magdalene's character. For some scholars her embrace of Jesus expresses a desire to hold onto that which is tangible.[85] For other scholars her embrace
expresses a desire to hold onto that which is only temporary.[86] Still other
scholars perceive in her embrace questions of purity and elements of danger for Jesus in his intermediary state between resurrection and ascension.[87] Jesus' correction of Mary Magdalene and his subsequent giving her
a message for his "brothers" also has had the patriarchal effect of allowing ancient, as well as modern, scholars to conclude that Jesus' appearance
to Mary Magdalene was only a preliminary appearance. These scholars
consider Jesus' later appearance to the disciples to be more important because it is at this resurrection appearance that Jesus breathes the Spirit
upon the disciples. Supporting this patriarchal interpretation is the fact
that, like her female counterparts in this text and other ancient texts, Mary
Magdalene disappears from the text immediately after she fulfills her literary purpose.[88]

One might see a positive element in the fact that Jesus uses the name
Mariam for Mary Magdalene. Such a usage may indicate that Mary Magdalene had become as much of a sister to Jesus (the new Moses) as the disciples had become "brothers." Yet, even this interpretation raises problems
of patriarchy. If such a correlation does exist, the primary purpose of Jesus'
calling Mary Magdalene "Mariam" would have been that of establishing
Jesus as the new Moses, not that of raising Mary Magdalene's status to

[84]Cf. chapter 4, pp. 108–9.

[85]Cf. D'Angelo, 530–1.

[86]Brown, *The Gospel According to John,* 2:1012.

[87]D'Angelo, 531–5. Cf. Okure "The Significance Today of Jesus' Commission to
Mary Magdalene," 177.

[88]Minear states that after Mary Magdalene's words about the resurrection had
been corroborated by Jesus' appearance to the disciples, Mary Magdalene disappears
from the scene; her work accomplished. I would say that she disappears before her
story had been corroborated. Cf. Minear, 130.

that of sister. Such a usage would also be patriarchal because the action of a man adopting his wife as a sister was one of the means by which the Hebrew Bible dealt with the matrilineal threat to patrilineal descent.[89]

Continuing the concept of patrilineal descent, Jesus' sends his bride to his "brothers" to tell them he is departing to their common heavenly Father. The *familia Dei* will continue to increase because Jesus' bride (the community of faith) is now in the hands of his "brothers" (cf. 21:1-17).

An Affirmation of the Female Mode of Relating

On the positive side of Mary Magdalene's characterization is the fact that her boldness and persistence paid off. Mary Magdalene was granted her heart's desire, not merely the body of her beloved, but her beloved himself. Jane Kopas has stated that, in the manner in which Mary Magdalene is characterized in the Fourth Gospel, the author affirmed the notion that seeking Jesus is not the whole story. One must also attentively wait. According to Kopas, receptivity is coupled with boldness in the character of Mary Magdalene.[90] Although I might describe Mary Magdalene's character more in terms of frantic persistence than attentive waiting, I would agree with Kopas that the implied author of the Fourth Gospel may have been encouraging the first-century male reader to adopt some aspects of a "feminine" model in his faith response. The manner in which the women in the Fourth Gospel approach Jesus eventually leads to success.[91] This positive aspect in the characterization of women supports the implied author's critique of the typical masculine mode of relating to God and others, a mode that was extremely concerned with a man's maintaining or increasing his own honor. This focus on earthly honor is consistently portrayed in the Fourth Gospel as being a block to true faith and relationship with God (cf. 5:41; 7:18; 9:50, 54; 12:25; 13:13-17).

Summary

Given the previous characterizations of Jesus and the women in his life, the characterization of Mary Magdalene at the tomb as a single frantic woman in search of Jesus' body would have encouraged an ancient reader to recognize that her character was developed along the lines of female lovers in the Greek love-novels and/or the woman of Canticle of

[89]Cf. Nancy Jay, "Sacrifice, Descent and Patriarchs," 57–9.
[90]Kopas, 205.
[91]Cf. chapter 2, pp. 40–1 (Mother of Jesus at Cana); chapter 3, pp. 73–5 (Samaritan woman); chapter 4, pp. 101–2 (Mary of Bethany) and pp. 104–7 (Martha of Bethany).

Canticles.[92] Such allusions would have led the reader to realize that in this scene, as well as in the crucifixion scene, Mary Magdalene fulfills the role of the bride of the messianic bridegroom and functions as a representative for the entire faith community. Jesus, who has already given his mother to the beloved disciple (the representative of the earthly residents of his kingdom) now sends his bride to his "brothers." Mary Magdalene, therefore, functions as an additional symbolic female bond between Jesus and his newly acquired family.

Until the moment of recognition, Mary Magdalene's function as the bride of the messianic bridegroom appears to be that of misunderstanding the significance of Jesus' missing body, alerting Peter and the beloved disciple to the fact that the tomb has been disturbed, and weeping because she cannot find the body of her beloved.[93] After the moment of recognition, her function changes to that of carrying Jesus' message back to his "brothers" and remaining with them, instead of resting in the embrace of her beloved.

Throughout the characterization of Mary Magdalene in the Fourth Gospel, androcentric and patriarchal overtones are evident. Her main function is to assist in Jesus' characterization as the messianic bridegroom who has fulfilled his role of establishing the new *familia Dei*. In the end she is marginalized as she is denied her embrace and sent to Jesus' "brothers" with the message that he is returning to their common heavenly Father. The disciples continue to appear in the text. Mary Magdalene, as bride, disappears.

[92]One could even perceive Jesus' words about love in his farewell speech, as well as his whole passion, death and resurrection, as a reflection of the phrase, "Love is stronger than death" (Cant 8:6).

[93] Cf. Rena, 143; Minear, 126–7.

7

Summary and Conclusion

Summary

The use of a historical-literary approach with the Fourth Gospel has led me to conclude that the main function of the female characters in the Gospel is that of supporting Jesus' role as the messianic bridegroom who has come to give those who believe in him the power to become children of God and therefore have eternal life (cf. 1:12; 3:15-16, 36; 6:40, 47; 10:28; 17:2-3). If one adds to this historical-literary approach a feminist critique, then it becomes apparent that, although the female characters help to further the plot of the Gospel and support the characterization of Jesus, their portrayals are inherently androcentric and patriarchal. First, their primary function of supporting the portrayal of the male hero as the messianic bridegroom (at times by being the literary link between Jesus and groups of men through the convention of patriarchal marriage) is highly patriarchal. In addition to this patriarchal element is the added factor that the christology of the implied author erases the recognition such patriarchal roles would ordinarily have accorded women in first-century texts. In the end, like most female characters in ancient texts, the female characters of the Fourth Gospel are marginalized after they fulfill their androcentric and patriarchal function.

Despite the inherent androcentric and patriarchal ideology in the characterization of women, however, the women in the Fourth Gospel generally function as positive paradigms of response to Jesus. They function as positive paradigms precisely because, except perhaps for the mother of Jesus, they represent communities of faith. This representational characterization, however, is patriarchal in itself because it is based

169

on the concept of a male God being in relationship to a faith community which must, therefore, be characterized as female. In their role as female representatives of faith communities, these women bring others to believe in Jesus, speak words of belief themselves, express love for Jesus, and move Jesus to act on behalf of others.

In chapter 2 of this book I demonstrated how the mother of Jesus at Cana (2:1-11) fulfills the function of supporting the portrayal of Jesus as the messianic bridegroom by being characterized according to the traits of a "mother of an important son" character-type from the Hebrew Bible. According to this character-type, a mother attempts to advance her son's status in the community and consciously or unconsciously ends up assisting her son in meeting his destiny with regard to the promise God made to Abraham that he would be the father of a great nation. At Cana the mother of Jesus endeavors to advance her son's status by insisting that he take care of a need that is actually the responsibility of the bridegroom (the lack of wine). Jesus' verbal response to his mother distances him from her and her aspirations for him. This distancing technique indicates that the mother of Jesus does not have the influence that a "mother of an important son" usually has over her son. According to the christology of the implied author, Jesus does not seek the earthly status that his mother desires for him. Rather, he seeks only the glory that comes from his heavenly Father. Although the persistence of his mother eventually moves Jesus to act, the manner in which he fulfills this mundane need for wine indicates that he is accepting the role of the messianic bridegroom who has come to bring abundant blessings. Thus, his action identifies him with his heavenly Father (the bridegroom of Israel), rather than his earthly mother.

Supporting this portrayal of Jesus as the messianic bridegroom who has come to give people the power to become children of God are the words of John the Baptist to his disciples, "He who has the bride is the bridegroom" (3:29), and Jesus' words to Nicodemus about the need to be born "from above" (3:1-10). Such a repeated portrayal of Jesus as the messianic bridegroom provides the opportunity for someone to play the role of Jesus' betrothed/bride. This role is first fulfilled by the Samaritan woman at the well on behalf of the Samaritan people (4:1-42), then by Mary of Bethany on behalf of the Jews (11:1-46; 12:1-11), and finally by Mary Magdalene on behalf of the entire community (19:25; 20:1-18).

As detailed in chapter 3, the implied author portrayed the Samaritan woman as the betrothed/bride of the messianic bridegroom on behalf of the Samaritan people through the adaptation of the betrothal type-scene from the Hebrew Bible. In this type-scene, a man or his surrogate travels to a foreign land and encounters a woman at a well. Usually, after one draws water for the other, the woman runs home to inform her family of the stranger's arrival. The family then invites the stranger in for a meal, after which the betrothal is finalized. By adapting the betrothal type-scene so that (1) Jesus gives "living water," (2) the Samaritan woman tells the townspeople of the stranger's presence, and (3) the townspeople invite Jesus to stay, the implied author was able to illustrate that Jesus was symbolically "wedding" himself to the Samaritan people as a whole, and not just to the Samaritan woman's extended family.

In chapter 4 I illustrated that the implied author portrays Mary of Bethany as the betrothed/bride of the messianic bridegroom on behalf of the Jewish people by having her anoint Jesus' feet with perfume and wipe his feet with her hair (12:3-4; cf. 11:2) and by consistently referring to her in conjunction with the Jews (11:31, 33, 45). By making Mary of Bethany the fictive betrothed/bride of Jesus, Lazarus becomes part of Jesus' family and is returned to life as a sign that all those who become part of the *familia Dei* will have eternal life. Martha, who fulfills the role of sister of the betrothed/bride, is the counterpart to the Samaritan townspeople who, as members of Jesus' family, express true faith in Jesus.

Besides the betrothal/marital motif in the individual pericopae mentioned above, one can identify within the overall structure of the Fourth Gospel a messianic betrothal followed by messianic marriage. As noted in chapter 3, the meal and subsequent betrothal is missing in the story of the Samaritan woman. Although the collapse of time allows the Samaritan woman within her own story to function both as betrothed and bride who subsequently produces offspring of faith (4:1-42), a reader could perceive a betrothal meal for Jesus in the meal given in his honor at Bethany six days before Passover, when Jesus' betrothed/bride (Mary of Bethany) anointed his feet with perfume and then wiped his feet with her hair (12:3). In as much as weddings generally took place soon after the betrothal meal in the first century C.E., the reader would have been predisposed to perceive the passion and death of Jesus as his wedding ceremony.

Beginning with the story of the wedding at Cana, the first-century reader was prepared to perceive Jesus' "hour" as the appropriate time for his "wedding." As described in chapter 5, various details in the crucifixion scene support this wedding motif in the passion narrative (e.g., Jesus' special "kingly" garment and crown, the king/garden terminology, the piercing of Jesus' side as a role reversal for the consummation of the marriage, and the flow of blood and water from his side combining with his spirit or the Spirit as the moment of conception of new life from above). The mother of Jesus at the cross supports the portrayal of Jesus as the messianic bridegroom by serving as the earthly symbol for the familial

relationship that Jesus' messianic marriage establishes with the entire
community of faith. By being given to the beloved disciple, who represents those who believe in Jesus, the mother of Jesus serves as a sign that
the disciples have truly become "brothers" of Jesus once he embraces his
hour/wedding.

Finally, chapter 6 explains how the implied author portrays Mary
Magdalene as the betrothed/bride of the messianic bridegroom on behalf
of the entire community of faith. Not only is she the only female character at the crucifixion (Jesus' hour/wedding) who can function as the bride
of Jesus (19:25), but she is also characterized as a woman obsessed with
searching for the body of her beloved (20:1-18). In this regard, the implied
author appears to have drawn upon popular Greco-Roman love-novels that
portray spouses being obsessed with finding the body/tomb of their
beloved and conclude with recognition scenes between husbands and
wives, as well as passages from the Canticle of Canticles that portray a
woman frantically searching for her beloved.

An androcentric and patriarchal ideology with respect to women per-
meates these portrayals of the women in Jesus' life. Androcentrism is evident in the mere fact that the main function of the female characters is that
of supporting a given portrayal of Jesus—the male hero. To this end, the
mother of Jesus and the Samaritan woman are not even referred to by
name. The narrator referred to the first only by her maternal relationship
to Jesus, the one character indicator that is necessary for her to function as
a "mother of an important son" and as a symbol for her son's fraternal relationship with believers. The narrator referred to the second only by her
ethnicity and gender, the two character indicators that are necessary for
her to function as the betrothed/bride on behalf of her own people. Androcentrism is also evident in the fact that different women are able to fulfill the role of Jesus' fictive betrothed/bride. This literary technique
emphasizes the fact that Jesus (the male messianic bridegroom) is the one
who is important, not his female bride(s).

Androcentrism is further indicated by the fact that, in each of the
pericopae involving female characters, the implied author first minimizes
their importance, even as they fulfill their role, and then marginalizes them
thoroughly after they have fulfilled their function in the text. The implied
author first minimizes the importance of the mother of Jesus at Cana by
distancing Jesus from her (having Jesus call her "woman") and by denying her the influence that a "mother of an important son" usually had over
her son. The implied author then marginalizes her at the end of the story
by removing her from the text until she is needed to fulfill another androcentric and patriarchal function in the crucifixion scene. The Samaritan

woman's importance is minimized by the fact that, unlike male disciples before her and after her, she expresses only a qualified belief in Jesus (4:29). She is then marginalized at the end of the story both by the words her own people speak to her (4:42) and by the fact that she too disappears from the text after she fulfills her function.

The importance of Mary of Bethany is minimized by the role her sister Martha has in the text. After first focusing on Mary to establish her role as betrothed/bride, the implied author listed Martha first in the statement regarding Jesus' love for these family members and referred to Mary only as Martha's sister, not by name (11:5). In addition, Martha is the member of the family who enters into a verbal conversation with Jesus and expresses faith in him, not his betrothed/bride Mary of Bethany. Although Martha makes a strong statement of belief in Jesus as a member of his fictive family, her importance is subsequently minimized by Jesus' rebuke of her when she resists his having the stone to her brother's tomb removed (11:39-40). After her brother is raised from the dead, Martha is then marginalized by being returned to a female (servant) role at a dinner in which her brother was a participant (12:2). Mary of Bethany, however, never escapes the female limitations of being betrothed/bride, as evidenced by her staying at home while her sister goes out of the village to meet Jesus.

The role of the mother of Jesus at the cross is minimized by the fact that the fraternal relationship that Jesus has with those whom the beloved disciple represents is not truly based on this dying king's exchange of a female relative, as is the fraternal relationship between Darius and Alexander and then Alexander and those he leaves in charge in the *Alexander Romance.* Rather, the fraternal relationship between Jesus and his disciples is based on the patrilineal descent that Jesus' blood sacrifice establishes. The mother of Jesus, as the female exchange item of a dying king, is but an earthly sign for the brotherly relationship that Jesus has with those whom the beloved disciple represents. The mother of Jesus is then marginalized by being placed in the care of the beloved disciple and disappearing from the text.

Mary Magdalene's importance as betrothed/bride at the crucifixion scene is minimized by the author's use of the mother of Jesus to indicate that Jesus was wedding himself to the community of faith at the cross (19:26-27). Mary Magdalene's importance as finder of the tomb and believer in the resurrection is then minimized by the Peter/beloved disciple interlude (20:1-10). The beloved disciple or Peter, not Mary Magdalene, is the first to observe that the tomb is actually empty, and the beloved disciple is the first to believe that Jesus had returned to his heavenly Father. Mary Magdalene is then marginalized by Jesus' refusal to embrace her as wife (20:17), an affirmation women in Greek love-novels usually receives upon finding their husbands after a long absence and search. Her importance lies not in her personal relationship with Jesus, but in her function as intermediary (levirate wife) between Jesus and his "brothers." Like the female figures before her, Mary Magdalene is merely a means by which Jesus is connected to a community of men (and maybe women).

A patriarchal world view is evident in the fact that the portrayal of women as the betrothed/bride of the messianic bridegroom both drew on and supported several common patriarchal conventions: the imagery of a male God loving a community that is characterized as female; the use of "the (sexual) sin of a woman" to represent the unfaithfulness of a nation (4:18); the use of the image of woman as "land to be sown" in order to represent the fruitfulness of Jesus' messianic marriage to the Samaritan people (4:35-38); and the silent presence of Mary Magdalene at the moment of her fictive wedding to Jesus (11:25-29). Such a use of patriarchal conventions gives evidence of a patriarchal world view on the part of the implied author, as well as the implied reader.

Besides the drawing on patriarchal conventions mentioned above, a patriarchal world view with respect to women is evident in the fact that the characterizations of the women are skillfully crafted according to patriarchal expectations. The portrayals of the mother of Jesus at Cana and at the cross, for instance, illustrate the patriarchal concepts that a widowed mother of a living son ought to be accompanied in public by a relative, preferably a son (cf. 2:12, 19:25), and that she should be taken into the home of a son (19:27). Similarly, patriarchal ideology is apparent in the fact that Martha, who had neither father, husband, son, nor brother at the time of Jesus' arrival at her village, was able to go outside the village to meet Jesus without being called by him (11:20, 30), whereas Mary of Bethany, the fictive betrothed/bride of Jesus, stayed at home (11:20), waited for Jesus to call her (11:28), and then left the village in the company of others (11:29-31). In fact, throughout chapter 11, Mary of Bethany, as the betrothed/bride, is portrayed as relatively quiet and passive, whereas Martha, the unattached female, is portrayed as talkative and assertive, (cf. the portrayal of the "technically unattached" Samaritan woman).

A certain amount of patriarchy is also reflected in the indirectness of women's communication with men in the Fourth Gospel. The mother of Jesus, as well as Mary and Martha of Bethany, present Jesus with only implicit requests (2:3; 11:3), unlike the male royal official who makes an explicit request (4:49). Such feminine "indirectness" is also apparent in the oblique manner in which the mother of Jesus at Cana asserts her maternal authority (2:5) and in the manner in which Mary and Martha of Bethany mask their disappointment regarding Jesus' absence with a statement of belief in his power to heal (11:21, 32). Finally, only a patriarchal world view on the part of the first-century reader would have enabled the reader to realize that Mary of Bethany was being portrayed as the betrothed/bride of the messianic bridegroom. Only a betrothed/bride could have anointed Jesus' feet with perfume, let down her hair in his presence, and then wiped his feet with her hair without receiving some kind of public rebuke for such otherwise shameless behavior (12:3).

Conclusion

What is evident throughout this entire analysis is that the women in the Fourth Gospel are important to the extent they advance the portrayal of the male hero, further the implied author's "heavenly" patriarchal ideology, and/or function as representatives of faith communities. In these respects, they are not unlike the female characters found in the Hebrew Bible, Hellenistic-Jewish literature, or the Greek love-novel.

Like their female counterparts in the Hebrew Bible,[1] the primary function of women of the Fourth Gospel is to put emphasis on the male hero, further the career or the hero, and/or support androcentric or patriarchal principles.[2] Because the Fourth Gospel can best be described as an ancient biography of Jesus,[3] the women of the Fourth Gospel are not the focus of attention in the same way that the heroines of Hellenistic-Jewish literature are.[4] Nevertheless, they do resemble the women in this literature in many respects.

[1] Cf. J. Cheryl Exum, *Fragmented Women: Feminist (Sub)versions of Biblical Narratives* (Valley Forge, Pa.: Trinity, 1993); Esther Fuchs, "The Literary Characterization of Mothers and Sexual Politics in the Hebrew Bible," *Feminist Perspectives on Biblical Scholarship,* ed. Adela Yarbro Collins (Chico, Calif.: Scholars Press, 1983) 117–36; Esther Fuchs, "Who is Hiding the Truth? Deceptive Women and Biblical Androcentrism," *Feminist Perspectives on Biblical Scholarship,* ed. Adela Yarbro Collins (Chico, Calif.: Scholars Press, 1983) 137–44; Amy-Jill Levine, "Ruth," *The Women's Bible Commentary,* eds. Carol A. Newsom and Sharon H. Ringe (Louisville: Westminster/John Knox, 1992) 78–84.

[2] The primary function of all the women in the Fourth Gospel is to support the portrayal of Jesus as the messianic bridegroom. Furthermore, the mother of Jesus, as "mother of an important son," acts in an assertive manner to further the status of her son in the community and Mary and Martha of Bethany act in a relatively assertive manner on behalf of their brother.

[3] Cf. chapter 1, pp. 11–12.

[4] Cf. Richard Pervo, "Aseneth and Her Sisters: Women in Jewish Narrative and in the Greek Novels," *Women Like This: New Perspectives on Jewish Women in the Greco-Roman World,* ed. Amy-Jill Levine (Atlanta: Scholars Press, 1992) 145–60.

Men in such Hellenistic-Jewish works as the Book of Judith, like men in Greek novels, are portrayed as relatively weak, inept, and less resolute than women.[5] A similar portrayal of men can be found in the Fourth Gospel (cf. the disciples' unwillingness to ask questions or enter into dialogue with Jesus and Peter and the beloved disciple going home after finding the tomb empty). The authors of this period tended to portray women as the successful characters in their literary works. Nevertheless, like the women in Hellenistic-Jewish literature,[6] Greek love-novels,[7] and Greek literature in general,[8] the women in the Fourth Gospel act in support of androcentric and patriarchal values.

Another similarity between the women in the Fourth Gospel and the female literary characters of the period is the fact that the female characters of the Fourth Gospel function in a symbolic manner and/or speak the beliefs of the author. Like Aseneth who functions as an appropriate bridal representative for all proselytes,[9] and Judith who appropriately represents

[5]Pervo, 157. Cf. Amy-Jill Levine, "Character Construction and Community Formation in the Book of Judith," *Society of Biblical Literature 1989 Seminar Papers,* ed. David Lull (Atlanta: Scholars Press, 1989) 564.

[6]Susanna speaks only to her maids and at her trail is silent; Aseneth, who in the beginning is boastful, arrogant, and contemptuous of men, is transformed into a woman who prays for courage and realizes her status through marriage; Only Judith, for the sake of the good of the community, turns the patriarchal world upside down for awhile. Cf. Pervo, 147–59.

[7]Pervo states that the heroines of the Greek novel tended to be portrayed in traditional sex roles and their rivals, who were portrayed as aggressive, independent, ruthless, willful, and domineering, were portrayed as "bad" women. He also notes, however, that the Greek love-novels of the Second Sophistic period tended to domesticate the women more than the non-sophistic Greek love-novels did. Cf. Pervo, 145–7.

[8]Cf. David Halperin, "Why is Diotima A Woman? Platonic Eros and the Figuration of Gender," *Before Sexuality: The Construction of Erotic Experience in the Ancient Greek World,* eds. David M. Halperin, John J. Winkler and Froma I. Zeitlin (Princeton: Princeton University Press, 1990) 257–308; Froma Zeitlin, "The Dynamic of Misogyny: Myth and Mythmaking in the *Oresteia,*" *Women in the Ancient World: The Arethusa Papers,* eds. J. Peradotto and J. P. Sullivan (Albany: State University of New York Press, 1984) 159–94; Helene Foley, "The Conception of Women in Athenian Drama," *Reflections of Women in Antiquity,* ed. Helene P. Foley (New York: Gordon and Breach, 1981) 127–68.

[9]Ross Kraemer notes that the transformation of Aseneth from a foolish and ignorant woman into the wise counterpart to Joseph might be a by-product of the author's need to characterize her as an acceptable wife for Joseph. Aseneth's negative femaleness is thus subordinated to her positive *theosebeia,* her inclusion into the community. Ross Kraemer, "The Book of Aseneth," *Searching the Scriptures—Volume 2: A Feminist Commentary,* ed. Elisabeth Schüssler Fiorenza (New York: Crossroad, 1994) 885–6. Cf. Pervo, 148–55.

the widowed Israel,[10] so the Samaritan woman, Mary of Bethany, and Mary Magdalene function as appropriate bridal representative for their respective communities.[11] Like Susanna who speaks the ideal sapiential principle that vengeance belongs to the most High,[12] Judith who is the model of Wisdom,[13] and Rebekah in *Jubilees* who articulates the most cherished ideals of the author (i.e., the purification of the Jerusalem Temple [25:21]),[14] so Martha of Bethany expresses the christological beliefs of the implied author of the Fourth Gospel (11:27). Just as women in early Jewish literature received revelations,[15] so too do the Samaritan woman, Martha of Bethany, and Mary Magdalene receive a self-revelation from Jesus. If one looks at the characterizations of Susanna, Aseneth, and Judith, however, one notices their positive and independent portrayals are connected with their symbolic function. Cheryl Anne Brown notes the same phenomena for Deborah, Jephthah's daughter, and Hannah in Pseudo-Philo's *Biblical Antiquities.* Their portrayals may be enhanced over their portraits in the biblical text, but they are also symbolic or typological

---

[10]Levine acknowledges that Judith (whose name means Jewess) is usually identified as a representation of or a metaphor for the community of faith because of her name, widowhood, chastity, beauty, and righteousness. Although Linda Bennett Elder does not agree with this interpretation, she acknowledges that commentators have a propensity for considering Judith an allegory or type of Israel or daughter of Israel. Levine, "Character Construction and Community Formation in the Book of Judith," 561, 565. Amy-Jill Levine, "Sacrifice and Salvation: Otherness and Domestication in the Book of Judith," *'No one Spoke Ill of Her': Essays on Judith,* ed. James C. Vanderkam (Atlanta: Scholars Press, 1992) 17, 21. Cf. Linda Bennett Elder, "Judith," *Searching the Scriptures—Volume 2: A Feminist Commentary,* ed. Elisabeth Schüssler Fiorenza (New York: Crossroad, 1994) 457.

[11]Each of these women are characterized in such a way as to further their ability to represent their respective communities. The Samaritan woman, as a representative of the Samaritan people, is characterized as a woman who has had five husbands/men plus one who is not her husband, meets Jesus' request with a "we-you" mentality, and misunderstands his words. Mary of Bethany, as a representative for the Jewish people, is characterized as a woman who weeps in the face of the death of a loved one, and Mary Magdalene, as a representative of the entire community of faith, is characterized as a woman obsessed with the physical presence of Jesus.

[12]Cf. Pervo, 148.

[13]Ibid., 154.

[14]Randall Chestnut, "Revelatory Experiences Attributed to Biblical Women in Early Jewish Literature," *Women Like This: New Perspectives on Jewish Women in the Greco-Roman World,* ed. Amy-Jill Levine (Atlanta: Scholars Press, 1992) 110.

[15]Chestnut comments on the revelatory experiences attributed to Rebekah in *Jubilees,* Aseneth in *Joseph and Aseneth,* and Job's wife and daughters in the *Testament of Job.* Chestnut, 107–25.

characters.[16] In the same way, the positive portrayal of female characters in the Fourth Gospel appears to be due to their representational function. Lest the active and positive elements in the characterizations of these women lead us to assume that such characterizations necessarily reflected reality, Helene Foley's statement regarding the portrayal of women in Greco-Roman drama is worth noting, ". . . women step out of the household in drama and act and speak publicly in a manner apparently denied them in life."[17]

Like Judith who departed from her female role when the community was threatened only to be returned to her female place,[18] so Martha of Bethany and Mary Magdalene are returned to their female role after they had exhibited a degree of independent behavior in the absence of a male relative.[19] Indeed, all the women in the Fourth Gospel are marginalized once they have fulfilled their role.

Implications for Johannine Studies

Prior to beginning this study, I had assumed that a historical-literary analysis of the female characters of the Fourth Gospel would have supported the findings of those feminist biblical scholars who, using the historical-critical method, state that the Fourth Gospel reflects a community whose discipleship of equals extended to women. Such, however, turned out not to be the case. Although a historical-literary analysis may indicate that a strong, vertical patriarchal relationship between believers and their heavenly Father resulted in a degree of horizontal equality among the "brothers" of Jesus, my historical-literary analysis of the fe-

---

[16]Cf. Cheryl Anne Brown, *No Longer Be Silent: First Century Jewish Portraits of Biblical Women* (Louisville: Westminster/John Knox, 1992) 212–9.

[17]Foley, "The Conception of Women in Athenian Drama," 135.

[18]Levine, "Character Construction and Community Formation in the Book of Judith," 567–9. In "Sacrifice and Salvation: Otherness and Domestication in the Book of Judith," Levine refines her views on this topic. Nevertheless, she still notes that the tension between Judith as the traditional representative of the community of faith through her name, widowhood, chastity, beauty and righteousness and her portrayal as an independent woman with sexuality is resolved through Judith's reinscription into Israelite society (i.e., her return to a female role) (cf. Jdt 16:21-23). Levine, "Sacrifice and Salvation: Otherness and Domestication in the Book of Judith," 24, 26–8. Cf. Pervo, 157–8.

[19]Martha could initially function independently because the death of her brother made her unrelated to father, husband, brother or son. Mary Magdalene, upon the death of her bridegroom, also exhibited a degree of independence by going to the tomb alone while it was still dark.

male characters in the Fourth Gospel does not indicate that this equality extended to women, at least not to women who were in any way connected to a man. Thus, although my analysis does not negate the possibility that a very early Johannine community maintained a discipleship of equals that extended to women, it does lessen that possibility. Androcentrism and patriarchy are simply too much a part of the warp and woof of the fabric of female characterization to be able to relate each individual instance of patriarchy or androcentrism to later additions to the text. Even if one could relegate each instance of patriarchy and androcentrism to later additions, and one could recognize the clear outline of a community behind this text, then, at least by the end of the first century C.E., that community had embraced an androcentric and patriarchal world view with regard to women. So, as my feminist friends would say, "Adeline, where is the hope?"

I believe the hope is in the future, not the past. I do not maintain that equality for women in the Church and society today is dependent upon proving that such equality existed in the past, either in the very early Church or in the views of the historical Jesus. The historical Jesus and the early Church existed in a culture that was dominated by patriarchy. This historical fact, however, in no way requires the normative conclusion that such patriarchy is divinely ordained and should continue indefinitely. My feminist friends, however, might then ask, "If we are against patriarchy now, what do we do with the patriarchal biblical text?"

The first thing I think we need is intellectual honesty. As I do not believe that an apologetic approach aimed at saving the historical Jesus or the biblical text is helpful, neither do I believe it to be helpful for feminists to uphold equality where it did not historically exist. Where patriarchy existed in the past, I believe that we should acknowledge it, mourn it, and move beyond it. In support of this process, I favor a combination of approaches to the biblical text.

Like Elisabeth Schüssler Fiorenza, I believe that we need to acknowledge the patriarchal oppression under which our predecessors suffered, and enter into a hermeneutics of remembrance, a hermeneutic that moves from androcentric and patriarchal texts to a reconstruction of women's history that focuses on the actual lives of women.[20] Like Rosemary Radford Ruether, I believe that we can utilize, in the service of the liberation of women, prophetic-messianic aspects of biblical texts that call

[20]Elisabeth Schüssler Fiorenza, *Bread, Not Stone* (Boston: Beacon, 1984) 15, 108–15. Elisabeth Schüssler Fiorenza, "The Will to Choose or to Reject: Continuing Our Critical Work," *Feminist Interpretation of the Bible,* ed. Letty Russell (Philadelphia: Westminster, 1985) 133–4.

for justice, but that do not necessarily refer to justice for women.[21] Finally, like Mary Ann Tolbert, I believe that we, as readers, can read biblical texts about women in a way that the original author(s) never meant.[22]

Alternative Readings for the Twentieth or Twenty-First Century

Having exposed the patriarchal and androcentric elements in the Fourth Gospel's characterizations of women through a historical-literary approach, I must now emphasize that a reader today does not have to read the text from a historical-literary perspective. As the reader-response approach to literature has emphasized, a reader always brings to a text his or her own cultural context and will always read from this perspective. Even if a reader makes a conscious effort to read from another cultural or historical context, some aspects of the reader's own current context will always be present.[23]

From a feminist perspective, a reader-response approach allows a reader to approach the text with a hermeneutic of suspicion, which entails being a resisting reader,[24] refusing to accept unquestioningly the androcentric and patriarchal ideology of the implied author.[25] Indeed, the utilization of cultural studies within biblical studies has led to a view that, because all interpretations by readers are constructs, real flesh-and-blood readers who are not from the dominant culture can construct the biblical text in a way that is liberating.[26] To illustrate how a reader today might read or "construct" the female characters of the Fourth Gospel in a way

[21]Rosemary Radford Ruether, "Feminist Interpretation: A Method of Correlation," in *Feminist Interpretation of the Bible,* ed. Letty Russell (Philadelphia: Westminster, 1985) 116–24.

[22]Cf. Mary Ann Tolbert, "Protestant Feminists and the Bible: On the Horns of a Dilemma," *Union Seminary Quarterly Review* 43 (1989) 10–4.

[23]Cf. E. D. Hirsch, *Cultural Literacy: What Every American Needs to Know* (New York: Vantage Books, 1988).

[24]Cf. Judith Fetterley, "Introduction: On the Politics of Literature," in *The Resisting Reader: A Feminist Approach to American Fiction* (Bloomington, Ind.: Indiana University Press, 1977) xi–xxvi.

[25]Cf. Patrocinio P. Schweickart, "Reading Ourselves: Toward a Feminist Theory of Reading," in *Gender and Reading: Essays on Readers, Texts, and Contexts* (Baltimore: Johns Hopkins University Press) 31–61.

[26]On the utilization of cultural studies within biblical criticism, see Fernando Segovia, "'And They Began to Speak in Other Tongues': Competing Modes of Discourse in Contemporary Biblical Criticism," in *Reading from this Place, Vol. 1: Social Location and Interpretation in the United States,* eds. Fernando Segovia and Mary Ann Tolbert (Minneapolis: Fortress, 1995) 28–32.

that does not embrace the androcentric and patriarchal ideology of the implied author, I will use the stories of the mother of Jesus at Cana and the Samaritan woman at the well.

A reader today could arrive at a more "attractive" view of the mother of Jesus than is presented in my historical-literary analysis if the reader were to

1) focus on that layer of the text that portrays the mother as being a catalyst for Jesus' beginning his work of helping people to become children of God,

2) accentuate an adapted version of the "from below" perspective for the mother of Jesus,

3) affirm those aspects in the female mode of relating that would be beneficial for one's faith life today.

By focusing on that level of the text in which the mother of Jesus acts as a catalyst for Jesus' sign that leads others to believe in him, biblical scholars have been able to declare that the mother of Jesus fits the description of a disciple who leads others to belief in Jesus. Martin Scott approaches the text in this way when he interprets the mother of Jesus as a disciple of Jesus Sophia because of her knowledge of where to go when the wine (a symbol in the Hebrew Bible for the gift of Sophia) runs out.[27] Gail O'Day acknowledges the mother of Jesus as a disciple by focusing on a fiducial faith perspective and affirming that the mother of Jesus trusted Jesus to act on her request and allowed him to act in freedom.[28] Schüssler Fiorenza affirms the mother of Jesus as an apostolic witness and exemplary disciple, not only for her reconstructed version of the original story of the wedding at Cana,[29] but also for the story in its final form, by asserting that Jesus' use of the appellation "woman" for his mother puts her in the company of other female apostolic witnesses and exemplary disciples whom he

[27]Martin Scott, *Sophia and the Johannine Jesus* (Sheffield: JSOT, 1992) 175–84.

[28]Gail O'Day, "John," *The Women's Bible Commentary,* eds. Carol A. Newsom and Sharon H. Ringe (Louisville: Westminster/John Knox, 1992) 295.

[29]Schüssler Fiorenza asserts that there was originally a shorter pre-Johannine version of the wedding story at Cana. This shorter version is reported to have had no verbal response from Jesus to his mother. Schüssler Fiorenza also asserts that this original story highlighted the mother's influence over her son as she compelled him to work a miracle. Elisabeth Schüssler Fiorenza, *In Memory of Her: A Feminist Theological Reconstruction of Christian Origins* (New York: Crossroad, 1983) 326, 342 n. 146. Cf. Raymond Brown, "Roles of Women in the Fourth Gospel," *The Community of the Beloved Disciple* (New York: Paulist, 1979) 194.

addressed as "woman," namely the Samaritan woman (4:21) and Mary of Magdala (20:13). Schüssler Fiorenza then maintains that the mother of Jesus, as a female disciple, instructs church leaders (the servants [diakonia]) to obey the commands of Jesus.[30]

Yet another way to view the mother of Jesus as a disciple, and the way that I prefer, is to read the text from a performative faith perspective, a faith that moves one to action. Although the implied author of the Fourth Gospel generally characterizes Jesus, the divine Logos, as remaining aloof in the face of human need,[31] emphasizing things "above" rather than "below" and, for the most part, characterizing him as not acting on the basis of human concern,[32] the mother of Jesus at Cana could be looked upon as someone who is truly concerned about the "below" needs of others. This concern for mundane matters could then be viewed in light of the love command that Jesus later gives to the disciples in the Fourth Gospel (13:34-35, 15:10-17).[33] From a praxis-oriented belief system, therefore, the mother of Jesus at Cana could be viewed as a woman who is aware of the needs of others, acts on that awareness, and refuses to allow her son to ignore the earthly needs of others simply because it was not his job. Although social expectations may have necessitated that she meet the need and assert her motherly influence in an indirect manner, she does meet the need. Viewed in this way, the mother of Jesus becomes a sensitive, assertive, and socially aware woman who will not take "no" for an answer when it comes to meeting the needs of others. Although she is not characterized as one who directly challenges the systemic, cultural constraints placed upon her, she can be viewed as a woman who works within the cultural constraints of her time to accomplish the "love command." Although a reader today can legitimately read the text in this manner, this reader-response approach is quite different from asserting that the implied author portrays the mother of Jesus as a disciple.

---

[30]The connection between the mother of Jesus and the female disciples leads Schüssler Fiorenza to question whether the Johannine community itself embraced this story's symbolic overtones that affirm a woman's ability to give orders to church leaders. Schüssler Fiorenza, *In Memory of Her,* 315–6, 326–7. Cf. Brown, "Roles of Women in the Fourth Gospel," 192–6.

[31]R. Alan Culpepper, *Anatomy of the Fourth Gospel: A Study of Literary Design* (Philadelphia: Fortress, 1983) 109–11. J. A. du Rand, "The Characterization of Jesus as Depicted in the Narrative of the Fourth Gospel," *Neotestamentica* 19 (1985) 29–30.

[32]Charles Giblin, "Suggestion, Negative Response and Positive Action in St. John's Portrayal of Jesus [John 2:1-11: 4:46-54; 7:2-14, 11:1-44]," *New Testament Studies* 26 (1980) 203.

[33]Cf. Bertrand Buby, "Mary in John's Gospel," *Mary, the Faithful Disciple* (New York: Paulist, 1985) 107–8.

Although the implied author led the ancient reader to a negative interpretation of the Samaritan woman as she resists Jesus' request for a drink, a present day reader could resist that inclination and affirm the Samaritan woman in her response. Using cultural criticism, a present day reader could perceive Jesus as being part of the dominant culture and the Samaritan woman as being doubly oppressed by being a female and a member of a minority group. Such a reader could then affirm the Samaritan woman in her refusal to acquiesce to the demands (N.B. the use of the imperative) of this unknown male member of the dominant group and affirm her in her continuing "to put him in his place," as he is presently on her turf, (1) in Samaria and (2) at a well (female territory). This reader could also affirm her for her willingness to move beyond her defensive posture to a qualified openness when she not only recognizes this person from the dominant culture and gender as a prophet, but also has the courage to instigate a theological discussion with him, during which time she is able to articulate well her own cultural traditions. The reader could also affirm her for her willingness to let go of her defensive position fully once Jesus articulates a relinquishment of the dominant position in favor of a position of equality in true worship. The Samaritan woman's ability to lead her own people to an acceptance of this person from the dominant culture who relinquishes hierarchical oppression and desires the unity of all persons can then also be affirmed by the reader.

Finally, regarding the response of the Samaritan people to the Samaritan woman once they experienced Jesus for themselves, a present-day reader could attest to the fact that this marginalizing verbiage comes from the mouth of the Samaritan people and not from Jesus himself. Thus, Jesus is not portrayed as necessarily supportive of this stance. Such a negating perspective of another's significance can be viewed as distorted and hopefully transitory. A present-day reader could hope that in time those who had come to encounter Jesus for themselves would no longer feel the need to downplay or discredit the one who brought them to Jesus. From a present-day feminist perspective, the reader may even see corollaries between the response to the Samaritan woman and the response to women in the Church today. From this perspective, a feminist reader might choose to enter into a hermeneutics of remembrance and pray for that time when a woman's contribution to another's faith journey will no longer need to be negated.

A variety of reading strategies are available today to readers who wish to embrace the women in the Fourth Gospel as models for social action or paradigms for the liberation of women in the Church and society. We are not limited to or by a historical-literary reading. Indeed, its very barrenness from the perspective of liberation for women becomes a strong impetus for theological creativity in the present. Illustrating the use of these reading strategies for each pericopae involving women, however, is material for another book and I invite others to join me in this task.

Bibliography

Abrams, Meyer H. *The Mirror and the Lamp: Romantic Theory and the Critical Tradition*. London: Oxford University Press, 1953.

Alter, Robert. *The Art of Biblical Narrative*. New York: Basic Books, 1981.

Archer, Léonie. "The Role of Jewish Women in the Religion, Ritual and Cult of Graeco-Roman Palestine." In *Images of Women in Antiquity,* edited by Averil Cameron and Amélie Kuhrt, 273–87. Detroit: Wayne State University Press, 1983.

Aristotle, *The Poetics*. The Loeb Classical Library Series, translated by W. H. Fyfe. Cambridge: Harvard University Press, 1953.

Athenaeus, *The Deipnosophists*. The Loeb Classical Library Series, translated by Charles Gulick. New York: G. P. Putman Sons, 1933.

Atwood, Richard. *Mary Magdalene in the New Testament Gospels and Early Tradition*. Bern, Germany: Lang, 1993.

Aune, David. *The New Testament in Its Literary Environment*. Philadelphia: Westminster, 1987.

_____. "Septem Sapientium Convivium." In *Plutarch's Ethical Writings and Early Christian Literature,* edited by Hans Dieter Betz, 51–105. Leiden: Brill, 1978.

Baker, James. "The Red-Haired Saint: Is Mary Magdalene the Key to the Easter Narratives?" *The Christian Century* 94 (1977) 328–32.

Bal, Mieke. *Death and Dissymmetry: The Politics of Coherence in the Book of Judges*. Chicago: University of Chicago Press, 1988.

Barrett, C. K. *The Gospel According to St. John,* 2nd ed. Philadelphia: Westminster, 1978.

_____. "The Old Testament in the Fourth Gospel." *Journal of Theological Studies* 48 (1947) 155–69.

Bauckham, Richard. "Mary of Clopas (John 19:25)." In *Women in the Biblical Tradition,* edited by George Brooke, 231–55. Lewiston, N.Y.: Edwin Mellen, 1992.

Bauer, Walter. *A Greek-English Lexicon of the New Testament and Other Early Christian Literature,* 2nd ed. Translated and augmented by William Arndt and F. Wilber Gingrich. Chicago: University of Chicago Press, 1979 (1957).

Beaton, Roderick. "Editor's Preface." In *The Greek Novel AD 1-1985,* edited by Roderick Beaton, vii–x. London: Croom Helm, 1988.

Bernard, J. H. *A Critical and Exegetical Commentary on the Gospel According to St. John.* 2 vols. Edinburgh: T & T Clark, 1976 (1928).

Bickerman, Elias. "Das leere Grab." *Zeitschrift für die Neutestamentliche Wissenschaft* 23 (1924) 281–92.

Black, C. Clifton, III. "Depth of Characterization and Degrees of Faith in Matthew." In *Society of Biblical Literature: 1989 Seminar Papers,* edited by David Lull, 604–23. Atlanta: Scholars Press, 1989.

Bligh, J. "Jesus in Samaria." *Heythrop Journal* 3 (1962) 329–46.

Boers, H. *Neither on this Mountain nor in Jerusalem: A Study of John 4.* Atlanta: Scholars Press, 1988.

_____. "Discourse Structure and Macro-Structure in the Interpretation of Texts: Jn 4:1-42 as an Example." In *Society of Biblical Literature: 1980 Seminar Papers,* edited by P. Achtemeier, 159–82. Chico, Calif.: Scholars Press, 1980.

Bonneau, N. R. "The Woman at the Well, John 4 and Gen 24." *Bible Today* 67 (1973) 1252–9.

Booth, W. *The Rhetoric of Fiction.* Chicago: University of Chicago Press, 1961.

Botha, J. E. *Jesus and the Samaritan Woman: A Speech Act Reading of John 4:1-42.* Leiden: E. J. Brill, 1991.

_____. "John 4:16: A Difficult Text—Speech Act Theoretically Revisited." In *The Gospel of John as Literature: An Anthology of 20th-Century Perspectives,* edited by Mark Stibbe, 183–92. Leiden: E. J. Brill, 1993. Reprinted from *Scriptura* 35 (1990) 1–9.

_____. "Reader 'Entrapment' as Literary Device in John 4:1-42." *Neotestamentica* 24 (1990) 37–47.

Bower, Robert and G. L. Knapp. "Marriage; Marry." *International Standard Bible Encyclopedia.* General Editor, G. W. Bromiley, 3:261–6. Grand Rapids: Eerdmans, 1986.

Brave, Stanley. "Marriage with a History." In *Marriage and the Jewish Tradition.* New York: Philosophical Library, 1951.

Brooks, James and Carlton Winbery. *Syntax of the New Testament Greek.* Lanham, Md.: University Press of America, 1979.

Brown, Cheryl. *No Longer Be Silent: First Century Jewish Portraits of Biblical Women.* Louisville: Wesminister/John Knox, 1992.

Brown, Raymond. "Roles of Women in the Fourth Gospel." Appendix II in *The Community of the Beloved Disciple.* New York: Paulist, 1979. First printed in *Theological Studies* 36 (1975) 688–99.

_____. "The Passion According to John: Chapters 18 and 19." *Worship* 49 (1975) 126–34.

_____. *The Gospel According to John.* The Anchor Bible Series, vols. 29, 29A. New York: Doubleday, 1966, 1970.

_____, ed. *Mary in the New Testament.* London: Geoffrey Chapman, 1978.

Buby, Bertrand. "Mary in John's Gospel." In *Mary, the Faithful Disciple.* New York: Paulist, 1985.

Buchanan, George Wesley. "The Samaritan Origin of the Gospel of John." In *Religions in Antiquity: Essays in Memory of Erwin Ramsdell Goodenough,* edited by Jacob Neusner, 149–75. Leiden: Brill, 1968.

Büchler, A. "The Induction of the Bride and the Bridegroom into the *Chuppah* in the First and Second Centuries in Palestine." In *Livre d'hommage a la memoire du Samuel Poznanski,* edited by Le Comité de la Grande Synagogue a Varsovie, 82–132. Leipzig: Varsovie, 1927.

Buck, H. "Redactions of the Fourth Gospel and the Mother of Jesus." In *Studies in New Testament and Early Christian Literature,* edited by David Aune, 170–80. Leiden: E. J. Brill, 1972.

Bultmann, Rudolf. *The Gospel of John: A Commentary,* translated by G. R. Beasley-Murray and edited by R.W.N. Hoare and J. K. Riches. Philadelphia: Westminster, 1971.

Burchard, C. "Joseph and Aseneth: A New Translation and Introduction." In *Old Testament Pseudepigrapha,* edited by James Charlesworth. Garden City, N.Y.: Doubleday, 1985.

Burnett, Fred. "Characterization and Reader Construction of Characters in the Gospels." *Semeia* 63 (1993) 1–28.

_____. "Characterization and Christology in Matthew: Jesus in the Gospel of Matthew." In *Society of Biblical Literature: 1989 Seminar Papers,* edited by David Lull, 588–603. Atlanta: Scholars Press, 1989.

Byrne, Brendan. "The Faith of the Beloved Disciple and the Community in John 20." *Journal for the Study of the New Testament* 23 (1985) 83–97.

_____. *Lazarus: A Contemporary Reading of John 11:1-46.* Collegeville: The Liturgical Press, 1991.

Cadman, W. H. "The Raising of Lazarus (John 10:40–11:53)." In *Studia Evangelica* I, Texte und Untersuchungen 73, edited by S. L. Cross, 423–34. Berlin: Academie-Verlag, 1959.

Cahill, P. J. "Narrative Art in John IV." *Religious Studies Bulletin* 2 (1982) 41–55.

Campbell, John Kennedy. "The Family: A System of Roles." In *Honour, Family and Patronage: A Study of Institutions and Moral Values in a Greek Mountain Community.* Oxford: Clarendon, 1964.

Canon, Katie Geneva. "Womanist Interpretation and Preaching." In *Searching the Scriptures: A Feminist Introduction,* edited by Elisabeth Schüssler Fiorenza, 326–37. New York: Crossroad, 1993.

_____. "The Emergence of Black Feminist Consciousness." In *Feminist Interpretation of the Bible,* edited by Letty Russell, 30–40. Philadelphia: Westminster, 1985.

Cantarella, Eva. *Pandora's Daughters: The Role and Status of Women in Greek and Roman Antiquity,* translated by Maureen Fant. Baltimore: Johns Hopkins University Press, 1987.

Cantwell, Laurence. "Immortal Longings in Sermone Humili: A Study of John 4:5-26." *Scottish Journal of Theology* 36 (1983) 73–86.

Carmichael, Calum. "Marriage and the Samaritan Woman." *New Testament Studies* 26 (1980) 332–46.

Cave, Terence. *Recognitions: A Study in Poetics*. Oxford: Clarendon, 1988.

_____. "Recognition and the Reader." In *Comparative Criticism: A Yearbook,* vol. 2, edited by Elinor Shaffer, 49–69. Cambridge: Cambridge University Press, 1980.

Chariton. *Chaereas and Callirhoe,* translated by Warren Blake. Ann Arbor: University of Michigan Press, 1939.

Chestnut, Randall. "Revelatory Experiences Attributed to Biblical Women in Early Jewish Literature." In *Women Like This: New Perspectives on Jewish Women in the Greco-Roman World,* edited by Amy-Jill Levine, 107–25. Atlanta: Scholars Press, 1992.

Cohn, Robert. "Convention and Creativity in the Book of Kings: The Case of the Dying Monarch (1 Kg 14; 2 Kg 1; 8; 20)." *Catholic Biblical Quarterly* 47 (1985) 603–16.

Collins, Raymond. "The Mother of Jesus in the Gospel of John." In *Mary in the New Testament,* edited by Raymond Brown, et. al., 179–218. Philadelphia: Fortress, 1978.

_____. "The Representative Figures of the Fourth Gospel." *Downside Review* 94 (1976) 26–46, 118–32.

_____. "Mary in the Fourth Gospel: A Decade of Johannine Studies." *Louvain Studies* 3 (1970) 99–142.

Corley, Kathleen. "Were the Women around Jesus Really Prostitutes: Women in the Context of Greco-Roman Meals." In *Society of Biblical Literature 1989 Seminar Papers,* edited by David Lull, 487–521. Atlanta: Scholars Press, 1989.

Cox, Patricia. *A Genre for the Gospels*. Philadelphia: Fortress, 1982.

Culley, Robert C. "Oral Transmission and Biblical Texts." In *Studies in the Structure of Hebrew Narrative*. Philadelphia: Fortress, 1976.

Culpepper, R. Alan. *Anatomy of the Fourth Gospel: A Study of Literary Design*. Philadelphia: Fortress, 1983.

_____. *The Johannine School*. Missoula, Mont.: Scholars Press, 1975.

Culpepper, R. Alan and Fernando Segovia, eds. *The Fourth Gospel From a Literary Perspective. Semeia* 53. Atlanta: Scholars Press, 1991.

D'Angelo, Mary Rose. "A Critical Note: John 20:17 and Apocalypse of Moses 31." *Journal of Theological Studies* 41 (1990) 529–36.

Darr, John. *On Character Building: The Reader and the Rhetoric of Characterization in Luke-Acts*. Louisville: Westminster/John Knox, 1992.

_____. "Glorified in the Presence of Kings: A Literary-Critical Study of Herod the Tetrarch in Luke-Acts." Ph.D. dissertation, Vanderbilt University, 1987.

Delaney, Carol. "The Body of Knowledge." In *The Seed and the Soil: Gender and Cosmology in Turkish Village Society*. Berkeley: University of California Press, 1991.

_____. "Seeds of Honor, Fields of Shame." In *Honor and Shame and the Unity of the Mediterranean,* edited by David Gilmore, 35–48. Washington, D.C.: American Anthropological Association, 1987.

Delling, Gerhard. "ὥρα." In *Theological Dictionary of the New Testament* edited by Gerhard Kittle, translated & edited by G. Bromiley, 9:675–81. Grand Rapids: Eerdmans, 1967.

Derrett, J. Duncan. "Miriam and the Resurrection (John 20:16)." *Downside Review* 111 (1993) 174–88.

_____. "The Samaritan Woman's Purity (John 4:4-52)." *Evangelical Quarterly* 60 (1988) 291–8.

_____. "The Samaritan Woman's Pitcher." *Downside Review* 102 (1984) 252–61.

Dewald, Carol. "Women and Culture in Herodotus' *Histories*." In *Reflections of Women in Antiquity,* edited by Helene Foley, 91–127. New York: Gordon and Breach Science Publishers, 1981.

Doherty, Thomas. *Reading (Absent) Character: A Theory of Characterization in Fiction.* New York: Oxford University Press, 1983.

Downing, Christine. "Athena." In *The Encyclopedia of Religion,* edited by Mircea Eliade, 1:490–1. New York: Macmillan, 1987.

Duke, Paul. *Irony in the Fourth Gospel.* Atlanta: John Knox, 1985.

du Rand, J. A. "The Characterization of Jesus as Depicted in the Narrative of the Fourth Gospel." *Neotestamentica* 19 (1985) 18–36.

Eilberg-Schwartz, Howard. *The Savage in Judaism, An Anthropology of Israelite Religion and Ancient Judaism.* Bloomington: Indiana University Press, 1990.

Elder, Linda Bennett. "Judith." In *Searching the Scriptures—Volume 2: A Feminist Commentary,* edited by Elisabeth Schüssler Fiorenza, 455–69. New York: Crossroad, 1994.

Eslinger, Lyle. "The Wooing of the Woman at the Well: Jesus, the Reader and Reader-Response Criticism." In *The Gospel of John as Literature: An Anthology of 20th Century Perspectives,* edited by Mark Stibbe, 165–82. Leiden: E. J. Brill, 1993. Reprinted from *Journal of Literature and Theology* 1 (1987) 167–83.

Exum, J. Cheryl. *Fragmented Women: Feminist (Sub)versions of Biblical Narratives.* Valley Forge, Pa.: Trinity, 1993.

_____. "'Mother in Israel': A Familiar Figure Reconsidered." In *Feminist Interpretation of the Bible,* edited by Letty Russell, 73–85. Philadelphia: Westminster, 1985.

_____. "'You Shall Let Every Daughter Live': A Study of Exodus 1:8–2:10." In *The Bible and Feminist Hermeneutics,* edited by Mary Ann Tolbert, 63–82. Chico, Calif.: Scholars Press, 1983.

Feuillet, André. "Les adiux du Christ à sa mère (Jn 19:25-27) et la maternité spirituelle de Marie." *Nouvelle Revue Théologue* 86 (1964) 469–89. Translated in digest form into English as "Christ's Farewell to his Mother." *Theology Digest* 15 (1967) 37–40.

_____. "The Hour of Jesus and the Sign of Cana." In *Johannine Studies.* New York: Alba, 1964. English reprint of "L'heure de Jésus et le signe de Cana." *Ephemerides Theologicae Lovanienses* 36 (1960) 5–22.

_____. "The Messiah and his Mother According to Chapter 12 of the Apocalypse." In *Johannine Studies.* New York: Alba, 1964. English reprint of "Le Messie et sa Mere d'apres le chapitre xii de l'Apocalypse." *Revue Biblique* 66 (1959) 55–86.

_____. "La recherche du Christ dan la nouvelle Alliance d'apres la Christophanie de Jo 20, 11-18." In *L'homme devant Dieu,* publiées sous la direction de la faculté de Théologie S.J. de Lyon-Fourviére, 93–112. Paris: Aubier, 1963.

Foley, Helene. "'Reverse Simile' and Sex Roles in the Odyssey." In *Women in the Ancient World: The Arethusa Papers,* edited by John Peradotto and J. P. Sullivan, 59–78. Albany: State University of New York Press, 1984.

_____. "The Concept of Women in Athenian Drama." In *Reflections of Women in Antiquity,* edited by Helene Foley, 127–68. New York: Gordon and Breach Science Publishers, 1981.

_____, ed. *Reflections of Women in Antiquity.* New York: Gordon and Breach, 1981.

Fortna, R. *The Fourth Gospel and its Predecessor.* Edinburgh: T. & T. Clark, 1988.

_____. *The Gospel of Signs.* Cambridge: Cambridge University Press, 1970.

Fowler, Robert. "Who is 'The Reader' in Reader Response Criticism." *Semeia* 31 (1985) 5–26.

Freund, Elisabeth. "Introduction: The Order of Reading." In *The Return of the Reader: Reader-Response Criticism.* New York: Routedge, Chapman & Hall, 1987.

Fuchs, Esther. "Structure and Patriarchal Functions in the Biblical Betrothal Typescene: Some Preliminary Notes." *Journal of Feminist Studies in Religion* 3 (1987) 7–13.

_____. "The Literary Characterization of Mothers and Sexual Politics in the Hebrew Bible." In *Feminist Perspectives on Biblical Scholarship,* edited by Adela Yarbro Collins, 117–36. Chico, Calif.: Scholars Press, 1985.

_____. "Who is Hiding the Truth? Deceptive Women and Biblical Androcentrism." In *Feminist Perspectives on Biblical Scholarship,* edited by Adela Yarbro Collins, 137–44. Chico, Calif.: Scholars Press, 1983.

Giblin, Charles. "Suggestion, Negative Response and Positive Action in St. John's Portrayal of Jesus [John 2:1-11: 4:46-54; 7:2-14; 11:1-44]." *New Testament Studies* 26 (1980) 197–211.

Gifford, Carolyn De Swarte. "American Women and the Bible: The Nature of Woman as a Hermeneutical Issue." In *Feminist Perspectives on Biblical Scholarship,* edited by Adela Yarbro Collins. Chico, Calif.: Scholars Press, 1985.

Goodman, Philip and Hanna Goodman. "Jewish Marriages Throughout the Ages." In *The Jewish Marriage Anthology.* Philadelphia: The Jewish Publication Society of America, 1965.

Grassi, Carolyn and Joseph Grassi. "The Resurrection: The New Age Begins; Mary Magdalene as Mystical Spouse." In *Mary Magdalene and the Women in Jesus' Life.* Kansas City, Mo.: Sheed & Ward, 1986.

Grimké, Angelina Emily. *Appeal to the Christian Women of the South.* New York: Arno and New York Times, 1969 (1836).

_____. *Letters to Catharine Beecher.* Boston: Isaac Knapp, 1838.

Grimké, Sarah M. *Letters on the Equality of the Sexes and the Condition of Women.* New York: Burt Franklin, 1970 (1838).

Hägg, Tomas. *The Novel in Antiquity.* Berkeley: University of California Press, 1983 (1980).

_____. *Narrative Technique in Ancient Greek Romances: Studies of Chariton, Xenophon Ephesius and Achilles Tatius.* Uppsala: Almqvist & Wiksells, 1971.

_____. "The Beginning of the Historical Novel." In *The Greek Novel AD 1-1985,* edited by Roderick Beaton, 169–81. London: Croom Helm, 1988.

Halperin, David. "Why is Diotima A Woman? Platonic Eros and the Figuration of Gender." In *Before Sexuality: The Construction of Erotic Experience in the Ancient Greek World,* edited by David M. Halperin, John J. Winkler, and Froma I. Zeitlin, 257–308. Princeton: Princeton University Press, 1990.

Hirsch, E. D. *Cultural Literacy: What Every American Needs to Know.* New York: Vantage Books, 1988.

Hoskyns, Edwyn. *The Fourth Gospel.* 2 vols. London: Faber and Faber Limited, 1940.

Isasi-Díaz, Ada María. "La Palabra de Dios en Nosotras—The Word of God in Us." In *Searching the Scriptures: A Feminist Introduction,* edited by Elisabeth Schüssler Fiorenza, 86–97. New York: Crossroad, 1993.

_____. "The Bible and Mujerista Theology." In *Lift Every Voice: Constructing Christian Theology from the Underside,* edited by Susan Brooks Thistlethwaite and Mary Porter Engle, 261–9. San Francisco: Harper and Row, 1990.

Iser, Wolfgang. *The Act of Reading: A Theory of Aesthetic Response.* Baltimore; Johns Hopkins University Press, 1978.

_____. *The Implied Reader.* Baltimore: Johns Hopkins University Press, 1974.

Jay, Nancy. "Sacrifice, Descent and Patriarchs." *Vetus Testamentum* 38 (1988) 52–70.

_____. "Sacrifice as Remedy for Having Been Born of Woman." In *Immaculate and Powerful: The Female in Sacred Image and Social Reality,* edited by Clarissa Atkinson, Constance Buchanan and Margaret Miles, 283–309. Boston: Beacon, 1985.

Jeremias, Jeremiah. "νυμφη, νυμφιος." In *Theological Dictionary of the New Testament,* edited by Gerhard Kittle and translated and edited by G. Bromiley, 4: 1099–106. Grand Rapids, Mich.: Eerdmans, 1967.

Jones, John R. *Narrative Structures and Meaning in John 11:1-54.* Ann Arbor: University Microfilms. Ph.D. Dissertation, Vanderbilt University, 1982.

Josephus. *Jewish Antiquities.* In *Josephus.* The Loeb Classical Library Series, edited by Allen Wikgren and translated by Ralph Maracus. Cambridge, Mass.: Harvard University Press, 1963.

Jowkar, Fourouz. "Honor and Shame: A Feminist View From Within." *Feminist Issues* 6 (Spring 1986) 45–65.

Käsemann, Ernst. *The Testament of Jesus: A Study of the Gospel of John in the Light of Chapter 17.* Philadelphia: Fortress, 1968.

Kermode, Frank. *The Genesis of Secrecy: On the Interpretation of Narrative.* Cambridge, Mass.: Harvard University Press, 1979.

Kolodny, Annette. "A Map for Reading: Or, Gender and the Interpretation of Literary Texts." *New Literary History* 11 (1980) 451–67.

_____. *The Lay of the Land: Metaphor as Experience and History in American Life and Letters.* Chapel Hill, N.C.: University of North Carolina Press, 1975.

Kopas, Jane. "Jesus and Women: John's Gospel." *Theology Today* 41 (1984) 201–5.

Kraemer, Ross. "The Book of Aseneth." In *Searching the Scriptures: A Feminist Commentary,* edited by Elisabeth Schüssler Fiorenza, 859–94. New York: Crossroad, 1994.

Krieger, Murray. *A Window to Criticism: Shakespeare's Sonnets and Modern Poetics.* Princeton: Princeton University Press, 1964.

Kuhn, Thomas S. *The Structure of Scientific Revolutions.* Chicago: University of Chicago Press, 1962.

Kysar, Robert. *John: The Maverick Gospel,* revised ed. Louisville: Westminster/John Knox, 1993 (1976).

Lagrange, M.-J. *Évangile selon saint Jean.* Paris: Gabalda, 1948 (1923).

Laqueur, Thomas. "Destiny Is Anatomy." In *Making Sex: Body and Gender from the Greek to Freud.* Cambridge, Mass.: Harvard University Press, 1990.

Lategan, Bernard C. "Introduction: Coming to Grips with the Reader in Biblical Literature." *Semeia* 48 (1989) 3–20.

Lee, Dorothy. *The Symbolic Narratives of the Fourth Gospel: The Interplay of Form and Meaning.* Sheffield: JSOT, 1994.

Lefkowitz, Mary. "Influential Women." In *Images of Women in Antiquity,* edited by Averil Cameron and Amélie Kuhrt, 49–64. Detroit: Wayne State University Press, 1983.

Levine, Amy-Jill. "Ruth." In *The Women's Bible Commentary,* edited by Carol A. Newsom and Sharon H. Ringe, 78–84. Louisville: Westminster/John Knox, 1992.

_____. "Sacrifice and Salvation: Otherness and Domestication in the Book of Judith." In *No One Spoke Ill of Her: Essays on Judith,* edited by James C. VanderKam, 17–30. Atlanta: Scholars Press, 1992.

_____. "Character Construction and Community Formation in the Book of Judith." In *Society of Biblical Literature 1989 Seminar Papers,* edited by David Lull, 561–9. Atlanta: Scholars Press, 1989.

Liddell, H. G. and Robert Scott. *An Intermediate Greek—English Lexicon.* Seventh Edition Oxford: Clarendon, 1989 (1889).

Lightfoot, R. H. *St. John's Gospel: A Commentary,* edited by C. F. Evans. Oxford: Clarendon, 1957.

Lindars, Barnabas. *The Gospel of John.* London: Oliphants, 1972.

Longus. "Daphnis and Chloe." In *Three Greek Romances,* translated by Moses Hadas, 3–68. New York: Macmillan, 1953.

Lonie, Iain M. *The Hippocratic Treaties: "On Generation," "The Seed," "On the Nature of the Child," "Diseases IV".* Ars Medica: Texte und Untersuchungen zur Quellenkunde der Alten Medizine. Berlin: Walter de Gruyer, 1981.

Mace, David. *Hebrew Marriage: A Sociological Study.* London: Epworth, 1953.

Mailloux, Steven. "Literary History and Reception Study." In *Interpretive Conventions: The Reader in the Study of American Fiction,* 159–91. Ithaca: Cornell University Press, 1982.

Malina, Bruce. "Dealing with Biblical (Mediterranean) Characters: A Guide to U.S. Consumers." *Biblical Theological Bulletin* 19 (1989) 127–41.

_____. *Christian Origins and Cultural Anthropology*. Atlanta: John Knox, 1986.

_____. *The Gospel of John in Sociolinguistic Perspectives. Forty-eighth Colloquy of the Center for Hermeneutical Studies,* edited by Herman Waetjen. Berkeley: Center for Hermeneutical Studies, 1985

_____. *The New Testament World: Insights from Cultural Anthropology*. Louisville: John Knox, 1981.

Martin, J. P. "History and Eschatology in the Lazarus Narrative: John 11:1-44." *Scottish Journal of Theology* 17 (1964) 332–43.

Martyn, Louis J. "Source Criticism and Religionsgeschichte in the Fourth Gospel." In *Jesus and Man's Hope,* edited by David Buttrick, 1:247–73. Pittsburgh: Pittsburgh Theological Seminary, 1970.

Matera, Frank. "John 20:1-18." *Interpretation* 43 (1989) 402–6.

Maynard, A. "Ti Emoi Kai Σοι." *New Testament Studies* 31 (1985) 582–6.

McGehee, Michael. "A Less Theological Reading of John 20:17." *Journal of Biblical Literature* 105 (1986) 299–302.

McHugh, John. "Mother of the Word Incarnate: Mary in the Theology of St. John." Part III in *The Mother of Jesus in the New Testament*. London: Darton, Longman & Todd, 1975.

McKane, W. *Proverbs*. Philadelphia: Westminster, 1970.

McNeil, B. "The Raising of Lazarus." *Downside Review* 92 (1974) 269–75.

Meeks, Wayne A. *The Prophet-King: Moses Tradition and the Johannine Christology*. Leiden: Brill, 1967.

Metzger, Bruce. *A Textual Commentary on the Greek New Testament*. Stuttgart: Biblia-Druck GmbH, 1975.

Michaels, J. Ramsey. "John 12:1-11." *Interpretation* 43 (1989) 287–91.

Minear, Paul. "'We Don't Know Where. . .' John 20:2." *Interpretation* 30 (1976) 125–39.

Mishnah. Translated by Jacob Neusner. New Haven: Yale University Press, 1988.

Mlakuzhyil, G. "Difficulties Against the Literary Unity and Structure of the Fourth Gospel." In *The Christocentric Literary Structure of the Fourth Gospel*. Roma: Editrice Pontificio Istituo Biblico, 1987.

Murphy-O'Connor, Jerome. "Sex and Logic in 1 Corinthians 11:2-16." *Catholic Biblical Quarterly* 42 (1980) 483–500.

Neyrey, Jerome. "What's Wrong with this Picture? John 4, Cultural Stereotypes of Women, and Public and Private Space." *Biblical Theology Bulletin* 24 (1994) 77–91.

_____. "Jacob Traditions and the Interpretation of John 4:10-26." *Catholic Biblical Quarterly* 41 (1979) 419–37.

Nolan Fewell, Danna. "Judges." In *The Women's Bible Commentary,* edited by Carol Newsom and Sharon Ringe, 67–77. Louisville: Westminster/John Knox, 1992.

O'Brien, Mary. *The Politics of Reproduction*. Boston: Routledge & Kegan Paul, 1981.

O'Collins, Gerald and Daniel Kendall. "Mary Magdalene as Major Witness to Jesus' Resurrection." *Theological Studies* 48 (1987) 631–46.

O'Day, Gail. "John." In *The Women's Bible Commentary,* edited by Carol Newsom and Sharon Ringe, 293–304. Louisville: Westminster/John Knox, 1992.

_____. *Revelation in the Fourth Gospel: Narrative Mode and Theological Claim.* Philadelphia: Fortress, 1986.

Okorie, A.M. "The Characterization of the Tax Collectors in the Gospel of Luke." *Currents in Theology and Mission* 22 (1995) 27–34.

Okure, Teresa. "The Significance Today of Jesus' Commission to Mary Magdalene [Jn 20:11-18]." *International Review of Mission* 81 (1992) 177–88.

_____. *The Johannine Approach to Mission: A Contextual Study of John 4:1-42.* Tübingen: Mohr, 1988.

Olsson, Birger. *Structure and Meaning in the Fourth Gospel: A Text-Linguistic Analysis of John 2:1-11 and 4:1-42.* Lund: CWK Gleerup, 1974.

Osborne, Basil. "A Folded Napkin in an Empty Tomb: John 11:44 and 20:7 Again." *Heythrop Journal* 14 (1973) 437–40.

Osiek, Carolyn. "The Feminist and the Bible: Hermeneutical Alternatives." In *Feminist Perspectives on Biblical Scholarship,* edited by Adela Yarbro Collins, 93–105. Chico, Calif.: Scholars Press, 1985.

Pazdan, Mary Margaret. "Nicodemus and the Samaritan Woman: Contrasting Models of Discipleship." *Biblical Theological Bulletin* 17 (1987) 145–8.

Peradotto, John and J. P. Sullivan, ed. *Women in the Ancient World: The Arethusa Papers.* Albany: State University of New York Press, 1984.

Peristiany, J. G. "Introduction." In *Honour and Shame: The Values of Mediterranean Society,* edited by J. G. Peristiany, 9–18. Chicago: University of Chicago Press, 1966.

Perkins, Pheme. "I Have Seen the Lord (John 20:18): Women Witnesses to the Resurrection." *Interpretation* 46 (1992) 31–41.

_____. "The Gospel According to John." In *New Jerome Biblical Commentary,* edited by Raymond Brown, et. al., 941–85. Englewood Cliffs, N.J.: Prentice Hall, 1990.

_____. *Resurrection: New Testament Witness and Contemporary Reflection.* Garden City, N.Y.: Doubleday, 1984.

Pervo, Richard. "Aseneth and Her Sisters: Women in Jewish Narrative and in the Greek Novels." In *Women Like This: New Perspectives on Jewish Women in the Greco-Roman World,* edited by Amy-Jill Levine, 145–60. Atlanta: Scholars Press, 1992.

Petersen, Norman R. *Literary Criticism for New Testament Critics.* Philadelphia: Fortress, 1978.

Pitt-Rivers, Julian. *The Fate of Shechem or the Politics of Sex: Essays in the Anthropology of the Mediterranean.* Cambridge: Cambridge University Press, 1977.

_____. "Honour and Social Status." In *Honour and Shame: The Values of Mediterranean Society,* edited by J. G. Peristiany, 19–77. Chicago: University of Chicago Press, 1966.

Platt, Elizabeth. "The Ministry of Mary of Bethany." *Theology Today* 34 (1977) 29–39.

Pliny. *Natural History*. The Loeb Classical Library Series, edited by H. Rackham. Cambridge, Mass.: Harvard University Press, 1945.

Plutarch, *Quaestiones Convivales*. In *Plutarch's Moralia*. The Loeb Classical Library Series, translated by Paul A. Clement and Herbert B. Hoffleit, vol. 8. Cambridge, Mass.: Harvard University Press, 1969.

Pollard, T. E. "The Raising of Lazarus (John xi)." In *Studia Evangelica* VI, Texte und Untersuchungen 112, edited by Elizabeth Livingstone, 434–43. Berlin: Academie-Verlag, 1973.

Pomeroy, Sarah. *Goddesses, Whores, Wives, and Slaves: Women in Classical Antiquity*. New York: Schocken Books, 1975.

Portefaix, Lillian. *Sister Rejoice: Paul's Letter to the Philippians*. Stockholm: Almqvist & Wilksell International, 1988.

Pseudo-Callisthenes. *The Romance of Alexander the Great by Pseudo-Callisthenes*, translated with Introduction by Albert Wolohojian. New York: Columbia University Press, 1962.

Quast, Kevin. *Reading the Gospel of John: An Introduction*. New York: Paulist, 1991.

Reardon, B. P. *The Form of Greek Romance*. Princeton: Princeton University Press, 1991.

_____. "The Form of Ancient Greek Romance." In *The Greek Novel AD 1-1985*, edited by Roderick Beaton, 205–16. London: Croom Helm, 1988.

Reed, Evelyn. *Woman's Evolution: From Matriarchal Clan to Patriarchal Family*. New York: Pathfinders, 1975.

Reinhartz, Adele. "The Gospel of John." In *Searching the Scriptures: A Feminist Commentary,* edited by Elisabeth Schüssler Fiorenza, 561–600. New York: Crossroad, 1994.

_____. "From Narrative to History: The Resurrection of Mary and Martha." In *Women Like This: New Perspectives on Jewish Women in the Greco-Roman World,* edited by Amy-Jill Levine, 161–84. Atlanta: Scholars Press, 1992.

Rena, John. "Women in the Gospel of John." *Église et Théologie* 17 (1986) 131–47.

Rensberger, David. *Johannine Faith and Liberating Community*. Philadelphia: Westminster, 1988.

Resseguie, James L. "Reader-Response Criticism and the Synoptic Gospels." *Journal of the American Academy of Religion* 52 (1984) 307–24.

Rissi, Mathias. "Die Hochzeit in Kana (Joh. 2:1-11)." In *Oikonomia: Heilsgeschichet als Thema der Theologie,* edited by O. Cullman, 76–99. Hamburg-Bergstedt: Reich, 1967.

Rochais, Gérard. "La résurrection de Lazare (Jn 11, 1-46)." In *Les Récits de résurrection des morts dans le Nouveau Testament,* SNTSMS 40. Cambridge: University Press, 1981.

Roth, Samuel. "The Blind, the Lame, and the Poor: An Audience-Oriented, Sequential Analysis of a Group of Characters Types in Luke-Acts." Ph.D. Dissertation, Vanderbilt University, 1994.

Rubin, Gayle. "The Traffic in Women: Notes on the "Political Economy" of Sex." In *Toward an Anthropology of Women,* edited by Rayna R. Reiter, 172–3. New York: Monthly Review, 1975.

Ruether, Rosemary Radford. "Feminist Interpretation: A Method of Correlation." In *Feminist Interpretation of the Bible,* edited by Letty Russell, 111–24. Philadelphia: Westminster, 1985.

_____. "Mary and the Mission of Jesus." In *Mary-The Feminine Face of the Church*. Philadelphia: Westminster, 1977.

_____. *Mary—the Feminine Face of the Church*. Philadelphia: Westminster, 1977.

Russell, Letty. *Household of Freedom: Authority in Feminist Theology*. Philadelphia: Westminster, 1987.

_____. "Authority and the Challenge of Feminist Interpretation." In *Feminist Interpretation of the Bible,* edited by Letty Russell, 137–46. Philadelphia: Westminster, 1985.

Safrai, S. "Home and Family." In *The Jewish People in the First Century,* vol. 2, edited by S. Safrai and M. Stern, 728–92. Philadelphia: Fortress, 1976.

Sakenfeld, Katherine Doob. "Feminist Perspectives on Bible and Theology: An Introduction to Selected Issues and Literature." *Interpretation* 42 (1988) 5–18.

_____. "Feminist Uses of Biblical Materials." In *Feminist Interpretation of the Bible,* edited by Letty Russell, 56–64. Philadelphia: Westminster, 1985.

Sanders, J. N. "Lazarus of Bethany." In *Interpreter's Dictionary of the Bible,* edited by George Arthur Buttrick et. al., 3:103. New York: Abingdon, 1962.

Schnackenburg, Rudolf. *The Gospel According to St. John*. 3 Vols. New York: Crossroad, 1980, 1982.

Schneiders, Sandra. *The Revelatory Text: Interpreting the New Testament as Sacred Scripture*. San Francisco: Harper, 1991.

_____. "Death in the Community of Eternal Life." *Interpretation* 41 (1987) 44–56.

_____. "Women in the Fourth Gospel and the Role of Women in the Contemporary Church." *Biblical Theology Bulletin* 12 (1982) 35–45.

_____. "The Veil: A Johannine Sign." *Biblical Theological Bulletin* 13 (1981) 94–7.

Scholes Robert and Robert Kellogg. *The Nature of Narrative*. London: Oxford University Press, 1966.

Schüssler Fiorenza, Elisabeth. "A Feminist Critical Interpretation For Liberation: Martha and Mary: Lk. 10:38-42." *Religion and Intellectual Life* 3 (1986) 21–36.

_____. "Remembering the Past in Creating the Future: Historical-Critical Scholarship and Feminist Biblical Interpretation." In *Feminist Perspectives on Biblical Scholarship,* edited by Adela Yarbro Collins, 43–63. Chico, Calif.: Scholars Press, 1985.

_____. "The Will to Choose or Reject: Continuing Our Critical Work." In *Feminist Interpretation of the Bible,* edited by Letty Russell, 125–36. Philadelphia: Westminster, 1985.

_____. *Bread Not Stone*. Boston: Beacon, 1984.

_____. *In Memory of Her: A Feminist Theological Reconstruction of Christian Origins*. New York: Crossroad, 1983.

_____. "Toward a Feminist Biblical Hermeneutics: Biblical Interpretation and Liberation Theology." In *The Challenge of Liberation Theology: A First Word*

Response, edited by Brian Mahan and L. Dale Richesin, 91–112. Maryknoll, N.Y.: Orbis, 1981.

_____. "Feminist Theology as a Critical Theology of Liberation." In *Churches in Struggle: Liberation Theologies and Social Change in North America,* edited by William Tabb, 46–66. New York: Monthly Review Press, 1986. Schüssler Fiorenza's meditation on Mary Magdalene found in this article was first printed in the *Union Theological Seminary Journal* April (1975) 22–3.

Schweickart, Patrocinio. "Reading Ourselves: Toward a Feminist Theory of Reading." In *Gender and Reading: Essays on Readers, Texts, and Contexts.* Baltimore: John Hopkins University Press, 1986.

Scobie, Charles. "The Origins and Development of Samaritan Christianity." *New Testament Studies* 19 (1972–1973) 390–414.

Scott, Martin. *Sophia and the Johannine Jesus.* Sheffield: JSOT, 1992.

Seckel, Marianne. "La Mère de Jésus dans le 4ᶜ Évangile: de la Lignée des Femmes-Disciples?" *Foi et Vie* 88 (1989) 33–41.

Segovia, Fernando. "'And They Began to Speak in Other Tongues': Competing Modes of Discourse in Contemporary Biblical Criticism." In *Reading from this Place, Vol. 1: Social Location and Interpretation in the United States,* edited by Fernando Segovia and Mary Ann Tolbert, 1–32. Minneapolis: Fortress, 1995.

_____. *The Farewell of the Word: The Johannine Call to Abide.* Minneapolis: Fortress, 1991.

_____. "The Journey(s) of the Word of God: A Reading of the Plot of the Fourth Gospel." *Semeia* 53 (1991) 23–54.

Seim, Turid Karlsen. "Roles of Women in the Gospel of John." In *Aspects on the Johannine Literature,* edited by Lars Hartman & Birger Olsson. Sweden: Alqvist & Wiksell International, 1987.

"Semahoth (Ebel Rabbath)." In *Babylonian Talmud,* translated by Michael Rodkinson, 8:1–62. Boston: New Talmud Publishing Company, 1899.

Shuler, Philip. *A Genre for the Gospels: The Biographical Character of Matthew.* Philadelphia: Fortress, 1982.

Sloyan, Gerard. "The Samaritans in the New Testament." *Horizons* 10 (1983) 7–21.

Smith, D. Moody. *The Theology of the Gospel of John.* Cambridge: Cambridge University Press, 1995.

Stählin, Gustav. "φιλέω." In *Theological Dictionary of the New Testament,* edited by Gerhard Friedrich, translated and edited by Geoffrey Bromiley, 9:113–71. Grand Rapids: Eerdmans, 1974.

Staley, Jeffrey. "Stumbling in the Dark, Reaching for the Light: Reading Character in John 5 and 9." *Semeia* 53 (1991) 55–80.

_____. *The Print's First Kiss: A Rhetorical Investigation of the Implied Reader in the Fourth Gospel.* Atlanta: Scholars Press, 1985.

Stanton, Elizabeth Cady, et al., The Revising Committee. *The Woman's Bible.* New York: European, 1898.

Stibbe, Mark. *John.* Sheffield: JSOT, 1993.

Suleiman, Susan R. "Introduction: Varieties of Audience-Oriented Criticism." In *The Reader in the Text: Essays on Audience and Interpretation,* edited by Susan. R. Suleiman, 3–45. Princeton: Princeton University Press, 1980.

Talbert, Charles. *Reading John: A Literary and Theological Commentary on the Fourth Gospel and the Johannine Epistles.* New York: Crossroad, 1994.

_____. "Once Again: Gospel Genre." *Semeia* 43 (1988) 53–73.

The New Oxford Annotated Bible with the Apocryphal/Deutero-canonical Books (New Revised Standard Version), eds. Bruce Metzger and Roland Murphy. New York: Oxford University Press, 1991.

Thompson, Marianne Meye. "'God's Voice You Have Never Heard, God's Form You have Never Seen': The Characterization of God in the Gospel of John." *Semeia* 63 (1993) 177–204.

Thomson, George. *Aeschylus and Athens: A Study in the Social Origins of Drama.* London: Lawrence & Wishart, 1941.

Thurian, Max. "Mary and the Church." In *Mary, Mother of All Christians.* New York: Herder & Herder, 1964.

Tolbert, Mary Ann. "How the Gospel of Mark Builds Character: Characterization in the Parable of the Sower." *Interpretation* 47 (1993) 347–57.

_____. "Social, Sociological, and Anthropological Methods." In *Searching the Scripture: A Feminist Introduction,* edited by Elisabeth Schüssler Fiorenza, 255–71. New York: Crossroad, 1993.

_____. "The Gospel in Greco-Roman Culture." In *The Book and the Text: The Bible and Literary Theory,* edited by R. Schwartz, 258–75. Cambridge: Basic Blackwell, 1990.

_____. *Sowing the Gospel: Mark's World in Literary-Historical Perspective.* Minneapolis: Fortress, 1989.

_____. "Protestant Feminists and the Bible: On the Horns of a Dilemma." *Union Seminary Quarterly Review* 43 (1989) 1–17.

_____. "Defining the Problem: The Bible and Feminist Hermeneutics." *Semeia* 28 (1983) 113–26.

Trenkner, Sophie. *The Greek Novella in the Classical Period.* New York: Garland, 1987.

Trible, Phyllis. "Five Loaves and Two Fishes: Feminist Hermeneutics and Biblical Theology." *Theological Studies* 50 (1989) 279–95.

van Bekkum, Wout, ed. *A Hebrew Alexander Romance According to Ms London, Jews' College no. 145.* Leuven: Peeters, 1992.

Votaw, C. W. "Some Example of Biography in the Ancient World Comparable to the Gospels." In *The Gospel and Contemporary Biographies.* Philadelphia: Fortress, 1970. Reprinted from "The Gospels and Contemporary Biographies in the Greco-Roman World." *American Journal of Theology* 19 (1915) 45–73.

Wead, D. W. *The Literary Devices in John's Gospel.* Basel: Reinhardt, 1970.

Weiss, Herold, "Footwashing in the Johannine Community." *Novum Testamentum* 21 (1979) 298–325.

Wikan, Uni. "Shame and Honour: A Contestable Pair." *Man* 19 (1984) 635–52.

Willard, Frances E. *Woman in the Pulpit*. Chicago: Woman's Temperance Publication Association, 1889.

Witherington, III, Ben. *Women in Ministry of Jesus*. Cambridge: Cambridge University Press, 1984.

Wolohojian, Albert. *The Romance of Alexander the Great by Pseudo-Callisthenes: Translated from the Armenian Version*. New York: Columbia University Press, 1969.

Wyatt, Nicolas. "'Supposing Him to Be the Gardener' (John 20:15): A Study of the Paradise Motif in John." *Zeitschrift für die Neutestamentliche Wissenschaft und die Kunde der Alteren Kirche* 81 (1990) 21–38.

Xenophon. "An Ephesian Tale." In *Three Greek Romances,* translated by Moses Hadas, 69–126. New York: Macmillan, 1953.

Zeitlin, Froma. "Travesties of Gender and Genre in Aristophanes." In *Reflections of Women in Antiquity,* edited by Helene Foley, 269–318. New York: Gordon and Breach Science Publishers, 1981.

_____. "The Dynamics of Misogyny: Myth and Mythmaking in the *Oresteia*." In *Women in the Ancient World: The Arethusa Papers,* edited by J. Peradotto and J. P. Sullivan, 159–94. Albany: State University of New York Press, 1984.

Zumstein, J. "Pourquoi s'intéresser a l'exégèse féministe?" *Foi et Vie* 88 (1989 no. 5) 5–7 for (l'exemple de Jean).

Index of Biblical
and Ancient Sources

The Fourth Gospel

12:2	83, 93 n.38, 99, 110, 173		18:35	77
12:2-3	4		19:2-5	123
12:3	88, 93, 98, 171, 175		19:2-6	137
12:3-4	171		19:12-15	137
12:4	101		19:14	120
12:4-5	100		19:16b-30	137
12:6	100		19:19	137
12:7	100, 101		19:21-22	137
12:9-11	1		19:23	120 n.14
12:20	143		19:24	133 n.61
12:23	53		19:25	95, 115, 132, 132 n.60,
12:25	166			133 n.61, 150, 170, 172,
12:27	53			174
12:32	127		19:25-27	23, 24, 40 n.58, 42, 43
12:32-34	53		19:25-28	1, 21
12:43	34		19:26	3, 134
13:13-17	166		19:26-27	134, 173
13:22	143		19:27	138, 174
13:33-35	182		19:28	4
14:2-3	123		19:29	120
15:9-10	162		19:30	130
15:10-17	182		19:31	120
15:15	41		19:33-34	149–50
15:19	92 n.31		19:34	41 n.63, 121, 127 n.42,
16:6	143, 162			128
16:14	34		19:34b	131 n.57
16:17-20	41		19:34-37	127 n.42
16:20	143, 162		19:38-39	41 n.62
16:21	31, 41 n.63		19:38-40	100
16:21-22	127		19:38-42	145
16:23	41		19:39	74
16:32	153 n.38		19:41	124, 157
ch. 17	47 n.10		ch. 20	145 n.7
17:1-5	34		20:1	93, 149 n.19, 150, 151
17:2-3	169		20:1-10	152 n.34, 173
17:6	122		20:1-18	1, 21, 145 n.7, 170, 172
17:6-26	162		20:2	128 n.43, 143 n.1, 145,
17:8	162			162 n.74
17:20	46, 77, 162		20:2b	154
17:22-24	34		20:2-3	151
17:26	18, 122		20:3-8	152
18:1	124, 157		20:4-6	152 n.33
18:4	143		20:7	152 n.34
18:7	143		20:8	152, 158 n.61
18:8	143		20:9	150, 152 n.34, 153 n.38
18:26	124, 157		20:10	41, 152 n.34, 153, 153 n.38
18:33-38	137		20:11	143, 151, 151 n.27, 154

Hebrew Bible and Apocryphal/Deutero-Canonical Books

New Testament

Ancient Authors and Writings

Index of Authors

Pomeroy, S., 14 n.54, 90 n.25, 99 n.62, 109 n.96
Portefaix, L., 88 n.14

Quast, K., 48–49 n.13, 50 n.18, 58 n.44

Räisänen, H., 24
Reardon, B., 146 n.11, 147 n.15, 156 n.51
Reed, E., 117 n.3, 122 n.20
Reinhartz, A., 14 n.56, 46 n.5, 61 n.51, 84, 84 n.3, 94 n.45, 96 n.52, 100 n.64, 101 n.69, 104 nn.75,78, 105 n.80, 106 n.81, 139–40 n.86, 143 n.2, 144 nn.3,5, 158 n.58
Reiter, R. R., 69 n.78
Rena, J., 24, 24 n.4, 33 n.33, 35 n.36, 74 n.90, 78 n.108, 79, 79 n.113, 92 n.34, 100 n.64, 106 n.81, 144 n.3, 152 n.34, 153 n.37, 154 n.43, 159 n.62, 162 n.76, 167 n.93
Rensberger, D., 47 n.10
Resseguie, J. L., 7 n.27
Reuther, R., 23
Ringe, S., 39 n.56, 46 n.7, 84 n.3, 129 n.49, 175 n.1, 181 n.28
Rissi, M., 30 n.23, 31 n.27
Rochais, G., 87 n.11, 105 n.80, 107 n.89
Rubin, G., 69, 69 n.78
Ruether, R. R., 23 n.3, 30 n.23, 141, 141 n.89, 179, 180 n.21
Russell, L., 3 n.9, 9 n.38, 25 n.10, 179 n.20, 180 n.21

Safrai, S., 85 n.4, 98 n.57, 101 n.68, 123, 123 nn.25,26
Sanders, J. N., 85 n.7
Schnackenburg, R., 4 n.10, 38 n.51, 58 n.45, 64 n.61, 65 n.66, 66 n.69, 87 n.11, 90 nn.22,23, 94 n.45, 97 n.54, 100, 100 nn.64,66,67, 102 n.70, 105 n.78, 107 nn.89,90, 108 n.93, 109 n.94, 110 nn.97,98, 111 n.102, 125 nn.31–33, 127 n.42, 128 nn.46,47, 131 n.57, 133 n.61, 138 n.80, 145, 145 nn.7–9, 146 n.10, 150 n.23, 151 nn.27,28, 152 nn.31,34, 154 n.41, 158 n.58, 160 n.67

Schneiders, S., 2 nn.2,5, 3 n.8, 4 n.13, 20 n.80, 30, 45 n.3, 46 n.6,8,9, 47 n.10, 49 n.17, 50 n.18, 55 n.39, 61 n.51, 65 n.65, 66, 67, 67 nn.71,73, 74 n.90, 79 n.114, 84, 84 n.3, 87 n.12, 92, 92 n.35, 94 nn.41,45, 96 n.52, 100 n.64, 104 n.75, 105 n.80, 106 n.82, 107 n.89, 109 n.95, 110–11 n.101, 134 n.65, 143 n.1, 144 n.5, 152 n.34, 153 n.35, 161 nn.72,73
Scholes, R., 12 n.46, 154 n.43
Schulz, S., 24
Schüssler Fiorenza, E., 2, 2 nn.2,6, 3, 3 n.9, 4, 4 nn.12–14, 5, 14 nn.53,55,56, 35 n.42, 35–36 n.44, 45 n.2, 46 nn.5,7–9, 47 n.11, 58 n.44, 78 n.106, 83, 84, 84 nn.2,3, 95 n.48, 96 n.50, 105 nn.79,80, 106 nn.81,83,86, 110–11 n.101, 111 n.102, 139–40 n.86, 143 n.2, 144 nn.3,5,6, 152 n.32, 153 n.37, 158 n.58, 176 n.9, 177 n.10, 179, 179 n.20, 181, 181 n.29, 182 n.30
Schwartz, R., 13 n.50, 146 n.11
Schweickart, P. P., 180 n.25
Scobie, C., 119–20 n.13
Scott, M., 2 nn.2,5, 6, 6 nn.18,19, 18 n.70, 19, 20, 23, 28 n.13, 46 nn.6,8, 50 n.18, 74 n.92, 84, 84 n.3, 104 n.78, 105 nn.79,80, 106 n.85, 111 n.102, 181, 181 n.27
Scott, R., 50 n.20
Seckel, M., 41 n.64
Segovia, F., 11 n.46, 12, 12 n.47, 13 n.51, 154 n.43, 180 n.26
Seim, T. K., 2 n.5, 20 nn.79,80, 24, 24 n.6, 47 n.11, 70 n.81, 84, 84 n.3, 102 n.70, 105 nn.80,81, 107 n.89, 108 n.93, 110–11 n.101, 111 n.102, 127 n.43, 139 n.85, 144 n.5, 163 n.79
Schaffer, E., 155 n.48
Shuler, P., 12 n.46, 15, 15 n.59
Sloyan, G., 66, 66 n.68, 119–20 n.13
Smith, D. M., 10 nn.39,41, 145 n.7, 153 n.37
Stählin, G., 91, 91 n.28, 92 n.31

Index of Terms and Characters

"above" point of view/perspective, **30–32**, 36, **65–66**, 80, 102, 182
adulterous woman (7:53–8:11), 20, 21
allegory/allegorical, 65 n.66, 177 n.10
allusion, 10, 13, 52, 53, 57, 93, 120, 121, 123, 124, 150, 157, 158 n.56, 159 n.65, 167
amplification, 15
  (*see also* mythologizing)
anagnorisis, 155, 156, 158 n.61
  (*see also* recognition)
Andrew, 77, 83
androcentric (androcentrism in)
  characterization/portrayal, 5, 6, 8 n.37, 20, 21, 25, **32–40**, **69–79**, **107–11**, **140–41**, **163–66**, 167, 169, 172, 175 n.1, 180
  ideology/bias/point of view, etc., 9, 39, 74, 113, 140, 169, 172, 175, 176, 179–81
  societies, 13
  texts, 2, 179
Aseneth, 95, 106, 106 n.88, 175 n.4, 176, 176 nn.6,9, 177, 177 n.15
Athena, 126, 126 n.36, 130

Bathsheba, 26 n.11
beloved disciple, 1, 8 n.32, 37 n.48, 40 n.58, 42, 83, 127, 128 n.43, 134, 137, 137 n.79, 138–42, 145 n.7, **150–53**, 154, 154 n.39, 158 n.61, 161 n.72, 162, 162 n.74, 163, 164, 167, 172, 173, 176

"below" point of view/perspective, **30–32**, 36, 42, 48, 58, **61–63**, 80, 102, **104–107**, 158, 158 n.59, 181, 182
betrothal, **49–52**, 53, 55, 55 n.37, 56 n.41, 58, 59, 63, 64, 64 n.62, 67, 69, 69 n.77, 70, 71, 71 n.84, 75 n.93, 92, 98, 112
betrothed, 20, 47, 58, 61, 71–73, 79–81, 84, 84 n.4, 85–87, 89–92, 92 n.32, 93–98, 99 n.62, 100–102, 107–109, 111–13, 113 n.104, 134, 170–75
Bilhah, 33
biography, 11, 11 n.42, 12, 12 nn.46,47, 15, 15 n.60, 16, 17, 135 n.69, 175
birth (born)
  general, 26, 26 n.11, 31, 32, 37, 41 n.63, 48, 56 n.40, 71, 116, 116 n.3, 117 nn.3,4, 118, 119 nn.11,12, 121, 121 n.18, 122, 122 n.19, 125 n.34, 126, 126 nn.36,37, 127, 128, 128 nn.45,46, 131, 138 n.81, 139–41
  from above, 43, 47–49, 71, 74, 86, 125, 127, 128, 131, 140, 170
  (*see also* conception & rebirth)
blood sacrifice(s), **116–21**, 122, 122 n.19, 131, 139–42, 161, 162, 173
bride(s), 20, 32, 47, 48, 49 n.13, 53, 54, 57, 58, 61, 67, 71–73, 79–81, 84–87, 89–92, 92 n.32, 93–98, 99 n.62, 100–102, 107–109, 111–13, 113 n.104, 123, 123 n.26, 124,